≈≈≈ Zora Neale Hurston

Zora Neale Hurston

≈≈≈ A LITERARY BIOGRAPHY

Robert E. Hemenway

WITH A FOREWORD BY ALICE WALKER

UNIVERSITY OF ILLINOIS PRESS
URBANA AND CHICAGO

Publication of this work was supported in part
by a grant from the Andrew W. Mellon Foundation.

Illini Books edition, 1980
© 1977 by the Board of Trustees of the University of Illinois
Manufactured in the United States of America

P 9 8 7

This book is printed on acid-free paper.

Grateful acknowledgment is made for permission to quote from the following works:

From *Dust Tracks on a Road* by Zora Neale Hurston. Copyright 1942 by Zora Neale
Hurston. Copyright © renewed 1970 by John C. Hurston. Reprinted by permission of J. B.
Lippincott Company.

From *Jonah's Gourd Vine* by Zora Neale Hurston. Copyright 1934 by Zora Neale Hurston.
Copyright © renewed 1962 by John C. Hurston and Joel Hurston. Reprinted by permission
of J. B. Lippincott Company.

From *Moses, Man of the Mountain* by Zora Neale Hurston. Copyright 1939 by Zora Neale
Hurston. Copyright © renewed 1967 by John C. Hurston and Joel Hurston. Reprinted by
permission of J. B. Lippincott Company.

From "Mule Bone: A Comedy of Negro Life." Published with the consent of the Langston
Hughes Estate and the Zora Neale Hurston Estate. These excerpts may not be reprinted
without permission.

From *Mules and Men: Negro Folktales and Voodoo Practices in the South* by Zora Neale
Hurston (Harper & Row, Publishers, Perennial Library edition). Copyright © 1935 by Zora
Neale Hurston. Reprinted by permission of Harper & Row, Publishers, Inc.

From *Tell My Horse* by Zora Neale Hurston. Copyright 1938 by Zora Neale Hurston.
Copyright © renewed 1966 by Joel Hurston and John C. Hurston.

From *Their Eyes Were Watching God* by Zora Neale Hurston. Copyright 1937 by J. B.
Lippincott Company. Copyright © renewed 1965 by John C. Hurston and Joel Hurston.
Reprinted by permission of J. B. Lippincott Company.

LIBRARY OF CONGRESS CATALOGING IN PUBLICATION DATA

Hemenway, Robert E.   1941-
    Zora Neale Hurston.

    Bibliography: p.
    Includes index.
    1. Hurston, Zora Neale. 2. Novelists, American—20th century—Biography.
PS3515.U789Z7   813'.5'2   [B]   77-9605
ISBN 0-252-00807-3

To Mattie

and for
Robin
Karintha
Matthew
Langston
Gina
Jeremy

What all my work shall be, I don't know that either,
every hour being a stranger to you until you live it.
I want a busy life, a just mind and a timely death.

Zora Neale Hurston, *Dust Tracks on a Road*

≋ Contents

Illustrations following page 353

 **Foreword**

I became aware of my need of Zora Neale Hurston's work some time before I knew her work existed. In late 1970 I was writing a story that required accurate material on voodoo practices among rural southern blacks of the thirties; there seemed none available I could trust. A number of white, racist anthropologists and folklorists of the period had, not surprisingly, disappointed and insulted me. They thought blacks inferior, peculiar, and comic, and for me this undermined—no, *destroyed*—the relevance of their books. Fortunately, it was then that I discovered *Mules and Men*, Zora's book on folklore, collecting, herself, and her small, all-black community of Eatonville, Florida. Because she immersed herself in her own culture even as she recorded its "big old lies," i.e., folktales, it was possible to see how she and it (even after she had attended Barnard College and become a respected writer and apprentice anthropologist) fit together. The authenticity of her material was verified by her familiarity with its context, and I was soothed by her assurance that she was exposing not simply an adequate culture, but a superior one. That black people can be on occasion peculiar and comic was knowledge she enjoyed. That they could be racially or culturally inferior to whites never seems to have crossed her mind.

The first time I heard Zora's *name*, I was auditing a black literature class taught by the great poet Margaret Walker, at Jackson State College in Jackson, Mississippi. The reason this fact later slipped my mind was that Zora's name and accomplishments came and went so fast. The class was studying the usual "giants" of black literature—Chesnutt, Toomer, Hughes, Wright, Ellison, and Baldwin—with the hope of reaching LeRoi Jones very soon. Jessie Fauset, Nella Larsen, Ann Petry, Paule Marshall (unequaled in intelligence, vision, craft by anyone of her generation, to put her contributions to our literature modestly), and Zora Neale Hurston were names appended, like verbal footnotes, to the illustrious all-male list that paralleled them. As far as I recall, none of their work was studied in the course. Much of it was out of print, in any case, and remains so. (Perhaps Gwendolyn Brooks and Margaret Walker herself were exceptions to this list; they were both poets of such obvious necessity it would be impossible to overlook them. And their work—due to the political and cultural nationalism of the sixties—was everywhere available.)

When I read *Mules and Men* I was delighted. Here was this perfect book! The "perfection" of it I immediately tested on my relatives, who are such typical black Americans they are useful for every sort of political, cultural, or economic survey. Very regular people from the South, rapidly forgetting their southern cultural inheritance in the suburbs and ghettos of Boston and New York, they sat around reading the book themselves, listening to me read the book, listening to each other read the book, and a kind of paradise was regained. For Zora's book gave them back all the stories they had forgotten or of which they had grown ashamed (told to us years ago by our parents and grandparents—not one of whom could *not* tell a story to make us weep, or laugh) and showed how marvelous, and, indeed, priceless, they are. *This is not exaggerated.* No matter how they read the stories Zora had collected, no matter how much distance they tried to maintain between themselves, as new sophisticates, and the lives their parents and grandparents lived, no matter how they tried to remain cool toward all Zora revealed, in the end they could not hold back the smiles, the laughter, the *joy* over who she was showing them to be: descendants of an inventive, joyous, courageous, and outrageous people: loving drama, appreciating wit, and, most of all, relishing the pleasure of each other's loquacious and *bodacious* company.

This was my first indication of the quality I feel is most characteristic of Zora's work: racial health—a sense of black people as complete, complex, *undiminished* human beings, a sense that is lacking in so much black writing and literature. (In my opinion, only Du Bois showed an equally consistent delight in the beauty and spirit of black people, which is interesting when one considers that the angle of his vision was completely the opposite of Zora's.) Zora's pride in black people was so pronounced in the ersatz black twenties that it made other blacks suspicious and perhaps uncomfortable; after all, *they* were still infatuated with things European—*everything* European. Zora was interested in Africa, Haiti, Jamaica—and, for a little racial diversity (Indians), Honduras. She also had a confidence in herself as an individual that few people (anyone?), black or white, understood. This was because Zora grew up in a community of black people who had enormous respect for themselves and for their ability to *govern* themselves. Her own father had written the Eatonville town laws. This community affirmed her right to exist, and loved her as an extension of itself. For how many other black Americans is this true? It certainly isn't true for any that I know. In her easy self-acceptance, Zora was more like an uncolonized African than she was like her contemporary American blacks, most of whom believed, at least during their formative years, that their blackness was something wrong with them.

On the contrary, Zora's early work shows she grew up *pitying* whites because the ones she saw lacked "light" and soul. It is impossible to imagine Zora envying anyone (except tongue-in-cheek), and, least of all, a white person for being white. Which is, after all, if one is black, a clear and present calamity of the mind.

Condemned to a deserted island for life, with an allotment of ten books to see me through, I would choose, unhesitatingly, two of Zora's: *Mules and Men*, because I would need to be able to pass on to younger generations the life of American blacks as legend and myth, and *Their Eyes Were Watching God*, because I would want to enjoy myself while identifying with the black heroine, Janie Crawford, as she acted out many roles in a variety of settings, and functioned (with spectacular results!) in romantic and sensual love. *There is no book more important to me than this one.*

Having committed myself to Zora's work, loving it, in fact, I became curious to see what others had written about her. This was, for the young, impressionable, barely begun writer I was, a mis-

take. After reading the misleading, deliberately belittling, inaccurate, and generally irresponsible attacks on her work and her life by
almost everyone, I became for a time paralyzed with confusion and
fear. For if a woman who had given so much of obvious value to all of
us (and at such risks: to health, reputation, sanity) could be so
casually pilloried and consigned to a sneering oblivion, what chance
would someone else—for example, like myself—have? I was aware
that I had much less *gumption* than Zora.

For a long time I sat looking at this fear, and at what caused it.
*Zora was a woman who wrote and spoke her mind—as far as one
could tell, practically always.* People who knew her and were
unaccustomed to this characteristic in a woman—one who was,
moreover, (a) sometimes in error, and (b) successful, for the most
part, in her work—attacked her as meanly as they could. *Would I
also be attacked if I wrote and spoke my mind? And if I dared open
my mouth to speak, must I always be "correct"? And by whose
standards?* Only those who have read the critics' opinions of Zora
and her work will comprehend the power of these questions to
riddle a young writer with self-doubt.

Eventually, however, I discovered that I repudiate and despise
the kind of criticism that intimidates rather than instructs the
young; and I dislike fear, especially in myself. I did then what fear
rarely fails to force me to do: I fought back. I began to fight for Zora
and her work, for what I knew was good and must not be lost to us.

Robert Hemenway was the first critic I read who seemed indig-
nant that Zora's life ended in poverty and obscurity, that her last
days were spent in a welfare home, and that her burial was paid for
by "subscription"; though Zora herself—as he is careful to point out
in this book—remained gallant and unbowed until the end. It was
Hemenway's efforts to define Zora's legacy and his exploration of
her life that led me, in 1973, to an overgrown Fort Pierce, Florida,
graveyard in an attempt to locate and mark Zora's grave. Although
by that time I considered her a native American genius, there was
nothing grand or historic in my mind. It was, rather, a duty I
accepted as naturally mine—as a black person, a woman, and a
writer—because Zora was dead and I, for the time being, was alive.

Zora was funny, irreverent (she was the first to call the Harlem
Renaissance literati the "niggerati"), good-looking, and sexy. She

once sold hot dogs in a Washington park just to record accurately how the black people who bought them talked. She would go any- where she had to go—Harlem, Jamaica, Haiti, Bermuda—to find out anything she simply *had* to know. She loved to give parties. Loved to dance. Would wrap her head in scarves as black women in Africa, Haiti, and everywhere else have done for centuries. On the other hand, she loved to wear hats, tilted over one eye, and pants and boots. (I have a photograph of her in pants, boots, and broad- brim hat that was given to me by her brother Everette. She has her foot up on the running board of a car—presumably hers, and bright red—and looks racy.) She would light up a fag—which wasn't done by ladies then (and thank our saints, as a young woman she was never a lady) on the street.

Her critics disliked even the "rags" on her head. (They seemed curiously incapable of telling the difference between an African- American queen and Aunt Jemima.) They disliked her apparent sensuality: the way she tended to marry or not marry men, but enjoyed them anyway, while never missing a beat in her work. They hinted slyly that Zora was gay, or at least bisexual—how else could they account for her drive?—though there is not a shred of evidence that this was true. The accusation becomes humorous —and, of course, at all times irrelevant—when one considers that what she *did* write about was some of the most healthily rendered heterosexual loving in our literature. In addition, she talked too much, got things from white folks (Guggenheims, Rosenwalds, and footstools) much too easily, was slovenly in her dress, and appeared maddeningly indifferent to other people's opinions of her. With her easy laughter and her southern drawl, her belief in doing cullud dancing *authentically*, Zora seemed—among these genteel "New Negroes" of the Harlem Renaissance—*black*. No wonder her pres- ence was always a shock. Though almost everyone agreed she was a delight, not everyone agreed such audacious black delight was permissible, or, indeed, quite the proper image for the race.

Zora was before her time—in intellectual circles—in the lifestyle she chose. By the sixties everyone understood that black women could wear beautiful cloths on their beautiful heads and care about the authenticity of things cullud *and* African. By the sixties it was no longer a crime to receive financial assistance, in the form of grants and fellowships, for one's work. (Interestingly, those writers who complained that Zora "got money from white folks" were often themselves totally supported, down to the food they ate—or, in Langston Hughes's case, *tried* to eat, after his white "godmother" discarded him—by white patrons.) By the sixties, nobody cared that marriage didn't last forever. No one expected it to. And I do believe that now, in the seventies, we do not expect (though we may wish and pray) every black person who speaks to *always* speak *correctly* (since this is impossible); or if we *do* expect it, we deserve all the silent leadership we are likely to get.

During the early and middle years of her career Zora was a cultural revolutionary simply because she was always herself. Her work, so vigorous among the rather pallid productions of many of her contemporaries, comes from the essence of black folklife. During her later years, for reasons revealed for the first time in this monumental work (as so much is!), she became frightened of the life she had always dared bravely before. Her work, too, became reactionary, static, shockingly misguided and timid. This is especially true of her last novel, *Seraph on the Suwanee*, which is not even about black people, which is no crime, but *is* about white people who are bores, which is.

A series of misfortunes battered Zora's spirit and her health. And she was broke.

Being broke made all the difference.

Without money of one's own in a capitalist society, there is no such thing as independence. This is one of the clearest lessons of Zora's life, and why I consider the telling of her life a "cautionary tale." We must learn from it what we can.

Without money, an illness, even a simple one, can undermine the will. Without money, getting into a hospital is problematic, and getting out without money to pay for the treatment is nearly impossible. Without money, one becomes dependent on other people who are likely to be—even in their kindness—erratic in their support and despotic in their expectations of return. Zora was forced to rely, like Tennessee Williams's Blanche, "on the kindness of strangers." Can anything be more dangerous, if the strangers are forever in control? Zora, who worked so hard, was never able to make a living from her work.

She did not complain about not having money. She was not the type. (Several months ago I received a long letter from one of Zora's nieces, a bright ten-year-old who explained to me that her aunt was so proud that the only way the family could guess she was ill or without funds was by realizing they had no idea where she was. Therefore, none of the family attended either Zora's sickbed or her funeral.) Those of us who have had "grants and fellowships from 'white folks'" know this aid is extended in precisely the way welfare is extended in Mississippi. One is asked, *curtly*, more often than not: How much do you need *just to survive*? Then one is— if fortunate—given a third of that. What is amazing is that Zora, who became an orphan at nine, a runaway at fourteen, a maid and manicurist (because of necessity and not from love of the work) before she was twenty, *with one dress*, managed to become Zora Neale Hurston, author and anthropologist, at all.

For me, the most unfortunate thing Zora ever wrote is her autobiography. After the first several chapters, it rings false. One begins to hear the voice of someone whose life required the assistance of too many transitory "friends." A Taoist proverb states that *to act sincerely with the insincere is dangerous* (a mistake blacks as a group have tended to make in America). And so we have Zora sincerely offering gratitude and kind words to people one knows she could not have respected. But this unctuousness, so out of character for Zora, is also a result of dependency, a sign of her powerlessness, her inability to pay back her debts with anything but words. They must have been bitter ones for her. In her dependency, it should be remembered, Zora was not alone. For it is quite true that America does not support or honor us as human beings, let alone as blacks, women, or artists. We have taken help where it was offered because we are committed to what we do and to the survival of our work. Zora was committed to the survival of her people's cultural heritage as well.

In my mind, Zora Neale Hurston, Billie Holiday, and Bessie Smith form a sort of unholy trinity. Zora belongs in the tradition of black women singers, rather than among the "literati," at least to me. There were the extreme highs and lows of her life, her undaunted pursuit of adventure, her passionate emotional and sexual experience, and her love of freedom. Like Billie and Bessie she followed her own road, believed in her own gods, pursued her own dreams, and refused to separate herself from "common" people. It would have been nice if the three of them had had one another to turn to in times of need. I close my eyes and imagine them: Bessie would be in charge of all the money; Zora would keep Billie's masochistic tendencies in check and prevent her from singing embarrassingly anything-for-a-man songs, thereby preventing Billie's heroin addiction; in return, Billie could be, along with Bessie, the family that Zora felt she never had.

We are a people. A people do not throw their geniuses away. If they do, it is our duty *as witnesses for the future* to collect them again for the sake of our children. If necessary, bone by bone.

December, 1976   ALICE WALKER

≈≈≈ **Preface**

When I began the research for this biography, only one of Hurston's books was in print, and much of the published information about her life, including her own autobiography, was inaccurate or misleading. Even basic details of her life were vague with mystery. What year was she born? When did she marry? Whom did she marry? All who had met Zora Hurston had a sharply etched memory of her, sometimes unflatteringly so, and the wide-ranging anecdotes often contradicted each other. Everyone remembered a dynamic, intelligent, witty, original human being. It was commonly held that *Mules and Men* was an important folklore collection, that *Their Eyes Were Watching God* was a remarkable, but mostly unread novel. Beyond this there was no agreement. One acquaintance called her "a ring-tailed roarer." A man who had met her only once thought she might be "a hundred-carat handkerchief head." A friend described her as a "black nationalist born before her time." A woman who knew her well said she was the "first black feminist." What were the facts?

In 1970–71, supported by a grant from the National Endowment for the Humanities, I drove a pickup camper thirty thousand miles from Key West to New Haven, from White Sulphur Springs, Montana, to Eatonville, Florida, seeking the documents and memories that might answer that question. By the time I stopped traveling, I owed an enormous debt to a wide variety of people who had helped the search, and the debt escalated in the last six years while I worked to write the book. The National Endowment for the Humanities awarded a second grant in 1974–75 for work in the Folklore Institute at Indiana University. Travel grants from the University of Wyoming and the University of Kentucky enabled me to stop writing periodically to track down new leads.

My intention has always been simple. Zora Neale Hurston is a literary artist of sufficient talent to deserve intensive study, both as an artist and as an intellect. She deserves an important place in American literary history. I have tried to demonstrate why this is so, not in the interests of producing a "definitive" book—that book remains to be written, and by a black woman—but in order to contribute to a new, closer examination of the unusual career of this complex author. This book provides an order to Hurston's life and an interpretation of her art; there are more biographical facts to be discovered, different interpretations to come.

After years of preoccupation with the Hurston personality, there has recently begun a serious examination of Hurston's career. Today, five of her books are in print, and established black writers like Alice Walker, June Jordan, Larry Neal, Addison Gayle, and Julius Lester testify to her influence. Hurston is widely regarded as one of the two or three collectors of black American folklore who have historical importance. The Modern Language Association, the professional arm of the academic literary establishment, held a special Hurston seminar during its national convention in 1975. All of this is recognition long overdue, a belated tribute to an author who committed her life's work to the celebration of Afro-American culture. My book is offered as a contribution to this new study of Hurston's commitment.

⟨≈≈≈⟩ Acknowledgments

This book has taken eight years to research and write, perhaps because I work slowly, perhaps because so much of the research had to be original, surely because each time I thought I was finished new information surfaced—often through the kindness of someone who shared an interest in Zora Hurston. I would like to thank the following, without whose help the effort would have been prolonged even further.

The late Arna Bontemps, Langston Hughes's literary executor, granted me access to letters Zora had written Hughes, consented to five hours of interviews, and helped me grasp the importance of the research when I spoke to his graduate seminar at Yale. Sterling Brown graciously shared an afternoon of Hurston anecdotes and Brown wisdom. Alan Lomax told fascinating stories about collecting with Zora. George Schuyler proved as helpful in person as he is abrasive in print. Arthur Huff Fauset reminisced about Hurston and Locke. Bruce Nugent spoke brilliantly into a tape recorder for six hours on two successive days, never once lapsing into cliché. Mr. and Mrs. Bertram Lippincott told about Zora's early days with her publisher, then let me pound on a Haitian voodoo drum Zora had given them thirty-five years earlier.

Arthur P. Davis and Saunders Redding talked of Hurston's visits to black campuses as a lecturer. Louise Thompson Patterson patiently explained what it was like to serve as typist and friend to Zora and to Langston Hughes. The poet and playwright May Miller spoke of Zora at Howard. The late Herbert Sheen told of his marriage to Zora. Paul Green remembered his dramatic collaboration with her, and compared it to his later collaboration with Richard Wright. Grant Reynolds described Zora's political organizing in his congressional campaign against Adam Clayton Powell.

A number of people shared their ideas about Hurston with me.

We have not always agreed, but I have always learned from them. I wish to thank Mary Burger, Richard M. Dorson, Gladys-Marie Fry, Patrick Gilpin, Trudier Harris, Evelyn Helmick, Nathan Huggins, Blyden Jackson, Gayl Jones, Lawrence Levine, Mary Ellen Lewis, William A. Stewart, and William Wiggins. Colleagues at the University of Wyoming and the University of Kentucky who gave special support were Lolita Burns, Herb Dieterich, Tillie Eggers, Walter Eggers, Duncan Harris, Janice Harris, Jerry Ranta, and Joseph Whittaker. Thomas Preston of the University of Wyoming graciously arranged for a summer office that enabled me to finish the last chapters.

The following people also aided my research in important ways—through interviews, correspondence, and sometimes just simple conversation. I wish to publicly thank Norton Baskin, C. C. Benton, C. E. Bolen, Walter S. Buckingham, Mrs. Kenneth Burritt, Rychard Cook, Carita Doggett Corse, Martin Duberman, W. Edward Farrison, Leroy Floyd, Ronald C. Foreman, Jr., Roland Gibson, Taylor Gordon, Montgomery Gregory, Herbert Halpert, Marilyn Hemenway, David Henderson, Tay Hohoff, Mary Holland, Eugene C. Holmes, Alan Jabbour, Bruce Kellner, Phyllis Klotman, John S. Knight, Adele Ferguson Lafayette, Mary Jane Lupton, Burroughs Mitchell, Henry Allen Moe, Henry Lee Moon, Frederick O'Neal, Don Pope, Percival Punter, Nora Holt Ray, Hiroko Sato, Marjorie Silver, John Szwed, Louis Waldman, Dorothy Waring, Jean Parker Waterbury, Armitage Watkins, Barbara Watson, Carolyne Rich Williams, and Norman Yetman.

The administrators and staff members of each library cited in the notes helped unselfishly in the gathering of materials. Staff in the libraries of the University of Wyoming, the University of Kentucky, and Indiana University have always been diligent and accommodating. Others who helped in special ways were Donald Gallup, Curator of American Literature, and Joan Hofmann of the Beinecke Rare Book and Manuscript Library, Yale University; Laura Monti of the University of Florida; Ann Allen Shockley and Sue P. Chandler of Fisk University; Dorothy Porter, Thomas C. Battle, and Esme Bhan of Howard University; Helga Eason of the Miami Public Library; S. A. Streit of the City College of New York; and Jean B. Hutson and Ernest Kaiser of the Schomburg Collection,

New York Public Library. A number of people not at libraries also helped me gather materials; these include the staff of the John Simon Guggenheim Memorial Foundation, Charles Scribner, Jr., of Charles Scribner's Sons, Armitage Watkins, Marjorie Silver, the late Herbert Sheen, and Paul Green.

I wish to thank the following libraries, institutions, and individuals for permission to quote from personal correspondence or from other Hurston materials in their possession: the James Weldon Johnson Memorial Collection and the Carl Van Vechten Papers, Collection of American Literature, Beinecke Rare Book and Manuscript Library, Yale University; Manuscript Division, the Moorland-Spingarn Research Center, Howard University; Rare Books and Manuscripts, University of Florida Library; the Archives of the University of Pennsylvania Library; the Humanities Research Center, University of Texas at Austin; the Florida Historical Society, and the depository for its papers, the University of South Florida Library; Special Collections, Fisk University Library; the Manuscript Division and the Archive of Folk Song, Library of Congress; the American Philosophical Society; the John Simon Guggenheim Memorial Foundation; Charles Scribner's Sons; and Alan Lomax.

Portions of the manuscript were read by Houston Baker, Barry Beckham, Alan Dundes, Michael Harper, and Phil Petrie; they all served me better than I deserved. My debt to Alice Walker is enormous; her foreword touches the book with a special grace. My main man, Tom Blues, not only helped preserve my sanity; he also read the manuscript with editorial precision and a bemused tolerance for creative syntax. Nikki Swingle, who typed the manuscript, served more as an editor than as a stenographer.

Above all, my debt is to the Hurston family for granting me permission to quote from Zora's correspondence and unpublished writings: to Everette Hurston, Sr., administrator of the Hurston estate, who has been both a friend and an advisor, and who provided some of the photographs for this volume; to his son, Everett, Jr.; to Myrtis Hurston, Zora's sister-in-law; to Mabel Hurston, widow of Zora's brother Joel; to the late John Hurston, who encouraged me, but who died before we ever met. May this book honor the memory of their extraordinary kinswoman.

≋≋ **Abbreviations**

The following abbreviations are used in the notes to refer to frequently mentioned persons and collections:

AL   Alain Locke
APS   American Philosophical Society Library
AS   Arthur Spingarn
AWRH   Armitage Watkins Files for ZNH, 1951, in RH's possession
CSJFisk   Charles S. Johnson Papers, Special Collections, Fisk University Library
CVV   Carl Van Vechten
EE   Edwin Embree
FB   Franz Boas
FHSP   Florida Historical Society Papers, University of South Florida Library
Fisk   Special Collections (other than CSJFisk and RosFisk), Fisk University Library
GgFnd   John Simon Guggenheim Memorial Foundation Files
HCUFla   Hurston Collection, Rare Books and Manuscripts, University of Florida Library
HUAL   Alain Locke Papers, Moorland-Spingarn Research Center, Howard University Library
JPW   Jean Parker Waterbury
JWJYale   James Weldon Johnson Memorial Collection, Collection of American Literature, Beinecke Rare Book and Manuscript Library, Yale University
LCAFS   Archive of Folk Song, Library of Congress
LCMD   Manuscript Division, Library of Congress
LH   Langston Hughes

LTP	Louise Thompson Patterson
MSRC	Moorland-Spingarn Research Center, Howard University Library
RH	Robert E. Hemenway
RosFisk	Rosenwald Foundation Papers, Special Collections, Fisk University Library
Scribner's	Charles Scribner's Sons Files
SCUFla	Special Collections, Rare Books and Manuscripts, University of Florida Library
Watkins	Armitage Watkins Files (other than AWRH)
ZNH	Zora Neale Hurston

In chapters 6, 8, 11, and 12, portions of the biography have been reconstructed from such an abundance of sources that to follow normal footnoting procedure would be too cumbersome. Rather than impede the narrative, I have indicated in a single note the documents upon which the passage in question is based. Quotations from Zora Neale Hurston for which no citation is given come from her autobiography, *Dust Tracks on a Road* (Philadelphia: J. B. Lippincott, 1942).

 Zora Neale Hurston

≋≋≋ Introduction

On January 16, 1959, Zora Neale Hurston, suffering from the effects of a stroke and writing painfully in longhand, composed a letter to the "editorial department" of Harper Brothers. She asked if the firm would be interested in seeing "the book I am laboring upon at present—a life of Herod the Great."[1] One year and twelve days later, Zora Hurston died without funds to provide for her burial, a resident of the welfare home of Saint Lucie County, Florida. She lies today in a segregated cemetery in Fort Pierce, Florida, somewhere near a granite marker reading

ZORA NEALE HURSTON
"A GENIUS OF THE SOUTH"
1901———1960
NOVELIST, FOLKLORIST
ANTHROPOLOGIST

The novelist Alice Walker placed that tombstone in the Garden of the Heavenly Rest in 1973, but she had no way of knowing exactly where her spiritual kinswoman had been buried. In a field of waist-high weeds there were only the depressions of unmarked graves to guide her to an approximate spot. Hurston's final resting place is symbolic of the black writer's historical fate in America. Alice Walker's homage to her sister in race and art protests this fact as it laments Hurston's untimely death.

Zora Neale Hurston died prior to the affirmation of Afro-American culture in the 1960s, and the letter to Harper's reveals how the bright promise of an earlier interest in black art—the Harlem Renaissance of the 1920s—deteriorated for many of those who had shared its exuberance. It also displays the personal tragedy of Zora Neale Hurston. The woman soliciting Harper's interest in her book was not accustomed to advertising manuscripts by unsolicited mail. She was a graduate of Barnard College, the author of four novels, two books of folklore, an autobiography, and more than fifty short stories and essays. She had been granted honorary doctorates, published in national magazines, featured on the cover of the *Saturday Review*, invited to speak at major universities, and praised by the *New York Herald Tribune* as being "in the front rank" not only of black writers but of all American writers. She had been the most important collector of Afro-American folklore in the country. She had published more books than any other black American woman.[2]

She was now sick and lonely, penniless and forgotten, without either the fame or the wealth such a career would seem to have earned. Her last book had been published eleven years before; in 1950 she was discovered working as a maid on the same day one of her stories appeared in the *Saturday Evening Post*. Yet her obscurity had nothing to do with drink, drugs, moral dissolution, or high living. Hurston died poor for the simple reason that near the end of her life she had no way to generate income while continuing to write. She was contacting Harper's in the hopes of an advance. The survival of three hundred pages of this final manuscript adds a poignant footnote to her literary legacy. Ordered to destroy her effects, the welfare-home janitor had begun to burn them, when a deputy sheriff extinguished the flame with a garden hose. Having heard that this indigent, part-time schoolteacher had once been an author, he thought the Herod manuscript might have monetary value and could be used to pay the many debts left behind.

"Herod the Great" is a good beginning for understanding Hurston's career, because it is unlike any of her previous books. It is a standard-English, straightforward, historical biography of the ruler of Galilee from 47 to 4 B.C., the father of the Herod to whom Christ was sent for trial by Pontius Pilate. Hurston spent most of her waning energy the last seven years of her life attempting to write this story, and yet even the most sympathetic reader concludes that the manuscript, lying now charred and incomplete in the University of Florida Library, would have been a minor work. It lacks the narrative effect that caused the *New York Times* to review one of her novels as "a well nigh perfect story."[3] Its spoken language is far from the skilled dialogue that moved the *Saturday Review* to claim in 1934, "No one has ever reported the speech of Negroes with a more accurate ear."[4] "Herod the Great" illustrates how far Hurston had retreated, or perhaps, more accurately, had been forced to retreat by circumstance, from the unique sources of her esthetic: the music and speech, energy and wisdom, dignity and humor of the black rural South.

Part of that retreat was a simple matter of economics, part of it a more complicated matter of personality. Of Hurston's contemporaries, Richard Wright and Langston Hughes were almost the only black authors who made a living by writing. During the thirties and forties, black authors did not receive big advances, and publishers did not court them; if their books were not about the "race problem"—as Hurston's were not—they seldom sold well. Yet Zora Hurston was a woman of fierce independence who lived for her writing; all of her jobs were simply stopgaps to support her between books. She never really compromised with the American economic system, and she spent a lifetime refusing to accept the roles prescribed for black women intellectuals. She was published mostly during the Great Depression, and the largest royalty any of her books ever earned was $943.75;[5] the only dwelling she ever owned was an old houseboat bought during World War II. She was married twice, briefly, and she could love hard; but she never let men, or their support, interfere with her career. Both marriages were short lived because she feared such encroachment.

Personally, Zora Hurston was a complex woman with a high tolerance for contradiction. She could occasionally manipulate people to aid her career, and she was a natural actress who could play many roles. Physically, she was a high-energy person, capable of intense work for long stretches of time, possessed of a personal effervescence that frequently overwhelmed. She had an instinct for publicity, and she was capable of commercially popularizing black culture, of taking white friends to storefront churches, telling down-home stories to those wishing to romanticize black life. Above all, she was a sophisticated writer who was never afraid to be herself. She was flamboyant and yet vulnerable, self-centered and yet kind, a Republican conservative and yet an early black nationalist. Her personality could seem a series of opposites, and her friends were often incapable of reconciling the polarities of her personal style. Aware of this, she came to delight in the chaos she sometimes left behind.

There was always, however, a central pattern to the apparent crazy quilt. Hurston remained committed to her work, and to the honest portraiture of her race, no matter how poorly that commitment paid. Her portraits were primarily drawn in a series of books published in the mid-thirties. She had collected folklore extensively in the rural South, and the collections were published in *Mules and Men* (1935), the first popular book about Afro-American folklore ever written by a black scholar; *Mules and Men* so compellingly displays the rich imaginative life in a black folk community that Alan Lomax has called it "the most engaging, genuine, and skillfully written book in the field of folklore." Her best novel, *Their Eyes Were Watching God* (1937), is regarded as one of the most poetic works of fiction by a black writer in the first half of the twentieth century, and one of the most revealing treatments in modern literature of a woman's quest for a satisfying life. The book has been favorably compared to *Native Son*, and it manages to express Zora Hurston's own hopes for a meaningful place in a male-dominated world much better than her autobiography, *Dust Tracks on a Road* (1942). Her other novels, the autobiographical *Jonah's Gourd Vine* (1934), the Moses legend from a black perspective, *Moses, Man of the Mountain* (1939), and her final book, about white southerners, *Seraph on the Suwanee* (1948), have also been highly praised; *Jonah's Gourd Vine* was described by one of the New York dailies at the time of its publication as the most "vital and original novel about the American Negro that has yet been written by a member of the Negro race." Despite such reviews, none of her novels sold more than five thousand copies before going out of print.[6]

An unmarked grave is a romantic, poignant resting place, but it represents a human tragedy. Zora Neale Hurston was a nontragic person, a woman who rejoiced in print about the beauty of being black. When her blues came, when bigots and rednecks and crackers and liberals and racial missionaries got her down, she retreated into a privacy that protected her sense of self; publicly, she avoided confrontation by announcing that she didn't look at a person's color, only one's worth. She personally believed in an integrated society, but she spent her career trying to preserve and celebrate black cultural practices. Her life testifies only for her particular black experience, but her career witnesses for contemporary black authors. Why did such a writer end up living on food vouchers from the state of Florida? Why did her body lie in wait for subscriptions to pay for a funeral? The answers are as complicated as her art, as paradoxical as her person, as simple as the fact that she lived in a country that fails to honor its black artists.

NOTES

1. ZNH to Harper Brothers, Jan. 16, 1959 (HCUFla). (For a list of abbreviations used in the notes, see pp. xxv-xxvi.)

2. Lewis Gannett, "Books and Things," *New York Herald Tribune*, May 3, 1934; Darwin T. Turner, *In a Minor Chord* (Carbondale: Southern Illinois University Press, 1971), p. 90.

3. Lucy Tompkins, "In Florida Glades," *New York Times Book Review*, Sept. 26, 1937, p. 29.

4. George Stevens, "Negroes by Themselves," *Saturday Review*, Sept. 18, 1937, p. 3.

5. Winnie Wong of J. B. Lippincott to RH, May 27, 1971, listing sales and royalty figures for ZNH books.

6. Margaret Wallace, "Real Negro People," *New York Times Book Review*, May 6, 1934, p. 6; Alan Lomax, "Zora Neale Hurston—A Life of Negro Folklore," *Sing Out!*, 10 (Oct.-Nov., 1960), 12.

1 ≋≋≋ Jump at the Sun: 1901-25

In the first week of January, 1925, Zora Neale Hurston arrived in New York City with one dollar and fifty cents in her purse, no job, no friends, but filled with "a lot of hope."[1] She came from Washington, leaving a steady job as a manicurist in a Seventh Avenue barbership to explore the opportunities for a career as a writer. As a part-time student at Howard University for the previous five years, she had been an aspiring English major, much praised for her short stories and poems, and she had a vague idea of studying writing in one of Manhattan's many colleges. She carried most of her belongings in her bag, including a number of manuscripts that she hoped would impress. Even if they did not, she was confident of her ability to survive in the big city; she had been on her own since the age of fourteen. Brown skinned, big boned, with freckles and high cheekbones, she was a striking woman; her dark brown eyes were both impish and intelligent, her voice was rich and black—with the map of Florida on her tongue.

She went first to the offices of the National Urban League on East Twenty-third Street, where she asked to be introduced to Charles S. Johnson, editor of the Urban League's magazine, *Opportunity: A Journal of Negro Life*. A month earlier he had published one of her short stories, and since September he had been encouraging her to submit material to the literary contest his magazine currently sponsored. Johnson, director of research for the league, had single-handedly turned *Opportunity* into an expression of "New Negro" thought. "New Negroes" were black people who made clear that they would not accept a subordinate role in American society, and Johnson believed that young writers like Zora Neale Hurston would help prove the cultural parity of the races. He urged her to stay in

New York, and as she settled in, he helped her find a series of odd jobs. Mrs. Johnson often gave Zora carfare to make sure she could accept the frequent dinner invitations at the Johnson house.[2]

For a young girl from rural Florida and provincial Washington who had been working for ten years to secure an education, this interest and help must have made all the sacrifice seem worthwhile. She had arrived at a hard-won sense of self built around the knowledge that because she was black her life had been graced in unusual ways, and she had confidence that she could express that grace in fiction. The story Johnson had printed a month earlier, "Drenched in Light," embodied this personal vision she brought to New York; it was her initial contribution to the cultural uprising that Johnson and others were calling a "Harlem Renaissance."

"Drenched in Light" was Hurston's calling card on literary New York, the tangible evidence she could point to that she was indeed a serious writer. It is also a statement of personal identity. It tells of a day in the life of Isie Watts, a "little brown figure perched upon the gate-post" in front of her Eatonville, Florida, home. Isie likes to race up and down the road to Orlando, "hailing gleefully all travelers." As a result, "everybody in the country" knows "Isie Watts, the joyful," and how she likes to laugh and play, beg rides in cars, and live to the fullest every minute of her young life. Isie gets into various scrapes, including an impish attempt to shave her sleeping grandmother, and eventually is given a ride by a passing white motorist, despite her grandmother's disapproval. There is no building toward a dramatic climax, and very little plot. The structure of the story is thematic. The point is that Isie, poor and black, is far from tragic; rather, she is "drenched in light," a condition which endears her to everyone, although it presents her grandmother with a discipline problem. Isie is persistently happy, and the implication is that whites suffer from an absence of such joy. Isie's white benefactor ends the story, "I want a little of her sunshine to soak into my soul. I need it."

Hurston may have been manipulating white stereotypes of black people here, but it is not a matter of satire. She remembered Eatonville as a place of great peace and happiness, identifying that happiness as a function of her family and communal existence. "Drenched in Light" refers to this sense of well being, and it repudiates any stereotyped notion that Zora Neale Hurston was a

JUMP AT THE SUN

tragically deprived black child, subject to any "mark of oppression" or self-hate. Coming at the start of her literary career, in her first nationally published story, it was her manifesto of selfhood, an affirmation of her origins.

Zora's identification with Isie Watts is almost total; the grandmother of the story had Hurston's own grandmother's name, Eatonville was her native village, and the events described were major memories of her childhood. If readers could have projected themselves into 1942 and read her autobiography, they would have found that Zora Hurston also "used to take a seat on the top of the gate-post and watch the world go by. One way to Orlando ran past my house, so the carriages and cars would pass before me. The movement made me glad to see it. Often the white travelers would hail me, but more often I hailed them, and asked, 'Don't you want me to go a piece of the way with you?'" If a vision into a future eighteen years away requires too much clairvoyance, a projection of only four years would reveal the same autobiographical content in her May, 1928, article in the *World Tomorrow*, "How It Feels to Be Colored Me." There Hurston stresses again that as a child "my favorite place was atop the gate-post. Proscenium box for a born first-nighter. Not only did I enjoy the show, but I didn't mind the actors knowing that I liked it." Although there is a good deal of pixie in that essay's title, since it addresses the unspoken question of many whites, her point is the same as in "Drenched in Light": "I am not tragically colored. There is no great sorrow dammed up in my soul, nor lurking behind my eyes. . . . I do not belong to the sobbing school of Negrohood who hold that nature somehow has given them a lowdown dirty deal."

"Drenched in Light" is a belligerent, combative statement of independence, intended to portray the value of an Eatonville memory for Zora Neale Hurston. Typically, it addresses both white paternalism and black self-pity. It suggests that Zora Hurston arrived in New York after considerable thought about who she was and where she came from; while other Harlem artists might grope for identity, she impressed all by being herself.

The sources of the Hurston self-confidence were her home town, her family, and the self-sufficiency demanded of her after she left home for the world. Eatonville, Florida, existed not as the "black backside" of a white city, but as a self-governing, all-black town, proud and independent, living refutation of white claims that black inability for self-government necessitated the racist institutions of a Jim Crow South. Incorporated since 1886, Eatonville was, in Zora Hurston's words, "a pure Negro Town," with charter, mayor, council, and town marshal; the only white folks were those who passed through.[3] As a result, she had been more or less isolated as a child in totally black surroundings, and the town became, as the black poet June Jordan has put it, "a supportive, nourishing environment," where people represented "their own particular selves in a Family and Community setting that permits relaxation from hunted/ warrior postures and that fosters the natural, person-postures of courting, jealousy, ambition, dream, sex, work, partying, sorrow, bitterness, celebration and fellowship."[4]

Adjacent to Maitland, five miles from Orlando, on the road that now connects Florida Highway 17 and Interstate 4, Eatonville was "a city of five lakes, three croquet courts, three hundred brown skins, three hundred good swimmers, plenty guavas, two schools, and no jail house."[5] It was a rich repository of the oral traditions preserved through slavery into the twentieth century, and as Hurston grew up she listened well to the "lying sessions" on the front porch of Joe Clarke's general store. In New York, even though she had been away from Florida for a decade, she could feel secure in the knowledge that the lies would not have stopped in her absence. The men and women on the store porch were not a function of time, history, population changes, or even Joe Clarke's dying and the store's going to Lee Glenn; their lying sessions were constant verbal rituals contributing order, beauty, and poetry to the community's life. They were as much a part of growing up as the two big chinaberry trees shading Zora's gatepost, or the Cape Jasmine bushes with hundreds of blooms on either side of her walk. Joe Clarke's store was the "heart and spring of the town," the place where people sat around on boxes, benches, and nail kegs, and "passed this world and the next one through their mouths." Here it was that God, Devil, Brer Rabbit, Brer Fox, Sis Cat, Brer Bear "walked and talked like natural men."[6] On the store porch even the Bible was made over; stories of creation became colorful explanations for the realities of day-to-day life: black people became black, Zora learned, by misunderstanding God's commandment in Genesis to "get back."

The store porch produced a whole cycle of tales about Marster and John, a quick-witted, powerful slave. If someone brought a guitar, the storytelling would stop, and the night would become haunted with the words of the blues, or reverberate with the rhythm of a railroad worksong learned from a "singing liner." Small children waiting for their mothers to call them to bed could listen to the elaborate guitar style of a man like Bubber Mimms, champion orange picker and one of the town's best "box" players. A mouth harp might suddenly appear, and the guitar solo became a duet. Before long others were joining in, beating out rhythm against the bottom of overturned nail kegs. The children might also tag after the turpentine workers who would stop to chat as they came through town on their way to another job. Zora remembered how "I'd run out and follow them. I thought they were the most exciting people in the world, stomping along, barefooted as a yard dog, playing their guitars and singing, and always the guitars had red ribbons on them."[7]

Hurston had been born in Eatonville on January 7, probably in 1901; birth records of the period do not survive, and she was purposely inconsistent in the birth dates she dispensed during her lifetime, most of which were fictitious. Depending on the document, and whether she was trying to impress someone with her youth or her age, she claimed to be born in 1898, 1899, 1900, 1901, 1902, or 1903. One family member says the year might be 1891. Zora was so deceptive about the real date that she once urged her youngest brother to list a birth date on the public record that would have made him older than her. The original deception may have occurred when she self-consciously entered high school at an advanced age, but the willful subterfuge is characteristic of her entire career—Zora Hurston always kept a portion of her life secret, and she always thought of herself as a young woman.[8]

She was brought into the world during "hog killing time" by a white man who arrived shortly before the mid-wife, intending to deliver only a ham for the Hurstons' meat house. She grew up as a highly inquisitive, almost belligerent child who took full advantage of the Florida sunshine. The Hurston yard was full of oranges, grapefruit, tangerines, and guavas; she chased away alligators and swam in the lake, discovered that she was extra strong for her age, and became "the one girl who could take a good pummeling without running home to tell." Her parents urged her to play with her Christmas dolls, but dolls caught the devil around Zora: "They got into fights and leaked sawdust before New Years." She was an unreconstructed tomboy who spied noble, grew like a gourd vine, and yelled bass like a gator.

Her belligerence, if we believe her characterization of herself in her autobiography, _Dust Tracks on a Road_, kept her constantly at odds with her father. While her mother was telling her to "'jump at de sun.' We might not land on the sun, but at least we would get off the ground," her father was counseling more realistic goals: "It did not do for Negroes to have too much spirit," or "The white folks won't stand for it." He frequently complained to her mother that Zora was going to be hanged before she got grown, that her mother "was going to suck sorrow for not beating my temper out of me before it was too late." One should not conclude from this that the Reverend John Hurston, moderator of the South Florida Baptist Association, was a passive participant in the Florida social structure; he was only attempting to inculcate the sensibilities of southern survival. Ralph Ellison, explaining why the young Richard Wright was often beaten, has called this process the "homeopathic" dose of violence administered to southern black children for their own good because the parent loves the child and wants him to live. Mayor of Eatonville for three terms, codifier of its laws, John Hurston's opposition to caste had never wavered. On at least one occasion during Zora's childhood he joined the men of Eatonville, gun in hand, to investigate moans and whipping sounds arising from a nearby lake shore. The anguished cries were discovered to come from a white recipient of Klan justice, rather than from a fellow townsman, but her father's action suggests much about the temper of Eatonville. John Hurston was one of the strongest men in the village, two hundred pounds of hard muscle, known for his bravery, leadership, and powerful, poetical preaching. A family legend told how he once "cold-conked" a mule with his fist. Although the illustrator of a modern paperback edition of her autobiography depicts Zora as a barefoot girl standing before a ramshackle dwelling, her father provided for his family well, building a sound eight-room house on his five acres, and always putting food on the table. The family had so many laying hens that the children sometimes boiled eggs in an iron kettle, then lay in the yard and ate until they were full. If the eight Hurston children went barefoot during the first years of Zora's life, it was by choice, something she did not always remember as she looked back with resentment on the disintegration of the family after her mother's death.[9]

It was her mother who made Zora her special child and had the most influence on her early life. She did not want to "squinch" Zora's spirit and turn her child into a "mealy mouthed rag doll." Small in stature, large in spirit, Lucy Hurston possessed the steely toughness she needed to deal with a philandering husband. She once took a horse whip to a feminine admirer of the Reverend Mr. Hurston, and it was her advice and counsel that helped him maintain his church despite an inability to deny the call of the flesh. Lucy Hurston was highly intelligent—Zora speculated that her father was frustrated by his inability "to whip her mentally"—with a commitment to education that was transferred to her five sons and three daughters; she gathered them each night in her bedroom to do lessons, carrying them herself past long division and "parsing sentences in grammar," the drills remembered from her days as a country schoolteacher. As they grew beyond such skills, the older children took over the lessons, but she remained in the room in order to insure the younger scholars' attention and acquire new knowledge herself. Taking root in a formidable natural intelligence, this training caused her youngest daughter to blossom. Zora learned to read before school age, and her quickness set her apart. Of all the school's students it was the fifth-grader Zora Hurston who so impressed two visiting Yankee ladies that they were moved to send her a box of books. Suddenly her single-volume library, the family's Bible, was augmented by Grimm's fairy tales, Greek and Roman myths, Norse legends, Kipling, and Robert Louis Stevenson.

Books simply confirmed her knowledge of another world, a hemisphere of the imagination. When she played in the moonlight, Zora was convinced that the moon followed her, specially shining on his special child. She liked to climb to the top of one of the huge chinaberry trees which guarded the front gate and search the horizon; she wanted to see what the end of the world was like: "My shoes had sky-blue bottoms to them, and I was riding off to look at the belly-band of the world." The green envelope protecting an ear of corn became "Miss Corn Shuck," who lived in Zora's special hiding place beneath the house. "Miss Corn Shuck" fell in love with a cake of scented soap, "Mr. Sweet Smell," which had disappeared from her mother's dresser. An abandoned door handle offered her "Reverend Door Knob"; her mother's sewing produced a whole family of "Spool People." They all stayed around the house for years, holding funerals and weddings and taking trips with their creator "to where the sky met the ground."

Her mother died when Hurston was nine, in a scene that was traumatic for the child. Near death, Lucy called Zora into the room and gave solemn instructions that no one was to take a pillow from under her head as she was dying, and neither the clock nor the looking glass in the room was to be covered with cloth. These were strange requests only because they indicate that on her deathbed Lucy Hurston wished to symbolically reject the folklore of her village. Eatonville, like many rural communities, believed that a person's dying hard was a bad sign, since the spirit might haunt the survivors; everything must be done to alleviate suffering. It was understood that a pillow under one's head prolonged dying, and that the looking glass should be covered because a reflection of the corpse might attach itself permanently to the glass. One covered the clock because it would be forever ruined if it was functioning when time ran out and the spirit looked upon the clock's face. The reasons for these beliefs, however, were ultimately unimportant. The community possessed a ceremony of dying, and Zora was unable to prevent the adults from carrying out their rites. Her father held her, and despite her protests the mourners softened dying by removing the pillow and turning the bed to the east (so that it would not be crossways of the world), while the hooded clock and mirror preserved the good fortune of the household.

The Eatonville world required those acts, and her father's physical restraint had preserved the sacraments. Unable to conquer Old Death, with his "big soft feet and square toes," the survivors created rituals to reassure the living and avoid admitting helplessness. Zora Hurston agonized over that moment for years, for she had failed her mother's dying request, thwarted by her father and her own community. As she put it: "If there is any consciousness after death, I hope that Mama knows that I did my best. She must know how I have suffered for my failure." She felt that her mother's death "was the end of a phase in my life": "That hour began my wanderings. Not so much in geography, but in time. Then not so much in time as in spirit."[10]

The years following her mother's death were extremely hard. Her father quickly remarried, and she was sent to school in Jacksonville. Eventually, opposition to her stepmother caused her relations with her father to deteriorate, and he even proposed that the Jacksonville school adopt her. She lived off and on with her father and other relatives, longed for books to read, attended school now and then, and worked a number of years for white people as a maid—none too successfully, since she did not act humble and she refused to entertain the advances of her male employers. She had a brutal fight with her stepmother, admitting thirty years later that she had longed to kill the woman. For the first time in her life she learned what poverty could be like, how people "could be slave ships in shoes." She grew self-conscious about her looks, feeling that no man could really care for her. At least one member of her family thinks she might have secretly married sometime during this period. Eventually she became a wardrobe girl in a Gilbert and Sullivan repertory company touring the South. More or less on her own since her mother's death, Hurston found the theatrical troupe the major educational experience of her youth, liberating her from the provincialism she had known all her life.

She traveled with the troupe for eighteen months, and learned enough of a larger world that when she left the show in Baltimore, she had a burning desire to attend high school and go on to college. Evening classes led to enrollment at Morgan Academy in Baltimore (the high school division of what is now Morgan State University) in September, 1917. A story is told that she was granted admission after she stopped a teacher on the street, asking him if he would support her schooling. When she entered classes in the fall, she owned only one dress, a change of underwear, and a pair of tan oxfords, but her raw intelligence glittered. Although in many ways only a rough working girl amid the sons and daughters of the middle class, she was encouraged at Morgan, her way eased with jobs arranged by school officials. She received credit for two years by exam, then enrolled in a college preparatory course, so excited about her opportunity that she once memorized Gray's "Elegy in a Country Churchyard" in a single night because she was afraid she might not get a chance to read it again. Doing well but not spectacularly, she graduated in June, 1918. She went on to Howard University, "the capstone of Negro education," where once again she quickly established herself, in the words of one former teacher, as a "rough edged diamond." Working part time as a manicurist, she plunged into her Howard studies, attending Howard Prep during the school year of 1918–19 in order to catch up in areas that her intermittent schooling had left untouched.[11]

The next year, as she went on to the college course, she met and fell in love with a fellow student, Herbert Sheen, of Decatur, Illinois. He had come to Washington with hopes of becoming a congressional page; when the job did not materialize, he began working his way through Howard as a hotel waiter. Both offspring of ministers, the two working students had much in common, and their romance blossomed even after Sheen moved to New York in 1921 to work for a physician who promised him help entering Columbia. When the doctor reneged, Sheen organized a jazz combo around his own hard-driving piano and played New Jersey resorts. While Zora stayed at Howard, he moved back to Illinois and the University of Chicago, eventually receiving his B.S. in 1924 and entering medical school. Through all their separations they remained close, and it was understood that they would marry sometime in the future.[12]

In the meantime, however, Hurston was much taken with university life. She worshipped her teachers and wanted to "be worthy to stand there under the shadow of the hovering spirit of Howard. I felt the ladder under my feet." She completed a year and a half of college course work during her intermittent study at Howard between 1919 and 1924. Her record was inconsistent, with A's in courses she liked, F's in courses that did not interest her, including physical education. Howard Academy granted her an associate degree in 1920. She worked constantly, but was frequently in debt;

she had at least one serious illness. In addition to her manicurist's job she also worked as a waitress at the exclusive Cosmos Club, and as a maid for distinguished black Washington families. She often spent her nights in marathon literary discussions at Halfway House, home of Georgia Douglas Johnson, a prominent black poet. Her literary aspirations were encouraged by a number of very good English teachers, and she was admitted to membership in the campus literary club, the Stylus. Alain Locke, a young philosophy professor, a Rhodes scholar and Harvard graduate, had formed this group and limited its membership to students of demonstrated talent, chosen in an annual competition. Montgomery Gregory, the dramatic arts instructor, was the other faculty sponsor, and both were excited about expressing the folklife of rural black people through plays, stories, and poems. Hurston was accepted as a Stylus member, and she published her first story, "John Redding Goes to Sea," in the group's magazine in May, 1921.[13]

"John Redding" is a groping, stumbling attempt to capture the folk ethos, overladen with sentimentality. The plot is trite, the saga of a young dreamer, John Redding, who from childhood dreams of leaving his rural, Eatonville-like village on Florida's Saint Johns River and sailing to "where the sky touches the ground." Encouraged in his hopes by his father, whose similar visions have never been realized, John is held by his mother, who in self-pity threatens to disown him if he leaves. The wanderlust remains, but circumstances beat him down, and marriage seems to seal his doom. The story ends in a flourish, however, with John going to labor on a new Saint Johns River bridge. A violent storm destroys the bridge during John's work shift, and he is last seen lying on his back on a piece of timber floating downstream: "His arms were outstretched and the water washed over his brogans. . . . A heavy piece of steel or timber had struck him in falling, for his left side was laid open by the thrust."

Every student author worth his pretense has created such a crucifixion, and neither Hurston's dialogue nor her self-conscious wisdom ("If time and propinquity conquered John, what then? These forces have overcome older men.") redeems the hackneyed story. What "John Redding" illustrates is that even as an apprentice, Zora Hurston was struggling to make literature out of the

Eatonville experience. It was her unique subject, and she was encouraged to make it the source of her art. Three years later, when Locke recommended her to Johnson, he knew already that she would bring unusual gifts to this Harlem Renaissance that Johnson was promoting. After the editor accepted her "Drenched in Light," she submitted another Eatonville story, "Spunk," and a play of Florida folklife, *Color Struck*, to the 1925 *Opportunity* contest. Both won prizes, earning her an invitation to the *Opportunity* contest award dinner. Less than five months after she introduced herself in the *Opportunity* offices, Zora Hurston found herself honored as one of the prominent talents in the new movement in the black arts.

A year before Zora arrived in New York, Charles Johnson had successfully arranged a dinner to display some of the "newer school" of black writers; he designed the award dinner in May, 1925, to provide a similar occasion for literary New York to meet the young authors. The dinner was attended by more than three hundred guests; the honorees were lionized, a fact that sometimes contrasted sharply with their circumstances. Mark Van Doren, editor of the *Century*, could chat with Langston Hughes, coming away much impressed, but unaware that the "bus boy poet" of Washington had used most of his forty-dollar prize to pay for his ticket to New York.[14]

Hurston shrewdly used this and subsequent dinners to make contacts, impressing those she met and encouraging a series of friendships that would significantly aid her career. "Spunk" won second prize for fiction and brought her to the attention of novelist Fannie Hurst, a contest judge. Discovering Zora's need of a job, Hurst eventually hired her as a live-in secretary, ignoring the fact that the D.C. manicurist did not type well, had little tolerance for detail, and was anything but self-effacing. Hurst was a very popular writer—her book in progress, the novel *Appassionata*, would become a best seller in 1926—but the new secretary was hardly humbled by her good fortune. Hurston's relations with her employer were more personal than professional, and Hurst, after throwing up her hands at "shorthand . . . short of legibility," and filing that was "a game of find the thimble," fired Zora as a secretary and kept her on as a chauffeur and companion. Zora stayed for more than a year, living "raffishly," according to Hurst, "with a blazing zest for life." She was late for appointments, utterly unimpressed by her employer's fame, and possessed of a quip for every occasion.[15]

Zora later described Hurst as "a little girl who is tall for her age." Although she admired the novelist's intelligence and talent, she found her a person of "contradictory moods and statements." She once referred to her famous friend as "a stunning wench" who was the complete "blend of woman and author," but who was also "one moment a serious worker controlled by her genii, the next instant playing make believe with all her heart." Privately, she expressed doubts about why Hurst was so interested in their appearing in public together; she told at least one friend that she thought it was because Hurst liked the way Zora's dark skin highlighted her own lily-like complexion.[16]

Hurst was taken aback when Zora would sometimes "race ahead of my thoughts and interject with an impatient suggestion or clarification of what I wanted to say." This quickness of mind impressed Annie Nathan Meyer, a socially prominent novelist and one of the founders of Barnard College, the women's division of Columbia University. Hurston had hoped to continue her schooling in New York, and shortly after their meeting at the awards dinner, Mrs. Meyer arranged for a Barnard scholarship to begin in the fall of 1925. For the first time since the age of thirteen, Zora Neale Hurston could attend school without financial worries. She would also be Barnard's only black student at the time.[17]

The Barnard experience was critical to Hurston's development, for she came to New York in 1925 as a writer and left Barnard two years later as a serious social scientist, the result of her study of anthropology under Franz Boas. In her "Record of Freshman Interest" she named writing as her major vocational interest, adding modestly, "I have had some small success as a writer and wish above all to succeed at it. Either teaching or social work will be interesting but consolation prizes."[18]

Although anthropology and art are not incompatible vocations, they can imply different uses of personal experience. When Hurston became fascinated with anthropology, she acquired the relatively rare opportunity to confront her culture both emotionally and analytically, both as subject and as object. She had lived Afro-American folklore before she knew that such a thing existed as a scientific concept or had special value as evidence of the adaptive creativity of a unique subculture. Hurston came to know that her parents and their neighbors perpetuated a rich oral literature without self-consciousness, a literature illustrating a creativity seldom recognized and almost universally misunderstood. The discovery of such scientific "facts" eventually made the imaginative truths of literature pale, and by 1927 her writing had become less interesting to her because of the growing sophistication of her anthropological study. During 1925 and 1926, however, Hurston thought of herself as an artist, a contributor to the literary movement that was the showpiece of the Harlem Renaissance.

This identity brought Zora a good deal of attention, and she was very quickly recognized in a number of New York circles as a special person. Not only was she Barnard's "sacred black cow," so cultivated by her classmates that she encountered little overt prejudice, but she was also a published writer, and secretary to a famous novelist. The black child who in Eatonville had begged for rides and followed turpentine workers down the road had traveled a considerable distance. She was now a New Negro, a part of the cultural movement illustrating the genius in black souls; her very presence exposed second-class citizenship as an absurd and irrational practice.

Zora Hurston was an extraordinarily witty woman, and she acquired an instant reputation in New York for her high spirits and side-splitting tales of Eatonville life. She could walk into a room of strangers, whether on Park Avenue or at a Harlem rent party, and almost immediately gather people, charm, amuse, and impress them, until it did not seem at all unnatural to be offering her whatever she might want. She was a perfect mimic, and she displayed a wide range of storytelling techniques learned from the masters of Joe Clarke's store porch. Added to this was her tendency toward the unorthodox act. She once took a nickel from the cup of the blind beggar at the 135th Street subway stop, explaining that she would repay later, but today she needed the fare more than he did. She could be tart, referring to racial uplifters as "Negrotarians," but she sometimes spent hours of a busy schedule reassuring a depressed fellow artist; her apartment was always open to someone needing a place to stay. All of this endeared her to most, and even before she entered Barnard, she had met the important people in black cultural circles, with the result that "Zora stories" circulated widely.

One does not know exactly how all the introductions took place. Dinners at Johnson's probably introduced her to James Hubert and Eugene Kinckle Jones of the Urban League. At socialite A'lelia Walker's townhouse in Harlem, nicknamed the "Dark Tower," she may have met writers Eric Walrond and Countee Cullen. William Pickens, her old dean from Morgan, now field secretary for the NAACP, probably was an entrée to the NAACP crowd, headed by W. E. B. Du Bois, the executive secretary, James Weldon Johnson, and Johnson's assistant, Walter White. Jessie Fauset, literary editor of the NAACP's magazine, the *Crisis*, was famous at the time for literary teas, and Hurston attended, meeting other young artists newly arrived in the city, like Arna Bontemps and Bruce Nugent. Nugent, who became a close friend, was familiar with the artistic life of Greenwich Village as well as less respectable parts of Harlem. Although Langston Hughes remembered Hurston as knowing everyone, especially celebrities, it is probably more accurate to say that she met more people, more quickly, with greater social results, than other newcomers.[19]

Zora still had many rough edges, and her ingenuous excitement contrasted—some thought by design—with New York sophistication. In the midst of her tenure as Hurst's companion, she took time in January, 1926, to send her prospective sister-in-law some matches shared one night by "Fannie Hurst, Stefannson (the explorer), Charles Norris, and myself," adding that Irvin S. Cobb "was there but he used another pack with Jessie Lasky and Margaret Anglin." The names mean little now, but in the twenties, some of them, like the humorist Cobb or the movie mogul Lasky, were widely known. A month later she would write again about all there was to see in New York, admitting, "I won't try to pretend that I'm not thrilled at the chance to see and do what I am. I love it." She added, "I am just running wild in every direction, trying to see everything at once."[20] The sending of used matchbooks hardly constitutes a designing cynicism or jaded sophistication, and although Hurston could frequently hide behind masks, the youthful excitement seems genuine.

Her intellectual talents were more prominent in New York than in Washington because of her *Opportunity* appearance and the new social circles she discovered. Washington and Howard had been largely a segregated existence, where she was limited to the carefully circumscribed world of job and school. Although her wit might impress a senator as she did his nails—the barbership had a distinguished clientele—she was still in the position of a personal service employee, exactly where the senator expected a black woman to be. He did not have to take her seriously, no matter how charming he found her, since she had done nothing as yet to document her talent. Her Howard professors might recognize her potential, but they encountered fine minds daily, some with similar talents and intellect. On campus, Hurston was still a sophomore.

In New York, as one of Charles S. Johnson's protégés at a time when there was great interest in black writers, Hurston's personality was not proscribed. Established artists accepted her as an equal. Even though she had published very little, it was in the right place. At Howard she had seen her fiction in the student magazine; now, her work appeared in one of the two major journals addressed to the national black community.

Johnson had designed the *Opportunity* contests and the award dinners for people in exactly Hurston's situation. It was part of his genius to know that New York was prepared to take Zora Hurston seriously, to cultivate her talent, and to support her monetarily. The recognition of Hurston's talent coincided with the time when "the Negro was in vogue,"[21] and it was no accident that Fannie Hurst wanted a black secretary or that Zora Neale Hurston would be sharing matches with famous New Yorkers.

Fannie Hurst was a sincere liberal. In 1933 she would publish *Imitation of Life*, a sensationalized novel of passing, earnestly if ineptly intended to explore the tragedy of race prejudice. She once took Zora on a trip to Vermont, passing her off as an African princess in order to integrate a local restaurant. Hurston finished the meal and remarked, "Who would think that a good meal could be so bitter."[22] Liberal principles were not the only reason whites were fascinated by black life during the twenties. It was a time when whites went out of their way to meet blacks, invite them to parties, ask them to serve as passports to Harlem. The black journalist George Schuyler, a sarcastic social critic, remembers it as a period when white folks "were adopting every Negro that displayed intelligence above that of the great ape."[23] The witty radiologist and novelist Rudolph Fisher said, "Negro stock is going up and everybody's buying."[24] Much of the interest had originated in the theater, where there was considerable excitement about black revues. *Shuffle Along* was a smash in 1921. One of the first performances by a black troupe on Broadway in a long time, it was followed by less successful imitations such as *Put and Take*, *Liza*, *Strut Miss Lizzie*, and *Runnin' Wild*. The interest in revue entertainers like Florence Mills, Ethel Waters, Bert Williams, Sissle and Blake, Miller and Lyles, and Creamer and Layton was quickly extended to the Bessie Smiths and the Duke Ellingtons, then to the race as a whole.

Particular "friends of the Negro" became widely known. Carl Van Vechten, a novelist, critic, and man-about-town, gave interracial parties that were routinely reported in the black press. Walter White referred to Van Vechten's apartment as the mid-town branch of the NAACP. Van Vechten's commitment to his black friends even caught the eye of *Time*, which reported on this dangerous figure in 1925: "Sullen-mouthed, silky haired Author Van Vechten has been playing with Negroes lately . . . writing prefaces for their poems, having them around the house, going to Harlem." Van Vechten was only the most prominent of many, for as Langston Hughes remarked in *The Big Sea*, Harlem parties often had enough white celebrities in attendance to turn any Nordic social climber green with envy. It was a time when a nationally known white journalist, Heywood Broun, was more easily recognized in some Harlem circles than was James Weldon Johnson, when stories were told of redcaps who carried the bags of their previous night's hostess, then waited, unrecognized, for their tip. Some whites, like Nancy Cunard, heiress to the steamship line, became such professional friends that they were a joke. "Do you know anything about Negroes," Salvador Dali was asked. "Everything," he replied. "I've met Nancy Cunard."[25]

Dali's flippancy was part of a general style of the twenties for both blacks and whites. It was the Jazz Age, and the music symbolized the freedom and frenzy of much behavior of that era. Part of discovering jazz was rotating one's hips to black dances; one of the most famous songs of the era was Ethel Waters's rendition of "Shake That Thing." Van Vechten arranged, through James Weldon Johnson, for Charleston lessons in his home. Jazz had been a forbidden music, and the people were given to smashing Victorian taboos. Rudolph Fisher claimed to envy the high-stepping "fays": "They camel and fish-tail and turkey, they geche and . . . scronch, they skate and buzzard and mess-around—and they do them all better than I!" When dancing the Charleston with abandon, one could be striking a blow for the new social freedom; it was a time of flappers and hip flasks, of "flaming youth," lost generations, and "revolutions in morals." Taylor Gordon, a singer from Montana, remembered being asked frequently if one could see his "black bottom"—a pun on the dance step reflecting the casual prurience of the age.[26] Hurston captured the flapper effect on a typical male in a song in one of her short stories:

> Skirt by skirt on every flirt
> They're getting higher and higher
> Day by Day in every way
> There's more to admire
> Sock by sock and knee by knee
> The more they show, the more we see
> The skirts run up, the socks run down
> Jingling bells run round and round
> Oh week by week, and day by day
> Let's hope that things keep on this way
> Let's kneel right down and pray.[27]

The speakeasy was the social club for the age, and places with such colorful names as "Basement Brownie's Coal Bin" were not special to Harlem, for they could also be found in the Financial District and Times Square. One Harlem cabaret was called "The Garden of Joy." Prohibition was considered another example of an outmoded morality, the federal government not being as up-to-date as the urban sophisticates, the most dedicated churchgoers making contacts with bootleggers. Historians have tried variously to explain the social history of the Roaring Twenties, but the dry prose never seems satisfactory. It was, as the clichés of this paragraph suggest, one of the most carefree periods in American national life.[28]

Hurston did not drink, but she was very much a part of this scene, and she was not restricted to its black division. Partially through contacts made with Hurst, partially because she was not afraid to court relationships with those who could help her, she became widely known in the Van Vechten circle. She wrote him frequent notes, inviting him to hear gospel groups discovered in storefront churches or blues singers new to town. She once offered to bring "the MOST MARVELLOUS SET OF SPIRITUAL SINGERS YET" to Van Vechten's apartment, promising him that if he heard just one song, he would "experience a revelation. I, Zora, vouch for it."[29] She became a common guest at the Van Vechten parties, where attendance was often a sign that Harlem artists had made their mark among upper-crust whites. Her white circle in the twenties included stockbrokers, journalists, publishing executives, artists, and editors who were fascinated by her rise from Eatonville. On the way back to New York from her first folklore collecting trip, she ended a letter to Van Vechten, "My love to the handsome 'debutante' broker of East 30th St., and the charming T.R.S. So eager to see you all. Hope Harry Block [a Knopf editor] is in town."[30] Hurston was not ashamed of her origins, and she made no effort to hide them, causing some black friends to accuse her of seeking patronage: why not help this poor girl from a rural Catfish Row? A more likely interpretation is that she refused to repudiate the folk origins that were such a rich part of her total identity. She abhorred pretense, and she had no desire to adopt a bourgeois respectability.

Hurston's association with the white cultural establishment was not unique among Harlem artists, for painting, literature, sculpture, music, and dancing created by black people became something of a white fad during the twenties—in much the same way that "Caucasians stormed Harlem," as Rudolph Fisher phrased it, in search of late-night excitement. Thinking that a trip uptown meant a safari into an exotic jungle, whites were titillated and exhilarated by Harlem spectacle. Harlem became an aphrodisiac, a place where whites could discover their primitive selves; many of the white fellow-travelers so often in attendance on the New Negro artists sought a vitality in the uptown night absent in their own lives. As one critic described it, "Caucasian dowagers . . . flocked

to Negro cabarets, drank gin supplied by Negroes with more business acumen than the race is generally credited with having, and
patronizingly gave individual Negroes bids to their homes. Nothing
was too good for the black man—as long as he expended his ener-
gies in song and dance."[31]

One way to legitimize this neurotic obsession with an exotic
primitivism was to claim an interest in the Afro-American creative
arts, and Hurston and her fellow artists were constantly faced with
determining the sincerity of the sudden white interest in their
work. The question of sincerity of white interest in the black arts,
however, must not be permitted to obscure the achievement of the
artists themselves. A great number of very talented black people
came to New York during the twenties, and they participated in a
literary uprising that forever changed the nature of black portraiture in American letters. Rejecting both the dialect school of Paul
Laurence Dunbar's plantation poetry and the slave-quarters sing-
alongs of white writers like Thomas Nelson Page, both nineteenth-
century stereotypes growing from the minstrel tradition, the young
black writers demanded a place for the creative expression of the
New Negro. Their attempt both contributed to and was a product of
special historical forces converging during the period. Although
these forces were not isolated from white influence, they were
largely the result of growing black assertions of cultural independence. Contrary to the popular notion, the Harlem Renaissance
was not a white fad, but an indigenous spiritual revolution.

Hurston thought of herself primarily as an artist, a writer of
essays, plays, and fiction, during her first year in the city while she
waited to enroll in Barnard, and she profited from the white interest
in black writing. As she devoted herself to her work, however, she
pledged allegiance to the young men and women who had arrived
in New York with steamer trunks full of short stories and poems to
offer this Renaissance. Although many whites were interested in
Harlem primarily for its exotic possibilities, it represented something quite different to the young artist. New York in general and
Harlem in particular become a mecca for black artistic hopes.

Harlem was created in the first two decades of the twentieth
century by black New Yorkers searching for new housing in de-

fiance of traditional discrimination. Black residential neighborhoods in Manhattan had begun in the seventeenth century at the tip
of the island and steadily migrated uptown as better accommoda-
tions became available. Between 1900 and 1910 the Harlem area
was overbuilt with new apartments, and in the face of empty rooms,
developers discovered the righteousness of open housing. Black
realtors purchased the buildings, and by the beginning of World
War I, after some bitter real estate battles between black buyers
and white owners, Harlem had been occupied. At the end of the
war, their ranks swollen by the steady migration of rural southern
blacks to northern industrial jobs, over one hundred thousand black
people had made Harlem a city within a city, designated it the
cultural capital of black America, and endowed it with youthful
exuberance and promise. Harlem indicated a new order of existence—a place where extraordinary things were commonplace.
"If my race can make Harlem," one man said, "Good Lord what
can't it do."[32]

In what became almost a cultural ritual, migrants from the Deep
South traveled by subway from Penn Station to the subway stop at
135th Street, where they emerged to be struck dumb by a sea of
blackness: black police, black taxicab drivers, black clerks in stores
that were (sometimes) owned by black businessmen, black doctors
and lawyers, even one or two black judges. Rudolph Fisher's ironic
short story "City of Refuge," about King Solomon Gillis, a North
Carolina youth bewildered and destroyed by this city, captured the
effect: Gillis anticipates that subway ride by thinking to himself, "In
Harlem black was white."[33] Fisher's story of shattered hopes was
appropriate, for often Harlem was patrolled by white policemen,
the white store owners sometimes refused to hire black clerks, and
white racketeers even kidnapped Casper Holstein, the Harlem
numbers king who paid for the *Opportunity* prizes, so that they
could take over his territory. King Solomon's anticipation of Harlem, however, was reflective of a national mood, and youths everywhere counted the days until they could emigrate to this concrete
symbol of a changed order. Langston Hughes admitted that he "was
in love with Harlem long before I got there."[34] A folk saying
captured a number of ironies as well as the Harlem effect: "I'd
rather be a lamppost in Harlem than Governor of Georgia." Most

black people in New York in the twenties, and to some extent black people in the entire nation, identified with the spirit that created Harlem. Claude McKay, a Jamaican who had made the trip via Alabama and Kansas, saw Harlem as the "Queen of Black belts, drawing Aframericans together into a vast humming hive. They have swarmed in from the different states, from the islands of the Caribbean, and from Africa. . . . Harlem is more than the Negro capital of the nation. It is the Negro capital of the world."[35] By 1930, when the Depression brought the Renaissance to a close, two hundred thousand men and women lived in this racial metropolis.

Zora Hurston identified with this "Negro capital." She studied its language, attended its parties, and joined in its spirit. She lived for a time on 131st Street, and she mastered the idiom of the streets. Later in her career she would begin a story, "Wait till I light up my coal-pot and I'll tell you about this zigaboo called Jelly. Well, all right now. He was a sealskin brown and papa-tree-top-tall." She quickly learned that a "Russian" was a southern black who had "rushed" up North, that "draped down" meant to be dressed in the Harlem fashion, and that "conk buster" could be either cheap liquor or an intellectual Negro. She had no fear of being alone on the streets. Once, dressed for a party in a flowing white dress and a wide-brimmed hat, she found herself sharing an elevator with a would-be Casanova. As they approached the first floor, he made his pass, and Zora responded with a roundhouse right that put him flat on the floor. She stepped out of the elevator, never looking back at the man laid out behind her. One of her early short stories, "Muttsy," was about the effect of the Harlem speakeasy world on a young Eatonville immigrant. Written in 1925 and published by Johnson in the August, 1926, *Opportunity*, "Muttsy" tells of a young girl entering Harlem as a bewildered ingenue and falling captive to "Ma Turner's back parlor," where people "danced on, played on, sang their 'blues' and lived on hotly their intense lives." A gambler named Muttsy is much taken with the innocent girl, but her resistance causes him to avoid seducing her; to win her hand he gives up his gambling ways for a job on the docks. In a nice ironic touch, his marriage does not lead to his reformation. The story ends with his going back to his gambling ways, since "what man can't keep one li'l wife an' two li'l bones?"[36]

"Muttsy" documents the bewilderment that could confront the

naïve migrant anticipating a city of refuge, but far more typical of Hurston's perception of Harlem was her comic story "Book of Harlem." It captures the high spirits that attended Harlem's growth, and spoofs the emigration process and the cabaret scene. Written in the form of a biblical chapter, "Book of Harlem" was never published; it is a series of short verses and includes an introductory gloss, as in many Bibles. A jeu d'esprit, the humor of "Book of Harlem" does not always work, but it can be very funny. There is a pestilence on the land of Hokum called Prohibition (a "mighty drought upon the land and many cried out"); Babylon is New York ("ruled by the tribe of Tammany"); and the hero, Mandolin, is a "Standardbottom, Georgia," youth urged to stay home by his father so that he can marry Gussie Smith ("for verily she is a mighty biscuit cooker before the Lord"). Mandolin and his father fight over his plan to go to Harlem ("Then strove they together all night"), but at daybreak Mandolin touches the old man upon the hip ("yea, verily, upon the pocket bearing joint") and gains his blessing. Arriving in New York and traveling to Harlem, he finds lodging with a youth named Toothsome and begins to take in the night life. His country clothes and hickish ways repel the Harlem ladies, however, and he does not become assimilated into city life until after a change of wardrobe and attitude, at which point his name becomes Panic ("for they asked one of the other, 'Is he not a riot in all that he doeth?'"). The youth becomes so adept that "both on One Hundred Thirty Ninth Street and on Lenox Avenue was he sought and his fame was great."[37]

Harlem in the twenties had its failed hopes, but the general tone, as perceived by the young writers, was joy in the assertion of a racial community. Alain Locke, Hurston's Howard philosophy professor, said: "In Harlem Negro life is seizing upon its first chances for group expression and self-determination." Harlem represented more than a destination, it symbolized a spirit of possibility. This was the mood of the novice writer, Zora Hurston, "when I set my hat at a certain angle and saunter down Seventh Avenue, Harlem City, feeling as snooty as the lions in front of the Forty-Second Street Library."[38]

NOTES

1. ZNH, *Dust Tracks on a Road* (Philadelphia: J. B. Lippincott, 1942), p. 176.

2. Ibid. See also Patrick Gilpin, "Charles S. Johnson: Entrepreneur of the Harlem Renaissance," in *The Harlem Renaissance Remembered*, ed. Arna Bontemps (New York: Dodd, Mead, 1972), pp. 215–46.

3. ZNH, *Dust Tracks*, p. 17; idem, *Mules and Men* (New York: Harper and Row, 1970), p. 29; idem, "How It Feels to Be Colored Me," *World Tomorrow*, 11 (May, 1928), 215.

4. June Jordan, "On Richard Wright and Zora Neale Hurston," *Black World*, 23 (Aug., 1974), 6.

5. ZNH, *Mules and Men*, p. 20.

6. ZNH, *Dust Tracks*, pp. 69, 71. See also ZNH, "Eatonville When You Look at It," manuscript, Florida Federal Writers' Project (FHSP).

7. Myrtis Hurston to RH, Aug. 30, 1976; Sally McDougall, "Author Plans to Upbraid Own Race," *New York World Telegram*, Feb. 6, 1935.

8. Hurston's deception about her birth date was consistent through her lifetime. On her second marriage license she claimed to be born in 1910. Her brother Everette Hurston, Sr., who has prepared a family genealogy, thinks that she was born in 1891. At various times she claimed to be either nine or thirteen at the time of her mother's death; most family members think that her mother died in 1904. She once asked her brother to list an erroneous birth date on his application for a New York driver's license so that he would appear older than she (RH interview with Everette Hurston, Sr., Jan. 13, 1976, Bristol, Conn.). I do not have a great deal of confidence in the 1901 date, although it does make the most sense in the context of the verifiable dates pertaining to her life, and it seems to be the date she most often used (with 1903 coming in a close second). If she were born in 1891, there is an unexplained ten-year gap in all the accounts of her life, including her own. It does not seem implausible that Zora may have been married for a decade, in much the manner of Janie Crawford and Logan Killicks in *Their Eyes Were Watching God*, and that she willfully forgot about that decade. This is, of course, sheer speculation, although based on the knowledge that Zora could be incredibly secretive about her private life. Witness the fact of her second marriage, hitherto unknown.

9. Ralph Ellison, "Richard Wright's Blues," in *Shadow and Act* (New York: Signet, 1966), p. 96; jacket copy for ZNH, *Seraph on the Suwanee* (New York: Charles Scribner's Sons, 1948); Myrtis Hurston to RH, Aug. 30, 1976.

10. ZNH, *Dust Tracks*, p. 97.

11. ZNH transcript, "Class: 1920," Morgan State College; RH telephone interview with Montgomery Gregory, Apr. 26, 1971, Washington, D.C.; RH interview with Phil Petrie, Jan. 14, 1976, New York City; Rayford Logan, *Howard University* (New York: New York University Press, 1969), p. 347. In *Dust Tracks* Zora says that she was at Morgan for two years; she may be including the year at night school. See also B. Alsterlund, "Zora Neale Hurston, a Biographical Sketch," *Wilson Bulletin for Libraries*, 13 (May, 1939), 586.

12. Herbert Sheen, undated autobiography, sent to RH on Mar. 21, 1975; RH interview with Sheen, Jan. 25, 1972, Los Angeles, Calif.

13. ZNH, *Dust Tracks*, pp. 164–76; Howard University Registrar's Records, in W. A. Sojourner, dean of admissions, to RH, Jan. 29, 1971; ZNH transcript, Howard University, given to RH by Everette Hurston, Sr.; RH interview with May Miller, Apr. 27, 1971, Washington, D.C.; ZNH, "John Redding Goes to Sea," *Stylus*, 1 (May, 1921), 11–22. ZNH attended Howard (university division)

each quarter between fall, 1919, and fall, 1923; she reported in her essay "The Hue and Cry about Howard University" (*Messenger*, 7 [Sept., 1925], 315) that she attended Howard Prep during the school year 1918-19.

14. See Gilpin, "Charles S. Johnson," and LH, *The Big Sea* (New York: Hill and Wang, 1963), pp. 214–16.

15. Fannie Hurst, "Zora Hurston: A Personality Sketch," *Yale University Library Gazette*, 35 (1961), 17–21.

16. ZNH, "Fannie Hurst," *Saturday Review*, Oct. 9, 1937, pp. 15–16, RH interview with Norton Baskin, Feb. 27, 1971, St. Augustine, Fla.

17. Hurst, "Zora Hurston," p. 17; ZNH, *Dust Tracks*, p. 177. Mrs. Meyer was an interesting figure in her own right and a real help to Hurston. See the profile of her by Robert L. Taylor, "The Doctor, the Lady, and Columbia University," in the *New Yorker*, Oct. 23, 1943, pp. 27–32, and Oct. 30, 1943, pp. 28–37.

18. "Record of Freshman Interest," Barnard College Records, Dec. 16, 1925.

19. LH, *Big Sea*, p. 239.

20. ZNH to Constance Sheen, Jan. 5, [1926], Feb. 2, 1926 (HCUFla).

21. LH, *Big Sea*, p. 223.

22. Hurst, "Zora Hurston," p. 20.

23. RH interview with George Schuyler, Dec. 29, 1970, New York City.

24. Rudolph Fisher, "The Caucasian Storms Harlem," *American Mercury*, 11 (May, 1927), 397.

25 .Bruce Kellner, *Carl Van Vechten and the Irreverent Decades* (Norman: University of Oklahoma Press, 1968), pp. 195–223; LH, *Big Sea*, pp. 252–53; CVV, Columbia Oral History Project, Mar.-May, 1960, no. 390, vol. 1, category IA (Columbia University Library).

26. Fisher, "Caucasian Storms Harlem," p. 398; Taylor Gordon, *Born to Be* (New York: Covici-Friede, 1929), p. 205; CVV, manuscript notes, "Introduction to the James Weldon Johnson Memorial Collection," p. 415 (JWJYale). The new edition of Gordon's book includes an account of his life after the Harlem Renaissance; see *Born to Be*, ed. RH (Seattle: University of Washington Press, 1975).

27. ZNH, "Book of Harlem," typescript (JWJ Yale).

28. Histories of the twenties are legion, and I have borrowed from many. See especially Nathan Huggins, *The Harlem Renaissance* (New York: Oxford University Press, 1971). I am particularly indebted to Huggins for the idea that Harlem in the twenties was an aphrodisiac and a place for an uptown safari. Another superb account of the period is George Kent, "Patterns of the Harlem Renaissance," in *Blackness and the Adventure of Western Culture* (Chicago: Third World Press, 1972).

29. ZNH to CVV, Jan. 5, 1926 (JWJYale).

30. Ibid., Aug. 26, 1927 (JWJYale).

31. Harold Preece, "The Negro Folk Cult," *Crisis*, 43 (1936), 364. This paragraph owes much to Huggins, *Harlem Renaissance*, and to Fisher, "Caucasian Storms Harlem." The white attitude toward Harlem is well illustrated by Edward Doherty's column entitled "Hot Harlem" in the *New York Daily Mirror*, Jan.–Feb., 1928.

32. James Weldon Johnson, *Black Manhattan* (1925; rpt., New York: Atheneum, 1968); Gilbert Osofsky, *Harlem: The Making of a Ghetto* (New York: Harper & Row, 1966), p. 123.

33. Rudolph Fisher, "City of Refuge," in *The New Negro*, ed. AL (New York: Albert and Charles Boni, 1925), p. 58.

34. LH, "My Early Days in Harlem," *Freedomways*, 3 (Summer, 1963), 312.

35. Claude McKay, *Harlem: Negro Metropolis* (New York: E. P. Dutton, 1940), p. 16. A major contributor to this spirit was Marcus Garvey. This mercurial West Indian was a powerful (some say the most powerful) force in Harlem during the era; yet he alienated many, especially leaders of the civil rights organizations.

36. ZNH, "Story in Harlem Slang," *American Mercury*, 55 (July, 1942), 84-96; idem, "Muttsy," *Opportunity*, 4 (Aug., 1926), 246–50; Myrtis Hurston to RH, Aug. 30, 1976.

37. ZNH, "Book of Harlem."

38. AL, "The New Negro," in *New Negro*, p. 7; ZNH, "How It Feels," p. 216.

The Harlem Renaissance was more a spirit than a movement, and because a spirit is ephemeral, generalizations about the Harlem Renaissance are either too hard or too easy. They have come easily enough to a whole generation of analysts, but the pithy summaries seldom reflect the wide divisions between blacks and whites, the black intelligentsia and the black masses, black artists and their bourgeois readers, that diversified the era. Indeed, when one studies the phenomenon of what was then called the Negro Renaissance or the New Negro Renaissance, and what is now called the Harlem Renaissance, he comes away with a bewildering complex of notions, statements, affirmations and manifestos. Although there is general agreement that the Renaissance is bounded by the armistice ending World War I and the beginning of the Depression, some historians have stretched the boundaries to before the war and after Roosevelt's second term. There has been a widespread tendency to consider the Harlem Renaissance as some sort of monolithic cultural movement, capable of reduction to an orthodoxy or a set of characteristic principles. This presumption reflects the bias in most American scholarship that postulates black people as "*the* Negro" and then poses theories ignoring individuation of thought and feeling.

Sometimes, however, the individual must be inferred from the age, and this is largely the case with Zora Neale Hurston. She spends exactly two paragraphs on the Renaissance in her autobiography, and her other writing, public and private, offers very little discussion of what the Harlem Renaissance meant to her. Yet her part in the Renaissance is well documented in the reminiscences of

others, with unanimous agreement that she was one of the most
memorable personages of the period. As Langston Hughes put it in
The Big Sea, she "was certainly the most amusing" of all the Harlem
Renaissance artists, "full of side splitting anecdotes, humorous tales
and tragi-comic stories." Hughes's words should not imply that she
was solely an entertainer. Although she was independent and
somewhat scornful of literary "movements," she shared in the
historical and cultural forces that made the Harlem Renaissance an
identifiable moment in American intellectual history, and she also
responded to and helped shape the esthetic assumptions of the era.

While the Harlem Renaissance was part of a historical process
which altered black life in America, the label has come to be a
literary one, a convenient reference to the extraordinary number of
books published by black writers during the decade. The Harlem
laborer may have known little about their success, but black writers
between 1919 and 1930 were published in greater numbers, and
received favorably by more publishers, than in any other single
decade in American life prior to the 1960s. The abundance of book
titles gives the literary orientation to generalizations about the
Renaissance, but the titles themselves, apart from the literature
they caption, were only symbols of the changing status of black
people in the United States. It was this awareness that contributed to Zora Hurston's "snootiness" as she walked the streets of
"Harlem City."

Hurston's arrival in Harlem came at the very end of a demo-
graphic shift called the Great Migration. During the decade preceding the end of World War I almost one million southern blacks
emigrated north. Between 1915 and 1918 alone, during the war-
time labor shortage, more than four hundred thousand black people
crossed the Mason-Dixon line. Hurston understood this migration,
and the opportunity and adventure it promised; she captured the
effect in her first novel: "And Black men's feet learned roads. Some
said good bye cheerfully . . . others fearfully, with terrors of unknown dangers in their mouths . . . others in their eagerness for
distance said nothing. The daybreak found them gone. The wind
said North. Trains said North. The tides and tongues said North,
and men moved like the great herds before the glaciers."[1]

Many people believed that leaving was an escape from the

South's irrational oppression and that the integrated North was a new frontier of racial equality. One group of Mississippians held a prayer meeting when their train reached the midpoint of the Ohio River, marking their deliverance with the hymn "I Done Come Out of Egypt Land with the Good News." Considerable evidence suggests that this was an illusion—labor unions were segregated, black men unfamiliar with the subtleties of northern bigotry were still lynched, the Ku Klux Klan was beginning a period of nationwide growth that would see it reach five million members by 1925—but the migration contributed to an undeniable sense of self-assertion among black Americans. Urged on by the NAACP and the Urban League, people began to refer to themselves as New Negroes.[2]

Zora Hurston was a New Negro, but this did not mean she was a revolutionary. The New Negro cast her lot with America and demanded that her vote be counted and her criticism be heard. New Negroes had very little patience with political stratagems that denied the possibility of first-class American citizenship. In 1928, Hurston wrote that the United States was "my country, right or wrong," and she satirized Marcus Garvey in an essay entitled "The Emperor Effaces Himself." Garvey's genius, Zora reported, was that he kept the money he collected, an act distinguishing him from other race leaders: "There had been some whisperings concerning W. E. B. Du Bois on account of his efforts to lower the violent mortality rate among his people, and advance their interests generally, but he never learned how to keep their money, and so missed true greatness."[3]

Hurston's criticism of Garvey came after he had lost much of his strength and had been repudiated by the major civil rights groups, and it illustrates how closely allied the Renaissance artists were to the intelligentsia of the Urban League and the NAACP, often without realizing it. She and other Renaissance writers made fun of the missionaries of racial uplift, but this was more a matter of personal style than of philosophy. Even though Zora might refer to the NAACP as a bunch of "Negrotarians," she was part of the organization's natural constituency, that segment of black America that Du Bois, a generation earlier, had called the "talented tenth"—those men and women who thirsted after higher education and the security it implied, and who had sufficient intellect and imagination to refuse the expected roles of "hewers of wood and drawers of water."[4]

Those who self-consciously sought a life of art during the Renaissance were conceived of as a talented tenth, and their esthetic aspirations became a part of the NAACP–Urban League policy offering the official definition of the New Negro. Those *Opportunity* dinners were more than mere social gatherings. Hurston and her fellow artists became known as New Negroes expressing a Negro Renaissance, although they were vague about the slogans and uncertain about their esthetic responsibilities to the New Negro movement. Rudolph Fisher tried to make fun of it all by threatening to christen his child "the New Negro." Hurston referred at a later period to "the *so-called* Negro Renaissance" (italics mine). The poet and novelist Arna Bontemps reminisced about meeting Zora and the others, remarking that "it did not take long to discover that I was just one of many young Negroes arriving in Harlem for the first time and with many of the same thoughts and intentions. Within a year or two we began to recognize ourselves as a 'group' and to become a little self-conscious about our 'significance.' When we were not too busy having fun, we were shown off and exhibited and presented in scores of places to all kinds of people. And we heard the sighs of wonder, amazement and sometimes admiration when it was whispered or announced, that here was one of the 'New Negroes.'"[5]

In entirely different ways, W. E. B. Du Bois and Alain Locke, two of those who were "exhibiting" and "showing off" the Hurstons and Bontempses, pronounced what was expected of this New Negro in art. A generation older than the artists emigrating to New York, Locke and Du Bois were the two most influential intellectuals urging an esthetic dimension to New Negroism. Some of the Renaissance artists accepted their directions with considerable discomfort, however, for they were unhappy with the idea that the esthetic geography of the Renaissance was to be bounded on the Du Bois side by propaganda and on the Locke side by "pure art." Zora Hurston was one of these. She was well aware that the apparent difference between the positions was mostly superficial, a fact overlooked by most analysts of the Renaissance, and one that caused considerable soul-searching when the artist tried, as Hurston did, to reject bourgeois values and identify with the folk. She was interested in folkloric fiction that did not treat "the race question." While both Locke and Du Bois encouraged the artist to be aware of folk origins, one was expected to do so with the future of the race in mind. To some extent, for both Locke and Du Bois, art became identified as Beauty in the service of Truth, the product of the elite artist articulating for an inarticulate race. Hurston's role in the esthetics of the Harlem Renaissance became part of the artistic politics of Locke, Du Bois, and the New Negro; she helped lead the revolt of the young artists against "propaganda" by interesting them in the "pure art" created by the black rural masses. All of this placed her under unusual and unique pressures as she began to formulate a personal esthetic.

The esthetic theory of W. E. B. Du Bois, like all his thinking, is exceedingly complex and difficult to summarize; in the twenties, however, he was best known for his refusal to distinguish between Truth and Beauty in the New Negro movement: both were part of the general struggle by black people to be "full fledged Americans with all the rights of other American citizens." Thus, Du Bois argued, "all Art is propaganda and ever must be, despite the wailing of the purists." He expected Hurston and her colleagues to create an art which could be used "for gaining the right of black folk to love and enjoy."[6]

Hurston's teacher at Howard, Alain Locke, edited the volume which has often been taken as the racial manifesto of the era, *The New Negro* (1925). In the title essay to that volume Locke identified the New Negro as a natural evolutionary phenomenon, gradually emerging as the "old Negro" became "more of a myth than a man . . . more a formula than a human being." The New Negro represented a "spiritual coming of Age," a "new soul" for black America, and its "heralding sign" was the "unusual burst of creative expression" in the works of younger artists like Zora Neale Hurston. This burst of creative expression differed significantly from what had come before; it was "a new aesthetic and a new philosophy of life," because it rejected the "cautious moralism and guarded idealizations" representative of an esthetic which "felt art must fight social battles and compensate social wrongs." The "newer motive" of the New Negro artist "in being racial is to be so *purely for the sake of art"* (italics mine). This phrase became a litany in Locke's own contributions to *The New Negro*, but his editorial policy did not become a strategy of "art for art's sake." In fact, his avowed purpose was to display the "creative expression" of young writers such as Hurston, Hughes, and Bontemps in order to further race relations: "The especially cultural recognition they win should . . . prove the key to that revaluation of the Negro which must precede or accompany any considerable further betterment of race relationships."[7]

Locke enjoyed his role as editor of *The New Negro*, for he consciously sought to be a literary arbiter. A brilliant, wide-ranging intellect, one of the most cultivated men in America, he was widely respected, even though many Harlem writers considered him proprietary. Hurston thought of him as a mother hen constantly clucking to keep his flock in line; yet she also sought his approval. Locke sometimes disapproved of Zora, harping on what he considered her lack of discipline; although he respected her talent, he was not hesitant to offer counsel. He told her, for example, that he liked her essay "How It Feels to Be Colored Me," but thought she had "opened up" to whites too readily. For her part, she solicited his help early in her career, then grew increasingly unhappy with him over the years, eventually calling him, in a moment of anger, "a malicious spiteful little snot that thinks he ought to be the leading Negro because of his degrees." At the time of *The New Negro* they were not so antagonistic; he asked for permission to reprint one of her *Opportunity* stories, and also considered her unpublished story "Black Death" for inclusion in the volume. She shared Locke's enthusiasm for the book and told him, "I hope the volume goes over with a bang."[8]

Most of the young writers Locke recruited for *The New Negro* were, like Hurston, anti-Garveyites, allied with the NAACP and the Urban League, college educated, with many of the materialistic goals of American society within their grasp. They welcomed the prestige and respectability of appearing with such older *New Negro* contributors as William Stanley Braithwaite, Robert R. Moton, and Kelly Miller. They also, however, were committed to the folk experience, which they tended to consider the life of the proletariat. Hurston's contribution to *The New Negro* was a short story, "Spunk," reprinted from the June, 1925, *Opportunity*.

"Spunk" explores the supernatural beliefs characteristic of black folklife. Set in an unnamed village that is obviously Eatonville, the story is dramatically structured so that the village store occupies the set and all the action takes place off stage. The store's loafers tell the tale, and they become both chorus and a catalyst for the action. Spunk is a hard-living, fearless community hero who rides the circle saw at the sawmill, the most dangerous work on the job. He openly steals Lena Kanty from her ineffectual husband, Joe, and dares him to do anything about it. When the store loungers humiliate him, the indecisive Joe takes his knife to Spunk, only to die when the more experienced fighter shoots him. Freed after a plea of self-defense, Spunk moves Lena into his own home and prepares to marry her. He has not reckoned, however, with the ghost of Joe Kanty, who haunts him, first in the form of a black cat, later as an invisible force pushing him into the circle saw. When Spunk falls and is killed, he dies cursing Joe for shoving him. The story ends on a note of continuity transcending the violence and tragedy of the moment, and with perhaps an ironic comment on the fickleness of the mob. The style is terse and effective: "The cooling board consisted of three sixteen inch boards on saw horses, a dingy sheet was his shroud. The women ate heartily of the funeral baked meats and wondered who would be Lena's next. The men whispered coarse conjectures between guzzles of whiskey."

Locke carefully explained why proletarian subject matter such as "Spunk" was appropriate for Harlem Renaissance artists, attaching the impulse to portray the masses to his notion that the motive of the black writer "in being racial is to be so purely for the sake of art." The established bourgeois position was that black art should avoid reinforcing racist stereotypes by refusing to portray the lowest elements of the race. Hurston should avoid writing about superstitious sawmill hands because white readers would believe that all black people were superstitious. Locke dissociated himself from such self-censorship, but he also placed a burden on Hurston and the other young writers. In his introductory essay to *The New Negro*, Locke had stressed that "no sane observer, no matter how sympathetic . . . would contend that the great masses are articulate as yet"; the major premise of his later essay "Negro Youth Speaks" is that the young writers will speak for these masses by expressing the race spirit. As he put it, "Youth speaks, and the voice of the New

Negro is heard." Hurston and her colleagues were to interpret the
race for the world: "What stirs inarticulately in the masses is already
vocal upon the lips of the talented few, and the future listens,
however the present may shut its ears." It was the same point Locke
had made in his title essay when he distinguished between the
multitude and the thinking few: "The multitude perhaps feels as yet
only a strange relief and a new vague urge, but the thinking few
know that in the reaction the vital inner grip of prejudice has been
broken."

When Locke spoke of a talented few, or a thinking few, he was
saying that a "talented tenth" would articulate for the inarticulate,
thereby helping secure a place for all in a revitalized American
system. As a member of the talented few, Hurston had special
responsibilities. It should have come as no surprise that Du Bois
would find no objection to Locke's volume, would contribute to it,
and could even tolerate its proclaimed purity of artistic intent. In
reviewing *The New Negro* favorably, Du Bois even chided Locke
for this new interest in Beauty, noting that "this is a book filled and
bursting with propaganda, but it is a propaganda for the most part
beautifully and painstakingly done. . . ."[9]

Locke's editing of *The New Negro* produced a volume that gave
lip service to pure art, but that in the end was similar in its esthetics
to the propagandistic tradition. This should not be construed as
a pejorative judgment. Black men and women were still being
lynched in 1925, not as an anomaly but as a frequent event, and the
Senate of the United States, in its collective wisdom and democratic
principle, could not even pass a federal anti-lynching bill. One
could reasonably argue that the race could not afford artists who
subordinated the social conscience. On the other hand, Hurston
and many of her fellow Harlem Renaissance artists felt uncomfortable with their "responsibilities," because they believed that a propagandistic motive vitiated artistic effects. They claimed that racial
appeals would compromise their art. Hurston later said she "was
and am thoroughly sick" of the "race problem." Illustrating the trap
of either/or thinking that often characterized the Renaissance debate between propaganda and esthetics, she once told a black critic
that she was interested in "writing a novel and not a treatise on
sociology."[10]

Partially in reaction to *The New Negro*, partially because they needed a forum for their views, a group of the younger writers, led by Hurston, Langston Hughes, and Wallace Thurman, created their own magazine, *Fire!!* While *Fire!!* did not grow from an explicit response to *The New Negro*, implicit in its very existence was the need for a magazine that really was, in Thurman's words, "purely artistic in intent and conception."[11] The proof of its purity, moreover, would be its commitment to the masses, or, in Hurston's terms, the folk.

Fire!! was a quarterly "devoted to the younger Negro artists." Organized during the summer of 1926, it published one issue before failing. It was primarily the creation of a group of energetic and talented people centered around Hurston, Hughes, and Thurman who enjoyed shocking the stuffy by calling themselves the "Niggerati." They met frequently to talk literature and politics, to gossip, and to party. Although these three were the most prominent members of the group, the circle almost always included Bruce Nugent, and on any given occasion the artist Aaron Douglas might be present, or John P. Davis, a Harvard law student, or Helene Johnson, one of the "teenagers" of the Renaissance, or Dorothy West, a writer from Boston, or Gwendolyn Bennett, a Howard art instructor and columnist for *Opportunity*, or the sculptor Augusta Savage, or, more rarely, Countee Cullen, one of the most widely published of the young poets, or Harold Jackman, a Harlem schoolteacher, or Dorothy Peterson, a stunning teacher and actress, or any number of hangers-on, friends, and acquaintances. Generally such festivities were raucous, with brilliant talk and, as the evenings wore on, outrageous good times.[12]

The good times have caused scholars to overlook the aspirations of these artists for a revolution in esthetic consciousness, but the error is understandable when one considers the personalities involved. Thurman was a tortured man, never able to create art measuring up to his own high standards, torn by an ambivalent sexual nature, tuberculosis, self-destructive alcoholism, sarcasm, cynicism, and a neurotic consciousness of his very dark skin. He was also the most gifted critic of the Renaissance generation, a novelist of promise, an identifiable genius, and a loyal friend. Nugent was a multitalented youth from a proper Washington family who was probably the most Bohemian of all the Renaissance artists. He seldom knew where he was going to sleep, dressed in whatever clothes were around when he woke up, and spent much of his time creating beautiful erotic drawings, shocking to even the most liberated viewer. Hughes was always a quiet observer of this scene, unfailingly kind, but never missing a thing, well embarked on a career that would make him the poet laureate of Harlem.[13]

Hurston was both a social and an intellectual force in the group. Probably the quickest wit in a very witty lot, she proclaimed herself "Queen of the Niggerati," and entertained entire parties with tales of Eatonville. She could mimic well, and often gave mocking accounts of the stuffed shirts she encountered on Park Avenue and labeled "Astorperious." Her apartment was always open for Niggerati meetings, with a pot on the stove that visitors were expected to contribute to in order to create a common stew. At other times she fried okra, or cooked Florida eel. Zora had moved into the apartment without furniture or money; yet within a few days it had been completely furnished by her friends with everything from decorative silver birds, perched precariously atop the linen closet, to a footstool for the living room. To celebrate she gave a "hand chicken dinner," so called, Hughes claimed, because she forgot to ask for forks. Arna Bontemps remembered her sometimes directing everyone in the singing of rousing spirituals. She constantly stressed a need for a "natural" art that did not emulate a bourgeois world, that was true to one's instincts of the moment, and she seldom hesitated to follow a whim. Still, Bruce Nugent felt that of all the *Fire!!* contributors only Hurston and Hughes had a sense of the magazine's historical importance.[14]

Fire!! had grown out of a series of Niggerati meetings in the summer of 1926. To reach the rooming house on 137th Street where both Hughes and Thurman lived, Hurston took the subway uptown from her apartment near Fannie Hurst on West Sixty-sixth Street. There the Niggerati sweated through the hot summer nights, working to create a magazine which would be unconcerned "with sociological problems or propaganda." *Fire!!* was to be a "noncommercial product interested only in the arts," and the editors thought of their magazine as part of an esthetic mission: "Hoping to introduce a truly Negroid note into American literature, its contributors had gone to the proletariat rather than to the bourgeoisie for characters and material, had gone to people who still retained some individual race qualities and who were not totally white American in every respect save color of skin."[15]

Fire!! has not been studied in depth by the literary analysts of the Renaissance, but it reveals more than *The New Negro* about the esthetic assumptions of younger writers like Zora Neale Hurston. *The New Negro* was under Locke's editorial control, unofficially sanctioned by the NAACP and the Urban League, and published by a major white publisher, Albert and Charles Boni. Representing the "artistic self-expression of the Negro" as the "truest social portraiture," it could be seen as a subtly designed piece of propaganda in the best Du Bois definition, Beauty and Truth serving the ideal of Justice for the New Negro in American life. Its title derived from the racial politics of the era. *Fire!!* was "devoted to the younger Negro artists," edited, paid for, and published by the artists themselves, and its politics were self-consciously esthetic. Its title came from a Hughes poem giving voice to a sinner's lament in the fashion of a spiritual. Appearing in November, 1926, a year after *The New Negro*, *Fire!!* represents the esthetic frustration of Hurston and her friends; their revolt against bourgeois subject matter had been easily co-opted in *The New Negro*. Faced with the appropriation of their talents by the racial propagandists, Hurston, Hughes, and Thurman self-consciously set out to liberate themselves from Du Bois, Charles S. Johnson, and even Alain Locke. As Hurston put it in a letter to Locke, there needed to be "more outlets for Negro fire." Although Locke had originally offered to be a patron for the magazine, the young editors very quickly went off on their own, and Locke's support was either discreetly withdrawn or discreetly rejected.[16]

The editorial board was headed by Thurman, who bore the major responsibility for getting the magazine into print. The other editors were Hurston, Hughes, Nugent, Gwendolyn Bennett, and Aaron Douglas; John Davis served as business manager. Each editor intended to contribute fifty dollars of his own money, with patrons expected to finance the remainder. As this shaky financing might imply, the whole enterprise was problem filled from the start. The editing was only partially completed when fall arrived, and Hurston began studying at Barnard, and Hughes returned to college in Pennsylvania. John Davis was at Harvard and helping edit the *Crisis* as well, while Gwen Bennett was busy at Howard and with her "Ebony Flute" column for *Opportunity*. Thurman himself switched magazine jobs from the *Messenger* to the *World Tomorrow* during this period. Neither Nugent nor Douglas, being artists, was much help with the editing, and Thurman was left with most of the preparation tasks. Short of material, he considered printing Hurston's play *Color Struck* under a pen name, since he was worried about the issue appearing too "Zoraish" with two of her contributions. When Nugent's story was destroyed accidentally while stored at Hurston's apartment, he rewrote it on a roll of toilet paper and handed it to Thurman. As Nugent has stated, the most amazing thing about *Fire!!* was that it came out at all.[17]

Because they could find only nine sponsors, and because only three of the seven editors contributed their fifty dollars (Hurston was among the slackers), Thurman signed a note to the printer and became personally responsible for a bill of nearly one thousand dollars. Incredibly, after borrowing $150 from the Harlem Community Church and another $150 from the Mutual League, he was held up on a Harlem street corner, losing not only his money, but most of his clothing as well. For more than four years Thurman's paychecks were periodically attached to meet the *Fire!!* debt. Hurston and the others tried to help, although no one had much money. She spent at least some time during a 1927 folklore-collecting trip soliciting subscriptions in the South in the hopes of publishing a second issue and recovering financial losses. She and Hughes contributed essays to the *World Tomorrow* to reimburse the magazine for money it had lent to *Fire!!* Hughes claimed that the chronically hungry Nugent, in charge of distribution, sometimes would eat up the receipts from the few copies sold. The long-suffering printer gave them the entire run of the magazine, apparently thinking that they might be able to sell them better in quantity, but this led to a final irony: several hundred copies burned while stored in the basement of an apartment house. Yet even this did not completely quell the young hopes. As Hurston put it, "I suppose that 'Fire' has gone to ashes quite, but I still think the idea is good."[18]

The one published issue was a mixture of intentions and subjects. Running throughout was an uncompromising race pride, a fascination with the masses, and an iconoclastic, belligerent attitude toward the accepted wisdom. Hurston's play *Color Struck* had won second prize in the drama division of the 1925 *Opportunity* contest, and the version printed in *Fire!!* had been reworked and submitted to the 1926 contest, where it won honorable mention. It is not a very effective drama, and its only memorable scene is a cakewalk. Its subject is the intraracial color-consciousness exercised by the bourgeoisie, and it addresses those who envy whites biologically or intellectually. It is an account of a poor woman so self-conscious about her dark skin that she is unable to accept the love of a good man. Really more a sketch than a play, it comes to life only when the folk of north-central Florida engage their wit in friendly verbal competition. On the whole, *Color Struck* is an apprentice work, but its theme was consistent with *Fire!!*'s aims. It celebrated the proletariat, and it condemned a common bourgeois attitude.

Hurston's short story in *Fire!!*, entitled "Sweat," is a remarkable work, her best fiction of the period. It builds a tragic structure around a washerwoman and her unemployed husband, dignifying her labor and his insecurity, making them victims of both their individual inadequacies and their larger fate. A perfect fusing of the Eatonville environment and the high seriousness of self-conscious literature, it illustrates the unlimited potential in Hurston's folk material when an organic form grew from the subject matter.

A story like "Sweat" might eventually have led to *Fire!!*'s success, assuring a continued life for the magazine. Despite all its troubles, *Fire!!* contained some first-class writing. By the time the apartment-house fire burned up the extra copies, however, the reviews of the magazine had been published, and it was unlikely that the reading public that *Fire!!* most specifically addressed intended to purchase copies. Benjamin Brawley, a pillar of the black literary establishment, disliked it intensely, and the whole issue of Du Bois's reaction forms an amusing but highly revealing chapter in the *Fire!!* story. Hughes reports in *The Big Sea*, "None of the older Negro intellectuals would have anything to do with *Fire*. Dr. Du Bois in *The Crisis* roasted it." But Hughes's memory is in error. Du Bois never reviewed the magazine in the *Crisis*, and I have been unable to find a Du Bois review anywhere else. The only notice the NAACP's journal gave to the magazine was a brief announcement in the January, 1927, issue noting that *Fire!!* had been received, was "a beautiful piece of printing," and was "strikingly illustrated by Aaron Douglas." The announcement concluded, "We bespeak for it wide support."[19]

What interests here is that Hughes *thought* Du Bois had panned it, revealing, one suspects, that this was what Hurston and her friends most desired. He was *supposed* to dislike it because the *Fire!!* editors, the Young Turks of the Harlem Renaissance, did not want him to praise *Fire!!* as he had *The New Negro*. Only Du Bois's disapproval would authenticate their "pure" esthetic purposes, proving that their art transcended both politics and morality. In fact, they had gone out of their way to challenge the Victorian morality of the older New Negro spokesmen with Thurman's story of a prostitute, "Cordelia, the Crude," and Bruce Nugent's elliptical monologue of a homosexual pondering his status, "Smoke, Lilies and Jade." Most of the New Negro spokesmen responded to these stories in exactly the way they were expected to, with moral outrage, and Du Bois was assumed to feel the same.

The manner in which these two stories came to be written was a part of the Bohemian impulse informing *Fire!!*'s proletarian esthetics. As Bruce Nugent tells the tale, after all submissions for the magazine were in and selections had been made, Thurman announced to the staff that they now had to find something that would get the issue banned in Boston—an idea Hurston endorsed. They began thinking of "what two things just will not take," and Thurman decided they would write about a streetwalker and a homosexual; after flipping a coin to determine the assignment, the final two stories for the magazine were completed.[20]

The casualness of this act is deceptive, revealing more about the *Fire!!* artists than even they recognized. Hughes wrote that the idea of *Fire!!* was "that it would burn up a lot of the old, dead conventional Negro-White ideas of the past, *épater le bourgeois* into a realization of the existence of the younger Negro writers and artists." Hurston said, "We can run the other magazines ragged." Nugent remembers *Fire!!* as the proof the young artists could offer that they "were going to do something big and black and wonderful." In a mimeographed letter soliciting money for a second issue, Thurman claimed that *Fire!!* "has established itself as a *tour de force* in the racial renaissance, and its searing motto of 'Fy-ah, Fy-ah, Lawd' is resounding through the country." Certainly there seems a paradox between these serious intentions and the casual decision to insure that the magazine was deliberately offensive to some readers. The key to the paradox, however, is that while self-consciously mining the proletariat, *Fire!!* required a bourgeois black readership for its esthetic and moral revolutions to make any sense. *Fire!!* was directed at the readers of what Zora called "the other magazines," those who would understand that the lack of "sociology and propaganda" contrasted with the pages of the *Crisis* and *Opportunity*, those who would feel that emphasis on the individual "race qualities" of the proletariat threatened their own lifestyle. As Hurston told Locke, "Don't you think there ought to be a purely literary magazine in our group? The way I look at it, 'The Crisis' is the house organ of the NAACP and 'Opportunity' is the same to the Urban League. They are in literature on the side."[21]

"Pure literature" was the key, and this meant that Victorian morality had to be confronted directly and shocked into retreat in order to free the artist. As Thurman's postpublication letter of solicitation proclaimed: "We want *Fire* to be provocative—want it to provide the shocks necessary to encourage new types of artistic interest and new types of artistic energy." Supposedly, Beauty could not be Truth if it was morally repelling, so Hurston, Thurman, and the *Fire!!* group became esthetic freedom fighters striking a blow for artistic integrity. The exclamation points in its title were not haphazardly placed. The *Fire!!* editors knew what would cause the greatest reaction, because it was their acquired legacy as the products of an upwardly mobile class. From childhood most of them had been told to comport themselves so that they would reflect honor on the race, exhibit moral behavior that could not be distorted into racist stereotypes. The *Fire!!* writers were working within a code of behavior as ritualized as a child's adolescent revolt against his parents. Their calculated offense and anticipation of Du Bois's rage constituted a behavioral ritual acted out to grant the illusion of liberation from class values.[22]

The last laugh, however, was on them. They were not really

taken seriously, and the negative reactions they liked to quote were mostly a condescending slap on the wrist. Locke, for example, criticized their "effete echoes of contemporary decadence," but also praised their anti-Puritanism. The bold *Fire!!* editors were considered so small a threat that Zora, Thurman, Bennett, and Hughes were invited to read from the magazine at a Civic Club tea on January 2, 1927. The NAACP even handled some of their prepublication publicity. Du Bois could afford to ignore *Fire!!*'s existence. *Les bourgeois* were not easily *épatés*, and the proletarian commitment and artistic purity of the magazine simply became a part of a larger issue: the Renaissance artist's allegiance to the folk. This was also an issue absolutely central to Zora Neale Hurston's development as an artist.[23]

There is the peril of arrogance in the belief that one articulates the race spirit, whether his intentions are pure (Locke) or propagandistic (Du Bois). The peril was most prominent when the writers looked to their folk heritage as a source for art, and it was here that Zora Hurston offered most to the Harlem Renaissance. She, more than any other Renaissance artist, struggled with the dangers of surveying the masses from the mountaintop, treating the folk material of the race as a landscape to be strip-mined in order to fuel the creative forge.

Urged on by Locke, most of the Renaissance writers rejected the notion that their art had to serve the race, always putting the best foot forward; but they had not always worked out the relationship between the artist and the folk. If one was not a "spokesman" for the race, what—if any—was the responsibility of the artist to those brothers and sisters without the talent or the opportunity to express themselves in print? Locke offered an apparent solution to the question by encouraging the writer to utilize his folk heritage, to carry "the folk gift to the altitudes of art."[24] One should be aware of the vertical assumptions in this phrase.

Locke's phrase grew from his conviction that the black artist should consciously strive for a pure rather than a propagandistic art, and should base this conscious creation on the unconscious esthetics manifested by the spirituals, the folk sermons, the folktales— the proletariat's artistic forms. This program would liberate the artist from the need to be representative in the old sense, because it would align him with what Locke variously called "the racial substance," the "racy peasant undersoil of the race life," the "race gift," and the "vast spiritual endowment" of the race. The young artist was to interpret this racial substance for the world.[25]

If the black folk constituted a class, it was unquestionably a proletariat, but few Renaissance artists—including Locke—had had prolonged firsthand contact with it. As critics of the Harlem Renaissance have often argued, the participants' bourgeois backgrounds suggested at least one generation of removal from the "racy peasant undersoil." Of them all, however, Zora Hurston was the closest, and her person and her fiction exhibited the knowledge that the black masses had triumphed over their racist environment, not by becoming white and emulating bourgeois values, not by engaging in a sophisticated program of political propaganda, but by turning inward to create the blues, the folktale, the spiritual, the hyperbolic lie, the ironic joke. These forms of expression revealed a uniqueness of race spirit because they were a code of communication—intraracial propaganda—that would protect the race from the psychological encroachments of racism and the physical oppression of society. Hurston knew that black folklore did not arise from a psychologically destroyed people, that in fact it was proof of psychic health. As she put it, the folk knew how to "hit a straight lick with a crooked stick," how to devise a communicative code that could simultaneously protest the effects of racism and maintain the secrecy of that very same protest. Hurston's remark upon learning that Countee Cullen and Eric Walrond were going to study in Europe reveals her sense of the cultural roots of black literature: "What, I ask with my feet turned out, are Countee and Eric going abroad to study? . . . A Negro goes to white land to learn his trade! Ha! That was inevitable for Countee. It will fit him nicely too. Nice, safe, middle class."[26]

Zora Hurston knew from childhood the quality of folklike and the esthetic forms it generated. She contributed an authentic folk experience to the esthetic mix of the Renaissance, a specific knowledge often underestimated when the Renaissance interest in the folk has been assessed. Folklore was fascinating to most Renaissance intellectuals, but they could also be vague and romantic about it. Hurston could not be sure what Locke meant when he said, "There is ample evidence of a New Negro in the latest phases of social change and progress, but still more in the internal world of the Negro mind and spirit. Here in the very heart of the folk-spirit are the essential forces and folk interpretation is truly vital and representative only in terms of these."[27] Are the "Negro mind" and the "folk spirit" one? What is "folk interpretation"? Hurston once made very clear the difference between herself and Locke: "Dr. Locke . . . had been born in Philadelphia, educated at Harvard and Oxford, and had never known the common run of Negroes. He was not at all sympathetic to our expression. To his credit, he has changed his viewpoint."[28]

Locke's shift in view overcame a tradition in black intellectual history. As Hurston demonstrated often during the twenties, the black intellectual had to challenge both the racist stereotype of folk experience in the American minstrel tradition and the historical neglect of the folk arts by black people themselves. The first generation of emancipated slaves often repudiated their folk heritage as a product of slavery, something that was to be forgotten as soon as possible. Music and poetry born of suffering were a too-painful reminder of the suffering itself. As Charles Johnson expressed it in *The New Negro*, "They would be expected to do just as they did: rule out the sorrow songs as the product of ignorant slaves, taboo dialect as incorrect English, and the priceless folklore as the uncultured expression of illiterates." Such attitudes had not died with subsequent generations, as Hurston well knew. She wrote an article in 1925 for the *Messenger* entitled "The Hue and Cry about Howard University." An affirmation of the school's aims, the essay analyzed the student and faculty unrest which had led to a recent strike; it also touched on the issue of the educated black response to folk origins. Howard's white president liked to hear his students sing, and his motives are suspect at best. When the students objected, however, they did so for the wrong reasons. According to Hurston, they argued that the spirituals were "low and degrading, being the product of slaves and slavery"; that they were "not good grammar"; and that "they are not sung in white universities." Although the Howard student revolt of 1925 had many motives, the students' response to the spirituals was symptomatic of the way many viewed the folk experience.

The response of the Renaissance intellectuals to such resistance to the folk heritage was to acknowledge the "crude" genius of the spirituals and to claim for them an emotional parity with "high" art. Locke, for example, praised the spirituals as "a classic expression of the religious emotion" comparable to Gregorian chants and "the rarest of German chorals"—despite their "crude vehicle."[29] His purpose was to establish a connection between black American folksongs and classical music. He wrote that the spirituals "have escaped the lapsing conditions and the fragile vehicle of folk art, and come firmly into the context of formal music. Only classics survive such things."[30] Locke was trying to reconcile folk art and "high art," and the best agents of reconciliation, those who could raise this folk form to the "altitudes of art," were the "conscious artists" who "interpreted" black spirituals.

Paul Robeson, Roland Hayes, Taylor Gordon, and J. Rosamond Johnson all became famous during the twenties for their interpretations of traditional Afro-American music. They, in turn, were building on the success of the Fisk Jubilee Singers and their imitators, who first arranged spirituals for the concert stage in the latter part of the nineteenth century. Many of these glee clubs remained popular during the twenties, and new groups were formed. The period saw a number of books published with spiritual arrangements; by far the most successful was *The Book of American Negro Spirituals*, compiled by James Weldon Johnson and his brother Rosamond. One of the first volumes issued by Viking Press, it was announced with considerable fanfare, unusual for a book of music. Johnson and Gordon even gave a concert to celebrate its appearance. James Weldon Johnson's introduction to the book stressed the way in which the individual artist who has "the capacity to *feel* these songs while singing them" will transform them into high art. He pointed out that "through the genius and supreme artistry of Roland Hayes these songs undergo . . . a transfiguration."

The spirituals' popular success reveals a number of paradoxes in formal representation of folk expression. Their interpreters usually performed them in black tie and tails, or some other formal dress, without stage settings, with only a piano as accompaniment. Such a setting removed them from their true context in the black church so that they could be "elevated" to the concert stage. The idea was that the transcendent artist would establish the folksong as a musical achievement of the same order as Beethoven symphonies. The formalized "concert"—the traditional repository of Western European aural culture—the fixed structure of the proscenium stage, the passive audience subordinating their own creativity to that of the "artiste," all emphasize how different the spirituals had been made, how dependent on the individual artist they had become. Gone was the shouting, moaning ecstasy which was a behavioral component of the spirituals. Absent was the phenomenon of group performance that operated from within a traditional frame but permitted extensive improvisation. The lack of a formal arrangement for the songs (the very rigidity of the word seems alien to the folk's understanding of the spiritual) had imbued them with great possibilities for both individual and collective expression. Johnson and Locke admitted that the spiritual concert had no way of tapping these resources, but that it was a necessary loss. The original context could not be captured, but Paul Robeson singing "Go Down Moses" could become the symbol of Afro-American manhood. His interpretation became a great triumph for the individual artist, because it was his vision that captured the "primitive" essence of the spiritual and consecrated it for the cultured audience.

What Johnson, Locke, and others stressed was the need for *conscious* art to display the *unconscious* artistry of black preachers and church singers. But in doing so they were also refusing to acknowledge what Hurston knew: that the folk were creating an art that did not need the sanction of "culture" to affirm its beauty. She once put the case succinctly when talking of Robeson: "Robeson sings Negro songs better than most, because, thank God, he lacks musical education. But we have a cathead man in Florida who can sing so that if you heard him you wouldn't want to hear Hayes or Robeson. He hasn't the voice of either one. It's the effect."[31]

Folk art arises out of the specific needs of a given community and is replicated through history because it satisfies a communal esthetic. Afro-American folksongs were perpetuated through the most oppressive of circumstances and became a major instrument of survival. Even though "sorrow songs" could profoundly express the race's anguish, they were not performed out of desperation or anxiety. They were not pathological in origin. Paraphrasing Ralph Ellison's definition of the blues, they were an autobiographical chronicle of group catastrophe transcending events through lyrical expression and biblical analogy.[32] They were behavior that satisfied a communal need, an opportunity for a group artistic expression. In their original social context, they projected an ethos, a characteristic sensibility. But as long as the spirituals were the captives of the concertizers, they suggested that this ethos was only a black peasant sensibility without the formal discipline of art. Such an assumption, widely held in the twenties, illustrates why Renaissance artists did not grasp the full possibilities of black folklore for their writing. Despite all the interest in the folk symbolized by the emphasis on spirituals, the writers did not really struggle with what Larry Neal has called "the consummate uses of the folk sensibility. . . . There was really no encounter and subsequent grappling with the visceral elements of the Black experience."[33]

Of all the Renaissance artists, Zora Hurston confronted these "visceral elements" most personally, and her grappling is illustrated in her essay "Spirituals and Neo-Spirituals," which appeared in Nancy Cunard's anthology, *Negro* (1934). Although written in the early thirties, the essay is only the final articulation of what Hurston was feeling between 1925 and 1927 in New York. Her article on Howard in the *Messenger* had stressed her commitment to the spirituals as an esthetic resource, but she was acutely aware that spiritual concerts were not the music of her father's Baptist church. In her 1926 note to Van Vechten offering to bring some nonprofessional church singers to his apartment, she told him, "Please hear them sing just one song . . . you will hear a spiritual done spiritually."[34] Her later essay elaborates on this theme, bringing the evidence of her folklore collecting to her earlier convictions.

She begins by distinguishing between "genuine" spirituals and "neo-spirituals." The latter are songs "sung by the concert artists and glee clubs and are the works of Negro composers or adapters *based* on the spirituals . . . all good work and beautiful, but *not* the spirituals." The genuine spirituals "are Negro religious songs, sung by a group, and a group bent on expression of feelings and not on sound effects. There never has been a presentation of genuine Negro spirituals to any audience anywhere." Above all, the genuine spiritual is not a lament for the race's condition: "The idea that the whole body of spirituals are sorrow songs is ridiculous. They cover a wide range of subjects from a peeve at gossipers to Death and Judgement." By stressing the ethnocentrism of the genuine article, Hurston emphasizes how far the genuine spiritual is from the concert version:

> Glee clubs and concert singers put on their tuxedoes, bow prettily to the audience, get the pitch and burst into magnificent song—but not *Negro* song. The real Negro singer cares nothing about pitch. The first notes just burst out and the rest of the church join in—fired by the same inner urge. Every man trying to express himself through song. Every man for himself. Hence the harmony and disharmony, the shifting keys and the broken time that make up the spiritual.
>
> I have noticed that whenever an untampered-with congregation attempts the renovated spirituals, the people grow self-conscious. They sing sheepishly in unison. None of the glorious individualistic flights that make up their own songs. Perhaps they feel on strange ground. Like the unlettered parent before his child just home from college. At any rate they are not very popular.
>
> This is no condemnation of the neo-spirituals. They are a valuable contribution to the music and literature of the world. But let no one imagine that they are songs of the people, as sung by them.

As a dedicated Harlem Renaissance artist, Zora Hurston searched hard for a way to transfer the life of the people, the folk ethos, into the accepted modes of formalized fiction. She knew the folkloric context better than any of her contemporaries, and this led to a personal style that many did not understand. To a large extent she personalized the Eatonville world of the "genuine" spirituals, relating it to the Renaissance conceptions of pure artistry exhibited in *Fire!!* and the "race gift" expressed by *The New Negro*. The result was a personal style that has deflected attention from the intellectual tensions shaping her art. While dividing her time between the activities of the Niggerati, the white interest in the New Negro, and the general frenzy of the Jazz Age, she worked hard to portray the Eatonville essence for the Renaissance readers, eventually discovering that the best one could do was *represent* the folklore process. She tried to reconcile high and low culture by becoming Eatonville's esthetic representative to the Harlem Renaissance, and when she discovered that this was an unsatisfactory role, she turned to the professional study of folklore as an alternative.

NOTES

1. ZNH, *Jonah's Gourd Vine* (Philadelphia: J. B. Lippincott, 1934), p. 232.
2. W. E. B. Du Bois, "Returning Soldiers," *Crisis*, 18 (May, 1919), 14. See also George Groh, *Black Migration* (New York: Weybright and Talley, 1972), and David Shannon, *The Twenties and Thirties* (Chicago: Rand McNally, 1974).
3. ZNH, "How It Feels to Be Colored Me," *World Tomorrow*, 11 (May, 1928), 216; idem, "The Emperor Effaces Himself," typescript (JWJYale). See also August Meier, *Negro Thought in America, 1880–1915* (Ann Arbor: University of Michigan Press, 1963), pp. 256–60; William Pickens, *The New Negro* (New York: Neale Publishing, 1916), p. 9 ff.; Howard Fullinwider, *The Mind and Mood of Black America* (Homewood, Ill.: Dorsey Press, 1969); Rayford Logan, ed., *The New Negro Thirty Years Afterward* (Washington, D.C.: Howard University Press, 1955).
4. RH interview with Arna Bontemps, Nov. 18, 1970, New Haven, Conn.; W. E. B. Du Bois, "Of the Training of Black Men," in *The Souls of Black Folk* (Chicago: A. C. McClurg, 1903).
5. Fisher's remark is quoted in Robert Bone, *The Negro Novelist in America* (New Haven: Yale University Press, 1958), p. 58; ZNH, *Dust Tracks on a Road* (Philadelphia: J. B. Lippincott, 1942), p. 176; Arna Bontemps, introduction to *Personals* (London: Paul Bremen, 1963), p. 6.
6. W. E. B. Du Bois, "The Criteria of Negro Art," *Crisis*, 32 (Oct., 1926), 296. See also W. E. B. Du Bois, "The Negro in Art: A Symposium," *Crisis*, 31 (Mar., 1926), 219; Du Bois may or may not have composed the questions to this symposium, but they reflect his editorial policies and esthetic concerns. For an excellent analysis of Du Bois's complicated esthetics, see Darwin Turner, "W. E. B. Du Bois and the Theory of a Black Esthetic," *Studies in the Literary Imagination*, 7 (Fall, 1974), 1-23; this appears in a special issue of the journal dedicated to the Harlem Renaissance.
7. AL, *The New Negro* (New York: Albert and Charles Boni, 1925), pp. 3, 16, xvii, 49, 50, 51, 15. The quotations are from Locke's foreword and his essays entitled "The New Negro" and "Negro Youth Speaks."
8. RH interview with Bruce Nugent (Richard Bruce), May 20, 1971, New York City; Wallace Thurman, *Infants of the Spring* (New York: Macauley, 1932), p. 233; ZNH, "The Chick with One Hen," typescript (JWJYale); ZNH to James Weldon Johnson, n.d. [ca. 1937–38] (JWJYale); AL to ZNH, June 2, 1928; ZNH to AL, June 5, [1925] (HUAL). See also Clare B. Crane, "Alain Locke and the Negro Renaissance," Ph.D. diss., University of California at San Diego, 1971.
9. W. E. B. Du Bois, "Our Book Shelf," *Crisis*, 31 (Jan., 1926), 141.
10. Clipping, "Zora Neale Hurston Reveals Key to Her Literary Success," *New York Amsterdam News*, Nov. 18, 1944 (MSRC); ZNH, *Dust Tracks*, p. 214; Nick Aaron Ford, *The Contemporary Negro Novel* (1936; rpt., College Park, Md.: McGrath Publishing, 1968), p. 96.
11. Cited in Mae Gwendolyn Henderson, "Portrait of Wallace Thurman," in *The Harlem Renaissance Remembered*, ed. Arna Bontemps (New York: Dodd, Mead, 1972), p. 151.
12. This portrait owes much to Dorothy West, "Elephant Walk," *Black World*, 20 (Nov., 1970), 77–87, and RH interview with Bruce Nugent, May 19, 1971, New York City.
13. RH interviews with Bruce Nugent, May 19, 20, 1971, New York City. See

also Arthur P. Davis, "Growing Up in the New Negro Renaissance," in *Cavalcade*, ed. Arthur P. Davis and Saunders Redding (Boston: Houghton Mifflin, 1971), p. 434.

14. CVV to Fannie Hurst, July 5, 1960 (JWJYale); RH interview with Taylor Gordon, Sept. 3, 1970, White Sulphur Springs, Mont.; Taylor Gordon, *Born to Be* (New York: Covici-Friede, 1929), p. 207; Carolyne Rich Williams (a friend of ZNH in the thirties) to RH, Feb. 16, Mar. 20, 1972; Myrtis Hurston to RH, Aug. 30, 1976; RH interview with Arna Bontemps, Nov. 18, 1970, New Haven, Conn.; RH interview with Bruce Nugent, May 20, 1971, New York City.

15. Myrtis Hurston to RH, Aug. 30, 1976; RH interview with Bruce Nugent, May 19, 1971, New York City; LH, *The Big Sea* (New York: Hill and Wang, 1963), pp. 235–37; Thurman folder (JWJYale); Henderson, "Portrait of Wallace Thurman," p. 151, quoting from Thurman, "Negro Artists and the Negro," *New Republic*, Aug. 31, 1927, p. 37.

16. AL, *New Negro*, p. xv; *Fire!!*, 1 (Nov., 1926), title page; ZNH to AL, Oct. 11, 1927 (HUAL); LH, *Big Sea*, p. 233. Thurman told Melvin Tolson, who was writing an M.A. thesis at Columbia, that Locke had originally offered to cover any of their debts. He did not appear as a patron in the published magazine, however, and Thurman's finances make clear that Locke's guarantee did not materialize. See Melvin Tolson, "The Harlem Group of Negro Writers," M.A. thesis, Columbia University, 1940.

17. RH interviews with Bruce Nugent, May 19, 20, 1971, New York City; LH, *Big Sea*, p. 236.

18. ZNH to LH, Mar. 17, 1927 (JWJYale); Henderson, "Portrait of Wallace Thurman," pp. 151–55; Tolson, "Harlem Group," pp. 110–15; LH, *Big Sea*, pp. 236–37; ZNH to AL, Oct. 11, 1927 (HUAL).

19. Benjamin Brawley, *The Negro Genius* (New York: Dodd, Mead, 1937), p. 264; LH, *Big Sea*, p. 237; "The Looking Glass," *Crisis*, 33 (Jan., 1927), 158.

20. RH interview with Bruce Nugent, May 20, 1971, New York City.

21. LH, *Big Sea*, p. 235; ZNH to LH, Mar. 17, 1927 (JWJYale); RH interview with Bruce Nugent, May 19, 1971, New York City; undated mimeographed letter from Wallace Thurman, addressed "Dear Friend," soliciting funds for *Fire!!* (Thurman folder, JWJYale); ZNH to AL, Oct. 11, 1927 (HUAL).

22. Thurman to "Dear Friend."

23. RH interview with Bruce Nugent, May 19, 1971, New York City; Scrapbook, Nov. 19, 1926 (Gumby Collection, Columbia University Library). See also Gwendolyn Bennett, "Ebony Flute," *Opportunity*, 5 (Mar., 1927), 91.

24. AL, *New Negro*, p. 48.

25. Ibid., pp. 47, 51.

26. ZNH to LH, Apr. 12, 1928 (JWJYale).

27 AL, *New Negro*, p. xv.

28. ZNH, "Concert," manuscript chapter of *Dust Tracks on a Road* (JWJYale); only part of this chapter appeared in the published book.

29. AL, "The Negro Spirituals," in *New Negro*, p. 201.

30. Ibid., p. 199.

31. Frank L. Hayes, "Campaigns Here for Negro Art in Natural State," *Chicago Daily News*, Nov. 16, 1934.

32. See Ralph Ellison, "Richard Wright's Blues," in *Shadow and Act* (New York: Signet, 1966), p. 90.

33. Larry Neal, "A Profile: Zora Neale Hurston," *Southern Exposure*, 1 (Winter, 1974), 162 (article reprinted from *Black Review*). I am indebted to Neal for the idea that folklore projects an ethos, a characteristic sensibility.
34. ZNH to CVV, Jan. 5, 1926 (JWJYale).

≋≋ **From the Earliest Rocking
of My Cradle**

Hurston had resident status in the Harlem Renaissance for only two and a half years, but she contributed much to its memoirs. A brilliant raconteur, a delightful if sometimes eccentric companion, she fit in well with the Roaring Twenties—both black and white divisions. Her presence was legendary. The playwright May Miller, who talked Hurston into transferring from Morgan to Howard when they were both in high school, remembers Zora's literally stopping a party following the 1925 *Opportunity* dinner. She had received a second-place prize for her play *Color Struck*, and she was not hesitant about reminding people. A long, bright-colored scarf hung over her shoulder, and as the party paused to note her arrival, she flung the scarf around her neck, dramatically calling out, "Calaaaah struuuck." Bruce Nugent remembers a bright summer day on Seventh Avenue when he and Zora were walking past the Lafayette Theater. In the twenties ladies were expected not to smoke in public, but Zora smoked a great deal, usually Pall Malls, and she asked Nugent, "Will you walk on the street with me if I smoke a cigarette?" He welcomed the challenge, and after lighting up, they began being stared at by passersby. Laughing, Zora wondered what would happen if they ran into the very proper foster father of their fellow *Fire!!* contributor, Countee Cullen; the Reverend Mr. Cullen had told his son to never let the man who wrote "Smoke, Lilies and Jade" into his house. A friend, Carolyne Rich Williams, remembers Zora's apartment as an "open house" where there was always a "motley group of Columbia students, creative people, song writers, authors, music arrangers and high spirited people." They would "sing together, laugh and talk and tell tall tales. They would play drums and sing old spirituals and Zora would have a harmonica." Dressing flamboyantly, "with lots of bangles and beads," Zora was the central figure, unless she had some work to do. Then, she would retire to the bedroom and amaze everyone by working with great concentration despite the noise in the next room. If she had an appointment, she would simply leave, saying that the last one out should lock the door.[1]

Much of Hurston's personal success was built around her storytelling, which more often that not emphasized the Eatonville milieu. She could become a living representative of the southern folk idiom. Although he did not meet her until later, Sterling Brown remembers that "when Zora was there she was the party." Arna Bontemps said, "In any group she was the center of attention. I don't know whether she was trying to, but . . . she somehow drew attention. . . . Almost before you knew it, she had gotten into a story."[2]

Her folktales and personal anecdotes seldom had been dramatized for the black artists of Hurston's acquaintance. In fact, few of the literary participants in the Renaissance knew intimately her rural South. Langston Hughes had arrived in New York for the first time after a midwestern childhood and a summer in Mexico; he would return after a European work experience. His friend Arna Bontemps was from California. Wallace Thurman had arrived from Utah via the University of Southern California. Cullen was from New York; Jean Toomer was from Washington, as was Nugent. Eric Walrond and Claude McKay were West Indians. Toomer had had to seek out a Georgia backwater for much of *Cane*, and even then had stayed only three months. Zora Neale Hurston represented a known but largely unexperienced segment of black life in America. Although it is impossible to gauge such matters, there seems little question that she helped remind the literary participants in the Renaissance—especially its more bourgeois members—of the richness in the racial heritage.

In one sense, of course, it is artificial to suggest a bourgeois-proletariat division to the black American community; by some measures, all black people are the proletariat no matter how many millions of dollars they may possess. Any black person is subject to discrimination no matter how cultured his accent; Malcolm X took great delight in reminding black professors that in white eyes they were still both literally and figuratively "niggers." Similarly, as Houston Baker has eloquently stated in *Long Black Song*, the race is the folk. Black people share their history to a much greater extent than do other Americans, and a part of that history is the folklore that has helped it survive. Arna Bontemps, growing up in California, was only one generation removed from Louisiana and a knowledge of hoodoo, and there were many folkloric residues in his experience. Hurston was not one generation removed, however, and she embodied a closer association with racial roots than any other Renaissance writer. Where they were Los Angeles or Cleveland, she was Eatonville. She was the folk.

Hurston's Barnard training in some ways militated against the expression of this folk experience in art. Hurston was in New York for only nine months before she entered Barnard and encountered anthropology; the academic discipline provided a conceptualization for her folk experience. The Eatonville folk became no longer simply good storytellers, relaxed in their lifestyles, remarkable in their superstitions, the creators of a profound humor—all the things that made for a rich source of exciting, local-color fiction. Now they became a part of cultural anthropology: scientific objects who could and should be studied for their academic value. As she put it in *Mules and Men*, "From the earliest rocking of my cradle, I had known about the capers Brer Rabbit is apt to cut and what the Squinch Owl says from the house top. But it was fitting me like a tight chemise. I couldn't see it for wearing it. It was only when I was off in college, away from my native surroundings, that I could see myself like somebody else and stand off and look at my garment. Then I had to have the spy-glass of Anthropology to look through at that."

This statement implies a certain dissociation of sensibility. The spy-glass enables Hurston to step back and see her experience from afar, but it also makes her see herself as somebody else. A dual consciousness comes to characterize her intellectual life, and a tension, perhaps latent since her removal from the Eatonville scene, stretched between the subjective folk experience and the abstract knowledge of the meaning of that experience; the tension was only complicated by the stress on scientific objectivity intrinsic to the Boas training. Barnard left Zora Hurston seeking a scientific explanation for why her own experience in the black rural South, despite all her education, remained the most vital part of her life, and why the black folk experience generally was the primary impetus for her imagination. Moving between art and science, fiction and anthropology, she searched for an expressive instrument, an intellectual formula, that could accommodate the poetry of Eatonville, the theories of Morningside Heights, and the esthetic revolt of *Fire!!*

According to her autobiography, she had entered Barnard as an earnest scholar, feeling "highly privileged and determined to make the most of it." She was particularly impressed with her admission—"not everyone . . . can enter these sacred iron gates" —and with Barnard's "high scholastic standards, equipment, the quality of her student body and graduates." As she came under the influence of Ruth Benedict, Gladys Reichard, and Franz Boas of Columbia's anthropology department, her image of herself as a writer dimmed. Boas became the most important figure in her academic life, not only because of his great personal magnetism, but also because he recognized her genius immediately and urged her to begin training as a professional anthropologist, concentrating on folklore. His science provided a taxonomy for her childhood memories, and she called Boas "the greatest anthropologist alive" and "king of kings." She admittedly idolized him. Hurston could be the victim of an easily aroused, indiscriminate enthusiasm, but the commitment to anthropology was no whim. She was dedicated enough to Boas's research to take a pair of calipers and stand on a Harlem street corner measuring people's skulls—an act that many contemporaries felt only Zora Hurston, with her relaxed insouciance, could have gotten away with. She was proud when Melville Herskovits cited her as a fellow scientist laboring on studies about "bodily form of the American Negro" in his 1927 review of anthropology and ethnology in *Opportunity* magazine.

Hurston did not abdicate the crown of the artist, however, and a kind of vocational schizophrenia began to complicate her life, calling for a compromise between her college career and her literary interests. Barnard came to represent scientific discipline and academic respectability; the life of the Harlem Renaissance artist came to symbolize imaginative freedom, social progress, and liberating iconoclasm. Holding both worlds together was her commitment to the folk experience and the artistic forms it generated.

Hurston's intellectual struggle was sometimes misunderstood by her friends, most of whom were exasperated with her denigration of her literary ambitions and with her tendency to dissipate her material in oral presentations. Langston Hughes, in *The Big Sea*, felt that of the whole Harlem group "Zora Neale Hurston was certainly the most amusing. Only to reach a wider audience, need she ever write books—because she is a perfect book of entertainment in herself." Thurman, in his novel *Infants of the Spring*, portrays Hurston as being cynical about both her white patrons and her literary ambitions. His fictional character Sweetie May Carr, a transparent Zora Neale Hurston, is "a short story writer, more noted for her ribald wit and personal effervescence than for any actual literary work. She was a great favorite among those whites who went in for Negro prodigies. . . . Sweetie May was a master of Southern dialect, and an able raconteur, but she was too indifferent to literary creation to transfer to paper that which she told so well. The intricacies of writing bored her, and her written work was for the most part turgid and unpolished." "Smoke, Lilies and Jade," the Nugent story that had so offended the Reverend Mr. Cullen, also stressed the personal performance in Zora's creative efforts: "Zora had shone again . . . her stories . . . she always shone . . . Everyone was glad when Zora shone."

Thurman was an excessively cynical man, but his view of Hurston, at least in regard to her literary ambitions, was not an uncommon one among Renaissance participants. Both Nugent and Arna Bontemps remembered her as running hot and cold on the subject of literature, and Bontemps thought at the time that it was impossible to tell where the folk left off and Zora began. He observed that she must have been a kind of folklore collector even before coming to New York, for she arrived there with a whole repertoire of tales, especially exaggerated stories that she called "lies." Although she occasionally wrote these out, more often she presented them in oral performance.[3]

What seems likely is that Hurston's presence at parties and in crowds was simply the behavioral manifestation of her intellectual dilemma, complicated by personality factors—she liked to be center stage—and the era's interest in the folk. She had grown up in a culture with an oral-aural tradition, where one's ability to entertain and hold an audience with metaphorical imagination and colorful language defined the role of artist. The folk artists on Joe Clarke's porch had no need to write down their tales, for they did not realize they were creating literature. Why was it so important for Zora Hurston to create *written* literature? Hurston's uncertainty about her own writing, and her embodiment of the role of taleteller, were acted out against a backdrop of general Renaissance interest in the folk, and to some extent a feeling that in these cultural roots were to be found the primary ingredients for black art. Locke had referred in *The New Negro* to the "slumbering gift of the folk temperament" and urged writers to look to the spirituals for the racial essence. Concert spirituals, however, were not the shouting hymns of an Eatonville Baptist church, and Hurston expressed dissatisfaction with what "conservatory concepts" had done to the native Afro-American music.[4] Yet how could she capture the Eatonville essence in fiction or in drama? How did one express the viability of black traditions? Hurston never satisfactorily answered this question during the Harlem Renaissance, but it informs all her fiction of the period.

Hurston's writing from the Harlem Renaissance is a mixed bag that culminates esthetically in *Fire!!*'s "Sweat" but looks back on a series of unsuccessful efforts to translate Eatonville into fiction, beginning with "John Redding Goes to Sea," her first story, for the *Stylus* in 1921. Republished in *Opportunity* in January, 1926, with only slight changes, it is what one might expect of the inexperienced author of five years earlier; but it should have been embarrassing to the more accomplished craftsman of 1926.[5]

What makes the story worth reading is the folkloric texture. Matty Redding believes that her son's dream of traveling to the horizon stems from a spell placed by a local witch who sprinkled "traveling dust" on the child at birth. The same night when John goes to work on the bridge that will kill him, a screech owl alights on the roof and "shivers forth his doleful cry." Matty's reaction to this sound is to burn salt in the lamp and turn her bathrobe inside out in an attempt to negate this omen of impending death. The world of witches and signs, superstitions and remedies, is not mocked or sensationalized, for it was an integral part of Hurston's childhood. *Mules and Men*, for example, cites the burning of salt as a surefire remedy for impending evil: "Nothing evil can't stand salt, let alone burnin' salt." The superstitions humanize and particularize the black folk of the rural village, capturing the rich literary possibilities in a world where natural phenomena have supernatural significance. Even though Matty's husband refers to conjure as a "low life mess," he too cannot escape belief, and when the owl screeches, Mr. Redding turns his sock wrong side out to aid the countercharm. Folk belief becomes a function of characterization for these country folk, and a part of John Redding's poignancy is that his intelligence directs him away from the communal trust. On the other hand, John's intellect stagnates in this self-sufficient village where "no one had ever been farther way than Jacksonville," where "life was simple indeed with these folk."

The story, in other words, depends for its effects on those traditional black folk beliefs that have become part of the survival mechanism of the village. The responses to the owl signify an unwillingness to stoically accept the pronouncement of death, a general characteristic of black folklore: there is usually an alternative to the verdict of the gods, and a remedy exists, if only it can be found in time. The traveling dust sprinkled on John was widely believed in, perhaps a manifestation of the slave's desire to travel away from bondage. The psychological effect of the belief also has a certain efficacy for people without legal resources: one's enemy can be forced to leave the vicinity although the person himself lacks the power to force the leave-taking. In "John Redding," however, traveling dust simply provides John's mother with a supernatural explanation for his seemingly irrational desire to search the horizon. It is a mother's response to the mystery of her child.

What "John Redding" reveals is that Hurston, with the encouragement of her Howard mentors, had begun to realize the literary potential in the life of southern black country folk. Whatever its faults, "John Redding" presents a sympathetic picture of a cultural milieu distorted by the neurotic racism of the dominant culture into stereotypes of ignorance, laziness, superstition, and sexuality. It also documents the tensions between a traditional world and a young generation wanting more than the simple life. Matty Redding's belief in conjure and superstition is not something to be laughed at; it is a literary device dramatizing her possessive dilemma. She fights to keep her son from encountering a modern life she does not understand. Her superstition is not ignorance, for if her initial premise is granted—that magic forces exist—then her response is appropriate. Superstition becomes a satisfying explanation for a world that is full of sudden changes of fate, threats to parental influence, and man's desire to explore the horizon. It is proper for the new bridge to contribute to her son's death, for it is a concrete and steel symbol of the threat to her pattern of family life and folk belief. It is also appropriate that the forces of nature conspire to destroy it, granting a dignity to Matty's supernatural faith. Matty becomes the most believable character in the story precisely because she is the representative of black folklore.

"Spunk," published first in the June, 1925, *Opportunity* and reprinted by Locke in *The New Negro*, shows Hurston's growth between 1921 and 1925.[6] She had learned that the mature artist shows rather than tells, and the story demonstrates her narrative strengths. In contrast to "John Redding," "Spunk" is almost entirely in dialogue, with all the characters speaking the rural black dialect of central Florida. Told with great economy (the story is only two and a half pages long), "Spunk" also points to Hurston's awareness that Eatonville and its beliefs were her special subject. Folklore again is the dominant factor in the story. Despite Spunk's physical supremacy and Joe's seeming helplessness, a remedy is available to the cuckolded husband, even if its magic can function only from beyond the grave. A supernatural force rights the wrongs of the natural world. An ironic tension is created between the naturalistic setting so specifically rendered—Spunk's cooling table consists of not two but three sixteen-inch boards on sawhorses—and the power of the supernatural. The men of the village believe without question in the ghost, and they do not think Spunk irrational when he concludes that the black cat is Joe "sneaked back from Hell." Nor do they suggest that Spunk's conscience has created the ghost, for in Hurston's fictional Eatonville there is no reason they should. Man's behavior is not the product of some subconscious motive no one can fathom; rather, it is action capable of being determined by magic powers. The symbol of this magic, the black cat, was one of the most common animals in conjure belief; the black-cat bone was a powerful fetish, and the black cat was frequently interpreted as an apparition. Such a specter is as much a part of one's life as ceremonies of dying, and as Spunk expires, the men turn him to the East, just as Lucy Hurston's neighbors turned her, so that the dying would not be prolonged by lying crossways of the world.

Hurston conceived of such rituals as expressions of religious belief, examples of how Eatonville could accommodate both native superstition and traditional Christianity. Her play *The First One*, submitted to the 1926 *Opportunity* contest and later printed in Charles S. Johnson's collectanea of Renaissance writing, *Ebony and Topaz* (1927), illustrates the folkloric process by which Judeo-Christian tradition was Afro-Americanized, the manner by which gods were made human. *The First One* is a biblical account of the Ham legend, comic in its presentation of Ham's curse as a product of the shrewishness in Shem and Japheth's wives. Ham is presented as a lover of dancing and music, a man of joy contrasted with his materialistic brothers. It is not a particularly good play, but it has interest as Hurston's first attempt to dramatize biblical stories. In Eatonville, biblical tales acquired great intimacy as the stories were personalized, Old Testament sagas becoming as familiar as the history of the family next door. Like a black preacher interpreting a text, Hurston improvised a play from the biblical discussion of race. Since black people were supposed to be the sons of Ham, Hurston could assign so-called black characteristics to Ham and make the play into a comedy about his curse and exile. In effect, the play pokes fun at all those who take seriously the biblical sanction for racial separation. It also revealed to Hurston the possibilities of presenting a black version of the Old Testament, a revelation which would reach fruition in Hurston's novel about Moses as a hoodoo man, *Moses, Man of the Mountain* (1939).

The writing which best illustrates Hurston's attempt to fuse folklore with fiction during the Renaissance is "The Eatonville Anthology," published in the *Messenger* in 1926. The anthology, in fourteen small segments, some only two paragraphs long, was printed in three installments, in the September, October, and

November issues. A printing mishap caused the last segment, "Pants and Cal'line," to go incomplete, the printer or editor apparently losing part of the story. Since the complete tale—an anecdote about Hurston's aunt confronting her husband in flagrante delicto and chasing him off with an axe—is printed in *Dust Tracks*, the error does nothing more than indicate some of the loose editorial practices of the understaffed, underpaid, overworked *Messenger* office. Billing itself as the "only radical Negro magazine in America," the *Messenger* was so poor that Wallace Thurman claimed that its editorial policy reflected whoever was paying best at the time. It eventually became the official organ of the Brotherhood of Sleeping Car Porters during A. Philip Randolph's drive to organize the porters.[7]

"The Eatonville Anthology" is the literary equivalent of Hurston's memorable performances at parties. The reader has the impression of sitting in a corner listening to anecdotes. Some of these are memorates (the folklorist's term for belief tales based on memories of actual events special to the teller); others are folktales or jokes known not only to Hurston but to many other traditional storytellers. For example, there are memories of Eatonville's town dog, an incorrigible cur named Tippy, and of Mrs. Tony Roberts, who always begged for her food instead of paying for it. Old Man Anderson is a backwoods farmer who reacts with great fright upon encountering his first train, a common folktale situation. Joe Lindsay, the greatest liar in the village, tells a tale so common that folklorists have classified it as Type 660, "The Three Doctors."[8] Joe's version tells of a doctor who removes every interior organ of a sick woman, washes out the body cavity, and replaces the organs so expertly that "she was up and about her work in a couple of weeks." Similarly, one segment explains why the dog chases the rabbit: the rabbit long ago split the dog's tongue, ruining his voice, in order to gain the upper hand in a lovers' rivalry. Hurston would publish this folktale later in *Mules and Men*.

There is some biographical interest in the vignette "Turpentine Love," since it is the kernel of a novel Hurston would not write for twenty years, *Seraph on the Suwanee.* It has special significance because it is about black people, while *Seraph* is about whites. The ninth sketch, a three-paragraph description of Mrs. Joe Clarke, became the root of *Their Eyes Were Watching God*, Hurston's novelistic masterpiece, published in 1937. The chief interest in "The Eatonville Anthology," however, is Hurston's lack of distinction between authentic folklore and the fiction she created from the Eatonville setting. The anthology is just that, a series of self-contained stories as they might be told in a night's lying session at Joe Clarke's store or at a meeting of the Niggerati at Hurston's apartment. The fourteen parts have no thematic, structural, or imagistic relationship beyond their general identification with Eatonville in a bygone age: "back in the good old days before the World War when things were very simple in Eatonville." Traditional tales are interspersed with contemporary anecdotes and imaginative fiction improvised for the moment, as was the case in any authentic tale-telling situation or at the gatherings where Hurston entertained.

"The Eatonville Anthology" is, finally, hardly fiction at all. It is pure Zora Neale Hurston: part fiction, part folklore, part biography, all told with great economy, an eye for authentic detail, and a perfect ear for dialect. It is the kind of performance that would lead a friend like Bruce Nugent, when pressed for a description of Hurston, to say simply that "Zora would have been Zora even if she was an Eskimo." Arna Bontemps called her "an original. . . . It seemed so natural to her." In other words, she could be herself without pretense, and, at its best, her art projects this same effortlessness. The anthology succeeds despite its lack of form; it is Hurston's most effective attempt at representing the original tale-telling context. If "Sweat" is the decade's finest example of her written art, "The Eatonville Anthology" is the best written representation of her oral art.

Fire!!'s "Sweat" is a story remarkably complex at both narrative and symbolic levels, yet so subtly done that one at first senses only the fairly simple narrative line. The account of a Christian woman learning how to hate in spite of herself, a story of marital cruelty and the oppression of marital relationships, an allegory of good and evil, it concentrates on folk character rather than on folk environment.

The story is about Delia, a washwoman, and her husband, Sykes. Sykes hates his wife, beats her, and openly courts another woman. He finds excuses to prey on Delia's obsessive fear of snakes; as the story opens, he throws his snake-like bull whip into the room to scare her. Sykes feels emasculated because his wife has earned much of their income by washing white people's clothes. This is a peril for unemployed black men, and Sykes sees the clothes as a constant challenge to his manhood, a recurring symbol of his inadequacy. Although he has told Delia "time and again to keep them white folks' clothes outa dis house," she has for fifteen years taken in washing in order that they both may survive. The result has been the loss of the love of her husband, and "sweat, sweat, sweat! Work and sweat, cry and sweat, pray and sweat!" Praying brings her the most solace, and her religious faith is connected, in Sykes's mind, to her work and its emasculating effects. In a speech logically irrational, but emotionally lucid with frustration, Sykes tries to hurt Delia: "You ain't nothing but a hypocrite. One of them Amencorner Christians—sing, whoop, and shout, and then come home and wash white folks clothes on the Sabbath." Searching for a characteristic that Delia can do nothing to change, Sykes finally decides that the thing he dislikes most about her is her gauntness: "Gawd! how ah hates skinny wimmen." His paramour, on the other hand, is quite the opposite: "Lawdy, you sho is got one portly shape on you." Hurston's favorite Eatonville businessman, Joe Clarke, understands Sykes's behavior with all the wisdom of a village philosopher:

> There's plenty men dat takes a wife lak dey do a joint uh sugar cane. It's round, juicy an sweet when dey gits. But dey squeeze an' grind, squeeze an' grind an' wring tell dey wring every drop uh pleasure dats in 'em out. When dey's satisfied dat dey is wrung dry, dey treats em jes lak dey do a cane-chew. Dey throws 'em away. Dey knows whut dey is doin' while dey is at it, an' hates theirselves fuh it but they keeps on hangin' after huh tell she's empty. Den dey hates huh fuh bein' a cane-chew an' in de way.

Sykes eventually tries to drive Delia from her own house by penning a rattlesnake near the back door. Then he attempts murder by moving the snake to the clothes hamper, hoping it will kill her when she reaches in to begin sorting the week's clothes. Delia escapes, however, and the released rattler kills Sykes as he returns to look for her body. Delia could have saved him, or at least comforted him in his dying moments, and we begin to understand

how high Delia's "spiritual earthworks" of Old Testament ven-
geance have been built against Sykes. As she tells him, "Ah hates
you, Sykes. . . . Ah hates you tuh de same degree dat Ah useter
love yuh. Ah done took and took till mah belly is full up tuh mah
neck. . . . Ah hates yuh lak uh suck-egg dog."

But this makes the story Delia's tragedy, too, for she does not
warn him about the loose snake, or help him when bitten; and when
Sykes dies at her feet with "his horribly swollen neck and his one
open eye shining with hope," a burden is not lifted but newly
imposed. Delia ends the story with great pity for Sykes, since his
dying glance focused on the clothes tubs that have destroyed him.
Even though her husband has attempted murder, her burden of
knowledge becomes two-fold: the awareness that his evil provided
the means for her to fulfill a wish for his death, and the recognition
that in his dying seconds Sykes learned that the immensity of her
hate precluded assistance—"She waited in the growing heat while
inside she knew the cold river was creeping up and up to extinguish
that eye which must know by now that she knew."

"Sweat" also illustrates a characteristic of Hurston's best fiction:
a complex imagistic structure, with Freudian overtones, that rein-
forces the thematic statement of the story. "Sweat" depends heavily
on traditional Christian symbolism, the snake being referred to
once as "Ol Satan," another time as "Ol Scratch." The serpent is
identified with Sykes's evil ways, and throughout the story the
imagery associated with the man evokes sinuosity. The very first
scene has Sykes throwing his bull whip at Delia: "Just then something long, round, limp and black fell upon her shoulder and
slithered to the floor beside her." The action is important because
Delia is deathly afraid of snakes, even having "a fit over a earth-
worm or a string," and Sykes cruelly exploits the fear. In the
context of Delia's unremitting faith, the snake comes to represent
the evil that lives inside despite her Christianity, a force she knows
and is afraid of, but which Sykes's cruelty will not permit her to
overcome. Sykes himself becomes a kind of devil, whose demonic
desires eventually lead to a struggle for Delia's life *and* soul, even
though he does not quite understand the dramatic part he plays.
The pity Delia can feel for Sykes as he dies in sight of the
clothes—"A surge of pity too strong to support bore her away from

that eye that must, could not, fail to see the tubs"—redeems her from her hate. Circumstances also cause Sykes to die knowing of her wish for his destruction. She ends the story holding to a chinaberry tree, a rigid, linear symbol that provides rootedness in a world of slithering sinuosity. Such contrasting imagery adds tension to Delia's struggle with herself and her husband—the evil both inside and out. The phallic resonates in this imagery, and the imagistic tension illustrates how Hurston's best writing assumes meaning at a variety of levels. Delia is frightened of Sykes not only because of his cruelty; he also represents male sexuality ominous in its desire.

"Sweat" contains little identifiable folklore. There are no references to conjure or hoodoo, and neither plot nor characterization depends on traditional behavior. Delia and Sykes are particularized by their love turned to hate, and their tragedy has little to do with forces outside themselves. The communal morality of Eatonville informs the story's movement—the men on Joe Clarke's store porch disapprove of Sykes and consider what punitive action the community should take toward him—but "Sweat" depends much less on the Eatonville scene than on the interplay between the two principals.

"Sweat" serves to illustrate why Hurston's fellow artists could become so exasperated with her seeming lack of literary commitment. When she depended less directly on the folklore of Eatonville and presented the folk characters in a drama of human motives, the result was superior art. But when she borrowed straightforwardly from the beliefs and customs of her village without integrating them into a literary design, the result was a "Spunk" or an "Eatonville Anthology"—interesting, but not overpowerful fiction. The difference is between the scrupulous reportage appropriate to anthropological description and the unprincipled selectivity characterizing esthetic construction. The reporter describes as much as she can of the event. The artist uses the event for her own selfish purposes. When Locke and James Weldon Johnson argued for a conscious art based on folk sources, they were advocating a disciplined irresponsibility to the folk idiom; Hurston had to reconcile licensed irresponsibility with her knowledge of the original source. The tension between these positions is well illustrated by "Black Death," a short story which is either a direct redaction of an Eatonville folktale, or a work of fiction Hurston permitted to masquerade as authentic folklore.

When Johnson contacted Hurston about the first *Opportunity* contest of 1925, she eventually submitted not only "Spunk" and *Color Struck*, both of which won prizes, but also another play, "Spears" (now lost), and "Black Death," both of which won honorable mention.[9] "Black Death" reveals the curious pressures Hurston felt as both writer and folklorist, making it in many ways her most interesting story of the 1925–27 period: it summarizes her uncertainty over how to use the Eatonville material. A manuscript of the short story, never published in its original form, is in the Charles S. Johnson collection at Fisk University, along with other submissions to the *Opportunity* contests. As submitted to Johnson, the story appears to be a fictional account of an Eatonville hoodoo man named Old Dan Morgan who can "kill any person indicated . . . without ever leaving his house or seeing his victim." Old Dan Morgan is called upon after Docia Boger, an Eatonville girl, is impregnated by Beau Diddeley (a traditional name for a village Lothario), who is a waiter in a Maitland hotel. Beau not only refuses to marry Docia, but also implies that he cannot be certain the child is his. He informs her that he is married anyway, and berates her: "Why I could pick up a better woman out of the gutter." Outraged, Mrs. Boger waits for darkness and consults the hoodoo man. Her daughter's tears have hardened her heart, and she wishes Beau dead, a fact divined by Morgan even before her late-night arrival. After a libation to the gods—she pours a gourd of water on the floor—the means of destruction are determined. Morgan produces a mirror and instructs Mrs. Boger to shoot to kill when Beau's face appears in the glass. She does so, and we learn that in the midst of wooing yet another local maiden, the youthful Beau has died of a heart attack. The strange thing about his death is a mysterious mark looking like a powder burn directly over his heart.

The story fascinates because the hoodoo setting becomes part of an African heritage surfacing during crisis. As Mrs. Boger sets out at midnight for Morgan's quarters, a world of witch doctors and drums is magically evoked: "In the swamp at the head of the lake, she saw a jack-o-lantern darting here and there, and three hundred years of

America passed like the mist of morning. Africa reached out its dark hand and claimed its own. Drums. Tom, Tom, Tom, Tom, Tom, Tom, beat in her ears. Strange demons seized her. Witch doctors danced before her, laid hands upon her alternately freezing her and burning her flesh." The jack-o'-lantern is a commonplace of black folklore; the tom-toms document Hurston's experimentation with the exotic-primitive theme informing Cullen's "Heritage" as well as a number of other poems and novels of the twenties. The theme itself flirts with racist stereotypes of black people as only partially civilized savages whose veneer of civilization slips away at times of stress, but its major purpose is to emphasize cultural difference. As Thurman's analysis of *Fire!!* made clear, black writers were interested in writing not about those who tried to emulate whites, but about people who maintained "racial qualities." The problem for the Renaissance writer was to determine what those qualities were. In "Muttsy," her story of a Harlem speakeasy, Hurston had associated them with jazz: "The piano in Ma Turner's back parlor stuttered and wailed. The pianist kept time with his heel and informed an imaginary deserter that 'she might leave and go to Halimufack, but his slow drag would bring her back,' mournfully with a memory of tom toms running rhythms through the plaint."

Such tom-tom beats were almost a cliché in Harlem Renaissance writing, and both blacks and whites became enmeshed in the cult of exotic primitivism. For the whites it was the idea that Harlem was an uptown jungle, a safari for the price of cab fare, with cabarets decorated in jungle motifs. They went to Harlem to see the natural rhythm and uninhibited grace of America's link with the heart of darkness. For the black artists it was a much more serious concern, an attempt to establish a working relationship with what Locke called in *The New Negro* the "ancestral" past. Countee Cullen would articulate the question well in "Heritage," one of his most famous poems: "What is Africa to me?" Hurston did not take a large part in this debate, and the "Halimufack Blues" that the piano played while the tom-toms beat was a song she remembered from Eatonville and would later collect throughout the South. Yet she was influenced by the emphasis on primitivism, as illustrated by her reaction to jazz in her 1928 essay, "How It Feels to Be Colored Me." Her response comes not only as a function of race, differentiating her from a white companion, but also as an archetype of history. Jazz, she implies, touches the racial memory of Africa:

> This orchestra grown rambunctious, rears on its hind legs and attacks the tonal veil with primitive fury, rending it, clawing it until it breaks through to the jungle beyond. I follow those heathen—follow them exultingly. I dance wildly inside myself; I yell within, I whoop; I shake my assegai above my head, I hurl it true to the mark yeeeeooww! I am in the jungle and living in the jungle way. My face is painted red and yellow and my body is painted blue. My pulse is throbbing like a war drum. I want to slaughter something—give pain, give death to what, I do not know. But the piece ends. The men of the orchestra wipe their lips and rest their fingers. I creep back slowly to the veneer we call civilization with the last tone and find the white friend sitting motionless in his seat, smoking calmly.

This description is so excessive that one wonders if its "yeeeeooww" effect is not slightly satiric, Hurston's response to some of the self-consciousness in the exoticism theme. The essay as a whole is serious, however, and the passage may indicate nothing more than her use of a common Renaissance technique; by stressing an instinctual Africanism, the black writer could easily symbolize a racial pride growing from a cultural difference. The Harlem Renaissance writer was proud of "individual race qualities," even if somewhat vague about their definition. The fact that they existed was seldom doubted. Despite a shared geography, the historical and spiritual legacy of black people was demonstrably different from that of whites, leading to a different cultural experience. Certainly, Eatonville, with its folk heritage, was different from bourgeois Washington and New-Negro New York, but all these communities were still more obviously different from white communities. That was the nature of American civilization.

The very first paragraph of "Black Death" establishes this cultural distinction: "We Negroes in Eatonville know a number of things that the hustling, bustling White man never dreams of. He is a materialist with little care for overtones." Hurston reported that white men do not believe in hoodoo; they scoff at it and consider it part of the black man's ignorance and superstition. Black people, however, *know* that hoodoo works. They *know* that Morgan has sold "himself to the devil over the powerful black cat's bone that alone will float upstream," and they *know* that "life and death are in his hands." White folks might say different, but "white folks are very stupid about some things. They can think mightily but cannot feel."

"Black Death" celebrates the very elements in the Eatonville culture that are made into stereotypes by an unfeeling, excessively materialistic, hopelessly rational white society. It suggests that Hurston had thought much about what was unique in Eatonville specifically and in Afro-American culture generally, and about how a black writer captured the sense of shared feeling characteristic of her community. "Black Death," however, is only about 20 percent fiction; it is 80 percent folklore. The plot, the rake's name, and much of the authenticating detail of the story are traditional, so much so that in 1931 Hurston would print "Black Death" in an altered form as a folktale about Eatonville hoodoo men. Significantly, this printing appeared in the country's major outlet for folklore research.

Late in 1931, Hurston published some of the results of her second collecting expedition in the *Journal of American Folklore*. Entitled "Hoodoo in America," her report took up almost the entire issue of the journal, more than a hundred pages, and was the first scholarly treatment of hoodoo by a black American folklorist. An important piece of scientific research, Hurston's article includes a number of "conjure stories" presumably collected from informants. One story concerns John Wesley Roberts, a hotel waiter who comes to Orange County as a stranger and helps create a baby. After he refuses to marry the girl, her mother goes to "Old Man Massey" and participates in the same ritual described in "Black Death," with the same results.

One wonders whether Hurston's informant for the variant 1931 text was not Zora Neale herself. The two versions are very close; the process by which Mrs. Boger's heart is hardened, for example, is almost identical in both 1925 and 1931 versions, the latter abbreviated to accommodate the limited space of the scientific report:

(from "Black Death")
Drip, drip, drip, went her daughter's tears on the old woman's heart, each drop calcifying a little the fibers till at the end of four days the

petrifying process was complete. Where once had been warm, puls-
ing flesh was now cold heavy stone, that pulled down pressing out
normal life and bowing the head of her.

(from "Hoodoo in America")
At the end of the week, her heart under the drip-drip from her
daughter's eyes had turned to stone.

What we have is the "Black Death" version of the tale presented
as fiction in early 1925—before Zora Neale Hurston ever studied
folklore. The "Hoodoo in America" version of 1931 is assumed to be
a folktale collected from informants in Eatonville, but no informant
is ever identified. Was Hurston lying in 1931, passing off her own
creative work as folklore? Or had the 1925 version been simply
a redaction of a folktale remembered from Eatonville, and given a
special telling by the young short-story writer? The logical interpretation, I think, is that Hurston, a product of a tradition in which
narratives were community property rather than any individual's
private possession, simply transferred a part of her repertoire to
the typed page. It was probably the same thing she had done with
the dog-and-rabbit tale of "The Eatonville Anthology" that later appeared in *Mules and Men*. There is certainly nothing wrong with
this, and it is appropriate to a folkloric process of creativity. In the
folk environment it is impossible to "steal" someone's idea for a
story; like a good joke, it is told for the delight of all, with the
understanding that if memorable it will be repeated and will become a part of the community's traditional verbal behavior. Each
oral tale-teller will then make the traditional story or joke uniquely
his, just as a blues singer gives a unique "signature" to a song well
known to his audience. Zora Hurston was making Old Dan Morgan
and Docia Boger a part of her special fictional world in the same way
she could claim that she was once arrested for crossing against a red
light but escaped punishment by explaining that she had seen the
white folks pass on green and therefore assumed the red was for
her. Perhaps the arresting officer had no way of knowing how
widely such a story is known among black people, but one should
not assume that it actually happened.[10] Zora Neale had used herself
as a character to give a traditional story a personal immediacy.

The number of traditional elements in "Black Death" also supports the folklore-to-fiction hypothesis. Among Morgan's other

conjures are the loveless curse on Della Lewis that has prohibited any of her seven husbands from remaining longer than twenty-eight days; a paralysis of Hiram Lester's left side after Morgan secures a track made by Hiram's left foot; the shed skin of a black snake in Horace Brown's shoe that made him as rootless as the Wandering Jew; a sprig of hair put in a bottle, then corked and thrown into a running creek with the neck pointing upstream, thereby making Lena Merchant go crazy; the fingernails buried with lizard's feet that caused Lillie Wilcox's blood to dry up. Every one of these episodes has been collected by other folklorists among conjure believers. They come from Hurston's imagination only in the sense that she selected them for her story from the repertoire of conjure stories in her memory, fitting them into her own imaginative retelling of the folktale.[11]

Finally, there is additional evidence that Hurston was engaged in a more-or-less conscious process of bringing Eatonville folklore to a wider audience during the Renaissance years. Arna Bontemps indicated that those who knew her during the twenties were not at all surprised by some of the tales in *Mules and Men*. They had heard them before during Zora's tale-telling feats at parties. When the *Forum* for September, 1926, printed her brief retelling of a widely known tale from the John-Marster cycle, it was simply a literary representation of her own oral performance. The tale itself was about the slave John's stealing a pig from his master, butchering it, and hiding it in a cooking pot. When the master searches for his pig and demands to see what is cooking, John reluctantly opens the pot, pointing out, "Ah put dis heah critter in heah a possum—if it comes out a pig, 'tain't mah fault." The *Forum*'s purpose in printing the tale is to affirm their "four square" stand "behind the New Negro" in his "literary as well as his economic progress." Referring to Hurston, they editorialize, "It is a wise writer who realizes that glints of the old time Uncle Remus 'native humor' are one of the richest contributions that the race has to offer." Hurston's "Possum or Pig" is not just a "glint" of traditional black humor, and it is certainly not an Uncle Remus story. It is a classic folktale known to many Afro-American storytellers, presented to the literary world as part of the creative output of the Harlem Renaissance. Like "Black Death," it demonstrates that Hurston's memory was overflowing with the acquired narrative legacy of her race, and that this was something she *brought to* the Renaissance. Since this fact has been largely misunderstood by previous commentators, it is appropriate to end the discussion of her contributions to the Harlem Renaissance with an analysis of those misapprehensions.

Nathan Huggins's *The Harlem Renaissance* (1971) traces the intellectual and social history of the era, and his extensive interviews and detailed research have contributed much that is new and valuable to our understanding of the period. When dealing with Zora Hurston, however, Huggins complains that Hurston's "common, rural Negro" with his "superstitions and habits of mind" did not give the reader fully developed characters but "folk types." Graced with "the speech of the lowly, rural Negro," Hurston's characters were "robust and passionate" men and women who "lived for the instant" and whose "life and mind were uncomplicated." Huggins considers this a sentimental view made even more artificial because Hurston's folktales were not even authentic: "The line between Zora Hurston's mind and her material was never clear."

Huggins makes an error of fact when citing the Hurston career, referring to an advanced degree from Columbia. But far more serious is his unwillingness to accept Zora Hurston as a creative artist struggling to embody the role of tale-teller to the Renaissance audience. The reason there was no clear line between Zora Hurston's mind and her material is that she operated from within a different esthetic, one which made no distinctions between the lore inherited by successive generations of folk and the imagination with which each generation adapted the tradition and made the lore its own. Hurston alone, among all the artists of the Harlem Renaissance, understood this principle of folk *process*. Folk tradition is not just a body of texts, melodies, and beliefs—materials—that the artist dips into, saving them from cultural obscurity by adding them to the written wisdom of Western Man. When one believed that it was, sorrow songs ended up as harmoniously arranged spirituals that were as far from authentic black religious music as Paul Whiteman was from Duke Ellington. Folk tradition involves *behavior*—performed interpretations of the world which influence action—and it does not easily transfer to a print-oriented tradition that conceives of art as something fixed, a symbol of status distinguishing the leisured classes from the peasants. There is no separation of subject and object, of mind and material in folk tradition. What appears from afar as material for the creative artist is simply behavior for the tale-teller, an activity as natural as thinking; traditional art is perpetuated without self-consciousness.

Zora Hurston was a young writer from the provinces confronted in New York with a conception of art antithetical to her experience. An objet d'art was assumed to be the personal product of the romantic egoist, forged in the smithy of her soul from bits and pieces of disjointed experience, then consecrated with talent for the sophisticated reader. If good enough, it became immortalized in an unchanging form, such as the text of *Hamlet*. This conception of the artist was held by virtually all her contemporaries—Hughes was a possible exception—and it made no difference if one were an iconoclast like Thurman or a traditionalist like Countee Cullen. Given these alternatives, Hurston turned away from fiction and plunged into anthropology, a science which offered an intellectual perspective, a "spy glass," for her emotional experience in Eatonville. She became Boas's student and a kind of proselytizer for anthropological knowledge. She even convinced Bruce Nugent, who loved learning and hated schools, to sit in for three years on Boas's classes.

The Boas training provided more than an explanation for Eatonville's existence. It also revealed how folklore could be preserved without transformation into conscious art. Many Harlem Renaissance intellectuals felt that because folk art was *un*conscious, it was being trampled into oblivion by the march of history. The downhome stories, the slave songs, the old-time religion were assumed to be the casualties of twentieth-century industrial life. As the environment changed, necessitating new modes of behavior, the old products of the folk imagination would be forgotten. Thus, the only way to preserve a portion of this dying heritage was to create a lasting, conscious art using the folk material as its base. James Weldon Johnson ended his introduction to *God's Trombones* with that explanation for his poems: "The old-time Negro preacher is rapidly passing. I have tried sincerely to fix something of him."

Hurston had tried to represent the folk process in fiction and had expressed her concern for folklore's survival. She represented in person the transformation of an Eatonville child into a modern urban woman, and she knew how quickly traditions could be lost. The systematic collection of folklore, however, offered an alternative to the view that the conscious artist salvaged the folklore of the race by using it for inspiration. A folklorist could live among her informants, just as Zora Hurston had lived in Eatonville as a child; the folklorist could assimilate the behavioral process that produced the lore, and the folklorist's collections would represent the traditions of one's people without the presumption of esthetic superiority. The artist need not speak for the masses, since the masses through their collected folklore could speak for themselves. If black folklore was dying, then the folklorist could become an essential tradition-bearer, reconciling the New Negro with the racial past, not as an elite artist interpreting the racial essence, not as an abstract intellectual with a vague and romantic commitment to the spiritual legacy, but as a careful scientist documenting the techniques of imagination in black American culture.

By February, 1927, when most of her Barnard course work was finished, Hurston had already expended great effort to create an art which would represent folklore in a fictional form. Her success had been uneven, and her reputation as a New Negro artist had come as much from personal performance as from fictional achievement; still, she had established herself as one of the Harlem literati. If at times her fiction displayed an uncertainty over exactly which fictional techniques were appropriate for representing the folk process, it could be excused because of her vocational commitment to anthropology. She had made a choice to subordinate art to science, and she was about to begin her career as a professional folklorist.

NOTES

1. RH interview with May Miller, Apr. 27, 1971, Washington, D.C.; Myrtis Hurston to RH, Aug. 30, 1976; RH interview with Bruce Nugent, May 20, 1971, New York City; Carolyne Rich Williams to RH, Feb. 16, Mar. 20, 1972.

2. RH interview with Sterling Brown, Apr. 29, 1971, Washington, D.C.; RH interviews with Arna Bontemps, Nov. 18, Dec. 11, 1970, May 4, 1971, New Haven, Conn.

3. RH interview with Bruce Nugent, May 20, 1971, New York City; RH interview with Arna Bontemps, Nov. 18, 1970, New Haven, Conn.

4. AL, *The New Negro* (New York: Albert and Charles Boni, 1925), p. 267;

ZNH, "Negro Religious Customs: The Sanctified Church," typescript, Florida Federal Writers' Project, p. 2 (LCAFS).

5. ZNH, "John Redding Goes to Sea," *Opportunity*, 4 (Jan., 1926), 16-21. Another less-than-successful ZNH story from this period is "Magnolia Flower" (*Spokesman*, July, 1925, pp. 26-29), about a school girl who loves her light-skinned teacher despite her father's opposition.

6. ZNH, "Spunk," *Opportunity*, 3 (June, 1925), 171–73. Robert Bone's *Down Home: A History of Afro-American Short Fiction* (New York: G. P. Putnam's Sons, 1975), pp. 141-50, contains an interesting analysis of "Spunk" and provocative remarks on Hurston's other short fiction of the period.

7. LH, *The Big Sea* (New York: Hill and Wang, 1963), p. 233–34. For a comprehensive account of the *Messenger*, see Theodore Kornweibel, *No Crystal Stair* (Westport, Conn.: Greenwood Press, 1975).

8. Antti Aarne and Stith Thompson, *The Types of the Folktale*, 2nd ed., rev., Folklore Fellows Communications, 184 (Helsinki: Suomalainen Tiedeakatemia, 1961), p. 231.

9. ZNH, "Black Death," typescript submitted to *Opportunity* contest (CSJFisk). This story was apparently also considered for inclusion in *The New Negro*; see ZNH to AL, June 5, [1925] (HUAL).

10. See Darwin Turner, introduction to *Dust Tracks on a Road* (New York: Arno Press, 1969), p. ii.

11. See Newbell Niles Puckett, *Folk Beliefs of the Southern Negro* (Chapel Hill: University of North Carolina Press, 1926); Harry Middleton Hyatt, *Hoodoo, Conjuration, Witchcraft, Rootwork*, 4 vols. (vols. 1 and 2, Washington, D.C.: American University Bookstore, 1970; vols. 3 and 4, St. Louis: Western Publishing, 1973); J. Mason Brewer, *American Negro Folklore* (Chicago: Quadrangle Books, 1968).

4 ≋≋≋ Do You Know Any Folktales?

In late February, 1927, Zora Neale Hurston boarded a southbound train at New York's Penn Station. Her destination was central Florida, where she planned to work in the field for the next six months, supported by a $1,400 research fellowship. She was sponsored by Columbia University's anthropology department. The Association for the Study of Negro Life and History was paying expenses, and Columbia's Franz Boas, the foremost anthropologist in America, was responsible for overseeing the expedition. The plan, worked out in his office over the winter, was for her to begin in Jacksonville and work south through such towns as Palatka and Sanford to Eatonville; if she had time, she would go on to Mobile and New Orleans. The task was to record the songs, customs, tales, superstitions, lies, jokes, dances, and games of Afro-American folklore.[1]

Hurston was returning to Eatonville under the aegis of an internationally known anthropologist, affiliated with a prestigious institution of higher learning, and supported by America's leading black historian, Carter G. Woodson, founder and director of the Association for the Study of Negro Life and History. The girl from Eatonville who had once believed that a neighbor's stroke came from the hoodoo spell of a local conjure man had indeed traveled a long journey in order to return to her origins. Now she would approach as a social scientist what she had lived as a child, and the folklore collected would reclaim her village from racist stereotypes.

Folklore is exceedingly difficult to define, and folklorists themselves quarrel over precisely what it is. Some claim simply to know it when they see it; all agree that folklore is not error, as in the phrase "That's only folklore." Two common definitions are "verbal art" and "literature transmitted orally." The well-known folklorist Francis Lee Utley once tried to define it by description, indicating that American folklore included the arts and crafts, the beliefs and customs of our lumber camps, city evangelical storefront churches, back-alley dives, farmers' festivals and fairs, hill frolics, carnivals, firemen's lofts, sailors' cabins, chain gangs, and penitentiaries. In other words, folklore touches everyone's life, whether it is a belief that a broken mirror brings seven years' bad luck, a tale of Brer Rabbit, or a song about the frog who goes a-courting. In an age of media, so much folklore is popularized for mass consumption that its origins are easily forgotten, and it is sometimes difficult to distinguish between authentic lore and creative art, between traditional heroes and popular imitations. "The Saint Louis Blues," published by W. C. Handy in 1914, is not a folksong, but a famous composition by a composer of genius; a spiritual such as "Swing Low, Sweet Chariot" *is* folklore, created by "black and unknown bards," then preserved as one slave generation taught the words and melody to the next. The northwoods demigod, Paul Bunyan, may or may not have originated in a folktale told by lumberjacks, but by the time he had been popularized in the advertising of the Red River Lumber Company of Minnesota and described by countless authors of children's stories, he had become a fictional rather than a folk hero.[2]

Separating genuinely traditional materials from those of contemporary authorship is only one of many factors making the study of folklore a challenging task. The collector may enter a community, often as a stranger, attempt to establish rapport, and then write down (or, now, tape-record) as many of the communal traditions as the people choose to share. *Tradition* is the key word, for the folklorist seeks especially those forms of communicative behavior —usually verbal, although they may also be evident in crafts or kinetic movements—that have survived through time by oral transmission. The hex signs on the barns of the Pennsylvania Dutch, the square dances of Texas ranchers, and the legend of John Henry, "the steel drivin' man," are all folklore. Put another way, folklore consists of unwritten traditions which cause people to perform in familiar ways, the performance of each generation and each individual contributing to the tradition from within the security of its familiarity. It is behavior replicated through history, and it reflects the common life of the mind existing at a level other than that of high or formal culture. Formal culture grows primarily from the presumption of the written heritage; traditional culture arises primarily out of the communicative expectations of a given group.

Since it was long held that traditions tend to survive best when a community has remained isolated and stable, the folklorist often searched for the backwater village uncorrupted by the modern world. The collector usually had to live with informants to establish good faith, becoming subject to their diseases and dangers, problems and pomposities. More than one folklorist has been run out of town, threatened with murder, or made the butt of local jokes. Even when the person is received well, the simple mechanics of collecting can be difficult; a classic anecdote tells about the folklorist who arranged to record some Appalachian ballads, only to discover that the rural cabin had no electricity to power his tape recorder.

Today the study of folklore has become much more sophisticated, no longer limited to out-of-the-way places and peoples, with a concern for everything from urban street culture to the shape of the entrance to the southern-mountain cabin. Students of Afro-American folklore study the ritualized insults of the dozens, the virtuoso rhyming abilities displayed by street people in toasts, the malign occultism of conjure practices, and the symbiosis of hoodoo and the numbers racket. In 1927, when Hurston began collecting, American folklore as a scholarly discipline was still in relative infancy; although the American Folklore Society had been founded in 1888, by 1927 not a single American university had a folklore department. Collections of Afro-American folklore, especially by black collectors, were almost nonexistent. William Wells Brown, the first black novelist, had reported on folksongs remembered by escaped or emancipated slaves in *My Southern Home* (1880); the black short-story writer Charles Chesnutt had written of the hoodoo practices of his native North Carolina; Hampton Institute had founded the first black folklore society, systematically queried its new students about customs and listed them in the school magazine, the *Southern Workman*.[3]

There was a sizable body of black folklore collected by whites, but often the collections carried interpretations twisting the material beyond recognition. Joel Chandler Harris had fictionalized animal tales in his Uncle Remus stories, reaching a large popular audience; but the plantation context for the tale-telling made the folklore seem a childish pastime. Various southern whites had sent to the *Journal of American Folklore* short accounts of behavior observed among their servants and sharecroppers, finding it quaint, curious, or mystifying.[4] Even when whites sympathized with black people and recognized black folklore as a major national resource, their eccentric collecting techniques led to artificial contexts for the lore. One of the financial angels of the American Folklore Society, Elsie Clews Parsons, had gathered songs and stories from the coastal islands in the Carolinas, inviting impoverished farmers to board her yacht to tell tales and sing songs.[5] One of the most scholarly studies in the field was a newly published book by Newbell Niles Puckett, a white Mississippian, called *Folk Beliefs of the Southern Negro*. Much of his information about hoodoo had been collected while he masqueraded as a hoodoo doctor himself. Puckett's interpretation of at least some of his material could not have charmed Zora Neale Hurston, based as it was on the belief that black personality was characterized by laziness, humor, and sexuality.

The field of Afro-American folklore was generally an untapped resource, never examined scientifically by a black scholar who had known prolonged, intimate contact with the rural South. Though Hurston was a complete novice at collecting when she took the train toward Florida in February, 1927, only one other member of her race, Arthur Huff Fauset of Philadelphia, had equivalent professional training and knowledge. Through a combination of luck, pluck, and accident, Zora Neale Hurston had the opportunity to become *the* authority on Afro-American folklore. Only once before had a black collector with similar training—again, Fauset—received such prestigious sponsorship or support. Never before had a black person with her particular creative talents and southern background undertaken such a study. The hopes for the trip and the promise of the person make Hurston's failure during this initial expedition especially interesting. Finding that she could not collect efficiently, torn by an ambivalence between the life of the creative artist and the demands of scientific study, beset by a marriage disintegrating almost before it began, Hurston struggled to gain control of a subject matter that would occupy her lifetime. Failing to do so, she committed that most grievous of academic sins—plagiarizing the work of another—and jeopardized her professional career at its very inception.

Hurston had first begun doing field work for Boas in 1926, and her measurements of Harlem physiognomy had become part of his research into physical characteristics of the race. Few Harlemites, however, needed the confirmation of a Columbia anthropologist's statistics to know that black people's skulls, despite the assertions of pseudo-scientific racist learning of the nineteenth century, had plenty of room for the brain. Boas's careful refutation of this ersatz science suggests both his commitment to "objective research"—the skulls must be measured—and his liberal racial views. Much of his research was directed toward establishing the equal capabilities of all races, and the very month Hurston left for Florida he published an article in *Current History* exposing the fallacies of racial inferiority. Boas had discovered early that Indians, presumed to be savages, maintained a highly complex, sophisticated belief system, and the evidence indicated that the same was true of illiterate black people. He was particularly interested in the African survivals in Afro-American culture, and Zora Hurston's field work would be part of the evidence documenting this unique Afro-American subculture; if the findings refuted ignorant racial stereotypes arising from the absence of anthropological data, so much the better.

The Barnard experience prepared Hurston well, but it was book-oriented study. She had little opportunity to actually go about the business of soliciting and collecting folklore. Her total field experience had been two summers in Harlem, working with specific directions from Boas and Melville Herskovits. Yet as she and her mentor talked about the material available in the South, both were excited about what she might find. In early November, 1926, knowing that Hurston would finish her full-time studies in February of the next year, Boas wrote to Carter G. Woodson of the Association for the Study of Negro Life and History, recommending his young student to the association and inquiring if a fellowship to support a field trip might not be available. He offered to oversee the work himself.[6] Boas knew that the association's budget was not large, but that Woodson was thoroughly committed to exploring all aspects of the Afro-American experience. Woodson, a Harvard Ph.D., had founded the association in 1915 and singlehandedly built it into a major research organization, counting virtually every important black intellectual in the nation in its membership. The organization's *Journal*, begun in 1916, rapidly gained the respect of scholars, and Woodson's own research was a model of scholarly documentation of black contributions to American history. His creation of Negro History Week in 1926, to be celebrated in the second week in February in most black schools of the country, honored all those black heroes so conveniently left out of the white man's textbooks. Woodson responded cautiously to Boas, indicating that he had been considering funding a more established scholar, Hurston's former teacher at Howard, Alain Locke, for a study of African art; after making sure that Columbia had no money for Hurston, and after consulting with Elsie Clews Parsons (who may have been donating some of the funds), Woodson eventually granted $1,400 for six months of collecting, February to August.[7] Hurston was to be in the field on her own for the first time in her career.

Boas's instructions had been fairly explicit, although he was worried that Hurston was a "little too much impressed with her own accomplishments." With some justification, she was never very modest. Boas assumed, however, that her "easy manner" would "work," meaning that she could enter the black folk milieu at a different level from that of most previous collectors.[8] The problem was that white collectors, no matter how earnest, liberal, kind, sympathetic, and well meaning, were always—by definition of race—outsiders looking in. Two of the most prominent collectors of the period, Guy Johnson and Howard Odum, authors of *The Negro and His Songs* (1925) and *Negro Workaday Songs* (1926), were frequently misled by their inability to penetrate to the center of their informants' experience. Odum even commercialized the folk speech of the black community in a kind of high-level, liberalized minstrel show, utilizing his research to produce dialect fiction for popular magazines. His "Black Ulysses in Camp," in the 1929 *American Mercury*, for example, portrays the ugliness of racial prejudice, while milking humor from knife fights and drunken sprees.

The difference that a black collector could make was well illustrated by Arthur Huff Fauset, whose collections of animal tales in the Mississippi Delta region in 1925 led him to reevaluate the Uncle Remus stories. Fauset found it "doubtful whether Negroes generally ever used the language employed in the works of Joel Chandler Harris."[9] The Uncle Remus stories were not folklore as Fauset conceived of it and collected it, and he explained in *The New Negro* how they contributed to white stereotypes. Animal tales in the pure folkloric state, Fauset argued, were quite different from the Uncle Remus tales, primarily because "the Harris variety of the Negro folk tale assumes to interpret Negro character instead of simply telling his stories." Since that interpretation depended on a plantation stereotype of the happy darky, it is easy to see how far from true folkloric sources Harris had gotten. Yet even the New Jersey–born Fauset, a Philadelphia schoolteacher, was not a native of the southern scene, and he, too, experienced problems penetrating to the roots of the southern folk experience. Despite white conceptions of a monolithic black culture, there are many black folk groups within the larger American culture, just as there are many black people, rather than "*the* Negro." Fauset's race was in some ways less important than his northern origins. Hurston, daughter of Eatonville, with the "map of Florida on her tongue" and a common experience with rural southern black people, presumably would make new breakthroughs.

Hurston arrived in Jacksonville in late February and began to search for material. She later admitted in *Dust Tracks* that her early difficulties arose because "the glamor of Barnard College was still upon me. I dwelt in Marble halls. I knew where the material was, all right. But I went about asking, in carefully accented Barnardese, 'Pardon me, but do you know any folk-tales or folk-songs?'" The results were unsatisfactory and dispiriting. She did not feel she could even write Boas to report, and by the end of March he was upset. Acting paternally, and obviously concerned about her progress, he wrote to complain that all he had received since her arrival was a letter from a Jacksonville finance company asking references for a loan application of $200. Had her arrangements with Woodson broken down? Hurston explained that the money was for a car to get around in, and that she was forwarding all the items she had thus far transcribed. She was especially concerned because most people had told her, "I used to know some of that old stuff, but I done forgot it all." She had concluded that "Negroness is being rubbed off by close contact with white culture."[10]

As these comments suggest, the collecting had been poor. By May, after reading two different batches of transcriptions, Boas was exasperated with his student, pointing out that "what you obtained is very largely repetition of the kind of material that has been collected so much." He stressed that what he was most interested in was manner rather than matter, style rather than substance: "You remember that when we talked about this matter I asked you particularly to pay attention, not so much to content, but rather to the form of diction, movements, and so on." Boas was implying that any white collector could obtain an accurate text of a folktale or folksong, but what Hurston could discover, since informants would be more natural with a member of their own race, was the actual folk style. "Habitual movements in telling tales, or in ordinary conversation," for example, would be more open to Hurston's observation than in a performance for white folks.[11]

Boas's admonitions were taken to heart, but the hurt was considerable. Hurston did not submit another report until her return to New York in the fall, and although she kept up her spirits, even Eatonville did not prove to be the rich storehouse that she remembered. People were friendly enough, but no one had all that much to contribute. She invited folks to a picnic, and charged Woodson $2.65 for a "watermelon cutting" on her expense account, but found very little that was really new.[12]

Eatonville was Hurston's turf, but she had not returned for a social visit. She was expected to be a serious, professional anthropologist-folklorist, meaning that she would follow a rigid methodology intended to obtain maximum scientific value from the Eatonville material. Hurston should collect a folksong not necessarily because she liked the words or melody, but so that she might classify its unique characteristics, compare it to the songs of other cultures, note its differences, and eventually combine it with a whole collection in order to determine the significance of music for Afro-American culture. She might enjoy the singing if she wished, but she would be expected to keep a keen eye out for the behavioral characteristics of the singer's performance. She had not yet mastered the field technique that would enable her to do this, and it was particularly hard to do among childhood friends. As she admitted in her autobiography, "O, I got a few items. But compared with what I did later, not enough to make a flea a waltzing jacket. Considering the mood of my going South I went back to New York with my heart beneath my knees and my knees in some lonesome valley. I stood before Papa Franz and cried salty tears."

Hurston later discovered that Boas was not all that disappointed, but her summary report of the "Florida expedition" shows how inadequate the collecting had been. When she complains about how "the bulk of the population now spends its leisure in the motion picture theatres or with the phonograph and its blues," she reveals not only her frustration, but also the common assumption among folklorists at the time that "race records" were a commercialization of traditional music. (The early blues artist is now considered a tradition-carrier of the Afro-American musical heritage, and some folklorists expend great effort trying to collect the records that Hurston complained about.)[13]

The insider's view had paid off in at least one area, the collection of conjure and hoodoo practices. Even in her disappointment, Hurston could see what had not been commonly acknowledged —that conjure believers studiously avoided admitting their belief because the conjure practitioner was widely known for magic powers. Trying to indicate the role of the hoodoo doctor in the community, she pointed out that he took the "place of the medical man, the priest, and the lawyer, with an added fear-power that none of the others have." This contrasted sharply with the paternalistic "science" of white collectors like Newbell Niles Puckett who tended to see the conjure man or root doctor as a cunning con man, open to exposure by any rational person; much of Puckett's scholarship laughed at the remedies he discovered. Hoodoo, however, even in Hurston's incomplete conception of it, was clearly a kind of secret religion to its believers, a religion that despite the snickers of the rationalists generated magic noted for its effectiveness. The whole question of black religion was beginning to fascinate Hurston, and her report to Boas stressed the need for prolonged study of black Christianity: "A careful study of Negro churches, *as conducted by*

Negroes, will show, I think that the Negro is not a Christian, but a pagan still . . . the formalized prayers, sermons, show . . . his concept of God as pre-Christian." Only a year later Hurston would be traveling to New Orleans to seek out power doctors who would admit her to hoodoo practice; only a short time after that, she would conceive of her first novel, an autobiographical account of her father's struggle with his so-called pagan instincts from the bulwark of his Christian belief. Clearly, the trip had influenced her, even if its collecting had been somewhat unsatisfactory.[14]

One conclusion the report on the Florida expedition certainly did not mention was Hurston's decision to separate from her husband of four months, Herbert Sheen. She had told neither of her sponsors about the marriage, maintaining a closeness about her private affairs that she would persist in all her life. (This closeness has misled many; at least one prominent critic has questioned whether she was ever married at all.) Perhaps she was afraid of the Boas-Woodson reaction, for resentment against promising women scholars' marrying and giving up their careers has long been strong in academic circles. Whatever the reason, neither of them knew that she planned to pause in her work, motor to Saint Augustine in the car she had purchased, and marry Sheen, her fiancé for the past six years. She did so on May 19, 1927.[15]

Their relationship had lasted throughout the Howard and Barnard years. Hurston described Sheen in *Dust Tracks*: "He could stomp a piano out of this world, sing a fair baritone and dance beautifully. . . . For the first time since my mother's death, there was someone who felt really close and warm to me." Hurston apparently saw no reason why a newlywed could not have her man and her research as well, but her reticence indicates that she doubted, probably correctly, that the two hard-driving scholars in Washington and New York would understand.

From the first, however, the marriage was endangered, primarily because Zora had almost immediate second thoughts. As she admitted to Sheen later, the night before he arrived in Florida, a dream "cast a dark shadow" over the upcoming ceremony. In the dream "a dark barrier kept falling between us and I sat up with the voice of your sister . . . calling my name in most unfriendly terms commanding me to leave you alone. Leave you alone or suffer

severe penalties. It was as vivid as noon, and it haunted me for a
very long time. It made me forever fearful that you would escape
out of my life. It all seemed unreal in a way, I mean our union. We
appeared like shadowy figures seen through an opal. It was terrible.
Therefore, I was not surprised when something came between
us."[16] Hurston's treatment of the marriage in her autobiography is
similar. She reports that she was "assailed by doubts" from the first
and wondered who had "canceled the well advertised tour of the
moon." Although she claims that her action caused the final separation after less than eight months of marriage, so that she could
return to the South to collect, the truth seems to be that two people
deeply in love could not share their careers. As late as 1953 Hurston
would tell Sheen, "Your own mother has never loved you to the
depth I have, Herbert, though I know that there came a time when
you did not believe it. . . ."[17] For all practical purposes the marriage was over by August, when Sheen returned to Chicago and the
Rush Medical School, and Hurston motored north with Langston
Hughes. Sheen had discovered that his bride resented interrup-
tions in her work and had no intention of following her husband in
his occupation. Hughes met Hurston by chance in Mobile, and she
saw nothing wrong with an unchaperoned auto trip to New York.
Perhaps it was the best way to make her feelings known. By
January, 1928, her relations with Sheen had been broken off, and
there was only intermittent, perfunctory communication before the
divorce on July 7, 1931.[18] Apparently they waited for the divorce
because neither could afford it at the time, although both may have
held thoughts of a reunion after their careers were established.
Hurston claimed in *Dust Tracks* that she used her second collecting
trip in the winter of 1927–28 to force Sheen to pursue his medical
career, but the real reason for the split probably was her feeling,
whether justified or not, that the marriage was inhibiting her work.
As she remarked to Langston Hughes at the time, "Herbert holds
me back."[19] Sheen reported, "The demands of her career doomed
the marriage to an early, amicable divorce." Two weeks after the
decree, Hurston wrote to a friend, "I hear that my husband has
divorced me, so that's that. Dont think I am upset, for your lil Zora
is playing on her harp like David. He was one of the obstacles that
worried me."[20]

Another factor contributing tension to the new marriage was the pressure generated by working for Carter Woodson. Woodson and Hurston did not get on well, perhaps partially because she was impatient with the historical research Woodson expected her to participate in as long as her job title was "investigator of the Association for the Study of Negro Life and History." A rigorous, careful historian, Woodson was genuinely interested in the folklore she was collecting. He was also mystified by his folklore scholar, who kept talking about buying a recording machine so that she could record what really had happened in black history. Woodson knew that people's memories were notoriously unsound and must be checked carefully by reference to written documents. Since he was holding the purse strings, Hurston had little choice but to further the association's historical research by consulting documents inaccessible to Woodson. She spent at least some time in June, shortly after her marriage, in the Duval County court records investigating the transactions of Jacksonville's black-owned traction company in the early 1900s.[21]

Woodson was a hard-working scholar who expected everyone to labor with as much dedication as himself, and as chief officer of the association, he demanded a strict accounting of expenses. Doling out Hurston's monthly allotment meant checking her accounts, and the idea of paying $2.35 for "railroad camp entertainment" or $3.00 for something labeled simply "music" no doubt caused raised eyebrows back in Washington. Near the end of the fellowship, Woodson paid for only two weeks' work instead of a month, leading her to refer to him, in a letter to Hughes, as an "improperly born wretch." Hughes himself had worked for Woodson in 1924, alphabetizing thousands of paper slips for Woodson's book *Thirty Thousand Free Negro Heads of Families*. He had found the older man such a hard taskmaster that, despite his "position" with the association, he quit to become a bus boy, "where meals were thrown in and it was less hard on the sight."[22]

Expecting Hurston to provide contributions for the *Journal of Negro History*, Woodson included in the October, 1927, issue her account of the black settlement established at Saint Augustine by the Spaniards in the seventeenth century, on which I. A. Wright had reported in 1924 in the *Journal*. Hurston's report was simply a transcription of records pertaining to the settlement, Fort Moosa, found in Florida archives, compiled from sources not cited in the original article. If this "communication" proves anything, it is that Woodson clearly intended to get his money's worth from his young scholar; Hurston could not have been happy mindlessly transcribing historical documents, and she no doubt resented the time taken away from her collecting.

This same October issue of the *Journal* included material from Hurston more relevant to her folklore collecting, an article entitled "Cudjo's Own Story of the Last African Slaver." Woodson introduced her fifteen-page essay by explaining that Hurston had made a special trip to Mobile to interview Cudjo Lewis, the only survivor of the last-known ship to bring African slaves to America in 1859. The essay which followed, while never stating precisely when Hurston spoke with Lewis, was filled with references to the interview: "Cudjo says," or "Cudjo thinks," or "Cudjo mentions," or "Cudjo in relating this breaks down in tears." There was an account of Cudjo's own memories of his African childhood and the beliefs and customs of his village, together with the narrative of how they were captured by Dahomeans, taken to the sea, sold to a Captain Foster of the *Clotilde*, auctioned off by the slave-trading Meaher brothers of Mobile, and enslaved for five years, from 1860 to 1865. It was the sort of thing both Woodson and Boas could be interested in, a combination of anthropology and history, Hurston's folklore interview supplemented by research in the written records of the Mobile Historical Society.

Cudjo Lewis was a remarkable figure, near eighty, with vivid memories of Africa, representing in person the process of acculturation that presumably created Americans out of Africans. A historical and anthropological anomaly, he was a major scientific resource, and Hurston's article should have been a culmination of her first collecting trip as a professional folklorist; it was an opportunity for her to focus all she had learned in the previous months. Apparently Boas and Woodson were pleased with the article, but if they had known the circumstances of its composition, their pleasure would have been considerably diminished.

Hurston's essay about Cudjo Lewis is 25 percent original research and the rest shameless plagiarism from a book entitled

Historic Sketches of the Old South. Written by Emma Langdon Roche, published in New York by the Knickerbocker Press thirteen years before Hurston's essay, this book was apparently available at the Mobile Historical Society. Despite her obvious use of it, Hurston nowhere acknowledges Roche as her source, and her plagiarism has remained undetected for almost a half-century. The linguist William Stewart first discovered it in 1972. What follows is the first public discussion of Stewart's discovery.[23]

Hurston had gone to Mobile in late July, and the interview with Lewis was her last task for Woodson. Her description of how to get to "African Town," now Plateau, Alabama, where Cudjo lived, includes references to highways and bridges built after Roche's study was printed. Since her essay includes quotations from Cudjo never published before, it is fair to assume that she actually interviewed him. One must conclude, however, that Hurston found herself without sufficient original material for her article, for whole portions of her narrative are from the Roche book, including, almost verbatim, the last seven pages of her essay.

The plagiarized passages are numerous and of the classic varieties found in freshman term papers. There is outright copying with only the slightest of changes; Hurston's third paragraph, for example, reads:

> Once on the African Coast, there was little trouble in procuring a cargo of slaves; for it had long been a part of the trader's policy to instigate the tribes against each other and in this manner keep the markets stocked. News of the trade was often published in the papers. An excerpt from *The Mobile Register* of Nov. 9, 1858, said. . . .

Compare this with the following passage from *Historic Sketches of the Old South*, from the chapter entitled "Preparations for Clotilde's Voyage" (p. 73):

> Once arriving on the African coast there was little trouble in procuring a cargo of slaves, for it had long been a part of the traders' policy to instigate the tribes against each other and in this manner keep the markets stocked. News of the trade was often published in the papers. The Meahers and Foster could have sought nothing more enlightening or to their purpose than an item published in *The Mobile Register*, November 9, 1858. . . .

There is a coy reference to the unacknowledged source when Hurston reports in 1927 that the hull of the *Clotilde* "lay in the marsh of Bayou Corne and could be seen for many years. It is now below water." Roche's 1914 book includes a photo of the hull lying in the water with the report that "her hull lies in the marsh at the mouth of Bayou Corne and may be seen at low tide." Of the sixty-seven paragraphs in Hurston's essay, only eighteen are exclusively her own prose. In one instance Hurston had to change her source in order to excise Roche's belief that Afro-American skulls accommodated smaller brains; Roche had favorably compared the African slaves to the "American negro" and reported that the survivors of the *Clotilde* "have more top head and there is a fullness indicating plenty of intelligence." Hurston altered this to read: "They have a very well developed forehead and back head and intelligent eyes."[24]

Though there might be other explanations for such passages—perhaps some footnotes were included with the article when she submitted it, but were lost by a secretary—Hurston's career needs no absurd apologetics. She never plagiarized again; she became a major folklore collector. Still, the Cudjo Lewis article is a dramatic example of initial failure, and what needs to be asked is why the incident took place. Why would a novice take such a risk, endangering her entire future? Even if she were going to depend heavily on a source, why do it so secretively, in such a dishonest manner?

One can only speculate. Hurston's lack of success in interviewing Lewis undoubtedly played a part, something she could not very well admit to either Boas or Woodson. Since Lewis was known to both folklorists and historians—Arthur Huff Fauset had collected an animal tale from him in 1925 and published it in *The New Negro*—admitting her failure would mean admitting that she had less skill than other scholars had. The interviewing *had* been difficult. Cudjo spoke in a heavily accented English that was hard to understand and took prolonged acquaintance to master. He was an old man, and although he was of good memory, the flow of reminiscence needed stimulation. Hurston had not asked the right questions. When queried about birth ceremonies, Cudjo replies, in Hurston's article, that he "thinks there probably were such ceremonies but he has no memory of them." Even more annoying was the old man's reticence about discussing religion, one of her major interests; she speculates, with some exasperation, "Cudjo is now an ardent Christian and is, I believe, hiding or suppressing what he knows about African religion for fear of being thought a heathen."

Plagiarism may be an unconscious attempt at academic suicide. The attempt is made because of a lack of respect for the writing one has to do. It seems plausible that some part of Hurston's self wanted to be caught, wanted to see her scientific integrity destroyed. If Boas and Woodson had detected the plagiarism, Hurston's academic career would have been finished. She also would never have had to worry again about capturing exactly the dialect in which the tale was told, the precise notations of the folksinger's music, or the nuances of style in the tale-teller's performance. She would be free of admonitions from Boas, scholarly demands from Woodson, and the frustration of interviewing a man like Cudjo Lewis. Folklore collecting had turned out to be tiresome, difficult, decidedly unglamorous labor.

Hurston was struggling with two concepts of culture. She was confronted on Morningside Heights with the implicit suggestion that although black folklore might be a valuable expression of unlettered people, it was still of a low order. Cultures are always evaluated ethnocentrically, and different cultural practices are assumed to be inferior simply because of their difference. The black critic Houston Baker has pointed out that "culture, like race, is little more than a superstition for most whites"; the idea that culture simply stands for a "whole way of life, and that there might be a multitude of wholes never occurs to most white Americans."[25] It was not so much what was taught in Columbia's anthropology department as it was the idea of Columbia itself—the elitism it encouraged and represented, the idea of culture of which it was inescapably a part. Zora Hurston had known firsthand a culturally different esthetic tradition. While she and her classmates revered Beethoven, she also remembered the box playing of Eatonville's Bubber Mimms. She enjoyed Keats, but recognized the poetry in her father's sermons; she read Plato, but told stories of Joe Clarke's wisdom. Her racially different folk culture was tolerated by whites as a primitive mode of apprehending experience; yet she knew that there was nothing primitive about it, that folk traditions enabled black people to survive with strength and dignity. Hurston sensed what Houston Baker has stated: that the world did not begin with Homer. Some of her fellow Harlem Renaissance artists did not realize this, but all the evidence suggests that Hurston did. She had known both written and oral traditions, had participated in American civilization at the levels of both "high" and "low" culture, and her commitment to folklore as a field of study was an inchoate challenge to the cultural imperialism that could declare these vertical judgments. This was perhaps not fully articulated in her mind; she sensed it in the way the student knows that the pieces of the academic puzzle do not quite fit together. Anthropology offered a conception of culture that dignified Joe Clarke by placing him in a tradition that included epic bards; it analyzed hoodoo doctors as examples of contemporary shamanism. Yet even the sophisticated social science of anthropology was a part of "high" culture, a discipline whose methods suggested periodic sorties among primitive folk followed by a return to the Heights for analysis and evaluation. What was the relationship between this Morningside perspective and the Harlem below, one generation removed from Eatonville, many generations removed from Cudjo's African memories? Only a skull's circumference in centimeters? Only an article in a scholarly journal?

Hurston had been a member of the Eatonville folk community, a New Negro seeking to repudiate racial stereotypes, a Barnard student fascinated with the collected knowledge of Western civilization, an anthropologist-folklorist documenting the existence of Afro-American cultural artifacts, and a creative writer contributing to the literary traditions of the English language. All these roles coexisted uneasily on the 1927 collecting trip, leaving Hurston with a vocational ambivalence; she wanted a career that would bridge the gap between Morningside Heights, 135th Street, and rural Florida. The question was how.

The irony in the Cudjo Lewis story is that she would later return to interview him again, with much greater success, and would eventually write a book-length study of him—a highly dramatic, semifictionalized narrative intended for the popular reader. Yet even this unpublished manuscript, written in 1931, makes extensive use of Roche and other anthropological sources; although it skillfully weaves together the scholarship and Hurston's own memories of Cudjo, it does not acknowledge those sources, and it is the type of book that Boas would have repudiated. The book purports to be solely the words of Cudjo; in fact, it is Hurston's imaginative recreation of his experience. Her purpose was to re-create slavery from a black perspective—"All these words from the seller, but not one word from the sold"—but she was doing so as an artist rather than as a folklorist or historian.[26]

Her uncertainty in 1927 about how she should react to the cultural artifacts in her possession is seen in letters she exchanged with Hughes. At the same time she was doing Woodson's hackwork in the Duval County courthouse and complaining to Boas about "Negroness" rubbing off in contact with whites, Hurston was writing Hughes with great enthusiasm, telling of her discovery of a self-taught wood carver who is the "greatest Negro artist in America." She added that she was "getting some gorgeous materials down here, verse and prose, *magnificent*. I shall save some juicy bits for you and me."[27]

This is not the language of a totally committed anthropologist. A social scientist dedicated to the presentation of authentic folk materials does not hold back the "juicy bits." Since Hurston and Hughes had discussed plans for an opera that would utilize folk expression, it was perfectly appropriate for Hurston to report to her collaborator on what she had found. It also reveals how ambivalent she was about the academic study of folklore, and how she had not yet reconciled "high" and "low" with the pluralistic premise of anthropological theory.

Hurston's ambivalence about folklore study grew from her dual identity between 1925 and 1927 as serious academic and active creative artist. Before going to the field in 1927, she had relatively little difficulty in maintaining both identities. Once removed from the abstractions of the anthropology books, confronted with the reality of a Cudjo Lewis, she had to make choices. The type of reportorial precision required of the scientific folklorist bored Hurston; she was used to assimilating the aura of a place and letting that stimulus provoke her imagination. Neither Boas nor Carter Woodson was that interested in her impressions; they wanted the facts as she had collected them. During the Harlem Renaissance, however, her subjective responses, her esthetic sensibility, had been what made her reputation. To what end was the folklore research? Did it really affirm black culture in the face of white cultural imperialism? Did not a short story about Eatonville better prove the genius of the folk?

While Hurston, of course, never used the phrase *cultural imperialism*, her hope to write an opera with Hughes represents her intellectual struggle with the colonizing influence of Western European culture. The opera was to use only authentic folksongs, dances, and tales; yet these were to be shaped into a vehicle thought to be among the most elevated of art forms. Their attempt reflected a general premise of Harlem Renaissance esthetics, a premise that Hurston always found dubious. The Renaissance artists were asked to conceive of themselves as an elite group dedicated to articulating the beautiful—if crude—voices of the folk. One should bridge the gap between high and low, between educated and illiterate. One should validate the unconscious art of the folk by transforming it into the conscious art of the novel, the poem, the opera. Such efforts, as the warrants of racial genius, would destroy the presumptions of racial inferiority. Hurston would eventually become a profoundly moving artist, but only after solving this dilemma of cultural imperialism. The primary experience responsible for that solution was her career as a professional folklorist between 1927 and 1931.

NOTES

1. FB to Carter G. Woodson, Nov. 6, 18, Dec. 7, 1926; Woodson to FB, Feb. 17, 1927 (APS).

2. See Jan Harold Brunvand, *The Study of American Folklore* (New York: W. W. Norton, 1968); Richard M. Dorson, *American Folklore* (Chicago: University of Chicago Press, 1959); Tristram Coffin, ed., *Our Living Traditions: An Introduction to Folklore* (New York: Basic Books, 1968); Francis Lee Utley, "A Definition of Folklore," ibid., pp. 3–15.

3. See Roger Abrahams, *Deep Down in the Jungle* (Chicago: Aldine, 1970); Thomas Kochman, ed., *Rappin' and Stylin' Out* (Urbana: University of Illinois Press, 1972); Charles Chesnutt, "Superstition and Folklore of the South," *Modern Culture*, 13 (1901), 231–35. See also the "Folklore and Ethnography" section of Hampton Institute's *Southern Workman* beginning in 1893, the year a chapter of the American Folklore Society was founded at Hampton.

4. See, e.g., Roland Steiner, "Observations on the Practice of Conjuring in Georgia," *Journal of American Folklore*, 14 (1901), 173–80; Mrs. William Preston Johnson, "Two Negro Tales," ibid., 9 (1896), 194–98.

5. Parsons was a distinguished folklorist who did much valuable collecting in
the early decades of the century; independently wealthy, she sponsored many
other folklorists. Her collecting techniques are not always clear, and I have been
unable to find documentation for the yacht singing, an anecdote often told among
folklorists; this version was told to me by William Wiggins, Indiana University,
fall, 1974.

6. FB to Carter G. Woodson, Nov. 6, Dec. 7, 1926 (APS).

7. Carter G. Woodson to FB, Feb. 17, 1927; FB to Woodson, Dec. 7, 1926;
FB to Elsie Clews Parsons, Dec. 7, 1926 (APS).

8. FB to Elsie Clews Parsons, Dec. 7, 1926 (APS).

9. Arthur Huff Fauset, "American Negro Folk Literature," in *The New Negro*,
ed. AL (New York: Albert and Charles Boni, 1925), p. 239.

10. FB to ZNH, Mar. 24, 1927; ZNH to FB, Mar. 29, 1927 (APS).

11. FB to ZNH, May 3, 1927 (APS).

12. ZNH to Carter G. Woodson, n.d. [July, 1927] (LCMD).

13. ZNH, "The Florida Expedition," typescript (APS).

14. Ibid.

15. See Arthur Davis, *From the Dark Tower* (Washington, D.C.: Howard
University Press, 1974), p. 119; marriage license, Herbert Sheen and ZNH, May
19, 1927, Marriage Book 5, p. 17 (Court Records, St. Johns County, St. Augustine,
Fla.).

16. ZNH to Herbert Sheen, Jan. 7, 1955 (Sheen Papers).

17. Ibid., Mar. 13, 1953 (Sheen Papers).

18. LH, *The Big Sea* (New York: Hill and Wang, 1963), pp. 296–300; Herbert
Sheen to RH, Mar. 21, 1975; divorce decree, July 7, 1931 (County Court Records,
St. Louis County, St. Louis, Mo.). See also ZNH to LH, Mar. 8, 1928 (JWJYale).

19. ZNH to LH, Mar. 8, 1928 (JWJYale).

20. Herbert Sheen, undated autobiography, sent to RH on Mar. 21, 1975; ZNH
to Mrs. Mason, July 23, 1931 (HUAL).

21. ZNH to Carter G. Woodson, n.d. [July, 1927] (LCMD).

22. LH, *Big Sea*, p. 211.

23. Stewart's discovery was conveyed to me by John Szwed of the University
of Pennsylvania. I am grateful to Professor Stewart for granting me permission to
cite his research and findings.

24. Emma Langdon Roche, *Historic Sketches of the Old South* (New York:
Knickerbocker Press, 1914), pp. 72–124; ZNH, "Cudjo's Own Story of the Last
African Slaver," *Journal of Negro History*, 12 (Oct., 1927), 648–63.

25. Houston Baker, *Long Black Song* (Charlottesville: University of Virginia
Press, 1972), p. 9.

26. ZNH, "Barracoon," manuscript (HUAL).

27. ZNH to LH, Mar. 17, 1927 (JWJYale).

≋ Godmother and Big Sweet:
1927-31

In mid-September, 1927, Zora Neale Hurston visited 399 Park Avenue at the invitation of Mrs. Rufus Osgood Mason, a very wealthy, beautiful, arthritic, elderly, generous, mystical patron of the Afro-American arts. Hurston presented Mrs. Mason with an idea she and Langston Hughes had casually talked about as early as July, 1926—an opera that would be the first authentic rendering of black folklife, presenting folksongs, dances, and tales that Hurston would collect. She went away from the meeting with high hopes and wrote Hughes immediately at Lincoln University, where he was beginning his junior year: "I went to see Mrs. Mason and I think that we got on famously. God, I hope so! She likes the idea of the opera, but says that we must do it with so much power that it will halt all these spurious efforts on the part of white writers."[1]

Mrs. Mason, born Charlotte van der Veer Quick, is one of the mysteries of the Harlem Renaissance, a patron who had such a powerful hold on Langston Hughes that breaking with her made him physically ill, a woman who would become a spiritual godmother to Zora Hurston, a figure of such charisma that a sophisticated intellectual like Alain Locke could become deferential in her presence. She had been the friend of presidents and ambassadors; possessed of family wealth for generations, she lived in an elegant apartment and thought of the Vanderbilts as nouveau riche. Yet, when younger, she had also spent long months covered with prairie dust, living among the Plains Indians while she financed Natalie Curtis in the field work that resulted in Curtis's volume of songs and legends entitled *The Indians' Book* (1907). Perhaps as a result of Curtis's later interest in black folksongs, Mrs. Mason paid special attention to the New Negro. Alain Locke became a trusted confidant, encouraging her to support painters Miguel Covarrubias and Aaron Douglas, as well as sculptor Richmond Barthé. A rough estimate is that Mrs. Mason contributed between fifty and seventy-five thousand dollars to New Negro writers and artists; she would give Zora Hurston approximately fifteen thousand over the next five years. In none of this philanthropy did she permit her protégés to publicly acknowledge her help, a stricture Hurston ignored as soon as she was removed from Mrs. Mason's influence; Langston Hughes never divulged her name.[2]

Her relationship with Hurston developed quickly. Zora made plans to take her to the small church in Harlem that had proved so interesting to Van Vechten and Fannie Hurst, and a number of get-togethers in October and November followed the initial meeting. Finally, on December 8, Zora arrived at 399 Park to attend a ceremony that was one of the most important events of the first thirty years of her life. She went there to sign a contract of employment with Mrs. Mason that would enable her to return south and collect folklore for the entire year of 1928; if she did well, there was talk of extending the pact through 1929. That contract reveals much about the nature of white patronage for black artists during the twenties, and it established the ground rules for a personal relationship that had an extraordinary influence on Hurston's career. Not only did Mrs. Mason's largesse enable Zora to do the basic field work that established her fame as a folklorist; it also eventually led to dependency and bitterness. In the end, the contract probably also had a great deal to do with the way that Hughes and Hurston's collaborative opera became "Mule Bone: A Comedy of Negro Life." "Mule Bone," in turn, became the center of a dispute between its authors that finally resulted in personal enmity and legal threats.[3]

In September, 1927, when she met Mrs. Mason, Zora and Hughes were very close, having just shared her car for the extended trip from Mobile to New York. She had received her last check from Woodson shortly before they left Alabama. On the way north they stopped at Tuskegee in the first week of August to lecture to the summer school students. Jessie Fauset was also there, and the Harlem literati had much to tell the Alabama students about the Renaissance in New York. Taking a leisurely trip, although Hughes was nearly broke, they relaxed and had a good time. In Georgia they visited the academy where Jean Toomer had taught for a short period and had received much of the inspiration for *Cane*. They also collected folklore along the way, to the delight of Hughes, who was fascinated by a hoodoo doctor from far back in the piney woods. They stayed over in Macon to talk with Bessie Smith and hear her sing, and by August 26 they had reached Cheraw, South Carolina, where Hurston wrote a note to Carl Van Vechten: "We rolled into this town tonight tired but happy. One or two mishaps on our run up from Charleston. 1. The car, known as Sassy Susie, had a puncture on a front tire, repaired at Columbia, S.C. 2. Somehow all the back of my skirt got torn away, so that my little panties were panting right out in public. I suppose this accident will be classed as more tire trouble." They hoped to be in New York within a week, Hughes to return to Lincoln University, Hurston to finish up a few incomplete credits for graduation from Barnard at the end of the fall semester.[4]

Once in New York, Hurston spent much of her time in the anthropology department at Columbia, organizing and sorting her six months of collecting. She received her formal dressing-down from Boas, then discovered that he was not as disappointed as she had thought. Within a month of her return she had been introduced to Mrs. Mason, probably by Alain Locke, and thereafter she cultivated the relationship. Mrs. Mason, herself an amateur anthropologist, and the young Eatonville folklore collector had much to talk about. They became very close very quickly. Mrs. Mason thought of Zora as an unspoiled child of nature, an impression that the younger woman did little to dispel. Hurston claimed that a psychic bond welded their souls: not only could Mrs. Mason read her mind, but Zora could do the same with the elderly white woman. Apparently the bond was part of a compulsion for naturalness and sincerity on the patron's part: "There she was sitting up there at the table over capon, caviar and gleaming silver, eager to hear every word on every phase of life on a sawmill 'job.' I must tell the tales, sing the songs, do the dances, and report the raucous sayings and doings of the Negro farthest down. She is altogether in sympathy with them, because she says truthfully they are utterly sincere in living."[5]

The problem with Mrs. Mason, as perhaps with all patrons, was that she expected some return on her money. In Hurston's case it was a report on the aboriginal sincerity of rural southern black folk; in Hughes's, it was the beating of tom-toms in the breast of the urban black poet. She asked Hughes to be "primitive and know and feel the intuitions of the primitive." She thought of him as Africa; eventually he replied that he could be only Cleveland and Kansas City.[6] Louise Thompson, another woman supported by Mrs. Mason for a time, eventually came to feel that the patron was "indulging her fantasies of Negroes," that she was in fact racist. Her black guests were either primitive, or they were not being themselves. Aaron Douglas reported similar feelings. Once Mrs. Mason even said that Locke acted too much like white folks. When a rich woman is interested in a person's work, pressing fifty-dollar bills into his hands without asking anything in return, it is not easy to see the self-satisfaction she needs. The situation becomes a power relationship; Hughes believed that her power was so great that she herself did not realize its dimensions. It is from the vantage of history that Mrs. Mason's kindnesses take on their clearest pattern.[7]

Because Hurston embodied the folk style and knew the world of the sawmill intimately, it was natural for Mrs. Mason to be drawn to her. From Hurston's perspective, the white woman assigned virtues to "the Negro farthest down" that most whites and many blacks were unwilling to grant. She seemed to confirm what Hurston sensed about Eatonville: it was a vital life which should be celebrated. Because she was highly intelligent and anthropologically informed, Mrs. Mason's self-gratification in primitive things was subtly manifest. Her off-hand refusal of a public role and personal aggrandizement disarmed the recipients of her largesse. Added to this was her awe-inspiring presence; Hughes described her as "an amazing, brilliant, powerful personality. I was fascinated by her, and I loved her." She even edited his first novel. Hurston saw her as a godmother, the appelation that both Hughes and she used, and that Mrs. Mason preferred. Mrs. Mason liked to sit in a throne-like chair, with her protégés on footstools at her feet, a fact that can be placed in perspective only when one remembers how strong were the Hughes and Hurston personalities. Hurston claimed that she often thought of herself as a child when in the great woman's presence. The key to any interchange was the ubiquitous sincerity: "Godmother could be as tender as mother-love when she felt that you had been right spiritually. But anything in you, however clever, that felt like insincerity to her called forth her well known, 'That is nothing! It has no soul in it.'"[8]

The soul Zora Hurston sought to define needed very little spiritual help from Mrs. Mason. The need was quite material, and Hurston knew it, whether she admitted it to herself or not. As she later told the president of Fisk University, at this time in her life she was "weighed down by this thought that practically nothing had been done in Negro folklore when the greatest cultural wealth of the continent was disappearing without the world ever realizing that it had ever been." To "do something," however, one needed money, and Mrs. Mason personified wealth. She once sent $500 to a black poet in Philadelphia whom she had never met, but whose verses she liked. Hurston apparently believed in the psychic bond between them, and we should be wary about mocking it. Both she and Mrs. Mason had unusual psychic powers, and they discovered some superrational kinship. Later in their relationship, when Godmother fell ill, Zora would light hoodoo candles and commune with Mrs. Mason's spirit, successfully praying her body back to health. Zora admitted to Godmother that if she became upset while writing, "I light a candle in your name and wait for you to send the peace." It is unfair to interpret such a bond simply as Hurston's willing belief to insure patronage. On the other hand, it is hard to believe that Hurston did not recognize Mrs. Mason's wealth as a key to her future. She knew that Mrs. Mason was given to supporting black artists and that she had funded folklore research before. Aware that she had just scratched the surface in her first trip, determined to prove herself as a folklorist, Hurston can hardly be blamed for pursuing the one source of funding open to her. She was not an established scholar, as the Woodson trip had proven. The foundations and scientific societies were not receptive to requests for support from black folklorists with undergraduate degrees and without academic affiliation.[9]

Hurston's relations with her patron would last longer than Hughes's did, because she spent most of her time away from New

York, using the money in places like Eau Gallie, Florida, Magazine
Point, Alabama, and Nassau, British West Indies. Throughout that
time she chafed under Mrs. Mason's restraints and schemed with
Hughes about ways to circumvent them; yet she still revered, even
loved, her Godmother. The relations with Mrs. Mason were hu-
manly inconsistent. As Hurston went farther away, the psychic
bond deteriorated, and her Godmother became a meddling patron.
When she was closer, the bond was an operative force in her life,
and Godmother was a soul mate, a woman whom Hurston could
address as her spiritual progenitor: "Flowers to you—the true
conceptual mother—not just a biological accident. To you of the
immaculate conception where everything is conceived in beauty
and every child is hovered [covered?] in truth. . . . I have taken
form from the breath of your mouth. From the vapor of your soul
am I made to be."[10]

It is startling to compare the intensity of Hurston's personal
correspondence with her patron and the December 8, 1927, employment contract that provided the wherewithal for her to begin a
serious career as a folklorist. Mrs. Mason apparently was afraid that
her young scholar-artist might use the materials she collected for
"commercial purposes"—meaning operas, plays, and novels. Zora
was still talking in terms of "juicy bits" that she and Langston could
use for the stage, and Mrs. Mason, sure that she knew what was best
for her charges, was not about to subsidize Hurston's independent
development. She needed some hold over the quixotic artist, and
the contract became that means of control. The white woman
agreed to pay Zora $200 per month for a year, and promised to
provide a motion picture camera and an automobile to facilitate the
collecting. Although this was a magnificent scholarship for a young,
untried folklorist, Mrs. Mason's grant was not exactly a disin-
terested scholarly stipend. Hurston was to collect Afro-American
folklore because *Mrs. Mason* was "unable because of the pressure of
other matters to undertake the collecting of this information in
person." Hurston was employed "as an independent agent" to
"collect all information possible, both written and oral, concerning
the music, poetry, folk-lore, literature, hoodoo, conjure, manifestations of art and kindred subjects relating to and existing among
the North American negroes." The contract instructed agent Hurs-

ton "to prosecute her search for said matters at the homes or gathering places of the said negroes in the Southern tier of states of the United States of America." It was so tightly drawn that it even removed Mrs. Mason from liability should Hurston injure anyone while driving the car.[11]

Such legalese would be comic if it did not represent the powerful, almost perverse control that Mrs. Mason exerted over Hurston's career for the next five years. The key to the document, and to the trouble ahead, lay in the closing paragraphs: Zora was bound "faithfully to perform her task" and "to return and lay before" Mrs. Mason "all of said information, data, transcripts of music, etc. which she shall have obtained." Mrs. Mason was going to preserve proprietary rights over the results of Hurston's labor. Having made an investment of capital, she wanted an exclusive, unique product in return. The young folklorist was forbidden "to make known to any other person, except one designated in writing by said first party, any of said data or information." Hurston's folklore collections would be exclusively the *property* of her patron—not because Mrs. Mason wanted to steal the material, but because she felt arrogantly certain that Zora Neale Hurston could not be trusted to know best what to do with it.[12]

On Wednesday, December 14, 1927, Hurston took the 3:40 train from Penn Station en route to Mobile. It was only three and a half months since she had returned from a similar trip to Florida, a trip that had ended in failure. With Mrs. Mason's money, she was returning to Cudjo Lewis, hoping to rectify the errors of that previous expedition. Not only was he old "and may die before I get to him otherwise," but this time she hoped to draw him out, to really converse with him, since she now admitted that he had not been too talkative before. She wrote to Hughes, urging him to join her when school let out, promising that it would be different this trip: "What I mean by it will be different, I will have a better car all PAID FOR and a better salary."[13]

Mrs. Mason eventually funded Hurston for an initial two years, from December, 1927, to December, 1929, and then granted a fifteen-month extension to March 30, 1931. Although Mrs. Mason then tried to remove her from the payroll, Zora held on irregularly until at least September of 1932. These were exciting, stimulating years. They provided Hurston with a lifetime of folk material to draw on, even though her fame was not established until her research was published in the mid-thirties. By the end of January, 1928, she had purchased a Chevrolet coupé, interviewed Lewis again near Mobile, spent a short time in Eatonville, and come to rest in the living quarters of the Everglades Cypress Lumber Company near Loughman, Florida. Two months after leaving Barnard, Hurston was exploring the jook joints of Polk County, where "de water drink lak cherry wine," and where people did not say "embrace when they mean they slept with a woman." Polk County's lumber and turpentine camps were natural repositories of folk tradition—isolated pockets of laborers, their families, and their camp followers, who all survived by the accumulated experience of black men and women creating a community on a job owned by whites. The Loughman camp included family men, fugitive murderers, honest workers, knife-wielding good-time girls, Christian mothers, hard-living gamblers, and jackleg preachers. It was all presided over by a two-gun white foreman who kept a tight rein, totaled accounts at the company store, tried to keep alcohol off the job, and six days a week ordered work parties into the woods at sunup.[14]

As on her first collecting trip, Hurston encountered initial hostility, but this time she was more than equal to the challenge. She convinced the hands that she was a Jacksonville bootlegger's woman on the run (thereby explaining the car and her clothes). After she traded verses of "John Henry" at the jook, revealing a considerable repertoire, she was accepted. She collected furiously for two months, ingratiated herself with Big Sweet, the job's fiercest woman, and managed to deflect the jealousies accompanying her frequent interviews of groups of men. The result was some of the most concentrated collecting of her career, from folktales to sayings to songs to jokes. Her very first lying session, announced by a notice at the post office promising four prizes for the four best lies, brought a wide response. Her first week in camp she heard Big Sweet "put her foot up" and "specify": "Big Sweet broke the news to him, in one of her mildest bulletins that his pa was a double-humpted camel and his ma was a grass-gut cow." Zora had seldom heard the dozens played so well.

Hurston left the job only after a knife in a woman's hand challenged her residence; she concluded that there were less dangerous locations for a serious social scientist. As one concession to her environment, she did begin packing a chrome-plated revolver in her purse. She returned to Eatonville for a period of rest and wrote Hughes enthusiastically. She was so excited about her collecting that she had not given much thought to their opera: "Now about the show. I have not written a line of anything since I have been down here and I left all of my manuscripts in Newark in storage. I have several good ideas, but nothing worked out. I am truly dedicated to the work at hand and so I am not even writing, but living every moment with the people. I believe I have almost as many stories now as I got on my entire trip last year." She sent Hughes an intercepted love letter from one informant to another, and a page of verses which demonstrated street rhymes: "A long engine / short caboose / that what you shooting ain't no use" and "Tea in de cup / coffee in de can / my gal ran away / wid de garbage man." What excited her most was how she had begun to build on her own knowledge of folklore: "I am getting inside of Negro art and lore. I am beginning to *see* really. . . . [This is] going to be *big*. Most gorgeous possibilities are showing themselves constantly." Then, to indicate that she had not entirely forgotten about their opera, only that she had become involved in something more important, she added, "I have the street scene still and two others in my mind—if you want them you can have them for yourself and its O.K. by me."[15]

A major reason for Hurston's willingness to give her materials to Hughes was her patron's demand that she not publish, but collect. Mrs. Mason and Alain Locke, her primary adviser, felt that Zora should concentrate first on collecting, with time allotted later for summary and publication, apparently in some kind of scholarly format. In the same letter to Hughes in which she gave over her street scenes Hurston added, "Godmother asked me not to publish and as I am making money I hope you can use them."

Hurston chafed over this prohibition, just as she must have had second thoughts about the contract she had signed. To think that she was not her own woman diminished the sense of triumph growing from her success as a collector. On the other hand, she knew she was onto something big that would have important cultural significance. The money certainly did not provide for an easy life—she was living in the style of her informants—but it was sufficient to further the research. Zora had come to think of herself as a woman with a mission: she would demonstrate that "the greatest cultural wealth of the continent" lay in the Eatonvilles and Polk Counties of the black South. Mrs. Mason was enabling her to fulfill that quasi-religious responsibility. Moreover, the pure adventure of the expedition was exhilarating. She was on her own, with a sure $200 per month, a car, and complete mobility; her only boss was a thousand miles away. Mrs. Mason's restrictions may have seemed a small price to pay, especially since Hurston felt that they were both interested in the same result. Godmother did not want fame for herself when the collections were published—in fact, she prohibited the use of her name; she wanted only to be able to help and advise Zora. Deciding not to publish for the present was Hurston's compromise with her future. What she was beginning to see had gone unseen for three hundred years, and she felt that she could become a Prometheus to those worlds, white or black, which felt above or beyond the folk. By April she would tell Hughes, "I can *really* write a village anthology now, but I am wary about mentioning it to godmother for fear she will think I am shirking, but *boy* I think [I] could lay 'em something now. I told you I must not publish without her consent."[16]

The reason for the prohibition against Zora's publishing her own fiction is difficult to determine. Since information about Mrs. Mason is sparse, we cannot know the extent of her commitment to scholarly, as opposed to popular, publication. We do know that Mrs. Mason interfered editorially with her protégés, and clearly, one reason for the restriction was to insure her editorial control over a person with a well-established reputation for independence. The ban against publication became a lever for her to govern her young folklorist. Predictably, she was outraged to discover Zora's essay "How It Feels to Be Colored Me" in the May, 1928, *World Tomorrow*. Zora had to ask Locke to intercede, explaining that the essay had been submitted months earlier to help defray the printing debts for *Fire!!* Mrs. Mason apparently felt that Hurston could not be trusted to go about her collecting business without imposed discipline. For her part, Hurston was collecting material she felt would change forever the conception of black folk culture. The key to her ability to carry on the project was continued financial support, and there was real need to tread softly around the throne-like chair on Park Avenue. Zora once angered her Godmother by saying that "white people could not be trusted to collect the lore of others." The fact that she was repeating one of Mrs. Mason's own statements did nothing to mitigate the white woman's anger. Fortunately, Locke was there again to mediate.[17]

None of this should imply that Hurston was a totally unwilling participant in any decision to wait for academic publication. At the same time she could muse about the esthetic possibilities of the folk scene, she was organizing material in her mind, classifying it for scientific analysis. She told Hughes:

> I am working hard and broadening some. I have come to 5 general laws, but I shall not mention them to Godmother or Locke until I have worked them out. . . .
>
> 1. The Negro's outstanding characteristic is drama. That is why he appears so imitative. Drama is mimicry. Note gesture in place of words.
>
> 2. Negro is lacking in reverence. Note number of stories in which god, church and heaven are treated lightly.
>
> 3. *Angularity* in everything, sculpture, dancing, abrupt story telling.
>
> 4. Redundance. Examples: low down, cap'n high sheriff, top-superior, the number of times—usually three—that a feature is repeated in a story. Repetition of a single, simple strain in music.
>
> 5. Restrained ferocity in everything. There is a tense ferocity beneath the casual exterior that stirs the onlooker to hysteria. Note effect of Negro music, dancing, gestures on the staid Nordic.
>
> 6. Some laws in dialect. The same form is not always used. Some { syllables are long before or after certain words and short in the { words same position. Example: You as subject gets full value but is short-

ened to yuh as an object. Him in certain positions and 'im in others depending on consonant preceding. Several laws of aspirate H.[18]

The "spy glass of anthropology" was focusing well, and Hurston surveyed a wide landscape. "I want to collect like a new broom," she said, and looked forward to the last half of the year, when she would deliberately go about interviewing conjure practitioners. A year earlier she had written to Boas to complain about the way black folklore was dying out, because people were spending too much time with their blues and phonographs. Now she knew that "Negro folklore is *still* in the making. A new kind is crowding out the old."[19]

Still, the impulse to go public, to bring these materials and their creators to a wider audience never left her mind. As a product of the Harlem Renaissance she had seen what well-meaning white playwrights like Eugene O'Neill, Paul Green, and DuBose Heyward had produced as "Negro drama." She had observed the Broadway froth of revues like *Rang Tang* and *Chocolate Beauties*. She had noted how brave Harlem theater groups like the Lafayette Players were often the captives of white materials, and how troupes like the Krigwa Players achieved only minor successes. She responded by asking Hughes what he thought of a true black theater: "Did I tell you before I left about the new, the *real* Negro art theatre I plan? Well I shall, or rather we shall act out the folk tales, however short, with the abrupt angularity and naivete of the primitive 'bama Nigger. Quote that with naive settings. What do you think?"[20]

Hurston's correspondence with Hughes during the first year of her collecting trip was frequent and conspiratorial. It provides an unintentional documentary of the expedition. She saw the two of them as secret sharers of racial lore and as conspirators for the dramatic vehicle that would make it public. In response to Hughes's enthusiastic reply to the "real Negro theatre," she wrote, "Of *course*, you know I didn't dream of that theatre as a one man stunt. I had you helping 50-50 from the start. In fact, I am perfectly willing to be 40 to your 60 since you are always so much more practical than I. But I know it is going to be *glorious*! A really new departure in the drama." At other times she imagined Locke together with them as a glorious artistic triangle; once she drew such a figure with *LH* and *ZH* at the base, *AL* at the apex. Yet even at these moments of great enthusiasm Godmother's presence loomed. The "real Negro theatre" did not meet with her approval; Zora told Locke, "Godmother was very anxious I should say to you that the plans—rather the hazy dreams of the theatre I talked to you about should never be mentioned again. She trusts her three children to never let those words pass their lips again until the gods decree that they shall materialize."[21]

Hurston was drawn to Hughes not only because they were close friends who had talked of writing an opera together, but also because she was learning how truly communicative Hughes's art could be. As she held lying sessions in towns throughout the South, she would read from Hughes's latest book of poems, *Fine Clothes to the Jew*. She reported to him, "Boy! they eat it up . . . you are being quoted in Railroad camps, phosphate mines, turpentine stills, etc." Because she brought the book to each lying session and purchased refreshments for the informants, *Fine Clothes* came to be called "de party book." At one such gathering a lead singer lined out the entire book for a community choir: "It was glorious." Hughes sent his suggestions for areas in which Hurston might collect, which she appreciated. With the extravagant enthusiasm that was a Hurston characteristic, she told him, "Without flattery, La——n, you are the brains of this argosy. All the ideas have come out of your head."[22]

Hurston's stay at the Cypress Company at Loughman was followed by a trip to the phosphate country around Mulberry, Pierce, and Lakeland, Florida, where she met Mack C. Ford, a former "singing liner" on a railroad gang. Now a phosphate miner, Ford provided a number of stories and songs, becoming one of her most memorable sources. Then it was back to Eatonville and more collecting from home folks. In late June she began making her way toward New Orleans and the collection of hoodoo. In her own mind there was only the slightest similarity between this 1928 trip and her expedition of a year earlier; yet her commitment to anthropology could still coexist with her visions of an authentic black theater. From Magazine Point, Alabama, she wrote Hughes in July, "Work going on well. I am getting much more material in a given area and space time than before because I am learning better technique. . . . I have about enough for a good volume of stories but I shall miss nothing. I shall go to New Orleans from here. Oh! Almost forgot. Found another one of the original Africans, older than Cudjo about 200 miles up state on the Tombigbee River. She is most delightful, but no one will ever know about her but us. She is a better talker than Cudjoe." Did Hurston wish to protect the woman from further scientific probes, conceal her anthropological sources, or hide her from Mrs. Mason in order to preserve this special material for her "new adventure in drama"? Even though she was much more successful this time than last, her vocational commitment remained unclear. She had begun to identify scientific publication of her collections with Mrs. Mason's stricture against publication without prior approval, and she was beginning to wonder if there might not be a better medium for the material. If Hughes's poetry satisfied the folk, might not the folk's poetry interest an educated audience? She added a final note in this July 10 letter from Alabama, indicating that she had wanted to let Knopf know what a hit Hughes was with the people; she had not done so because Godmother "doesn't want *me* to say anything at present. But I shall do it as soon as this is over."[23]

"This" would not soon be over, for New Orleans was an eye-opening, mind-wrenching experience. Arriving in the city in early August, 1928, during the worst of the summer's heat, she sought contacts among people Hughes had met during his brief stay there the year before. While waiting for these to develop, she contemplated into what categories she might divide the material collected so far: "My plans: 1 volume of stories. 1 children's games. 1 Dance and the Negro. 1 'Mules and Men,' a volume of work songs with guitar accompaniment. 1 on religion. 1 on words and meanings. 1 volume of love letters with an introduction on Negro love." Becoming intimate with the world of Marie Leveau, the legendary hoodoo queen, was slow work, but by September Hurston could report to Hughes that "things are beginning to go well now. I am getting in with the top of the profession. I know 18 tasks, including how to crown the spirit of death, and kill. It makes me sick to see how these cheap white folks are grabbing our stuff and ruining it. I am almost sick—my one consolation being that they never do it right and so there is still a chance for us." She told Locke that she was "just in the knick of time too, for I find its greatest era is about forty years in the past." Initial collecting went so well that by October she told Hughes that from then on she expected only duplication of what she had learned so far. Much of the collecting had been hard physical work under less than perfect conditions; bedbugs had routed her from at least one furnished room, and her finger had been cut to make her a blood brother to a rattlesnake. Still, she had a "marvelous dance ritual from the ceremony of death," and many other things. She had been going to every conjure doctor she heard of, "for the sake of thoroughness," despite the cost and duplication. She wrote Locke, "I am using the vacuum method, grabbing everything I can see." By the end of November she knew that her initial estimates were wrong and that there was much more than she had first realized: "I have the most marvelous ceremony. The dance of the 9 snakes. Just you wait till you see that. You were right again in saying that it would take 6 months to do the conjure. I am knee deep in it with a long way to go."[24]

Hurston collected conjure lore in the same way she collected anything else, by totally immersing herself in the lives of the people who lived it, by what anthropologists call the participant-observer technique. Only rarely to that time had any observer been taken into full participation in hoodoo rites. Comparing Hurston's collecting technique with that of Newbell Niles Puckett reveals why she was so much more successful. Puckett had masqueraded as a conjure man himself, trading remedies and rituals with the doctors who would talk with him. He was a white man challenging the black man's power. Hurston was a black woman of great sympathy offering herself as an apprentice to the experienced sorcerer. She wished to learn, beginning with the simple and advancing to the complex. As a result, she not only gained a holistic view of the hoodoo process, but also experienced a series of impressive initiation ceremonies marking her acceptance into the occult world.

Hoodoo and *conjure* are collective terms for all the traditional beliefs in black culture centering around a votary's confidence in the power of a conjure, root, two-head, or hoodoo doctor to alter with magical powers a situation that seems rationally irremediable. At its most basic level it is sympathetic magic; at its most complex, a highly complicated religion. Many scholars believe that some practices are of African origin. Although whites sometimes believe in hoodoo, especially in the rural South and particularly in New Orleans, conjure beliefs are widespread and traditional in Afro-American culture, and hoodoo believers are predominantly black. Conjure has historically provided an access to power for a powerless people, and many of its traditions are ancient. It is an alternative mode for perceiving reality, contrasting sharply with what is perceived as the white man's excessive rationality.

One resorts to hoodoo for many things, most commonly the healing of various ailments, especially when the patient believes that science cannot help and that an enemy is responsible for the illness by placing a hex. Other common supplications are for resolving tangled love affairs and insuring favorable legal decisions; occasionally, the hoodoo doctor is asked to cause the death of an enemy. Synonymous terms are *conjure, goopher, tricking, hexing,* and *fixing.* A "hand" or "mojo" is a magic charm that wards off a hex. Supernatural effects are produced in a variety of ways, depending on the power of the practitioner, and formulas are myriad: an egg in a murdered man's hand causes the murderer to wander around the death scene; nine needles, each broken into three pieces, can help break up a love affair; a special hot-foot powder sprinkled under a doorstep will cause an enemy to leave the vicinity.

Although many hoodoo people are also "root doctors," some root workers have nothing to do with hoodoo. Root doctors have received the traditional legacy of Afro-American folk medicine that identifies certain roots as capable of curing certain diseases, and root work in its strictest interpretation is fundamentally different from hoodoo and conjuring, although they are often intermingled. A root doctor's prescription for the clap might be a concoction of blackberry root, sheep weed, bluing, and laundry soap; no incantation endows the medicine with its healing effects. Roots are intended to have a specific medicinal function; hoodoo is sympathetic magic used to alter psychic and physical conditions. The problem with such textbook definitions it that they rarely apply precisely to actual hoodoo-conjure-rootwork practices. "Root work" sometimes also means magic, and roots are often used to produce supernatural results. John-the-conqueror root, for example, when soaked in whiskey and mixed with perfume, can anoint a litigant with the power of success. Hurston saw very soon that this complex of beliefs was a serious religious practice that has only a distant connection with notions of superstition. Modern interest in psychic phenomena has confirmed her feeling that the power of this belief could produce events unexplainable by rational means. An index of the faith's efficacy was the tenacity of its believers: "Nobody knows for sure how many thousands in America are warmed by the fire of hoodoo, because the worship is bound in secrecy. It is not the accepted theology of the Nation and so believers conceal their faith. Brother from sister, husband from wife. Nobody can say where it begins or ends. Mouths don't empty themselves unless the ears are sympathetic and knowing." She believed that hoodoo was "burning with a flame in America, with all the intensity of a suppressed religion. . . . It adapts itself like Christianity to its locale, reclaiming some of its borrowed characteristics to itself."[25]

In New Orleans the hoodoo world was presided over by the spirit of Marie Leveau, a legendary Creole conjurer. Hurston claimed that Leveau was descended from three generations of hoodoo queens and that she was born on February 2, 1827, and died near the beginning of the twentieth century after a long life of extraordinary spiritual feats. She was said to have been consulted by Queen Victoria, to be attended by a huge rattlesnake, and to have the ability to rise from the depths of Lake Pontchartrain and walk on its water. She once mesmerized an entire police force. Official records list a Marie Leveau who was married in 1819 and died in 1881, but her historical reality was less important than her spiritual presence. Marie Leveau summed up a whole era of hoodoo: "She was the great name in its golden age." The real "power doctors" in New Orleans claimed some sort of kinship or apprenticeship with Marie Leveau; it was a purported grandnephew who in the fall of 1928 provided Hurston with a most impressive "crowning" ceremony.

Hurston gave two accounts of this experience, one in her article "Hoodoo in America" in the 1931 *Journal of American Folklore*, another in *Mules and Men*. In the former, Leveau's descendent is named Samuel Thompson; in the latter, Luke Turner. Thompson was probably his correct name, but by whatever appellation, he was a figure of demonstrable power. He claimed to have the skin of the great rattlesnake that served Marie Leveau's altar, and he always wrapped this around him before attempting serious work. Thompson was at first very reluctant to accept Hurston as a novitiate; he relented after being impressed with her sincerity and persistence. He still had to determine, however, if she had "the soul to *see*":

> He bade me sit before the altar for an hour. We sat there silently facing each other across the candles and incense, for those sixty minutes. Then he rose and put the sacred snake skin about his shoulders and stood behind me with his hands upon my head. It seemed a long time to me. I was full of anxiety lest he tell me he had nothing to say to me. After a while I forgot my fears, forgot myself, and things began to happen. Things for which I can find no words, since I had experienced nothing before that would furnish a simile. I became conscious after a while of a rhythmic tremor that communicated itself to me through his hands on my head. He murmured in low syllables in some language very rapidly. A violent retching of his body all but threw me from the chair. He held still and stood silent for a minute listening. Then he answered: "Yeah, I goin' tell her. Yeah, I tell her all you say—yeah, unhunh, yeah."

No one approached the altar of the spirit without the "crown of power," and the crown was something that must be earned. In Hurston's case it was earned by lying nude for sixty-nine hours, face downward on a couch at Thompson's house, without food or water, with her navel touching a snake skin beneath her. "Three days I must lie silently, that is, my body would be there. My soul would be standing naked before the spirit to see if he would have me." There was more to the ceremony, but it is useful to contemplate that scene. It is as far from a literary tea at Jessie Fauset's or a dinner at Charles S. Johnson's as one is likely to get. It is a suspended moment of high seriousness, of another order of existence from a night on the town with the Niggerati. One cannot imagine Alain Locke in the same position. It is the act of a dedicated anthropologist willing to place herself in both physical and psychic peril. One does not participate in such rites for pure adventure. The act is not casual, and a person enters into it with fearful knowledge of its dangers and an anxious sense of its possibilities. It is the kind of act that separates Zora Neale Hurston from the Harlem literati and adds a different dimension to the sources of her imagination. Her very reticence in describing it indicates that she could not maintain a completely analytical attitude in order to capture the details of the experience. She had become for the moment the spiritual descendent of Marie Leveau, and one did not talk in books about the nature of that transformation. Hurston's report on the climax of this preparation is virtually the same in the 1931 and 1935 versions; the experience is summarized in a single paragraph: "For 69 hours I lay there. I had five psychic experiences and awoke at last with no feeling of hunger, only one of exaltation." It is true that the folklorist within was not completely quiet, that she could observe after the fact that her preparation had been akin to that of all mystics, a cleansing of body and mind. And she provided an objective report of the remaining initiation ritual, which included the painting of lightning symbols across her back, the drinking of blood mixed with wine, and the sacrificial killing of a black sheep. But the preparation paragraph reveals most, not for what it says, but for what it does not say. What happened during those psychic experiences? Hurston's only answer was, "I shall not detail them here; but I knew that I had been accepted before the sixty nine hours had passed."

The hoodoo sections of *Mules and Men* are derived from her "Hoodoo in America" article; they are as close to an objective account of black folklore as Hurston could make them and still satisfy her publisher's demands that the book be accessible to the general reader. What lies behind that reticent paragraph is Hurston's awareness of the spiritual possibilities in the hoodoo experience, and what informs the paragraph is her *belief* in the magic. Although very subtly done in both *Mules and Men* and the *JAF* article—so as not to alienate a rationalistic audience—Hurston ultimately reveals her conviction that these men and women, considered irrationally superstitious by most observers, have discovered many of nature's secrets. Time after time she reports that her 1928 trip found hoodoo rituals to be successful. Without commenting on the reasons for success, she documents the efficacy of the charms, spells, and mojos she encountered. In *Mules and Men* she tells a friend "with assurance": "Don't fool yourself. . . . People can do things to you. I done seen things happen." The reader has the feeling that her confidence is more than a collecting technique. She tells us of another order of existence: "Three days my body must lie silent and fasting while my spirit went wherever spirits must go that seek answers never given to men as men." When Pierre Anatole, another doctor she studied with, sleeps for ninety days in a black-draped coffin in order to bring about a death, she concludes, simply, "And the man died." Readers are left to draw their own conclusions.

This five months between August and December of 1928 was a dramatic time for Hurston, transforming her from an enthusiastic artist-folklorist into a mature, thoughtful scholar. There were no striking changes in her behavior, and she remained excited about her material. But the quality of her enthusiasm changed; she began to see more serious implications in her research. Alan Lomax, collecting folksongs with her in 1935, remembers her as guarded and mysterious about her conjure experiences, maybe even a little frightened by them; the New Orleans ceremonies marked her for the rest of her life.[26] There was real sadness when she made ready to leave the city, and Luke Turner/Samuel Thompson told her that the spirit had spoken: she was the last doctor he would make, for in one year and seventy-nine days he would die; could she stay with him to the end? There is no phony pathos in *Mules and Men* when she reports, "It has been a great sorrow to me that I could not say yes."

Hurston's success as a folklore collector was occurring in secret. Almost no one knew of her discoveries, and she wanted to share the excitement with others. If one has a considerable ego, as Hurston had, and if one has previously failed in his chosen profession, as Hurston had in the field of folklore, then pride demands that others be made aware of the new triumphs. This was not always easy for a black scholar in New Orleans in 1928. Locke had suggested that she get in touch with the Tulane University faculty, but the result was not promising. She wrote him, "Thanks a lot for the Tulane U contact. They sent an application blank in case I might wish to enroll in one of the social science classes. Dont laugh." In an attempt to establish contact with her scientific community, so that she could then inform it of her accomplishments, Hurston sent Boas a box of oranges for Christmas in 1928, the first time she had communicated with Papa Franz for over a year. As she undoubtedly expected, he replied immediately that he appreciated the gift, adding, "I wish you would write to me from time to time. I should like to know what you are doing."[27] Her quick reply accomplished many ends, though it was vague about exactly what she was doing:

My dear Dr. Boas,

I was very proud to hear from you. I have wanted to write you but a promise was exacted of me that I would write *no one*. Of course I have intended from the very beginning to show you what I have, but after I had returned. Thus I could keep my word and at the same time have your guidance.

I am finding lots of things which will intrigue you. I find Odom [*sic*] and Johnson in error constantly. A too hasty generalization. The subject of sympathetic magic is being looked into thoroughly as I can, and folk-lore collected, religious expression noted.

This is confidential. I accepted the money on the condition that I should write no one. It is unthinkable, of course, that I go past the collecting stage without consulting you, however I came by the money. I shall probably be in New York by the Fall. I have not forgotten your interest in Creole languages, but I have had little time to note anything. I am getting on very well. The experience that I had under you was a splendid foundation, for whereas, I got little for you, now, I know where to look and how. Sometimes I have gotten in a week as much as I gathered for you through out. I regret it too, but I know that you understand, and will be pleased with me when I return.

Most affectionately yours,
Zora Hurston[28]

This brief note informed the leader of the American anthropological profession that his former student was working very well, thank you, despite the 1927 failure. She had now established that she was under wraps, and implied that, once free of the fetters of patronage, there would be glorious results. She was also contracting with her mentor for his help in her summarizing. Boas would no longer think of her as a promising failure, and her work would be broadcast in informal, professional ways—"Have you heard that Boas's former student Zora Neale Hurston is doing some work with sympathetic magic in New Orleans?"

Hurston stayed in Louisiana for most of the winter of 1928–29. After Mrs. Mason renewed her contract for another year, she began making her way back to Florida. By April she was staying with her brother John in Jacksonville and gathering material about an African princess who married a white man beyond the three-mile limit and lived on an island off the coast. Her major effort was organizing her field notes. She was proud that her data would destroy existing theories: "I am sitting down to sum up and I am getting on very well at it. I feel full of subjects, but there are [sic] going to be lots of hollering as various corns get stepped on."[29]

Later that month she settled in a small cabin in Eau Gallie, a tiny coastal village near Saint Augustine, and stopped collecting altogether. She wrote Boas, "I have more than 95,000 words of story material, a collection of children's games, conjure material and religious material, with a great number of photographs." She wished to insure scientific accuracy, and she wanted the distinguished scholar's advice:

Is it safe for me to say that baptism is an extension of water worship as a part of pantheism just as the sacrament is an extension of cannibalism? Isn't the use of candles in the Catholic church a relic of fire worship? Are not all the uses of fire upon the altars the same thing? Is not the christian ritual rather one of attenuated nature worship, in the fire, water, and blood? Might not the frequently mentioned fire of the Holy Ghost not be an unconscious fire worship. May it not be a deification of fire?

May I say that the decoration in clothing is an extension of the primitive application of paint (coloring) to the body?

May I say that all primitive music originated about the drum, and that singing was an attenuation of the drumbeat. The nearer to the primitive, the more prominent the part of the drum. Finally the music (the singers) reach that stage where they can maintain the attenuation independently of, and unconscious of the drum. Such is the European grand opera. Unrithmic attenuation. I mean by attenuation, the listener to the drum will feel the space between beats and will think up devices to fill those spaces. The between-beat becomes more and more complicated untill the music is all between-beat and the consciousness of the dependence upon the drum id [is] lost.

Hurston's questions demonstrate her interest in the universality of human behavior, whether in Eatonville or New York, and the ties all civilizations have to so-called primitive practices. Implicit in her religious questions is the assertion that hoodoo is no more primitive than Catholicism. Boas's reply was that of the careful scholar, warning her that her questions "contain a great deal of very contentious matter" and adding that he did not think her suppositions about primitive music would explain the origin of intervals.[30]

The caution of Boas did not dampen Hurston's enthusiasm, and near the end of April she wrote Hughes: "I am just beginning to hit my stride. At first I tried to do too much in a day. Now I am satisfied with a few pages if they say what I want. I have to rewrite a lot as you can understand. For I not only want to present the material with all the life and color of my people, I want to leave no loop-holes for the scientific crowd to rend and tear us." On the other hand, "I am leaving the story material almost untouched. I have only tampered with it where the story teller was not clear. I know it is going to read different, but that is the glory of the thing, don't you think?"[31]

Hurston's rewriting and tampering with material, even done solely for the purposes of clarity, would be anathema to most modern folklorists, although the requirements for accurate, authentic transcriptions of folk narratives were not always as exacting in 1929 as they are today. Her rewriting grew out of her desire to emphasize the esthetic significance of the folklore performance. She was trying to set down an entire Baptist service "word for word and note for note" from her field notes, and found that the prayers were best rendered in blank verse, "for thats what they are, prose poetry." She planned to "cut the dull spots in the service to the minimum and play up the art."[32] She had heard a magnificent sermon from the Reverend C. C. Lovelace in Eau Gallie on May 3, and it reaffirmed her conviction that the black minister was a true poet.

A month later Hurston wrote Hughes that she had finished a first draft of both the "lore and the religion. I shall now set it aside to cool till it grows inside me." She made plans to go to Miami and collect children's games and Seminole Indian lore. But before she could leave, she became seriously ill, entering the hospital at Saint Augustine with a liver ailment that had bothered her for the past two years. At first the doctors felt they would have to operate, but the decision was stayed at the last minute, when she began to recover.

By August, 1929, she was in Miami, employing a stenographer to type second and third drafts.[33]

Freed from collecting and summarizing, she turned her efforts again to the Hughes-Hurston play, which had not been abandoned, despite Mrs. Mason. "Do you want to look over what I have on our show?" she wrote Hughes. "Let's call it 'Jook.' That is the word for bawdy house in its general sense. It is the club house on these saw mills and turpentine stills. Then we can bring in all of the songs and gags I have. Shall we work it at once? I am willing if you are. I know that G[odmother] would never consent for me to do so, so you will have to take it all in your name. Man, I got some jook songs! I am getting enough for a volume by itself and I am pushing it close. The folks call playing and singing those songs 'jooking.' For ex.[ample] 'Man, he sho kin jook.'"[34]

She stayed in Miami and thought further about their show. She proposed a brace of skits, one called "White Folks Love" in which a black man tries to win his girl by making "dicty love," and fails; then "he gits real common and is a knockout." She also thought they might try redoing the railroad coach scene from her play *Color Struck*; in all she had seven skits "about ready." She was thinking of the musical content of the show: "I am now writing music, and if I do say so, I have one or two snappy airs. I am trying to get the whole together so that you can have a copy and make your additions ad lib."[35]

Hurston did not stop collecting, however, and found much material around Miami during September. She also began to see links between Afro-American and Afro-Caribbean folklore. She had met so many West Indians in the Miami area that she was sure "their folklore definitely influences ours in South Florida." In October she traveled to Nassau in the Bahamas to collect material that would both reinforce and contrast with her previous collections. While there, she went through one of the worst hurricanes to hit either the islands or Florida in many years, an experience that made her think she would never get back to the mainland, but a memory that would become fiction in *Their Eyes Were Watching God*. Both songs and hoodoo were in great abundance in the Bahamas, and until she ran out of money, Hurston pursued both with characteristic energy. On the day before she left Nassau, she finally found one of the island's most powerful hoodoo men. She had only a return ticket and twenty-four cents in her pocket, and she had to leave her work with him for a second trip.[36]

When Hurston returned to Miami in mid-October of 1929, she became involved in a dispute with Mrs. Mason that tells us much about her patronage arrangement. In May, Boas had written her about research being done by Columbia under the supervision of Otto Klineberg into "mental characteristics" of ethnic groups. Boas told her he was interested in the "special" musical ability of black people; he wanted Hurston to help find black communities in the New Orleans area where "a great deal of singing is still going on." The pay would be $150 per month plus expenses. Hurston did not respond immediately, perhaps because she knew that Boas was going to be in Europe until October, but she had decided to lend a hand. On October 20, 1929, a week after returning from Nassau, she wrote Boas that she would be in New Orleans by November 1 and would meet with Klineberg. Her letter also spoke of her own projects, and she went to considerable effort to impress upon him her scientific exactness; the same person who could tell Hughes that she was tampering only when her stories were unclear told Boas: "I hope that you will have time to read the material soon. I have tried to be as exact as possible. Keep to the exact dialect as closely as I could, having the story teller to tell it to me word for word as I write it. This after it has been told to me off hand until I know it myself. But the writing down from the lips is to insure the correct dialect and wording so that I shall not let myself creep in unconsciously." She also wanted Boas to know that her research was exposing the shallow inaccuracy of two of her favorite whipping boys: "I have been following the works of Odum and Johnson closely and find that they could hardly be less exact. They have made six or seven songs out of one song and made one song out of six or seven. . . . Let them but hit upon a well turned phrase and another volume slops off the press. Some of it would be funny if they were not serious scientists; or are they?" (She was even more specific in a letter to Locke, telling him that Odum and Johnson's *Negro Workaday Songs* [1926] was no threat to her own folksong collecting: "They have done the book just about like Nicholas Murray Butler would do the black bottom.")[37]

Hurston had not fully arranged, before she wrote Boas, for release from Mrs. Mason's employ, but she must have felt that most of her work was done. The original contract, extended for a second year, was due to expire in a month. She had collected a complete volume of folktales, written them up, and sent them on to New York. A religion volume, dealing with spiritualists and evangelical preachers, was also nearing completion. Locke and Mrs. Mason had read the folktale manuscript and determined that it merited publication. Hurston knew this by at least October 15, for she told Hughes in a letter of that date, "G[odmother] told me we are going to press with the stories." Apparently Mrs. Mason also served as censor. Zora admitted to Hughes, "Godmother says the dirty words must be toned down. Of course I knew that, but first I wanted to collect them as they are." Even though a planned song volume was still incomplete, Hurston had every right to think that Mrs. Mason would not object to her participating in the Columbia project, thereby furthering her career on an independent basis. Her assumption that she was a free agent in this matter was very quickly rejected. By either wire or telephone Mrs. Mason made it clear that Zora was not to shirk her duties. Hurston had to write Boas almost immediately about "what I am up against. I thought I might drop my work and do this thing with Dr. Klineberg, but I find that I am restrained from doing anything of the sort." She added, "I have been brought up so shortly." In a telegram to Klineberg she said, "I find I am restrained from leaving the employ of my present employers."[38]

What Hurston also did, however, was to assure both Boas and Klineberg that she would give them as much help as possible—in an unofficial capacity. She sent Klineberg a list of her informants, and left for New Orleans on October 23 in her Chevrolet coupé, representing the trip to Mrs. Mason as nothing more than the further collecting of conjure. Once in the city, Hurston spent considerable time with the Columbia scholar; he believed that she was there to join his research team. Klineberg wrote Boas that Hurston might be able to finish her own work in a couple of weeks and work full time with him.[39]

Why not simply tell Mrs. Mason she was through? The answer lies in the original contract. Hurston had not officially been collecting for herself. Although she had done all the field work and interpretation, Mrs. Mason still had a legal hold over the collected material; in fact, the folktale volume, tentatively entitled *Mules and Men*, was in one of Godmother's safe-deposit boxes in New York. If Hurston wanted to see the results of her two years of labor in print, under her name, she had to accede to her patron's wishes. Godmother felt that the collections needed more work, and she was not about to lose control over either folklore or folklorist. The pressure was great, and it came at a bad time. Before leaving for Nassau and the final collecting, Zora had told Hughes that she felt "forlorn": "Too tired, been working two years without rest, and behind that all my school life with no rest, no peace of mind." She admitted to Boas that Mrs. Mason's action had put her in "a terrible nervous state."[40]

Hurston's resentment only led to her surreptitious aid for the Columbia team—a small rebellion, but one that suggests the difficulty she had begun to know as a salaried scholar. She stayed in New Orleans through November and part of December, assisting the Columbia research and continuing her own work. She wrote Hughes, "I am running here with my tongue hanging out to get everything I see." She planned to go to the Bahamas around Christmas for carnival season and then sail from there for New York. She told Boas, "I want to make this conjure work very thorough and inclusive. As soon as I have the latest material assembled in some order, I shall let you have it"—a promise that would be unremarkable were it not in direct defiance of Godmother's prohibition against letting anyone else see the collections.[41]

Hurston collected in the Bahamas during January and February, 1930, returning to the hoodoo doctor she had been forced to leave, and then sailed for New York. By March she was living in a rooming house in Westfield, New Jersey, and frequently seeing Hughes, who was also living in Westfield, in quarters rented for him by Mrs. Mason. Westfield sometimes became a kind of artist's colony for Mason people. Joining the group was Louise Thompson, a young intellectual who had been working as a secretarial science teacher at Hampton Institute; she had been hired by Mrs. Mason as a literary secretary to the two young writers. Hurston had all her field notes with her, and she began the task of organizing and selecting, which would occupy her for the next two years. The material was so extensive that Thompson often typed half the night to prepare Zora's manuscripts. [42]

Hurston worked most closely with Alain Locke, and the relationship did not always go well. She resented his editorial responsibilities, perhaps because he was there as a representative of Mrs. Mason. Locke was very close to Mason, serving as a talent scout for her, and in Zora's case Mrs. Mason made clear from the start that she should consult with him. Beginning in April of 1929, when Hurston began to transcribe story material, he took a great interest in the work, apparently reading each manuscript sent to New York from the South. Hughes also read portions, and his presence at conferences where her work was discussed proved valuable. Hurston solicited Hughes's advice about the politics of her situation, and he provided reports on what was being said about her. During the summer of 1929 Hughes intimated that she should be careful about what she told Locke, and Hurston replied, "I told him nothing but asked him about editing the material, and I only asked him that because G[odmother] said she wanted me to be more cordial to him. I have only written him foir times since I have been down. But thanks for the tip. I shall be even more reticent from now on. I'll keep my big mouf shut." She assured Hughes that she would be discreet about anything he told her because "I know that you tell me things to guard my relations with G[odmother]." As she thought over Locke's actions, she added a postscript: "The trouble with Locke is that he is intellectually dishonest. He is too eager to be with the winner. . . . He wants to autograph all successes, but is afraid to risk an opinion first hand."[43]

Hurston's reaction to Locke was part of her complex emotional struggle with Mrs. Mason. From the time she left for the South, she had tried to return Mrs. Mason's kindnesses. During the same winter when Zora began collecting, Hughes began the visits to New York that led to Godmother's support for the writing of his novel *Not without Laughter* during the summer of 1928. He reported to Hurston on what seemed to please in New York and what did not. When some unusual wood carving she sent was well received, he apparently suggested that she find more. Thereafter, whenever she discovered a native carver with talent, Hurston commissioned a piece, perhaps because she was well aware of Mrs. Mason's sense of property. From Florida, Hurston sent orange blossoms to Park Avenue; from New Orleans it was melons. She once sent some wood from the *Clotilde*, the scuttled ship that had brought Cudjo Lewis to America. When Hughes thought a lighter report might be in order, Hurston sent "a bit of intended-to-be-humorous manuscript, as you suggested." Before Godmother sailed for Europe in the summer of 1928, Zora sent her some wit and wisdom from Joe Wiley, one of the "Magazine Point boys" she had collected from in Alabama. When Hughes warned that infrequent reports were causing rumblings, Hurston assured him she would write every week now, adding, "Yes, I do think that she is wonderful."[44]

Wonderful though Mrs. Mason might be, Hurston was obviously hurt by her manner in the Klineberg-Boas matter, and Zora's bonds often chafed. When she left for the final Bahamian leg of the expedition in December, 1929, she told Hughes, "I may have to ask for more time but I hope not"—apparently meaning that she hoped her contract would be over. Hurston did ask for more time, partially because "G[odmother] said that I may have it if I wish" and partially because the stacks and stacks of field notes were not easily condensed into book form, but mainly because she had little choice. Mrs. Mason still had control over the material.[45]

Working out of the rooming house in Westfield, Hurston began to take material to Boas for his advice, apparently at first without Mrs. Mason's knowledge. In April she wrote him, "I have just received a word from headquarters telling me to come over Friday at three and bring materials for discussion." She would have to retrieve the essay Boas was reading, but she presumed that the summons was "merely intended to see how I am coming on." She added, "I am urged to do things as quickly as possible and so at present I am working furiously." Boas, who never learned Mrs. Mason's name and who frequently asked about the publication plans of the "people for whom you are working," was impressed enough with the collections to suggest that Zora ask Mrs. Mason about supporting her toward a Ph.D. in anthropology at Columbia. In June she wrote him that "the 'angel' is cold towards the degrees but will put up money for further research. I have broached the subject from several angles but it got chill blains no matter how I put it." Boas was persistent, asking her to urge her "angel" to combine the degree with research: "Make it clear to her that your research work under the direction of a university would be more profitable than without it and that she will further your own welfare considerably by making the combination." (For whatever reason, the idea did not take, and Hurston would have to wait until 1935 before returning to Columbia for a short-lived attempt at being a graduate student.)[46]

Hurston spent the rest of 1930 working on her collections, splitting them into folk narrative and conjure practices, and deciding that a separate volume of songs was unnecessary. All the publishers she contacted liked the material but demanded something more than the mere transcription of collected tales. She did transcribe a few dance songs and tales from the Bahamas for publication in the *Journal of American Folklore* in the July–September issue of 1930. Largely unrelated to her Afro-American collections, the article gives every appearance of being Hurston's sop to the demand for scientific publication—something quick and easy, done to illustrate her academic interests. By the time her employment for Mrs. Mason officially ended, on March 31, 1931, she had finished a new version of the volume of folktales and had prepared the scholarly article about hoodoo for the *Journal of American Folklore* that would eventually be revised and incorporated in *Mules and Men*.[47]

Hurston did not, however, work exclusively on folklore for the five months she spent in Westfield in the winter and spring of 1930. Before returning to Florida for the summer, she also became involved with Langston Hughes in the writing of a play called "Mule Bone." Just as with Zora's collecting trip, Mrs. Mason's powerful personality stood behind this effort, and this time the Hughes-Hurston friendship did not withstand the effect.

NOTES

1. ZNH to LH, Sept. 21, 1927 (JWJYale).

2. RH interview with LTP, June 22, 1976, New York City; Natalie Curtis, *The Indians' Book* (New York: Harper and Row, 1907). See also Clare B. Crane, "Alain Locke and the Negro Renaissance," Ph.D. diss., University of California at San Diego, 1971, p. 174; Natalie Curtis Burlin, *Negro Folk-Songs (Hampton Series)* (New York: G. Schirmer, 1918–19); correspondence between Mrs. Mason and ZNH, 1928–31 (HUAL).

3. Contract between Mrs. Mason and ZNH, Dec. 8, 1927 (HUAL).

4. Gwendolyn Bennett, "The Ebony Flute," *Opportunity*, 5 (Sept., 1927), 277; LH, *The Big Sea* (New York: Hill and Wang, 1963), pp. 293–300; ZNH to CVV, Aug. 26, 1927 (JWJYale).

5. RH interview with LTP, June 22, 1976, New York City; ZNH, *Dust Tracks on a Road* (New York: J. B. Lippincott, 1942), p. 185.

6. LH, *Big Sea*, p. 325.

7. Nathan Huggins, *The Harlem Renaissance* (New York: Oxford University Press, 1971), pp. 129–36; LTP to RH, Mar. 19, 1976; RH interview with LTP, June 22, 1976, New York City; RH interview with Arthur Huff Fauset, Jan. 16, 1976, Philadelphia.

8. ZNH, *Dust Tracks*, p. 185; RH interview with LTP, June 22, 1976, New York City.

9. ZNH to Thomas E. Jones, Oct. 12, 1934 (CSJFisk; copy in JWJYale); RH interview with Arthur Huff Fauset, Jan. 16, 1976, Philadelphia; ZNH to Mrs. Mason, Oct. 10, Apr. 18, 1931 (HUAL).

10. ZNH to Mrs. Mason, May 10, 1931 (HUAL).

11. Contract between Mrs. Mason and ZNH, Dec. 8, 1927 (HUAL).

12. Ibid.

13. ZNH to LH, Dec. 9, 1927 (JWJYale).

14. ZNH postcard to LH, Jan. 31, 1928; ZNH, *Mules and Men* (New York: Harper and Row, 1970), pp. 79–200. The official dates of Mrs. Mason's funding (1927–31) come from applications ZNH filled out when applying for a Rosenwald Foundation Fellowship (1934) and two Guggenheim Fellowships (1935–36) (RosFisk, GgFnd). There are some inconsistencies on these applications. The Hurston-Mason correspondence at MSRC makes clear that she continued to receive money until the fall of 1932, while in *Dust Tracks* Zora says, "In May, 1932, the depression did away with money for research so far as I was concerned" (p. 216).

15. ZNH, *Mules and Men*, pp. 85–200; RH interview with Everett Hurston, Jr., June 23, 1976, Brooklyn, N.Y.; ZNH to LH, Mar. 8, 1928 (JWJYale).

16. ZNH to LH, Apr. 12, 1928 (JWJYale).

17. RH interview with Arthur Huff Fauset, Jan. 16, 1976, Philadelphia; ZNH to AL, June 14, 1928 (HUAL).

18. ZNH to LH, Apr. 12, 1928 (JWJYale). Hurston was to closely follow these observations when she wrote "Characteristics of Negro Expression" for Nancy Cunard's *Negro: An Anthology* (London, Wishart, 1934).

19. ZNH to LH, Apr. 12, 1928 (JWJYale); "The Florida Expedition," typescript (APS).

20. ZNH to LH, Apr. 12, 1928 (JWJYale).

21. Ibid., May 1, 1928 (JWJYale); ZNH to AL, Dec. 16, [1928] (HUAL).

22. ZNH to LH, July 10, 1928 (JWJYale).

23. Ibid.

24. Ibid., Aug. 6, Sept. 20, Oct. 15, 1928 (JWJYale); ZNH to AL, Oct. 15, 1928 (HUAL).

25. ZNH, *Mules and Men*, pp. 229, 231, 332–43.

26. RH interview with Alan Lomax, May 15, 1971, New York City.

27. ZNH to AL, May 10, 1928 (HUAL); FB to ZNH, Dec. 18, 1928 (APS).

28. ZNH to FB, Dec. 27, 1928 (APS).

29. ZNH to LH, Apr. 3, 1929 (JWJYale).

30. ZNH to FB, Apr. 21, 1929; FB to ZNH, Apr. 24, 1929 (APS).

31. ZNH to LH, Apr. 30, 1929 (JWJYale).

32. Ibid.

33. Ibid., May 31, July 23, Aug. 17, 1929 (JWJYale).

34. Ibid., n.d. [July–Aug., 1929] (JWJYale).

35. Ibid., Aug. 17, 1929 (JWJYale).

36. Ibid., Oct. 15, 1929 (JWJYale).

37. FB to ZNH, May 17, 1929; ZNH to FB, Oct. 20, 1929 (APS); ZNH to AL, May 10, 1928 (HUAL).

38. ZNH to LH, Oct. 15, 1929 (JWJYale); ZNH to FB, Oct. 20 and ca. 20–22, 1929; ZNH telegram to Otto Klineberg, Oct. 22, 1929 (APS).

39. ZNH telegram to Otto Klineberg, Oct. 22, 1929; Klineberg to FB, Nov. 18, 1929 (APS).

40. ZNH to LH, Oct. 15, 1929 (JWJYale); ZNH to FB, Oct. 20–22, 1929 (APS).

41. ZNH to LH, Dec. 10, 1929 (JWJYale); ZNH to FB, Dec. 10, 1929 (APS).

42. LH, *Big Sea*, p. 320; ZNH to LH, Dec. 10, 1929 (JWJYale); RH interview with LTP, June 22, 1976, New York City.

43. ZNH to LH, Apr. 3, 1929, n.d. [July–Aug., 1929] (JWJYale).

44. Ibid., Mar. 8, Aug. 6, 1928, n.d. [July–Aug., 1929], Sept. 20, 1928 (JWJYale); ZNH to AL, May 10, 1928; ZNH to Mrs. Mason, July 25, 1928 (HUAL).

45. ZNH to LH, Dec. 10, 1929 (JWJYale).

46. ZNH to FB, Apr. 16, 1930; FB to ZNH, May 3, 1930; ZNH to FB, June 6, 1930; FB to ZNH, June 13, 1930 (APS).

47. Correspondence between ZNH and Mrs. Mason, 1930 (HUAL).

6   ≋≋≋ "Mule Bone"

"Mule Bone" has never been produced, and only its third act has ever been published. Fewer than ten copies of the play survive, all deposited in private papers. Still, despite the fact that it has been read in full by only a few, it is a notorious work, the center of a quarrel that transformed Hughes and Hurston from intimate friends to lifelong enemies. "Mule Bone" is the reason Langston Hughes, a kind, gentle, forgiving man, never forgave Hurston for what he considered theft and dishonesty. "Mule Bone" caused Zora Hurston, who had high hopes of making their collaborative efforts famous, to accuse her partner of stealing ideas and of sabotaging the play's production. "Mule Bone" explains why, after February 3, 1931, Zora Neale Hurston and Langston Hughes avoided each other for the rest of their lives.

The "Mule Bone" episode is not so important in itself, perhaps, but it provides an intimate glimpse of the kinds of pressures Hurston struggled to control all her life. The tale is worth focusing on because its true history has gone unreported, and also because it illuminates complex tensions in Hurston's life that arose from patronage and personality. These tensions illustrate why Zora Hurston's career would be at times controversial, at times puzzling, occasionally inconsistent.

The "Mule Bone" story is tangled, filled with bad behavior, shrill voices, and feigned innocence. When Hughes accused Hurston of claiming sole authorship of a play they had written together and of marketing it for the stage without consulting him, he acted from a legitimate sense of outrage. She had done both—whether out of misunderstanding, ambition, or malice, it is hard to say. Hughes's representation of the facts in *The Big Sea*, however—up to now the only public account of the dispute—oversimplifies an incredibly complicated affair. Hughes actually gave two versions of his side of things, one in his autobiography, another in correspondence with his lawyer. Hurston never gave a public account, and only a partial private one. The narrative that follows has been pieced together from a variety of sources, including the private correspondence of the principals.[1]

"Mule Bone" was written largely between March and June of 1930. Living near each other in rooming houses in New Jersey, seeing each other almost every day, Hughes and Hurston apparently talked about some of their plans for a "real Negro theatre." At a party in late February or early March, Hughes met Theresa Helburn of the Dramatists Guild; Helburn complained that practically all the plays about black people offered to the guild were serious problem dramas. Why didn't someone write a comedy—not a minstrel show, but a real comedy? Hughes took the idea back to Hurston, and they began to work, meeting at Zora's place in Westfield; they decided to build a three-act comedy around a folktale she had collected.

The tale was about two hunters who shot simultaneously at a wild turkey and then quarreled over who had killed it. In the ensuing fight, one hunter knocked the other unconscious with the hock bone of a mule found by happenstance during the struggle. The bone wielder was charged with assault and battery and brought to trial. When it was asserted that a mule bone could hardly be considered a lethal weapon, a minister read to the jury the biblical story of Samson's slaying three thousand Philistines with the jawbone of an ass. Pointing out that a mule is more dangerous the farther to the rear one goes, the minister concluded that a bone from the hind legs must be considered a very dangerous weapon indeed. The hunter was convicted and expelled from town.

How Hughes and Hurston shaped this story into a comic play —the division of responsibility, who wrote what—is unknown. Hughes claimed that he was to do the construction, plot, some characterization, and some dialogue, and that Hurston was to provide the authentic Florida color, give the dialogue a true southern flavor, and insert turns of phrase and "highly amusing details" from her collecting trips. By early April they were working together intensely, dictating to Louise Thompson. The three of them had a wonderful time, Zora sometimes reducing the others to helpless laughter as she acted out all the parts. In four weeks they completed drafts of the first and third acts and at least one scene of the second act. The turkey was dropped (over Hurston's objections) and a girl made the root of the argument. The combatants became members of different churches, and the trial became part of a sectarian struggle. In May, Hurston left Westfield. In June she returned to the South for the summer, taking with her notes and outlines for the trial scene of act 2; she was to complete this act over the summer, and they would polish it in the fall.

Hughes contended that he saw nothing unusual in this departure just when things were nearing completion, and he claimed to be surprised and disappointed when Hurston returned in September and brushed him off when asked about beginning work again. According to him, she canceled appointments, said she had no time, and by early December was no longer seeing him at all. However, this autumn coldness was consistent with her breaking off work in late spring when things were going smoothly; neither action had anything to do with the need for a trip south or the press of other business. She was angry over the growing friendship between Hughes and Louise Thompson, and she felt, rightly or wrongly, that Hughes was trying to make Thompson a part of their collaborative effort. Hurston broke off their partnership because she was angry over the way things were working out between them and their stenographer.

Her complaint, not voiced until later, was over Hughes's proposal that Thompson assume more than a stenographer's role in their effort, that perhaps she even be made business manager of any Broadway production. Hurston did not admit it, but this new partner was a considerable distraction to a creative collaboration looked forward to for years. She had already given up the racial opera they had talked about; Mrs. Mason decided that Hughes could do it better with a composer, and she had sent him to Cuba to look for a new collaborator. Hughes later claimed that he attributed Hurston's behavior that fall to nerves and to the rush of getting her folklore collections organized for publication. It seems more likely that he knew what was bothering his co-worker and had concluded that it was best to let their long friendship cool.

The other factor complicating the Hughes-Hurston relationship at the time was Hughes's growing uneasiness with Mrs. Mason.

During the fall and winter of 1930 Hughes began to feel guilty about eating caviar above Park Avenue while apple vendors hawked for survival on the street below. Hughes's poem "Advertisement for the Waldorf-Astoria" had addressed this feeling:

> Have luncheon there this afternoon, all you jobless.
>   Why not?
> Dine with some of the men and women who got rich off of your
>   Labor, who clip coupons with clean white fingers because your
>   hands dug coal, drilled stone, sewed garments, poured steel to let
>   other people draw dividends and live easy.

Mrs. Mason not only had clean white fingers, she also clipped coupons regularly. She was bound to disapprove of the poem, and Hughes probably knew it. Her disapproval led to his rethinking their relationship, with the result that in late December or early January he went off the payroll. There was a final traumatic scene at 399 Park, and the parting was bitter, Mrs. Mason accusing him of ingratitude and disloyalty. Hurston knew about Hughes's dissatisfaction and probably foresaw the breakup. It may be that she was trying to protect her own relationship with her patron, hoping that Mrs. Mason's unhappiness with Hughes would not rub off on her. She had apparently made her peace with Mrs. Mason and did not wish to sever the patronage arrangement until her field work was organized. If this sounds as though Hurston abandoned a friend, it is important to remember that Louise Thompson—in Zora's mind at least—had already come between them. Complicating it all was Thompson's support from Mrs. Mason while typing the play and her growing dissatisfaction with Mrs. Mason's interest in black people as primitives. Hurston herself was not entirely easy with this aspect of the Mason personality, but she knew how to play to Godmother's preferences. She once addressed Mrs. Mason as the "guard-mother who sits in the twelfth heaven and shapes the destinies of the primitives." Thompson, who was very close to Zora before the "Mule Bone" blowup, remembers how, whenever Mrs. Mason sent an exotic dress for Zora to wear, Zora called Park Avenue to report that it looked stunning on her; then she would hang up and turn to her companion, remarking with a laugh that she would not think of wearing such a thing.

Hughes's reaction to the breakup with Mrs. Mason was to become psychosomatically ill. He spent his remaining money on doctors and radiologists who could find nothing wrong with him. One New York physician, a specialist in diagnosing Oriental ailments, identified his as a Japanese tapeworm. When Hughes returned home to Cleveland to live with his mother in early January, 1931, a general practitioner attempted to solve his problems by removing his tonsils. As Hughes admitted, his real illness was in his wallet; he began recovering the moment the last of Mrs. Mason's money was gone.

Hughes's tonsillitis did not stop him from visiting Cleveland's Karamu House shortly after his return. A settlement playhouse run by Rowena and Alexander Jelliffe, Karamu was the home of a black acting company called the Gilpin Players, nationally known for the quality and vigor of their productions. When Rowena Jelliffe told Hughes on January 15 that she had just obtained the rights to a play called "Mule Bone," a comedy of "Negro life" by Zora Neale Hurston, he was mystified. When the script arrived and proved to be clearly the play they had worked on together, he was angry. And when he could get no satisfactory explanation from Hurston by phone call or letter, he was outraged. He immediately copied act 2 from the script received, added his own copies of acts 1 and 3, and sent the play off to be copyrighted in both their names. He also sent Hurston a registered letter threatening litigation.

What actually happened was that Hurston had given the play to Carl Van Vechten to read. Although the script was in a very unfinished form, he had, without her knowledge, sent it to Barrett Clark, a reader for the Theatre Guild. Clark was sure that the guild would reject it, but in his capacity as an employee of Samuel French, the theatrical producer, he had written Mrs. Jelliffe to ask if the Gilpin Players would be interested. When she said yes, he had sent the script on, indicating that a letter explaining rights to the play would follow.

Was Hurston thinking of marketing the play as her own? It seems likely, since the script read by the Theatre Guild carried only her name. Moreover, she, too, had submitted the play script for copyright, but in October of 1930, using her own second act, reinserting the turkey as the object of contention, and listing herself as the sole author. Still, she had not sent the play anywhere herself, and when she received an angry phone call from Hughes on January 16, she truthfully denied knowing anything about the play's being in an agent's hands or in Cleveland. Hughes found this hard to believe, and the phone conversation degenerated rapidly.

The Gilpin Players wanted very much to do the play. Mrs. Jelliffe was enthusiastic. Even though the script was in a rough state—the turkey had been reinserted, but the girl remained; there were two endings, with the suggestion that the performers take their pick—one of its authors was in Cleveland and available for rewriting. A number of phone calls followed, the upshot being that Barrett Clark promised Mrs. Jelliffe that he would try to obtain Hurston's permission for a production. On January 20, 1930, a wire came from French's saying that Hurston had refused to authorize the production and that the script should be returned at once. Within twenty-four hours, however, three wires came directly from Hurston authorizing the production and indicating that she would collaborate with Hughes on script changes. Within that same twenty-four-hour period, Hughes received a letter from Hurston, written on January 18, saying that no part of the play was his. Understandably confused, he contacted New York attorney Arthur Spingarn, one of the chief supporters of the NAACP, to protect his interests.

The letter that Hughes received from Hurston claiming he had no rights in the play was not vicious, although it undoubtedly angered him.[2] Hurston said that she wanted to have a heart-to-heart talk about the play, and finally expressed her resentment about Louise Thompson: "In the beginning, Langston, I was very eager to do the play with you. ANYthing you said would go over big with me. But scarcely had we gotten underway before you made three propositions that shook me to the foundation of myself. First: that three way split with Louise. Now Langston, nobody has in the history of the world given a typist an interest in a work for typing it. Nobody would think of it unless they were prejudiced in favor of the typist." According to Hurston, Hughes's second proposition was that Thompson be paid more than the usual typist's fee, and his third that she be made the business manager of the Broadway production. The effect, Hurston claimed, was to make her feel as though she were "among strangers, and the only thing to do was to go on away from there." (In a letter written two days later, she added a touch of melodrama to her exile: "I just went off to myself and tried to resolve to have no more friendships. Tears unceasing have poured down inside me.")

Having adopted the role of the betrayed partner, Hurston then told Hughes: "Now about the play itself. It was my story from beginning to end. It is my dialogue; my situations. But I am not concerned about that. Langston, with God as my judge, I don't care anything about the money it might make nor the glory. I'd be willing to give it all to you off-hand. But the idea of you, LANGSTON HUGHES, trying to use the tremendous influence that you knew you had with me that someone else might exploit me cut me to the quick." Then Hurston added her trump card, a veiled hint that although they both knew that her claim to the play was questionable, she had the money and power to back it up: "I told Godmother that I had done my play all by myself, and so I did, and for the reasons stated before."

Godmother's entry into the proceedings was not by happenstance. She apparently knew that Zora was now working alone on a play that had been written in collaboration, and she chose to back Zora in the dispute. In the spring of 1930 the authors' uncertainty over whether Mrs. Mason would approve of their theatrical venture had led directly to one of their first arguments over Louise Thompson. Neither Zora nor Langston had enough money to pay her for the typing, and Thompson offered to wait for payment until the play was produced. This seems generous, but Zora saw it as a ploy; she complained to Hughes, "She resisted pay and tried to put it on a sentiment and royalty basis. Establishing the record of being the first stenog.[rapher] to try to collect royalties." Finally they spoke to Mrs. Mason about the play and obtained her permission to work together with Thompson as their typist.

Hurston's report to Hughes that Godmother was on her side was probably designed to scare him. They had already had a nasty telephone conversation during which Hughes threatened to sue her, and she was replying in kind. He was just now beginning to find some peace of mind after the breakup with his patron, and it must have been unsettling to think that Mrs. Mason might express her resentment toward him by backing Hurston's claim of authorship—perhaps even accusing him of trying to steal folklore material from her. Hurston, who knew of the anguish in his departure, may have been more than a little designing; but then, she also felt wronged. She told Arna Bontemps years later that she had been jealous of Louise Thompson, that this was a key to the dispute.

Exactly what Hurston meant is unclear; she also told Bontemps that she was not in love with Hughes.[3] In a letter to Hughes, dated January 20, 1931, Zora said, with some feeling: "Now get this straight, Langston. You are still dear to me. I don't care whom you love nor whom you marry, nor whom you bestow your worldly goods upon. I will never have any feeling about that part. I have always felt that if you had married anyone at all it would make no difference in our relationship. I *know* that no man on earth could change me towards you." She explained that she had gone off in June because "I couldn't hear myself saying unpleasant phrases to you." She had worked "the play out alone—carefully not using what was yours."

This claim to sole authorship melted away quickly when confronted by the good offices of Arthur Spingarn, when gentle persuasion brought the two friends back together again. Sorting out the sequence of events with help from Van Vechten, telling them they both were acting foolishly, Spingarn urged mutual apologies and a renewed attempt to polish the play; after all, it was a theatrical property that Van Vechten, at least, felt could be as great a popular success as *Green Pastures*. Things were smoothed over. Hurston consulted with her agent, Elizabeth Marbury, and although the preparation for the Cleveland production was tension filled, primarily because the signals from New York kept changing, it was finally agreed that Hurston would come to Cleveland by February 1 for last-minute work with Hughes. The first performance was scheduled for February 15.

Zora represented this accommodation to Godmother as a way for her to bring Langston to his senses and back into the Mason Holding Company. On January 20 she wrote Mrs. Mason that Hughes wanted to make up with his Godmother but was too emotional to come forth: "Personally I think that he has so much in him, that it is worth my swallowing and forgetting if by extending a friendly hand I can bring him back into the fold." She assured Mrs. Mason that Hughes "is ashamed of his attitude about the play," and that this enabled her to accept him once again as a co-author: "Godmother, I am so happy Langston has taken an honorable view of the thing, that I would give him part. I shant say that to him right now, but it takes all the sting out of the thing. The money didn't mean anything, Godmother, really."

Hurston arrived in Cleveland on the first of February and in a meeting with Hughes resolved their differences. They agreed to the Gilpin Players production—provided the players still wanted to do it. The players had held a conference the same evening and voted to discontinue; they were uncertain of Hurston's attitude, and the whole production had become problematical. When Mrs. Jelliffe and the leader of the players promised to reconsider, all seemed settled. "Mule Bone" could be performed in Cleveland and, if financial backing was obtained, taken to Broadway; eventually, they hoped, it would become a movie.

Overnight, however, Hurston learned that Louise Thompson had recently been in Cleveland to visit Hughes. Although Thompson's visit was part of some interracial seminars she was conducting and had nothing to do with the play, it is logical that Zora Hurston would think otherwise. She concluded that Hughes and Thompson were scheming to pirate her play, and her reaction was total anger. According to Hughes, she called Mrs. Jelliffe and berated her. She went the next afternoon to a conference at Hughes's house, where his tonsillitis had confined him to bed, and berated him, the Gilpin Players, and the Jelliffes. She even complained about the playground next door to the settlement house. She abused Hughes's mother and generally stormed and raged. Since Hughes is the only participant who left a reminiscence of this event, publicly or privately, we are dependent on his account, which obviously would not be favorable to Hurston; it is doubtful if she was quite as emphatic as his descriptions imply, or, if she was, that her behavior was without provocation. Nevertheless, Hurston's capacity for outrage was considerable, and in this instance she felt deeply wronged. She told friends in New York that she would tear Louise Thompson limb from limb the next time she saw her. Carl Van Vechten claimed that she once threw herself to the floor of his study in a tantrum over Hughes's betrayal. Needless to say, the production was called off. Hurston wired Mrs. Mason to tell of the betrayal, then left for New York, still angry, accusing Hughes of double-crossing her once again.[4]

Spingarn and Van Vechten did make some preliminary attempts to patch up the quarrel; Hurston became reconciled with Louise Thompson; and Zora and Hughes exchanged letters of a less hostile nature than their last meeting. Despite all this, "Mule Bone" was dead as a dramatic production. In March, 1931, in response to one of Spingarn's queries, Hurston replied acerbically, sending a copy of her letter to an approving Godmother:

> This is to deny your assertion that you have seen the original script. You have seen what your client *says* is the original script. You evidently forget that your client had my script out in Cleveland and I see did not hesitate to copy off some "emendations." The whole matter is absolutely without honor from start to finish and this latest evidence of trying to make a case by actual theft, "emendations" as you call them, makes me lose respect for the thin[g] altogether. From the very beginning it has been an attempt to build up a case by inference and construction rather than by fact. But all the liberal construction in the world cannot stand against certain things which I have in my possession.
>
> I think it would be lovely for your client to be a playwright but I'm afraid that I am too tight to make him one at my expense. You have written plays, why not do him one yourself? Or perhaps a nice box of apples and a well chosen corner. But never no play of mine.[5]

Hughes still had to assert his rights to the play as late as August, 1931, in conversations with Hurston's agent. In 1933 Hurston told Harold Jackman that she was thinking of revising "Mule Bone" again, and in January, 1934, she assured Van Vechten that a new version of the play was being prepared. But she more or less gave up hope for the play's production, as did Hughes. After Hurston's death he permitted the third act to be published in *Drama Critique*, but the play has never been performed or printed in full.[6]

Hughes's account of this whole episode in *The Big Sea* is discreet to the point of being self-serving. With his usual gallantry he chose not to mention Louise Thompson by name, and he nowhere suggests that a dispute over a typist was a central issue. He portrays Zora as a lively "girl," who was inhibited by village-like Westfield but made to stay there by "those backing her folklore project" who felt that it would be good for her to work quietly. He adds, "So she was restless and moody, working in a nervous manner. . . ." There are also factual errors in the *Big Sea* account, some probably resulting from slips of memory, some reflecting the interests of Hughes's case. Hughes leaves the impression that Mrs. Jelliffe had a copy of the script in hand when she first told him about it. Actually, he had to wait to see if it was the same script they had worked on together.

He nowhere mentions that in the script sent to Cleveland, Hurston had somewhat rewritten all three acts. He denies that he talked with Hurston on the phone; yet he admitted privately that this was the first thing he did on January 16 when he saw the script. He does not mention that at one point he was willing to accept only a one-third interest in the play, granting that two-thirds of it was Hurston's work. He claims that Hurston's original folktale was about two rival church factions, but he told Arthur Spingarn that the tale was about two hunters and that the idea of making them representatives of the Baptist and Methodist faiths was his own. He also claims that there was a first draft finished before Hurston went south and that it was he who was supposed to work out a final version. He reports that Hurston wrote him that she gave the play to her agent—she gave it only to Van Vechten—because he would "only take my half of the money and spend it on a girl she didn't like." He concludes in *The Big Sea,* "Girls are funny creatures."

Apart from the factual errors in this account, Hughes's construction of events is subtly designed to make Zora Hurston appear a fickle woman, representative of her sex, nervous and moody in New Jersey, and, above all, a "funny creature." In short, he presents a chauvinistic interpretation of their collaboration. Hughes's greatest omission, however, is his failure to admit that both parties were thinking of Mrs. Mason sitting in her throne-like chair on Park Avenue. When he reports in *The Big Sea* his dismay over Alain Locke's siding with Hurston, he presents Locke as a man who is as mysteriously unfair as Hurston is unstable. But Hughes knew that Locke had heard the story of the play only from Mrs. Mason and Zora. Hughes's fear of Mrs. Mason's power was such that when Spingarn reported that Locke was backing Hurston, Hughes came to doubt even Spingarn. Convinced that his lawyer was siding with the money and power in New York, at one point he asked for the return of his private papers from Spingarn's files. Zora kept Mrs. Mason abreast of the entire matter by letter—including copies of her letters to Hughes; a common refrain runs throughout: "I'd love for Langston to face me in your presence," and "I wish it were possible for Locke to get him before you and then call me in and let him state his claims."

What one is left with, finally, is speculation about an honest misunderstanding exacerbated by the special pressures both writers experienced at the time. Although Louise Thompson served as a typist, she was also a talented, brilliant woman, in the beginning a good friend to both Hughes and Hurston. She undoubtedly made suggestions as they dictated, which Hughes, at least, appreciated. Hurston, seeing her as both a personal and an artistic rival, probably did not. On the other hand, she was primarily a typist, and Hurston had every right to resent Hughes's suggestions for her participation in the production. Yet one senses that Hughes's proposal probably arose as the two young writers grew excited about their play, imagined its Broadway production, and dreamed of its success. Envisioning fame and wealth for the authors, it seems perfectly plausible for Hughes to want the third person in the room not to feel left out. "And we'll make Louise business manager" seems a logical reaction, but one that a collaborator, already suspicious of that third person, might view skeptically. Since Louise Thompson had also been supported by Mrs. Mason while working with them on the play—and since both Hughes and Louise Thompson left Mrs. Mason in late 1930, shortly before the "Mule Bone" dispute, while Hurston stayed on—Mrs. Mason's presence had to have some effect on everyone's behavior. Arna Bontemps, working on a Hughes biography up to the time of his death, felt that Mrs. Mason was the key to the entire squabble and that Zora thought Louise Thompson might pose a threat to her relations with Mrs. Mason. Apparently the play arrived in Cleveland by pure happenstance, without Hurston's approval, making Hughes's initial willingness to accuse her of wrongdoing a bit unfair. Moreover, there is little question that most of the material in the play came from Hurston, including the basic characters and situation, which were Eatonville material. Still, though Hughes admitted that it was more hers than his, this does not justify her claim to sole authorship. At one point Hughes asked, with some exasperation, why she had not asked him to bow out of their work sessions if she was so convinced that the play was hers. Zora's reply was to accuse him of stealing from her for his first novel, *Not without Laughter*.

None of this fully explains the behavior of all involved, and the circumstances surrounding the play will always remain a mystery. Hurston and Hughes were never entirely candid about their motives. One wonders if the dispute had something to do with Hurston's officially going off the payroll in March of 1931. Zora did ask Bontemps in 1939 to tell Langston that their quarrel was "the cross of her life," but the bitterness stayed with Hughes to the end. Although he tried hard to be fair to her in his autobiography, he could not easily forget the pain she had caused. Hurston never really forgave, either; when Hughes went to Cuba to regain his health and try to forget the whole episode, she remarked to God-mother: "I know Langston says he was going to Cuba, but I suspect that he is really gone to hunt up Eatonville to pretend that he knew about it all along."

The play is the thing, however, and "Mule Bone" is an interesting attempt to transcend black dramatic stereotypes. The play is set in Eatonville, the porch of Joe Clarke's store serving as the set for the first act, and the village lifestyle providing the key to the action. "Mule Bone" tries to convey the humanity of this experience from its comic side. It rejects the stock comic types of the minstrel tradition, replacing them with real human beings who get a good deal of fun out of life, but who unconsciously order their existence and give it special meaning with elaborate verbal rituals. The play's effect depends largely on the devices of verbal improvisation—sounding, rhyming, woofing—that are central to Afro-American folklore.

The major characters of the play are described by the authors as follows:

Jim Weston: Guitarist, Methodist, slightly arrogant, aggressive, somewhat self important, ready with his tongue.
Dave Carter: Dancer, Baptist, soft, happy-go-lucky character, slightly dumb. . . .
Daisy Taylor: Methodist, domestic servant, plump, dark and sexy, self-conscious of clothes and appeal, fickle.
Joe Clark: The Mayor, storekeeper and postmaster, arrogant, ignorant and powerful in a self-assertive way, large fat man; Methodist.[7]

The setting is the raised porch of Joe Clark's general store and the street in front. The porch is to stretch almost completely across the stage, with a plank bench at either end. At the center of the porch three steps lead up from the street. At the rear of the porch, in the center, is a door with Post Office painted to the left and General Store to the right. Soapboxes and small kegs are on the porch for townspeople to lounge on during the action. To one side is a large kerosene street lamp.

The time of the play is Saturday afternoon. "The villagers are gathered around the store. Several men sitting on boxes at edge of porch chewing sugar cane, spitting tobacco juice, arguing, some whittling, others eating peanuts. During the act the women all dressed up in starched dresses parade in and out of the store. People buying groceries, children playing in the street, etc. General noise of conversation, laughter and children shouting."

The first scene begins with a number of village men on the porch chewing their sugar cane and aimlessly talking. One of the regulars soon arrives carrying a hock bone of "Brazzle's ole yaller mule," an animal that is an Eatonville legend: "so skinny you could do a week's washin on his ribs for a washboard, and hang 'em up on his hip bones to dry," so mean that he died on his back with his feet straight in the air, "too contra'y to lay down on his side like a mule orter and die decent." The bone was found down by the lake, where the village had gone to give the mule a mock burial only a few months earlier; its discovery produces a number of stories that illustrate the verbal talents of the porch sitters and the mulish nature of the animal. When the mule is finally buried as a conversation topic, Daisy Taylor enters the scene, much to the delight of the middle-aged men on the porch. She has a "mean walk on her," prompting one of them to say, "Yeah, man. She handles a lot of traffic! Oh, mama, throw it in de river . . . papa'll come git it." Joe Clark says that Daisy puts him in mind of "I God, a great big mango . . . a sweet smell, you know, with a strong flavor, but not something you could mash up like a strawberry. Something with body in it." The stage directions at this point are particularly interesting: the authors feel compelled to warn that the scene must be played to avoid sexual stereotypes. After Joe Clark's remarks there is to be "general laughter, but not obscene," and the actors are directed to comment admiringly but not lasciviously on Daisy's sexuality.

The play's two major conflicts are introduced, first, when the men remark on how Jim Weston and Dave Carter seem to be losing their friendship over Daisy, an unavoidable circumstance since "wimmen is something can't be divided equal," and second, when the Methodists and Baptists on the porch begin playfully to dispute each other. One Methodist says, "Y'all Baptist carry dis close-communion business too far. If a person ain't half-drownded in de lake and half et up by alligators, y'all think he ain't baptized, so you can't take communion wid him." In response, one of the Baptists tells a story about a Methodist minister's son who, because he can never get enough to eat, leaves home and goes to hell. He returns on a wintry day after seven years, and his father is overjoyed to have him back. The father invites him into the house where eight fellow Methodist pastors are sitting around the fireplace and eating. The minister asks his son how hell was, and his son replies, "It's just like it is here . . . you cain't git to de fire for de preachers."

The major conflict in act 1 is between Jim and Dave. They enter as the best of friends, good-natured rivals for Daisy's affection. When one of the men on the porch suggests that Daisy may be after their money, Jim assures him that there will be no gold dug from him, since he "wouldn't give a poor consumpted cripple crab a crutch to cross the river Jordan." Dave agrees that this will not work with him either, for he "wouldn't give a dog a doughnut if he tree a terrapin." In their attempt to impress Daisy they sing for her:

> Got on the train
> Didn't have no fare,
> But I rode some,
> I rode some.
> Got on de train,
> Didn't have no fare,
> But I rode some,
> But I rode some,
> Got on de train,
> Didn't have no fare,
> Conductor asked me what I'm doing there
> But I rode some.
>
> Grabbed me by the neck,
> And led me to the door
> But I rode some,
> But I rode some.
> Grabbed me by the neck

> And led me to the door
> But I rode some,
> But I rode some.
> Grabbed me by the neck,
> And led me to the door,
> Rapped me cross the head with a Forty-Four,
> But I rode some!

The two men begin to argue over Daisy, and their rivalry becomes intense. A child calls out, "Fight, fight, you're no kin. Kill
one 'nother, won't be no sin." The argument comes to blows, and in
the course of the fight Jim reaches down, picks up the mule bone,
and knocks Dave out. This causes an uproar. Some of the
townspeople exit to minister to the wounded Dave; the others
arrest Jim and escort him to Joe Clark's barn, where he will be kept
until trial on Monday. Daisy is left in stage center at the curtain,
asking petulantly, "Now, who's gonna take me home?"

The setting for act 2 is the interior of the Macedonia Baptist
church, where the trial will take place. The scene begins with the
townspeople filing in to take their places on either one side of the
church or the other, Jim's Methodist supporters on the right and
Dave's Baptists on the left. The two groups begin to trade insults as
they wait for the mayor and the principals to arrive. When these
men do enter, it is suggested that the trial begin with a hymn, and
the two congregations rise to sing simultaneously—the Baptists
using "Onward Christian Soldiers" to try to drown out the
Methodists' "All Hail the Power of Jesus' Name."

The legal niceties of the trial center around whether or not a
crime was committed. Jim admits to hitting Dave but denies that it
is a criminal offense. The Methodist minister argues persuasively
on this point: "Naw, he ain't committed no 'ssault. He jus' lammed
Dave over de head, dat's all. (Triumphantly) Yuh see y'all don't
know whut yuh talkin 'bout. Now I done set in de court house an'
heard de white folks law from mornin till night. . . . You got tuh
have uh weapon to commit uh 'ssault. An' tain't in no white folks'
law and tain't in dis Bible dat no mule bone is no weapon."

The Methodists are not to have the final word, for the Baptist
minister then quotes Judges 18:18 about Samson's warfare. Since
the jawbone killed three thousand, the hock bone, coming from the

dangerous part of the animal, must be a lethal weapon; thus there
was a crime. The Methodist minister still objects, but is squelched
when Joe Clark tells him to be quiet: "You may be slick, but you kin
stand another greasin." Jim is banished from the town for two years
as punishment. The mayor ends the trial, and the act, by announcing that those in the audience who are near blows must get off the
church grounds before they start to fight, and they can't "use no
knives, an' no guns, an' no mule bones. Court Dismissed."

The setting for act 3 is a high stretch of railroad track through
a luxuriant Florida forest. It is near sundown. At the rise of the
curtain

> there is no one on stage, but there is a tremendous noise and hubbub
> off-stage right. There are yells of derision and shouts of anger. Part of
> the mob is trying to keep Jim in town and part is driving him off. After
> a full minute of this, Jim enters with his guitar hanging around his
> neck and his coat over his shoulder. The sun is dropping low and red
> through the forest. He is looking back angrily and shouting at the
> mob. A missile is thrown after him. Jim drops his coat and guitar and
> picks up a piece of brick and makes threatening gestures of throw-
> ing it. He runs back the way he came, hurling the brick with all
> his might.

Jim's opening speech indicates how drastically the town's harmony has been disrupted: "I'm out o' yo' ole town. Now just let
some of you ole half-pint Baptists let yo' wooden God an' cornstalk
Jesus fool you into hittin' me. . . . I'm glad I'm out o yo ole town
anyhow. I ain't never comin back no mo, neither. You ole ugly-
rump niggers done ruint de town anyhow. Lawd, folks sho is
deceitful. I never woulda thought people woulda acted like that."

Before long Daisy enters, claiming that she has been worried
about him. He does not believe her: "Ashes to ashes, dust to dust,
show me a woman that a man can trust." She convinces him of
her affection, however, and they have made up by the time Dave
enters. The two men, sobered by the violence of their quarrel,
become involved in a courting ritual designed to prove to Daisy
who loves her most. Dave says to Daisy, "I love you harder than de
thunder can bump a stump—if I don't—God's a gopher." Jim
complains to Daisy, "You ain't never give me no chance to talk wid

you right," and Daisy says, "Aw, you'all better stop dat. You know you don't mean it." Dave responds, "Who don't mean it. Lemme tell you somethin, mama, if you was mine, I wouldn't have you countin no ties wid you pretty lil toes. Know whut I'd do. . . . I'd buy a whole passenger train and hire some mens to run it for you." Jim is not about to be outdone: "De wind may blow, de door may slam, Dat stuff you shooting ain't worth a dam. I'd buy you a great big ole ship—and then, baby, I'd buy you a ocean to sail yo ship on." Dave's reply is in kind: "A long train, a short caboose, Dat lie whut you shootin, ain't no use. . . . Miss Daisy, know what I'd do for you? . . . I'd come down de river ridin a mud cat and leadin a minnow." But Jim will not be topped: "Naw he ain't—he's just lyin—he's a noble liar. Know whut I'd do if you was mine? . . . I'd make a panther wash you dishes and a gator chop yo wood for you." This verbal play goes on for some time. When Dave asks Jim how much time he would do for Daisy on the chaingang, Jim answers, "Twenty years and like it." Dave exults, "See dat, Daisy, Dat nigger ain't willin to do no time for you. I'd beg de judge to gimme life."

Again, a significant stage direction interrupts the dialogue. By telling us that "both Jim and Dave laugh," Hurston and Hughes were trying to show the sense of verbal play and rhetorical improvisation characteristic of Eatonville generally, and Joe Clark's storefront porch specifically. To use a term from the professional folklorist, Hurston and Hughes were attempting to dramatize the "oral-aural worldview" of a black community that contrasts with the typographic-chirographic structure of white middle-class thought. The contest is a ritual, designed to defuse the violence implicit in the conflict, to channel the aggression into mental rather than physical terms. The manner in which the courting contest ends suggests its ritualistic nature: Dave says to Daisy, "Don't you be skeered, baby. Papa kin take keer o you [To Jim: suiting the action to the word] Countin from de finger back to de thumb. . . . Start anything, I got you some." Jim is taken aback: "Aw, I don't want no more fight wid you, Dave." Dave replies, "Who said anything about fighting? We just provin who love Daisy de best."

The courting rapidly ends when the men discover that Daisy expects that whoever she chooses will work for her white folks —washing windows, sweeping the sidewalk, hoeing, raking, and gardening. Although she has tentatively chosen Jim, the prospect of such employment causes her charms to diminish in his eyes. Dave has a similar reaction. The two men are reconciled, and Daisy is left without either of her lovers.

Daisy tells them, "Both of you niggers can git yo' hat on yo' heads and git on down de road. Neither one of y'all don't have to have me. I got a good job and plenty men beggin' for yo' chance." Jim heaves a sigh of relief: "Dat's right, Daisy, you go git you one them mens whut don't mind smellin' mules—and beatin' de white folks to de barn every mornin'. I don't wanta be bothered wid nothin' but dis box." Dave supports his buddy: "An' I can't strain wid nothin' but my feets." The good friends return to Eatonville, daring any townsman to deny them access to their community.

Although much could be said about this play, the most pertinent commentary has to do with authorial intention. Hughes claimed that they were trying to create "the first real Negro folk comedy"; what he meant, I think, was that the play could be contrasted with the black low-life comedy familiar to American theatergoers as the minstrel show. The minstrel stereotypes of the lazy, sensual, ignorant, laughing darky had been challenged by revue performers of the twenties such as Bert Williams; they had triumphed in spite of the tradition, on the basis of sheer talent rather than their stage roles. Hughes and Hurston, however, attempted to create a play that would be a part of what Larry Neal has called "a truly original Black literature," an attempt to portray the black folk in such a way as "to establish some new categories of perception; new ways of seeing a culture which had been caricatured by the white minstrel tradition, made hokey and sentimental by the nineteenth century local colorists, debased by the dialect poets, and finally made a 'primitive' aphrodisiac by the new sexualism of the twenties."[8] "Mule Bone" did not quite achieve this new mode of perception, but one wonders if its authors' continued collaboration might not have produced a breakthrough. The play that was originally titled "The Bone of Contention" turned out to be truer to its title than to its purposes.

One example will suffice to show the subtlety of the authors' attempt. The courting ritual in the final scene is a traditional mode of verbal lovemaking among southern rural black folk, very possibly

African in origin. Some of the first recorded rituals appeared in 1895 in the *Southern Workman*, Hampton Institute's monthly magazine, written by a man remembering the tradition-bearer role that an old slave named Uncle Gilbert contributed to the quarters. Young slaves would go to Uncle Gilbert to learn "courtship's words and ways." The old man believed that to "git a gal wuth havin'" a man "mus' know how to talk fur her." Such talking involved a combination of testing the girl's availability, her willingness to be courted, her skill in solving riddles, and the suitor's ability to display verbal improvisation. Certain formulas and rhymes were set, others improvised at the moment. The slave's proof of his affection is similar to Dave's purchase of a passenger train or Jim's buying an ocean; yet the point is not the implausibility, but the imagination that thought of the example: "Kin' lady, ef I was to go up between de heavens and de' yearth an drop down a grain of wheat over ten acres of land an' plow it up wid a rooster fedder, would you marry me?" Courtship testimony from the folklorist in 1895—"Dear Miss, ef I was starvin' an' had jes one ginger cake, I would give you half, an' dat would be de bigges' half"—is similar to "Mule Bone"'s "If I was dead and any other woman came near my coffin de under taker would have to do his job all over—'cause I'd git right up and walk off." A direct connection between act 3 of "Mule Bone" and traditional courting rituals is found in Dave's question to Daisy following one of his boasts: "Miss Daisy, ma'am, also ma'am, which would you ruther be—a lark a flyin' or a dove a-settin, ma'am, also ma'am?" In 1895 Portia Smiley reported the following as a part of courting rituals in Alabama: "Kin' lady, are yo' a standin' dove or a flyin lark? Would you decide to trot in double harness, and will you give de most excrutish pleasure of rollin' de wheels of de axil, accordin' to your understandin'?" In *Negro Folk Rhymes* (1922), Thomas W. Talley includes a similar exchange in the section on courtship rhymes:

> (He) Is you a flyin' lark or a settin' dove?
> (She) I'se a flyin' lark, my honey Love.
> (He) Is you a bird o' one fedder, or a bird o' two?
> (She) I'se a bird o' one fedder, w'en it comes to you.
> (He) Den, Mam:
>   I has desire, an' quick temptation,
>   To jine my fence to yo' plantation.[9]

Hurston had collected such rituals and had sent some examples to Hughes. They were both aware that the genre was traditional, and they were consciously trying to represent for the stage the folk-loric context. If successful, they would be able to undermine the minstrel image of the ignorant black man using long words he did not understand, the stereotyped conception of black verbal art. If done well, the verbal duel would prove the rhyming ability, the ingenious improvisation, and the general wit of black folk, who were anything but ignorant or inarticulate. A play like "Mule Bone" could challenge racist preconceptions by remaining true to the traditions of "lowly" black peasants; it could destroy stereotypes by entertaining a "cultured" audience with the functional comedy of the Eatonville community. The courtship rituals were behavioral manifestations of a unique aspect of Afro-American subculture, and "Mule Bone" could represent that behavior in a way never realized on the stage before. Contrary to Van Vechten's hope that "Mule Bone" might become another *Green Pastures*, the effect of the play was intended to be quite different. *Green Pastures*, a well-meaning play by a white author, was redeemed from comic stereotypes by black actors. As Du Bois pointed out, it was "de Lawd," Richard Harrison, who had "guided a genial comedy into a great and human drama."[10] "Mule Bone" was "Negro folk comedy" written by two black authors who designed the play around the traditional verbal behavior of black people. Its comedy came not so much from the authors' wit as from the skillful verbal communication of the folk. It never came to the stage because of the authors' quarreling over authorship. Yet in a sense it was written by neither Hurston nor Hughes. Much of the language in the play belonged to the race itself, making the argument over its ownership even more ironic.

The "Mule Bone" quarrel took place at the same time Hurston was working hard to prepare her field notes for public attention, and the play was influenced by an uncertainty about the best medium for popular consumption of Afro-American folklore. The presentation model offered by Boas and Locke was the scientific article—a most unliterary genre—in which the scholar subordinated personality in order to report factually on phenomena observed. The audience addressed was narrow and extraordinarily fickle, with a minimal capacity for an immediate effect on popular attitudes. Fretting scrutiny would follow the announcement of her findings, and even scholarly acceptance would be no guarantee of validity; as Hurston had seen with scientists like Odum and Johnson, truth was a culturally determined commodity. The adaptation of folklore for the stage in "real Negro theatre" was a possibility she had been drawn to for years. Yet the form necessarily compromised the authenticity of the lore; a hunter's quarrel had to become a lover's triangle to heighten dramatic conflict. The personal essay, published in forums accessible to the general public, had much to recommend it, but most mass-circulation magazines were controlled by whites, and if black material was accepted at all, it had to deal with the "race problem."

Hurston knew that her collections were unique and that she could write well enough to publish her findings in whatever form she chose. She spent considerable effort searching for the most appropriate medium. Songs and dances lost all life when confined to the written page. The communal participation in a tale-telling session disappeared when the folklorist intruded on the event. Yet a collector was not faceless. How did she report dispassionately on what she called the "boiled down juice of human living"? How did she camouflage a belief that "the greatest cultural wealth of the continent" was being ignored, and that she was the person who could save it from obscurity? Hurston used many presentational media in the next few years; all her efforts were characterized by an evangelical zeal for the form and substance of black folk art. Her missionary spirit was submerged in her scholarly attempts, left implicit in her career as a producer of folk drama, and proudly proclaimed in popular essays and *Mules and Men*. Hurston came to speak for the esthetic consciousness of the "Negro farthest down," and her message was broadcast in many creative forms. "Mule Bone" was only one attempt to find an individual art commensurate with the native esthetics of her people.[11]

NOTES

1. This chapter is based primarily on a file of letters and documents found in HUAL, including a twelve-page explanation of the entire "Mule Bone" episode written by Hughes and sent to Spingarn on Jan. 21, 1931; a complete version and

other partial versions of "Mule Bone" in HUAL; LH, *The Big Sea* (New York: Hill and Wang, 1963), pp. 311-34; and my interview with LTP, June 22, 1976, in New York City. In reconstructing the episode from these materials and other published and unpublished sources, I have noted only those documents not in HUAL, and I have quoted directly only from Hurston's letters. My account comes chiefly from the following in HUAL: ZNH to LH, Jan. 18, Jan. 20 (two telegrams), Feb. 14, Mar. 18, 1931; ZNH to Mrs. Mason, Jan. 20, Mar. 25, Apr. 18, Aug. 14, 1931, Mar. 27, 1932; ZNH to AS, Mar. 25, 1931; ZNH to AL, Oct. 29, 1934; LH to ZNH, Jan. 16, 22, 27 (two letters); LH to AS, Jan. 21, 24, 26, 27, 30, Feb. 3, Mar. 6, 15, Aug. 14, 1931; LH to AL, Jan. 28, 1931; AL telegram to LH, Jan. 29, 1931; AS to LH, Jan. 24, 27, 28, Feb. 5, Mar. 5, 1931; LTP to LH, Jan. 28, 1931; Rowena Jelliffe to AS, Jan. 30, 1931; return receipt, registered mail, for LH to ZNH, Jan. 18, 1931; copyright notification for "Mule Bone," received Jan. 22, 1931.

2. This letter is not complete. Apparently Hughes kept the last page of the letter for personal reasons. As it has survived, the letter breaks off at this point: "I didn't intend to be evasive. With anyone else but you I could have said a plenty. Would have done so long ago but I have been thinking of you as my best friend for so long, and as I am not in love with anyone, that [rest of letter missing]."

3. Arna Bontemps to LH, Nov. 24, 1939 (JWJYale).

4. RH interview with LTP, June 22, 1976, New York City; Bruce Kellner (CVV's biographer) to RH, Sept. 1, 1972, quoting a letter from CVV to LH.

5. ZNH to AS, Mar. 25, 1931 (HUAL).

6. ZNH to Harold Jackman, Dec. 15, 1933; CVV, manuscript notes, "Introduction to the James Weldon Johnson Memorial Collection," p. 224; ZNH to CVV, Jan. 22, 1934 (JWJYale).

7. "Mule Bone: A Comedy of Negro Life," by LH and ZNH, mimeographed (HUAL).

8. Larry Neal, "A Profile: Zora Neale Hurston," *Southern Exposure*, 1 (Winter, 1974), 162.

9. Portia Smiley, "Folklore and Ethnography," *Southern Workman*, 24 (1895), 15; Frank D. Banks and Portia Smiley, "Old Time Courtship Conversation," ibid., pp. 14–15, 78, reprinted in *Mother Wit from the Laughing Barrel*, ed. Alan Dundes (Englewood Cliffs, N.J.: Prentice-Hall, 1973), pp. 251-57 (Dundes's notes to this article are especially valuable); Thomas W. Talley, *Negro Folk Rhymes* (New York: Macmillan, 1922), p. 135.

10. W. E. B. Du Bois, "Besides the Still Waters," *Crisis*, 38 (May, 1931), 169.

11. ZNH, "Folklore," typescript, Florida Federal Writers' Project, ca. 1938 (FHSP); ZNH to Thomas E. Jones, Oct. 12, 1934 (Fisk); ZNH, *Dust Tracks on a Road* (Philadelphia: J. B. Lippincott, 1942), p. 185.

7 ≋≋ The Will to Adorn

Folklore, Hurston said, is the art people create before they find out there is such a thing as art; it comes from a folk's "first wondering contact with natural law"—that is, laws of human nature as well as laws of natural process, the truths of a group's experience as well as the principles of physics.[1] These interpretations of nature, called "unscientific" or "crude," often turn out to be wise and poetic explanations for the ways of the world. The parable of the hog under the oak tree—he eats and grunts but never looks up to see where the acorns are coming from—teaches less about the laws of gravity than about the importance of looking for the sources of good fortune; "Ah means tuh prop you up on ev'y leanin' side" is a more graceful explanation of peer support than the jargon of the behavioral psychologist. The folklorist learns to respect these wondering beliefs as artistic expressions which teach one how to live, and Hurston had learned a good deal about both art and life by the time she returned to New York in March, 1930.

She was faced, however, with a scholarly problem: what was her responsibility in explaining the lore? What stance should she take in relation to the folk? How could she make others see this great cultural wealth? The final answers to these questions came in *Mules and Men*. Not published until 1935, the book was largely completed between March, 1930, when Mrs. Mason first paid her rent for the room in Westfield, and September of 1932, when Zora received her last payments from her patron. By the time readers shared in her discoveries, some of her ideas were six years old, and Hurston had gone on to a career as a novelist and dramatist. As she organized her field notes during 1930–32, she conceptualized black folklore, exploring the ways black history affected folk narratives, hypothesizing about racial characteristics in traditional communication. This mature conception of folklore changed only slightly over the years, and it antedates her best work as an artist. Even though her first novel was published prior to *Mules and Men*, it was written after she had completed the folklore research. In a sense, her career as a folklorist ended when she finished with her field notes, and after the fall of 1932 she usually conceived of herself as a creative writer—even when writing about folklore.

The struggle to shape a book, or, more accurately, a series of books, from her mass of folklore texts became increasingly difficult. She worked fiercely for the remainder of 1930, producing a number of different drafts; by the end of the year she was still confident, but much more tentative than when she had returned from her travels. She told Mrs. Mason, "I shall wrassle me up a future, or die trying." Publishers had various ideas for revision, but no one was ready to publish. Mrs. Mason's support could not go on forever, and the white woman was growing less patient with each rejection. Zora told her, "I am trying to get some bone in my legs so that you can see me standing so that I shall cease to worry you." Publishers had been telling her that she was too impatient, that "large sums are not invested without due thought." In the child-like imagery that Mrs. Mason enjoyed and Hurston knew would charm, she told her Godmother that she would be more aggressive: "So watch your sunburnt child do some shuffling. That is the thing that I have lacked—the urge to push hard and insist on a hearing."[2]

Early in 1931 Hurston decided to forget about her folktale manuscript and write up the story of Cudjo Lewis. A second manuscript, on conjure, was making the rounds after extensive editing by Locke, but the initial reports were not promising. Soon she had a hundred-page manuscript about Lewis entitled "Barracoon," but her old friend, the editor Harry Block, said it was not ready. Her strength was being stolen by infected tonsils, and she felt "only half of me at least a third of the time." Block also read the conjure manuscript and urged her to make it less a mere collection, more a "geographical and chronological narrative." It all added up to rejection—a failure symbolized by Mrs. Mason's formal severance of their contract on March 31. Zora could continue to work her manuscripts, but she would do so without regular subsidy.[3]

In June the city of New York began to tear up the street outside her apartment on West Sixty-sixth, and the noise "disorganized" her; she fled upstate to a friend's house in Pleasantville, struggling again with *Mules and Men*, the folktales that seemed to have the best chance of publication. Mrs. Mason gave her $100 for the month, but it was not enough. She asked for more, and assured Godmother that "by July first I can make some arrangements that will help tide me over." Zora was troubled at being suddenly thrust out from under the Mason umbrella, and the peace of mind she needed to work was frequently missing. She searched for employment, even proposing to Godmother that she be provided capital so that she could "set up as a chicken specialist" who would "be ready to supply hot fried chicken at a moment's notice to the carriage trade." She explained, "Why do I think of this? I firmly believe that I shall succeed as a writer, but the time element is important."[4]

One of the Great Depression's unemployed, Zora still wrestled with *Mules and Men* during the summer of 1931; she felt that she was beginning to find herself: "It has been a most intense summer, not a moment of relaxation, but I like working hard." In the fall the hard work began to pay off. George Antheil, the French composer, contacted her on behalf of Nancy Cunard, to ask if she had any folklore essays that Cunard might use in an anthology she was putting together. Zora was waiting for a chance to demonstrate the richness of her material, and after getting Godmother's approval, she met with Antheil. He went away with six essays, charmed and dazzled by this dynamic woman who he believed "would be the most stolen-from Negro in the world for the next ten years at least."[5]

The daughter of British nobility, Nancy Cunard was a flamboyant personality who made frequent trips to Harlem in the late twenties and early thirties, much to the delight of the journalists who luridly reported her every move. Despite her family's opposition, she had fallen in love with a black musician, and a major reason for assembling the anthology was to dedicate it to him. She solicited contributions world wide, ending up with a massive volume entitled *Negro* that took years to prepare for publication.

Hurston's essays in *Negro* probably were written in 1930, since there are a number of favorable references to Hughes that would not have been likely after "Mule Bone." The most analytical part of her series, "Characteristics of Negro Expression," represents her first attempt to summarize her field work. The article is disorganized, indicating that the task proved difficult. Its thesis, however, is clearly stated: creativity is the distinguishing characteristic of black American culture. In an assimilationist era, when black intellectuals stressed the similarities between the races, Hurston proudly affirmed the cultural differences. She believed that an esthetically oriented black subculture provided a striking contrast to the imaginative wasteland of white society. Although she did not use the phrase, she was really saying that whites were culturally deprived because they lacked soul.

Hurston's emphasis throughout *Negro* is on communicative forms as distinctive black art. She identifies one of the key characteristics of Negro expression as the "will to adorn." Hurston speaks of black people's taking what white civilization offered and ornamenting it for their own use. She cites how the "American Negro has done wonders to the English language" by introducing unusual metaphors and similes ("one at a time, like lawyers going to heaven") double-descriptive adjectives (*low-down, kill-dead*), and verbal nouns (*funeralize*). Her explanation for this behavior is that "the stark, trimmed phrases of the Occident seem too bare for the voluptuous child of the sun, hence the adornment. It arises out of the same impulse as . . . the making of sculpture."

However interesting, Hurston's *Negro* essays were not a comprehensive account of black American folklore, and *Mules and Men* remains her primary expression of the extensive research of 1927–32. It sought a publisher in several versions between 1929 and 1934, although the book's core—seventy folktale texts—remained the same. Zora left New York for Eatonville in the spring of 1932, and the change in scenery became a major factor in enabling her to complete the book. She told friends that she was happier in Eatonville than she had been for years: "The air is sweet, literally sweet." She planted a garden with black-eyed peas, watermelons, pole beans, and okra, then got to work again on the book, revising all day and sitting on her porch at night to listen to the mockingbirds and smell the honeysuckle. By July the garden had been victimized by dry weather, but *Mules and Men* was finished and being typed.

By September the manuscript was looking again for a publisher. The tales that in 1929 were "going to press" became, in 1932, "folk tales with background so that they are in atmosphere and not just stuck out into cold space. I want the reader to see why Negroes tell such glorious tales. He [the Negro] has more images within his skull than any other human in circulation. That is why it makes me furious when some ham like [Octavus Roy] Cohen or Roark Bradford gets off a nothing else but and calls it a high spot of Negro humor and imagery." She told another correspondent that she was leaving out all the theory and restricting the book to the folktales themselves and how they were collected. The manuscript made the rounds for the next two years; not until her first novel, *Jonah's Gourd Vine*, had been accepted by Lippincott's did it find a publisher. Even then, her editor, Bertram Lippincott, asked her to revise the manuscript, "so that it would not be too technical for the average reader." Since the publisher wanted a "$3.50 book," she also selected and condensed from her earlier hoodoo article to add to the volume, the hoodoo section forming the last third of the book. This material (discussed earlier) was changed only slightly from the 1931 version in the *Journal of American Folklore*.[6]

With *Mules and Men* scheduled for publication in February, 1935, she became afraid that Papa Franz might not endorse such an unscientific work:

> Longwood, Fla.
> Aug. 20, 1934

Dear Dr. Boas,

I am full of tremors, lest you decide that you do not want to write the introduction to my "Mules and Men." I want you to do it so very much. Also I want Dr. [Ruth] Benedict to read the ms. and offer suggestions. Sort of edit it you know.

Mr. Lippincott likes the book very much and he will push it. His firm, as you know probably publishes more text-books than any other in America and he is conservative. He wants a very readable book that the average reader can understand, at the same time one that will have value as a reference book. I have inserted the between-story conversation and business because when I offered it without it, every publisher said it was too monotonous. Now three houses want to publish it. So I hope that the unscientific matter that must be there for the sake of the average reader will not keep you from writing the introduction. It so happens that the conversations and incidents are true. But of course I never would have set them down for scientists to read. I know that the learned societies are interested in the story in many ways that would never interest the average mind. He needs no stimulation. But the man in the street is different.

So *please* consider all this and do not refuse Mr. Lippincott's request to write the introduction to *Mules and Men*. And then in addition, I feel that the persons who have the most information on a subject should teach the public. Who knows more about folk-lore than you and Dr. Benedict? Therefore the stuff published in America should pass under your eye. *You* see some of the preposterous stuff put out by various persons on various folk-subjects. This is not said merely to get you to write the introduction to my book. No. But an enormous amount of loose writing is being done.

My best to Drs. [Otto] Klineberg and [Gladys] Reichard.

Most Sincerely
Zora Hurston[7]

Boas granted his approval after checking the manuscript for authenticity. He stressed in his preface that it offered "the intimate setting in the social life of the Negro" absent from previous folklore books.

The intimacy of *Mules and Men* is an obtained effect, an example of Hurston's narrative skill. She represented oral art functioning to affect behavior in the black community; to display this art in its natural setting she created a narrator who would not intrude on the folklore event. A semifictional Zora Neale Hurston is our guide to southern black folklore, a curiously retiring figure who is more art than life. The exuberant Zora Hurston who entertained the Harlem Renaissance is seldom in evidence in *Mules and Men*. In her place is a self-effacing reporter created by Hurston the folklorist to dramatize the process of collecting and make the reader feel part of the scene.

Mules and Men begins in Eatonville as the young collector returns to her native village to listen to "all them old-time tales about Brer Rabbit and Brer Bear" and "set them down before it's too late." Her next stop is Polk County, "where they really lies up a mess and . . . where dey makes up all de songs." By the time she leaves central Florida, her seventy tale texts have been recorded and two-thirds of the book written. She then heads for New Orleans to collect hoodoo. This last section describes the rituals of five different power doctors she studied with, supplemented by an appendix listing conjure paraphernalia and root doctors' prescriptions.

It is easy to overlook Hurston's craft as she mediates between self and material in this presentation; yet she shaped *Mules and Men* in somewhat the same manner in which Henry David Thoreau created a unified experience in *Walden*. His two years of residence at Walden Pond were condensed into a book structured around one year's seasonal cycle. Hurston condenses a two-and-a-half-year expedition into one year and nine months, with a one-year segment (Florida) and a nine-month segment (New Orleans). Her two return trips to Eatonville in 1927 and 1928 are telescoped into a single dramatic homecoming. At the end of the Florida section she claims to have "spent a year in gathering and culling over folk tales." Actually, she spent only six months in Florida before heading for New Orleans; but a year makes possible an orderly transition to the new section: "Winter passed and caterpillars began to cross the road again. . . . So I slept a night, and the next morning I headed my toe-nails toward Louisiana."

Hurston had to provide a frame for the adventures and insights of a complicated experience; she had to select from a multitude of situations and personalities. One way to unify could have been, like Thoreau, to stress the personal significance of the various encounters. Yet *Mules and Men* is ultimately a book very different from *Walden* precisely because Hurston did not choose the personal option. Her adventures go purposely without analysis. While Henry David Thoreau embarks on a voyage of spiritual discovery, Zora Neale Hurston always remains close to the shore, her description directed away from the inner self toward the words of her informants.

The scholarly folklorist of the thirties was expected to subordinate self to material in the interests of objectivity. The intent was to leave the emphasis on the folklore texts that were being added to the "body of knowledge." After describing the corpse, the folklorist could perform an autopsy in order to learn how the living organism functions. The cold text, isolated on the page for scientific study, implied the living folk, but the folk themselves were secondary to the artifact collected. Hurston knew such training, and she had written two articles for the *Journal of American Folklore* in a proper scholarly manner, dispassionately reporting her texts and offering theories about the relationships between Afro-American and Afro-Caribbean folklore. As she acknowledged in the letter to Boas, she was well aware of how *Mules and Men* departed from this accepted mode, and she worked hard to make sure that her personal saga did not become the book's focus. Much of *Mules and Men* is a simple reporting of texts, an approach similar to that of another prominent black folklorist of the era, J. Mason Brewer. Yet Hurston also breathed life into her narrative by presenting herself as a master of ceremonies, a transitional voice. Instead of observing a pathologist perform an autopsy, the reader keeps in sight a midwife participating in the birth of the body folklore. The effect is subtle and often overlooked. *Mules and Men* does not become an exercise in romantic egoism; it celebrates the art of the community. Where the reader of *Walden* comes away with visions of separating from society in order to gain spiritual renewal, the reader of *Mules and Men* learns a profound respect for men and women perpetuating an esthetic mode of communication; the impulse is not to isolate oneself, but to lose the self in the art and wisdom of the group.

From the very first pages Hurston creates a self-effacing persona inviting the reader to participate in collective rituals. She arrives in Eatonville knowing that even if she had given birth to a "Kaiser baby" (that is, had had a child by the Kaiser), she would still be John and Lucy's daughter; college degrees mean nothing to the loafers on the store porch, for they will define their community in their own terms, identify people according to kin. They are like African *griots* who preserve the genealogy of a tribe which has not developed a written language. Hurston portrays herself as a town prodigal returned to collect "them big old lies we tell when we're jus' sittin' around here on the porch doin' nothin." She is an educated innocent whose memory of the village folklore has been diminished by her urban experience and academic study; she must renew community ties.

Yet Arna Bontemps testified that many of the *Mules and Men* tales were a vivid part of Hurston's storytelling repertoire when she arrived in New York, well before she ever studied or collected folklore. A short story like "Black Death" confirms the accuracy of that memory. The Zora Neale Hurston of *Mules and Men*, then, is deliberately underplaying her knowledge of Eatonville so that the reader will not feel alienated. Because she saw from a dual perspective, both from within the community and from without, Hurston the writer could select those experiences which would attract the reader and let the folk speak for themselves. Hurston the narrator admits only to a desire to hold a microphone up to nature.

This technique, which falls somewhere between scientific reporting and personal journalism, produces a repeated pattern of experience. Zora becomes a member of each community she encounters, accepted by virtue of race and her sympathy with communal ways. As she is accepted, so is the reader. Each experience in the book begins with her admission into a group. She starts in Eatonville not only because she can collect there without harm or danger, but also because she is by definition of birth a part of that village. When she travels to Polk County she must establish a right to be in the lumber camp before she can retire and listen. She is accepted only after a fugitive status is created, an extensive repertoire of folksongs is demonstrated, and her "$12.74 dress from Macy's" is put away. The dress is an obvious example of Hurston's narrative posing for the benefit of her readers. Given her collecting experience, it seems extremely unlikely that Zora Neale would actually be wearing such a dress in a lumber camp. Yet by suggesting a certain distance between herself and her informants—symbolized by her clothes—the narrator manages to ease the reader into the alien environment.

There is an ambivalence here that has sometimes been criticized. Is *Mules and Men* about Zora Hurston or about black folklore? If the former, the self-effacement makes the reader want to know more about what was going on in her mind, more about her reaction to the communities that embraced her. If the latter, there is a need for folklore analysis. Are hoodoo candles a form of fire worship comparable to the use of fire in Christian ritual? What is the cross-cultural structure of the folktale? These deficiencies are the price Hurston paid for her two-fold purpose. On the one hand, she was trying to represent the artistic content of black folklore; on the other, she was trying to suggest the behavioral significance of folkloric events. Her efforts were intended to show rather than tell, the assumption being that both behavior and art will become self-evident as the tale texts and hoodoo rituals accrete during the reading.

Hurston presents the artistic content in the communication by stressing how "facile" is the "Negro imagination." The participants in a tale-telling session are all capable of verbal adornment: "A'nt Hagar's son, like Joseph, put on his many-colored coat and paraded before his brethren and every man there was a Joseph." A story-teller is someone who can "plough up some literary and lay-by some alphabets." The scholar never steps in to stress the ingenuity of a particular metaphor or the startling effectiveness of an image. She wants to reveal, in her words, "that which the soul lives by" in a rural black community; although there was a need for a transitional voice, only by stepping to the background could she allow unhampered expression. She did not want her readers reminded too often that a folklorist was there to take it all down, a fact that is reflected in her collecting technique. When Alan Lomax asked her, in 1935, "How do you learn most of your songs?" he got a precise reply: "I just get in the crowd with the people and if they sing it I listen as best I can and then I start to joinin' in with a phrase or two and then finally I get so I can sing a verse. And then I keep on until I learn all the verses and then I sing 'em back to the people until they tell me that I can sing 'em just like them. And then I take part and I try it out on different people who already know the song until they are quite satisfied that I know it. Then I carry it in my memory. . . . I learn the song myself and then I can take it with me wherever I go." Hurston's technique, in other words, was to become one of the folk, a position which did not allow for the detachment of the analytical observer.[8]

This deliberate lack of analysis places a special responsibility on the reader. The tales of *Mules and Men* are *not* quaint fictions created by a primitive people. They are profound expressions of a group's behavior. Readers have frequently overlooked the fact that Hurston represented this in a tale-telling context; because context is often essential to understanding an orally rendered story, they have also failed to perceive the behavioral significance of the particular tale. The following story illustrates the point:

You know Ole Massa took a nigger deer huntin' and posted him in his place and told him, says: "Now you wait right here and keep yo' gun reformed and ready. Ah'm goin' 'round de hill and skeer up de deer and head him dis way. When he come past, you shoot."

De nigger says: "Yessuh, Ah sho' will, Massa."

He set there and waited wid de gun all cocked and after a while de deer come tearin' past him. He didn't make a move to shoot de deer so he went on 'bout his business. After while de white man come on 'round de hill and ast de nigger: "Did you kill de deer?"

De nigger says: "Ah ain't seen no deer pass here yet."

Massa says: "Yes, you did. You couldn't help but see him. He come right dis way."

Nigger says: "Well Ah sho' ain't seen none. All Ah seen was a white man come along here wid a pack of chairs on his head and Ah tipped my hat to him and waited for de deer."

The tale is best understood as that of a slave outwitting his master, thwarting his plans, then escaping punishment by retreating behind the mask of stupidity. The mask is effective because the white man's racism disables him; to believe that the black man is intelligent enough to trick him would destroy his presumption of superiority. It is the time-honored technique of "puttin' on ole massa." The key to this interpretation of the tale is the context Hurston established for it. It is told on a day when the men in the logging camp discover that they will not have to work because the train to transport them to the woods has been sent away. This occasion produces a series of tales about how white men have imposed labor on blacks, and how black men and women, since slavery, have both suffered from the imposition and cunningly escaped it. Directly preceding the antlers–pack-of-chairs story are an account of a field hand saying "More rain, more rest," then changing his line to "more rain, more grass" when asked to repeat by the overseer; speculation that there "must be something terrible wrong" at the lumber camp "when white folks get slow about putting us to work"; a story about a straw boss "so mean dat when the boiler burst and blowed some of the men up in the air, he docked 'em for de time they was off de job"; a tale about John's tricking Ole Massa into holding a bear by the tail; and a story about how the white man obtained pen and ink from God and "so ever since then de nigger been out in de hot sun, usin' his tools and de white man been sittin' up figgerin', ought's a ought, figger's a figger, all for de white man, none for de nigger." Hurston's context emphasizes white unfairness and black ingenuity. Applied to the story, this context suggests that when the slave refuses to shoot, he is escaping from labor, just as the field hand did when it rained; his action protests the presumption that a white skin endows one with the right to give orders or demand a Jim Crow acknowledgment —the tip of the hat—of white authority. The slave's explanation enables him to gain ascendency in a situation where those orders have not been carried out. The ludicrous picture of a white man with a rack of chairs on his head undermines the image of white dominion. The denouement places the master in a situation where his wishes have been thwarted, his appearance has been mocked, and his own labor has been made as unrewarding as that of his slaves.

One characteristic of folktales is that they lose their original context. Like ancient religious rituals, the form is kept while the function changes; the meaning gets lost. Hurston knew that this was a characteristic of all folklore, and her immediate report of this revolutionary tale, no doubt taken from her field notes, reveals how the function of the tale may have been distorted. Providing an interpretation of the tale that sharply contrasts with Hurston's context, the teller concludes, "Some colored folks ain't got no sense, and when ah see 'em like dat, ah say, 'My race but not my taste.'"

It may be that this was simply the closing formula for the tale, passed from generation to generation, insuring that its ironic content would not be detected. If so, the closing lines mean exactly the opposite of what they say. But as one commentator has argued about the phrase "if you're black get back," expressions like "some colored folks ain't got no sense" may feed racial self-hate and encourage a group inferiority complex.[9] There is a fine line between seeing the tale as cunning and seeing it as ignorance.

One must challenge any interpretation of ignorance because there are so many overt protest tales in *Mules and Men* of the same form and structure as the antlers–pack-of-chairs story. The pattern is basically that a dutiful slave performs a task and the situation results in a thwarting of the master's wishes. The tales from the

John-Marster cycle are almost all of this general structure; the emphasis is upon John's ingenuity in turning a situation to his advantage. As one storyteller puts it, "John sho was a smart nigger now. He useter git de best of Ole Massa all de time." Hurston observed that this quality makes John "the wish fulfillment hero of the race."

The following story makes a mockery of the myth of the dutiful slave and the legend of the good master; it also makes comic reference to the stereotype of white womanhood and the illusions of obedience:

> Ole John was a slave, you know. And there was Ole Massa and Ole Missy and de two li' children—a girl and a boy.
>
> Well, John was workin' in de field and he seen de children out on de lake in a boat, just a hollerin'. They had done lost they oars and was 'bout to turn over. So then he went and tole Ole Massa and Ole Missy.
>
> Well, Ole Missy, she hollered and said: "It's so sad to lose these 'cause Ah ain't never goin' to have no more children." Ole Massa made her hush and they went down to de water and follered de shore on 'round till they found 'em. John pulled off his shoes and hopped in and swum out and got in de boat wid de children and brought 'em to shore.
>
> Well, Massa and John take 'em to de house. So they was all so glad 'cause de children got saved. So Massa told 'im to make a good crop dat year and fill up de barn, and den when he lay by de crops nex' year, he was going to set him free.
>
> So John raised so much crop dat year he filled de barn and had to put some of it in de house.
>
> So Friday come, and Massa said, "Well, de day done come that I said I'd set you free. I hate to do it, but I don't like to make myself out a lie. I hate to git rid of a good nigger lak you."
>
> So he went in de house and give John one of his old suits of clothes to put on. So John put it on and come in to shake hands and tell 'em goodbye. De children they cry, and Ole Missy she cry. Didn't want to see John go. So John took his bundle and put it on his stick and hung it crost his shoulder.
>
> Well, Ole John started on down de road. Well, Ole Massa said, "John, de children love yuh."
>
> "Yassuh."
>
> "And Missy *like* yuh!"

"Yassuh."

"But 'member, John, youse a nigger."

"Yassuh."

Fur as John could hear 'im down de road he wuz hollerin', "John, Oh John! De children loves you. And I love you. De Missy *like* you."

John would holler back, "Yassuh."

"But 'member youse a nigger, tho!"

Ole Massa kept callin' 'im and his voice was pitiful. But John kept right on steppin' to Canada. He answered Old Massa every time he called 'im, but he consumed on wid his bag.

Mules and Men is not all folktales and hoodoo. It also contains many sayings, fragments of songs, rhymes, and legends. There is little explanation, however, of how all this folklore assumes any significance beyond the immediate entertainment. When a story ends "Stepped on a pin, de pin bent / And dat's de way de story went," it is up to the reader to speculate about the traditional closing formulas of the folktale. In actuality, the rhyme functions like "and they lived happily ever after." When one man tells another, "Don't you like it, don't you take it; here's mah collar, come and shake it," there is no explanation of how verbal formulas direct aggression into socially acceptable forms. Rhyme as a creative response to a prosaic world goes unanalyzed. Brer Rabbit is not discussed as an allegorical figure symbolizing black cunning. Hoodoo as an alternative science with a worldview as valid as any other goes unexplored. The universality of trickster figures like John goes unanalyzed. There is deliberately no cross-cultural reference, although many of the tales also appear in other cultures. There is no reference at all to the scholarship in the field.

These remarks are not necessarily criticisms, for Hurston makes *Mules and Men* a very readable folklore book. But the subordination of Hurston the scholar to Hurston the narrator can cause the reader to miss her attempts to provide the data for scholarly study. There is a consistent and subtle attempt, for example, to demonstrate how traditional tales are perpetuated. A small boy is encouraged to speak, then praised for the "over average lie" he contributes to the lying session. Presumably he will grow up a storyteller. When Joe Wiley asks if anyone has heard the story about "Big Talk," the reply is, "Yeah, we done heard it, Joe, but Ah kin hear it some 'gin." When a man says he will tell a tale for his wife, his listener responds, "Aw, g'wan tell de lie, Larkins if you want to. You know you ain't tellin no lie for yo' wife. No mo' than de rest of us. You lyin' cause you like it." There is psychic satisfaction in the repetition of narratives.

Similarly, Hurston summarized the difference between an active and a passive tradition-bearer:

> "Didja ever hear de White man's prayer?"
> "Who in Polk County ain't heard dat?" Cut in Officer Richardson.
> "Well, if you know it so good, lemme hear *you* say it," Eugene snapped back.
> "Oh, Ah don't know it well enough to say it. Ah just know it well enough to know it."

The active tradition-bearer produces the text; the passive tradition-bearer is a self-correcting force insuring that the text will not be altered in any significant way. [10]

The tale-telling context is often humorous, a kind of game-playing; but tales can also be used to deflect a potentially violent encounter. Hurston chose such an event to give one of her infrequent, indirect explanations of folkloric process: how proverbs serve as religious texts for a secular moment, and how specially gifted storytellers function as secular priests. The following exchange demonstrates Hurston's contextualism; the explanation occurs in the form of an argument between the storytellers:

> Jim Allen commented: "Well, you know what they say—a man can cackerlate his life till he git mixed up wid a woman or git straddle of a cow."
> Big Sweet turned viciously upon the old man. "Who you callin' a cow, fool? Ah know you ain't namin' *my* mama's daughter no cow."
> "Now all y'all heard what Ah said. Ah ain't called nobody no cow," Jim defended himself. "Dat's just an old time by-word 'bout no man kin tell what's gointer happen when he gits mixed up wid a woman or set straddle of a cow." "I done heard my gran'paw say dem very words many and many a time," chimed in Larkins. "There's a whole heap of them kinda by-words. Like for instance:
> "'Ole coon for cunnin', young coon for runnin',' and 'Ah can't dance, but Ah know good moves.' They all got a hidden meanin', jus' like de Bible. Everybody can't understand what they mean. Most

people is thin-brained. They's born wid they feet under de moon. Some folks is born wid they feet on de sun and they kin seek out de inside meanin' of words."

"Fack is, it's a story 'bout a man sittin' straddle of a cow," Jim Allen went on.

The narrative which follows concerns a man who sends his son to college and upon his return asks him to help milk a troublesome cow. The boy "scientifically" concludes that to kick the milking bucket the cow has to hump her body; thus, the way to stop the hump is to tie his father astraddle her back. The cow breaks loose and goes down the road with her rider, to the great amusement of the "uneducated."

While logically this story has little to do with the argument preceding it, imagistically it is appropriate. The lying session provides for exactly this kind of free association. By the time the tale is finished, the argument, which was playful to begin with, has been forgotten. The listeners are ready for another story. One of the effects here is to emphasize folklore as a dramatic vehicle for community expression. There is a drama involved in all tale-telling contests, and the potential violence of these actors is disarmed by the verbal ceremonies they participate in. They are performing before an audience in a ritualized way, just as the tale-teller becomes the main actor and the story spun is a form of one-act "play"—the verbal noun being particularly appropriate. The dispute becomes both a serious matter and a game. Hurston's attempt to recreate this dramatic context in *Mules and Men* was informed by considerable thinking about the relationship between folklore and drama.

She had written earlier about the dramatic properties of black expression. She saw drama permeating "the Negro's entire self" and felt that "every phase of Negro life is highly dramatized. No matter how joyful or sad the case there is sufficient poise for drama. Everything is acted out. Unconsciously for the most part of course. There is an impromptu ceremony always ready for every hour of life. No little moment passes unadorned."[11] Later she would state, "To those who want to institute the Negro theatre, let me say it is already established. . . . The real Negro theatre is in the jooks."[12]

Mules and Men, for all her attempts to indicate a context for each tale and to hold together the disparate experience, left out much of the drama. The storyteller gestured, postured, winked, and laughed during the story; yet it was difficult to present these actions without distracting from the texts themselves. At the time, Hurston considered the presentation of texts her primary responsibility.

"Mule Bone," however, had opened her eyes to the possibilities of representing black folklore on the stage, and she became increasingly interested in the theatrical potential in her collections. While the material was inherently dramatic, it needed a context for true understanding. That context was not a formal concert of spirituals, or even a volume of prose, but a social performance. The beauty of the performance derived not from the melodious arrangement of musical notes, or from the colorful presentation of tale texts or hoodoo rituals; it came from the living racial genius informing the behavior of the folk community. Hurston turned to drama in order to represent that genius.

Hurston's employment for Mrs. Mason formally ended on the last day of March, 1931, but Godmother continued to support her on an irregular basis until September of 1932, when *Mules and Men* was finally completed. She may have done so because of Zora's frustration with her manuscripts and her increasing interest in the theater; Mrs. Mason feared that Zora would use the materials in a way she did not approve of. What "Mule Bone" symbolized—a dramatic representation of the texts and contexts of black American folklore—was very much on Hurston's mind in the fall of 1931. She had completed one prose account of her folktales, but no one wanted to publish it; the idea of presenting folklore on the stage became especially attractive, despite Mrs. Mason's reservations. She began to seek out theatrical people, and, as usual, her talent was quickly recognized. She was contacted by Forbes Randolph, a producer preparing a revue called *Fast and Furious*. Scheduled for September, with an all-star cast, *Fast and Furious* billed itself as "a colored revue in thirty-seven scenes." At first Zora hoped to write the book for the revue. In the end, she wrote three sketches, and made her dramatic debut as a pompom girl in a sketch about a football game; her sister cheerleader was a pre-"Moms" Jackie Mabley.[13]

Hurston's other job on *Fast and Furious* was to assist with the directing—a task that must have been educational. The level of entertainment can be gathered from her courtroom scene, in which Tim Moore served as "his honery of the court" and sentenced a prisoner to serve nine years wearing a muzzle in a watermelon patch. "At Home in Georgia" shows Hurston's more serious touch, the program carefully explaining that the version of "John Henry" rendered in this segment was probably the oldest in America.

Fast and Furious opened on September 15, 1931, received poor reviews, and folded in a week. The expectations for a black show during the period are well illustrated by the review in the *Brooklyn Eagle*. Trying to praise, the reviewer described movement without frenzy, "a novelty among darky entertainments"; its relaxed tempo revealed that "these Negroes do not perspire nearly so much as most of those who have come before."[14]

Hurston was not surprised by the reviews. She had complained bitterly that Randolph was a "stupid and trite" showman who "squeezed all Negro-ness out of everything and substituted what he thought out to be Negro humor." But her attempt to earn a living independent from Mrs. Mason suffered a blow in the show's closing, for she collected only $75 instead of the $500 she had expected. Broke again, she was forced to submit a detailed expense account to an increasingly parsimonious Godmother to secure additional living expenses; not only was she expected to list purchases of string beans and canned fruit, she also felt compelled to cite expenditures for colon medicine (three dollars) and sanitary napkins (sixty-five cents).[15]

There were many theater people interested in her talent, and she soon began writing sketches for another revue, *Jungle Scandals*. As the title suggests, it was less than satisfactory labor and she had no illusions about her employment: "I do not consider either of the revues as great work, but they are making the public know me and come to me, and that is important." After *Jungle Scandals* died a mercifully early death, she began to think about a revue that would be artistically true to the folk situation, without Broadway adulteration. Tentatively titled "Spunk," the songs and dances would be of the people. She told Mrs. Mason: "I like the idea of going from the light and trivial to something better, rather than coming down from a 'Spunk' to 'Fast and Furious.' The public will see growth rather than decline." Later she said that Mrs. Mason had once suggested she restrict her collecting to folktales and hoodoo rituals, but that she had found music an integral part of all folkloric events: "My people are not going to do but so much of anything before they sing something." She possessed a great deal of music by the time she returned to New York and began shaping her collections into book form, and it was the chief reason she was so much in demand. When she decided to organize her own show, she took this musical material to the composer, arranger, and choir director Hall Johnson.[16]

The twenties had been an era of black choirs, and Johnson was probably the most famous choral director in the country. The Hall Johnson Choir had been prominent in the success of *Green Pastures* in 1930. Hurston wanted Johnson to prepare the music for performance by his choir, but after holding it for a number of months he returned it. She claimed he did so with the statement, "The world was not ready for Negro music unless it were highly arranged. The barbaric melodies and harmonies were simply not fit for musical ears." She may have overstated Johnson's reaction, but there is little question that they had different conceptions of folk music. The son of a Georgia minister, Johnson knew the original settings for the spirituals, and he had made his career stylizing them in highly arranged concerts. His drama *Run Little Chillun*, a success on Broadway in 1933, was praised highly; reviewers called it a collection of "beautifully sung spirituals at a concert," pointing out that "in their singing the voices of men and women and children are blended perfectly."[17]

Hurston envisioned a more authentic performance than Johnson was interested in, and she took his rejection as a personal challenge. In October, 1931, after the demise of *Jungle Scandals*, she collected a group of performers and began rehearsing them in her apartment. She organized some of her best material for presentation in revue form, adding Bahamian dances to worksongs, children's games, conjure ceremonies, and jook scenes. The dancers were a special find, recruited largely from among immigrants born in Bimini. With names like Motor Boat and Stew Beef, and with great exuberance, they added a flavor of Caribbean carnival to the staging. Hurston put it all together in a show called *The Great Day*, loosely structured around a single day in the life of a railroad work camp. Then she went back to Johnson with troupe and script and asked him to reconsider. He agreed to give it a try, but after a December, 1931, concert had been set, the collaboration fell apart. She claimed that he deliberately sabotaged the arrangement, then stole some of her material for adaptation in *Run Little Chillun*. Indeed, the ending of Johnson's play was staged exactly as Zora had staged the finale for *The Great Day*.

Without funds of her own, Hurston sought help from Mrs. Mason once again, asking for the money to finance a performance. She needed $200 for advertising and $250 for costumes. The car Mrs. Mason had given her was being sold to put a deposit on the theater, and she had pawned her radio to pay subway fares for her group of dancers and singers. With fifty-two people in the cast, Zora was desperate: "I am on the brink of putting the thing over and it will break my heart to fall down." The *Great Day* concert had become so important because it was Hurston's opportunity to bring authentic black folk culture to a New York audience. The folklore she had collected, which no one wanted to publish in written form, would live in music and movement. She admitted that she had "worked harder on this than anything else except collecting it . . . now that I have gone thru the rigors of it, and worked so hard to get it into shape, I am willing to make any sacrifice, meet any terms to give it a chance of success." Mrs. Mason came through once again; her backing was for a single evening at the John Golden Theater on Sunday, January 10, 1932.[18]

The advertisement for *The Great Day* stressed that the material was "true Negro music" rather than "highly concertized" spirituals: "the spirituals in 'Great Day' are fresh and without the artificial polish of re-arrangement. The dancers have not been influenced by Harlem or Broadway." Mrs. Mason's adviser, Alain Locke, wrote the program notes for the concert; he emphasized that Hurston was providing a special glimpse into life behind the veil. From Stephen Foster to contemporary Broadway, black people had been presented in "adulterated approximations," primarily because "these folk have always had two arts—one for themselves and one for the amusement and beguilement of their masters." Few people have been able to break through that "instinctive make believe and 'possum play' of the Negro peasant." Referring to Hurston's "three years of intimate living among the common folk in the primitive privacy of their own Negro way of life," Locke found *The Great Day* a rare sample of the "pure and unvarnished materials from which the stage and concert tradition has been derived." He concluded that "all who wish to know the true elements of this Negro heart and soul" should welcome the performance.[19]

This enthusiasm, according to Zora, was late in coming; but Locke's interest in the authenticity of the material was appropriate. The show included much of the material from *Mules and Men*, and the sequence of the day's activities follows roughly the sequence of events in the sawmill camp portion of that book: rising, work, sermon, jook. Although a full script has not survived, the content can be inferred from the program, reviews of the performance, and reminiscences of the audience and performers. Hurston was often to use the same materials in the next few years, as *The Great Day* became the core of a continuing effort to bring legitimate folklore to theater and concert audiences.[20]

The show began with daybreak, a shack-rouser awakening the railroad camp by knocking on doors and singing:

> Wake up, bullies, and git on de rock.
> 'Tain't quite day light and it's four o'clock.
>
> Wake up, Jacob, day's a breakin'.
> Git yo' hoe cake a bakin and yo' shirt tail shakin'.

The workers were next seen laboring to build a railroad, punctuating their efforts with the songs of a singing liner; they worked in a rhythm fitting the task at hand—the swinging of a pick, driving of a spike, or lining of a rail. (The settings from *Savage Rhythm*, which was currently playing at the John Golden, added a mossy backdrop.) Their verses frequently had both rhythmic and social significance:

> Cap'n got a pistol and he try to play bad,
> But I'm going to take it if he make me mad.
> Shove it over! Hey, hey, can't you line it?
> Ah, shack-a-lack-a-lack-a-lack-a-lack-a-lack-a-lack.
> Can't you move it? Hey, hey, can't you try?

At dusk, after a hard day's work, the men returned to the quarters to rest, while their children played traditional games such as "Chick-Mah-Chick" and "Mister Frog." "Chick-Mah-Chick" was a counting game Hurston had collected all over the South; the accompanying chant ran:

> Chick-mah-chick-mah-craney-crow
> Went to the well to wash my toe
> When I got back my chick was gone
> What time, old witch?[21]

As night fell, an itinerant preacher gave a hard-driving sermon. The first act ended with two nonchoral spirituals from his congregation: "All You People Got to Go" and "You Can't Hide."

The second part of *The Great Day* began later in the evening at the jook. Blues were played and sung, including "Frankie and Albert," and "Cold Rainy Day": "Oh the rocks may be my pillow / Lawd, the sand may be my bed / I'll be back some cold rainy day." Also included was "Halimufack," the same blues that provoked the tom-tom beat in the short story "Muttsy":

> You may leave and go to Halimufack
> But my slow drag will bring you back
> Well-uh you may go
> But this will bring you back.
>
> I been in the country but I moved to town
> I'm a tolo-shaker from head on down
> Well-uh you may go
> But this will bring you back.
>
> Ah, some folks call me a tolo-shaker
> It's a doggone lie, I'm a back bone breaker
> Well-uh you may go
> But this will bring you back.[22]

The jook scene was supposed to be followed by a midnight conjure ceremony, but Mrs. Mason put her foot down when she saw the program; the conjure was much too special to be wasted on a Broadway audience. Thus, the finale was a rendition of "Deep River" by part of the cast on one side of the stage, counterpointed by a blues from the jook, performed by the rest of the cast on the other side.[23]

The Great Day was an unqualified success. Hurston later exulted, "The world wanted to hear the glorious voice of my people." It received good reviews, and the *Herald Tribune* hoped it would become a regular show. Sterling Brown remembers traveling from Washington to see it and being impressed with the reception. In the midst of the final applause Hurston was pushed on stage, not unwillingly, to take some bows. She spoke briefly, explaining that one reason she had staged the production was "that music without motion was unnatural with Negroes, and what I had tried to do was to present Negro singing in a natural way—with action."[24]

The only problem with *The Great Day* was at the ticket window. Although the theater was nearly filled, it did not produce enough revenue to cover expenses. After the theater rental was deducted, only $261 remained. Finding herself without enough money to pay the cast, Zora asked for an additional loan. Godmother paid grudgingly, adding the $80 owed the performers to the $530 she had previously lent for costumes, advertising, and stage settings. Zora had hoped that a Broadway producer would pick up the show, but no one came forth. Mrs. Mason made clear that her $610 was a loan, and she asked her lawyer to draw up legal papers to confirm the transaction. That agreement illustrates again the unusual pressures on Zora Hurston as she attempted to bring Afro-American folklore to a popular audience.[25]

Zora knew that the concert had been an artistic success. She also knew that Godmother thought of the theater as a sordid, "commercial" enterprise. Mrs. Mason still held technical legal rights to the fruits of Hurston's labor—the very songs, dances, and tales that had fascinated the audience at the John Golden—and she was determined to force Zora to publish these materials in books, no matter what her dramatic inclinations. When the concert was over, Hurston made another attempt to liberate her collections. She asked Mrs. Mason, "Now, I wish to know your pleasure as to the future of the material in the concert. It is yours in every way, and while I know it has great commercial value, I have no right to make a move except as you direct." She added that she could not pay off her loan without some freedom to develop these materials.[26]

Mrs. Mason's reply was a legal agreement, signed in January, 1932, which listed the portions of the concert program which Zora could use for "theatrical purposes." It also specified that "the other data and material which you have collected on the mission for which I sent you shall not be used for any purpose without further permission from me, particularly that dealing with the conjure ceremony and rituals." The agreement ended with Godmother's admonition to Zora: "In all that you do, Zora, remember that it is vital to your people that you should not rob your books which must stand as a lasting monument in order to further a commercial venture." Nothing could describe the perils of patronage more clearly. From an academic perspective Mrs. Mason's concern was legitimate, and her assessment correct: *Mules and Men* is indeed a "lasting monument" to black people. Yet could Mason money really *purchase* the traditions of black folk, along with the imaginative uses Zora Hurston might make of them? A stage version of *Mules and Men* might have had the same impact as the televising of Alex Haley's *Roots*. The lost possibilities illuminate Hurston's personal plight. In 1932, at the height of the Depression, she was expected to write books about the folklore she had collected, while she was also restricted from using that same folklore to prepare a presentation for a mass audience, or even to buy the time to enable her to write the books. One might argue that Zora should have repudiated Mrs. Mason's arrogance and challenged her rights; but if she had done so, would *Mules and Men* have been published? For better or worse, Zora did what seemed easiest at the time. She took what was left her and used the liberated portions of the *Great Day* program to earn a living while she waited for her books to be written, her talents to be recognized.[27]

The Great Day became one of Hurston's chief preoccupations for the next three years, and a major source of both money and fame, although she claimed that she had no intention of making concert "her field." *Theatre Arts* took photos of the cast and published one of them in the April issue. On March 29 the troupe gave a performance at the New School for Social Research; the Folk Dance Society presented the West Indian dances at the Vanderbilt Hotel. It was almost impossible to keep a group together for infrequent appearances, and Hurston disbanded the troupe after the New School performance. There was a good deal of enmity in the parting, primarily because the West Indians claimed that she still owed them money. The dancers refused to give up the drums and snake-skin costumes until she made restitution.[28]

Hurston's immediate future was uncertain, and both Mrs. Mason and Locke were losing patience. In April, 1932, Locke came to New York for a talk, apparently to explain to Zora that she could no longer expect money from Godmother. He pointed out, like a professor to a student, that her apartment was far too expensive for her reduced income, and that she should be writing to black colleges about employment. The country was in the midst of economic disaster, and even Mrs. Mason was feeling it. Locke found Hurston at loose ends, without prospects, lacking even the money to buy the medicine she needed for her recurring bouts of intestinal illness. It had not helped her state of mind when Godmother arranged for her to see an expensive internist in Brooklyn; Zora had been ushered into a laundry closet, quickly examined, and then hurried out of the office. She remembered it as her "most humiliating" Jim Crow experience, and she went away feeling the "pathos" of Anglo-Saxon civilization.[29]

What she wanted to do was go south. She asked Godmother for the fare, apologizing for not making a success of her career: "I understand that both you and Alain feel that I have lost my grip on things." After some hesitancy Mrs. Mason agreed to pay her bills. On April 28 she gave Zora a ticket to Eatonville and enough cash to purchase a new pair of shoes; Zora's big toe had burst through her only pair, the ones she had been wearing since the first of the year.[30]

In late May, after she was established in Eatonville, growing her garden and working on the folktales once again, Zora received a letter from Walter White of the NAACP. He was assisting in the casting of an opera based on *Batouala*, the prize-winning novel of an African village by René Maran. Maran had done a libretto, Paul Robeson was cast in the lead, Leopold Stokowski of the Philadelphia symphony was backing it; and when the subject of dancers came up, everyone thought of Zora Hurston. She assured White that she could provide all the dancers needed and looked forward to participating. She personally offered to be a witch doctor or one of Robeson's partners in polygamy. She also deviously asked White to retrieve her drums and costumes, which he did after a great deal of negotiation ("I never heard so much West Indian in my life," he said). The production, however, never came off, and another dramatic possibility faded away.[31]

Hurston had left New York for Florida in search of the peace of mind to finally revise *Mules and Men*. She went to her native village for "quiet, atmosphere, and economical existence." Shortly after returning she made contact with faculty members at Rollins College in Eatonville's neighboring city, Winter Park, and she wrote at once to determine Rollins's interest in supporting another *Great Day*. Telling of the New York concert, she explained that "seeing the stuff that is being put forth by overwrought members of my own race, and well meaning but uninformed White people, I conceived the idea of giving a series of concerts of untampered with Negro folk material so that people may see what we are really like." She wondered if Rollins would be interested in "putting the world right on Negro expression," and she stressed that "the real Negro theatre . . . yet to be born" could come from Eatonville and their own Orange County.[32]

Robert Wunsch of the Rollins English department became interested in the concert idea, and in the late fall of 1932, after the *Mules and Men* manuscript was finished, the two of them began to train a cast for another *Great Day*. They received some financial support from the college, but Hurston made do on a shoestring budget. She recruited her performers largely from Eatonville friends and relatives, cajoling them with her own enthusiasm and the promise of the publicity. She even convinced her uncle, the Reverend Isiah Hurston, to give the sermon sequence. When her intestines flared up, she rehearsed the troupe while sitting on an inner tube to ease the pain.[33]

The concert was scheduled for a small, experimental theater. In January, 1933, the performance was given, with a new title, *From Sun to Sun*, but with virtually the same program as *The Great Day*. It was such a hit that in early February a second performance was given at Recreation Hall, the main auditorium on campus. Zora wrote Locke, "Personally I am growing. Now I am doing some of the things that we used to dream of. For one thing I have the chance to build a Negro theatre. Not just the building but the heart, the reason for the building to be." In the midst of her excitement over this success, Hurston was reminded of where she was, and of how difficult it would be to establish a "Negro theatre" in the South. She wrote Mrs. Mason, "Tickets to the general public—except Negroes. I tried to have the space set aside, but find that there I come up against solid rock."[34]

From Sun to Sun was well received, and concerts were scheduled for other Florida cities, usually to segregated houses. When they took the show to Eatonville, it was a special source of community pride. Hurston had found a way to dramatize the material she had collected, and her skill in producing folk concerts became widely known through the area. Her hope was to "work out some good nigger themes and show what can be done with our magnificent imagery." She told Mrs. Mason, "Perhaps I will never roll in wealth. That is not the point. If we can give *real* creative urge a push forward here, the world will see a New Negro."[35]

In 1933, however, theatrical producing was not a steady job in central Florida, and Zora turned again to fiction; she had not written serious fiction for six years, but she was desperate. It so happened that her own art, based on the folk arts of her people, finally won for Zora Hurston the public attention that not only established her career, but also liberated her from the entanglements of patronage.

NOTES

1. ZNH, "Folklore," typescript, Florida Federal Writers' Project, ca. 1938 (FHSP).
2. ZNH to Mrs. Mason, Nov. 25, Dec. 15, 1930 (HUAL).
3. Ibid., Mar. 25, Apr. 18, Mar. 9, 10, 1931 (HUAL).
4. Ibid., June 4, Sept. 25, 1931 (HUAL).
5. Ibid., Sept. 25, Oct. 15, 1931 (HUAL).
6. Ibid., Apr. 4, 27, May 8, 17, July 20, Sept. 28, 1932 (HUAL); ZNH to Walter White, n.d. [ca. Aug., 1932] (LCMD); ZNH to Edwin Osgood Grover, June 15, 1932 (HCUFla); ZNH to FB, Oct. 23, 1934 (APS); ZNH to CVV, Mar. 24, 1934 (JWJYale).
7. ZNH to FB, Aug. 20, 1934 (APS).
8. ZNH, *Mules and Men* (New York: Harper and Row, 1970), p. 18; Darwin Turner's introduction to this edition provides an excellent overview of the Hurston career. Alan Lomax's interview of Hurston (transcribed here by RH) and her singing folksongs may be heard on the following LCAFS recordings: 337 B1, 1879 A1-3, 3135-39, 3144 B1-4.
9. Eldridge Cleaver, "As Crinkly as Yours," *Negro History Bulletin*, 25 (1962), 127-32.
10. Hurston may be reflecting earlier folklore scholarship that asserted the

idea of an essentially immutable text transmitted from culture to culture. See, e.g., Walter Anderson, *Kaiser und Abt*, Folklore Fellows Communications, 42 (Helsinki: Suomalainen Tiedeakatemia, 1923), and Stith Thompson, *The Folktale* (New York: Holt, Rinehart and Winston, 1946), pp. 367–412.

11. ZNH, "Characteristics of Negro Expression," in *Negro: An Anthology*, ed. Nancy Cunard (London: Wishart, 1934), p. 39.

12. Ibid., p. 46.

13. Playbill, *Fast and Furious*, New Yorker Theatre, Sept. 15, 1931.

14. Arthur Pollock, review of *Fast and Furious*, *Brooklyn Eagle*, Sept. 16, 1931.

15. ZNH to Mrs. Mason, Sept. 25, Aug. 14, 1931 (HUAL).

16. Ibid., July 23, 1931 (HUAL); ZNH, "Concert," manuscript chapter of *Dust Tracks on a Road* (only part of this chapter appeared in the published book) (JWJYale).

17. ZNH, "Concert"; ZNH to Thomas E. Jones, Oct. 12, 1934 (Fisk); review of *Run Little Chillun*, *New York Times*, Mar. 2, 1933, p. 21; "Negro Folk Drama," *New York Sun*, Mar. 2, 1933.

18. ZNH to Mrs. Mason, Dec. 16, 1931 (HUAL).

19. Advertising flyer–program, "Announcing Great Day," Jan. 10, 1932 (HCUFla). See also ZNH, "Concert."

20. RH interview with Everette Hurston, Sr., Jan. 13, 1976, Bristol, Conn.; RH interview with "P" (name withheld by request), cast member of *The Great Day*, Jan. 15, 1976, New York City.

21. The "Chick-Mah-Chick" game is described in full in ZNH, "New Children's Games," typescript, Florida Federal Writers' Project (FHSP). It is a widely known game; see, e.g., William Wells Newell, *Games and Songs of American Children* (1903; rpt., New York: Dover, 1963), pp. 215–21. See also ZNH, *Mules and Men*, pp. 93, 174–82, 316–18.

22. ZNH, LCAFS 3138 B2 (RH transcription).

23. Letter of agreement between Mrs. Mason and ZNH, Jan. 20, 1932 (HUAL); RH interview with Everette Hurston, Sr., Jan. 13, 1976, Bristol, Conn.

24. ZNH to Thomas E. Jones, Oct. 12, 1934 (Fisk); review of *The Great Day*, *New York Herald Tribune*, Jan. 17, 1932; RH interview with Sterling Brown, Apr. 29, 1971, Washington, D.C.; ZNH, "Concert."

25. Balance sheet for *The Great Day*; ZNH to Mrs. Mason, Jan. 14, 21, 1932 (HUAL).

26. ZNH to Mrs. Mason, Jan. 14, 1932 (HUAL).

27. Letter of agreement between Mrs. Mason and ZNH, Jan. 20, 1932 (HUAL).

28. ZNH, *Dust Tracks*, p. 216; ZNH to Walter White, n.d. [June-July, 1932]; Walter White to ZNH, Aug. 9, 1932 (LCMD).

29. ZNH to Mrs. Mason, Apr. 4, 1932 (HUAL); ZNH, "My Most Humiliating Jim Crow Experience," *Negro Digest*, 2 (June, 1944), 25-26.

30. ZNH to Mrs. Mason, Apr. 14, 27, 1932 (HUAL).

31. ZNH, *Dust Tracks*, p. 216; Walter White to ZNH, May 31, 1932; ZNH to White, n.d. [June-July, 1932]; White to ZNH, Aug. 9, 1932 (LCMD).

32. ZNH to Thomas E. Jones, Oct. 12, 1934 (Fisk); ZNH to Edwin Osgood Grover, June 8, 1932 (HCUFla).

33. ZNH to Mrs. Mason, Jan. 6, 1932 [letter misdated by ZNH; should be 1933] (HUAL).

34. Ibid., ZNH to AL, Mar. 20, 1933 (HUAL).

35. ZNH to Thomas E. Jones, Oct. 12, 1934 (Fisk); program, *From Sun to Sun*, Feb. 11, 1933 (HCUFla); ZNH to CVV, Jan. 22, 1934 (JWJYale); ZNH to Mrs. Mason, Jan. 6, 1932 [1933] (HUAL).

8 ≋ Plough Up Some Literary

In early 1933 Zora wrote a short story entitled "The Gilded Six-Bits" and gave it to Robert Wunsch to read. He liked it, read it to his writing class at Rollins, and sent it to *Story* magazine. Published in the August, 1933, issue, the story so impressed Lippincott's that Bertram Lippincott sent her a letter inquiring if she were also working on a novel.[1]

"The Gilded Six-Bits" is one of Hurston's best short stories, an ironic account of infidelity and its human effects. A young Eatonville wife, Missie May, is seduced by a traveling Lothario whose main appeal is a gold watch charm. He promises her this gold coin, but at the moment of submission they are discovered by her husband, Joe. The cheapness of the affair and the tarnish of the marriage is represented by the coin left behind—instead of a ten-dollar gold piece it turns out to be only a gilded half-dollar. Joe cannot verbalize his grief and Missie May cannot articulate her sorrow, but they work during the next year to recapture their love, growing together again after the birth of their first child—who strongly resembles Joe. The story ends as Joe goes to the white man's store to buy his wife some candy kisses, a symbol of his forgiveness, paying for the purchase with the gilded six bits kept as a reminder of her infidelity. The clerk later says to a customer: "Wisht I could be like these darkies. Laughin' all the time. Nothin' worries em."

Hurston claimed that she had not written a word on a novel when this story caught Lippincott's attention. Still, she told him that she was indeed working on a book, and "the very next week I moved up to Sanford where I was not so much at home as at Eatonville and could concentrate more and sat down to write *Jonah's Gourd Vine*." She also admitted that the story had been in her mind since 1929, "but the idea of attempting a book seemed so big, that I gazed at it in the quiet of the night, but hid it away from even myself in daylight." She began writing on July 1, and by September 4 she could tell Lippincott that she was within a week of finishing. She completed the manuscript on September 6, talked a woman into typing it for a deferred fee, then discovered that she could not afford to mail it. She borrowed two dollars from the treasurer of the local Daughters of the Elks and sent the manuscript to Lippincott's in early October. By October 16 she had a letter of acceptance and the offer of a $200 advance.[2]

The writing of *Jonah's Gourd Vine* is a good example of Hurston's dedication to her craft. She had no means of support while writing. She lived in a one-room house in Sanford renting for $1.50 per week. She composed on a flimsy card table and survived on the fifty cents for groceries her cousin lent her each Friday. By the time the manuscript was completed, she owed eighteen dollars in rent, and on the morning of October 16 the landlord evicted her, despite the fact that she was about to earn her first money in three months by booking some folksingers for a city festival. She opened the publisher's telegram in the afternoon while purchasing shoes to replace her worn scraps of leather, and when she saw the figure $200 she "tore out of that place with one old shoe and one new one on and ran to the Western Union office." The book was published in the first week of May, 1934.[3]

Jonah's Gourd Vine is an autobiographical novel, not a document for understanding Hurston's private life. It is usually dealt with as a fictionalization of her parents' marriage—complete with her father's philandering, her mother's steady strength, and Zora's reaction to them both. The novel's main characters are named John and Lucy; their history is the Hurston family history. The plot takes John from life on an Alabama plantation to a ministerial position in Eatonville. Zora even uses the deathbed scene that she remembered as a major trauma of her youth, when her dying mother asked her to stop the neighbors from removing her pillow at the moment of passing. Having observed such parallels between art and life, the reader should be wary of accepting Hurston's fictional characters as autobiographical admissions. Often the novel portrays John and

Lucy in ways in which she apparently never thought of her parents, and the novel's plot does not follow exactly the family story. For example, there is more than a hint that Lucy's death is caused by the workings of a hoodoo doctor, an idea with dramatic potential but apparently no basis in fact.

The novel is basically John's story. He rises from a life as an illiterate laborer to become moderator of a Baptist convention in central Florida. The seeds of his tragedy are sown early: he cannot resist women, and although he is a powerful man of God when in the pulpit, he is a man among women when his inspiration ends. Lucy, who is in many ways the strongest character in the novel, serving as both a mainstay for John and a cohesive force for her family, all but wills him the backbone necessary to rise in the world. But after she dies, his lusts predominate. Eventually his congregation rejects him, and he dies just as he has begun to understand both his success and his failure.

John is the bastard child of Amy Crittenden, a slave on the Pearson plantation before Emancipation. His father was probably the master, Alf Pearson, but John never knows it, and Amy never admits it. After the Civil War, Amy struggles to make a life with her cruel husband, Ned, and it is his rejection of John that causes the teenager to leave home for work at Pearson's. John is such a strong, handsome, striking figure that he is soon sent to school and put in a position of responsibility. He also falls in love with his schoolmate, Lucy Potts, the smartest girl in the class. Even though she is barely past puberty, they become engaged. Her parents object because John is from "over the creek," without money or status; but the lovers persevere, Lucy showing great courage in the face of the familial opposition. After their marriage, John is unfaithful, although he continues to express his love. He always returns to Lucy, and he violently defends wife and family when they are endangered. The Alabama portion of the novel ends when John savagely beats Lucy's brother for collecting a debt at the time she is having her third child. John is arrested and arraigned, but Pearson secures his release, advising him that "distance is the only cure for certain diseases." He runs away, ending up in Eatonville where "uh man kin be sumpin' . . . 'thout folks tramplin' all over yuh. Ah wants mah wife and chillun heah." After they arrive, Lucy encourages John in his preaching, and he becomes a major figure in the community. The family prospers despite John's indiscretions. Eventually Lucy grows sick, and all John can think of, despite the intensity of their love, is the release her death will bring from the guilt she instills in him.

After Lucy's death John marries his mistress, to the distress of his children and parishioners. The church begins to plot his downfall, and his enemies are eventually joined by his new wife, Hattie, who has become a woman scorned. John realizes that her attraction is only physical, and he is bewildered to even find himself married. After he beats Hattie for attempting to conjure him, she asks for a divorce. John refuses to contest because he recognizes the racism of the white court. He tells his friend: "Dey thinks wese all ignorant as it is, and dey thinks wese all alike, and dat dey knows us inside and out. . . . De only difference dey makes is 'tween uh nigger dat works hard and don't sass 'em, and one dat don't." Although the church tries again to remove him, John deflects their efforts with powerful preaching. Finally, he voluntarily removes himself from the pulpit and discovers how quickly people relish the hardship of the dispossessed. One man says, "Well, since he's down, less keep 'im down." After moving to a nearby town he meets a good woman, who becomes his third wife and helps him understand some of the forces within him. He returns to preaching, but is killed accidentally just as he approaches his greatest self-awareness.

The title of the novel is addressed not so much to this total story as to a specific act of cruelty caused by the "brute-beast" in John. In a crucial scene Lucy is lying sick, on a bed that will shortly be turned to the East so that she can die peaceably. John resents this illness because it makes him feel guilty about his mistress, and he tries to take out his frustrations on Lucy. He accuses her of always complaining, "always doggin' me bout 'sumpin." When she replies with references to his love affairs, he tells her to "shut up! Ahm sick an' tired uh yo' yawin and jawin'. 'Taint nothin ah hate lak gittin sin throwed in mah face dat done got cold. Ah do ez Ah please. You jus' uh hold back tuh me nohow . . . uh man can't utilize hisself." When she replies, "Big talk ain't changin' what you doin'. You can't clean yo self wid yo tongue lak uh cat," he hits her for the first and only time of their marriage. From this moment John's descent begins. He dreams of Lucy, begs her forgiveness, and tries to forget his act. He cannot do so, and it seems likely that this scene was what

Hurston had in mind when she explained the novel's title to Carl Van Vechten: "Oh yes, the title you didn't understand. (Jonah 4:6–10). You see the prophet of God sat up under a gourd vine that had grown up in one night. But a cut worm came along and cut it down. Great and sudden growth. One act of malice and it is withered and gone."[4]

This sort of conventional analysis for *Jonah's Gourd Vine* does not address what seems most important in reading the novel. There is little preparation for the horror in the scene; for all his faults, John has not been portrayed as a man likely to slap his wife on her deathbed. Although the episode is intended to haunt John, the haunting gets lost in the hypocrisy he encounters; he becomes as much the victim of others as of himself. This is a good example of why *Jonah's Gourd Vine* cannot be properly represented by a plot outline or a discussion of character development. The novel is less a narrative than a series of linguistic moments representing the folk-life of the black South. A statement of one's independence is "Ahm three times seben and uh button." At parting people say, "See yuh later, and tell yuh straighter." At birth a child's "nable string" is buried under a chinaberry tree. A game of "Hide and Seek" is accompanied by a standard rhyme, probably adapted from jump-rope chants:

> Ah got up 'bout half-past fo'
> Forty fo' robbers wuz 'round mah do'
> Ah got up and let 'em in
> Hit 'em ovah de head wid uh rollin' pin.
> All hid? All hid?

In the critical speeches of the novel, characters express themselves in the traditional metaphors of the culture. An enemy of Lucy's announces, "Ah means tuh beat her 'til she rope lak okra, and den again Ah'll stomp her 'til she slack lak lime." When John proposes, he asks Lucy if she pays attention to birds. She deliberately misunderstands him, referring to a folk belief about the blue jay, who goes "to hell ev'ry Friday and totes uh grain uh sand in his mouf tuh put out de fire." But what John wants to know is, "Which would you ruther be, if you had yo' ruthers—uh lark uh flyin', uh dove uh settin?" He proposes in a ritual (discussed earlier) handed down from slavery; somewhere he was taught the words and ways of courtship, the poetic ceremonies that adorned life under an oppressive system.

Hurston's purpose in the novel, as she stated in a letter to James Weldon Johnson, was to emphasize this quality in her characters' lives. John was to be "a Negro preacher who is neither funny nor an imitation Puritan ram rod in pants. Just the human being and poet that he must be to succeed in a Negro pulpit. I do not speak of those among us who have been tampered with and consequently have gone Presbyterian or Episcopal. I mean the common run of us who love magnificence, beauty, poetry and color so much that there can never be too much of it."[5] The preacher as poet is the dominant theme in the novel, and it is the quality of imagination—his image-making faculty—that always redeems John's human failings. When in the pulpit, John is an inspired artist who consecrates language. He can speak as God creating the world:

> I am the teeth of time
> That comprehended de dust of de earth
> And weighed de hills in scales
> That painted de rainbow dat marks de end of de parting storm
> Measured de seas in de holler of my hand
> That held de elements in a unbroken chain of controllment.

Yet this inspiration is only an elevated form of the verbal skill common to the group; he can also say, "Ahm jus' lak uh old shoe —soft when yuh rain on me and cool me off, and hard when yuh shine on me and git me hot."

As the two passages indicate, John's poetic powers operate in both spiritual and physical worlds; he is a poet who attempts to reconcile the secular and the religious, the spirit and the flesh. Hurston told James Weldon Johnson shortly after the book was published:

> I suppose that you have seen the criticism of my book in The New York Times. He means well, I guess, but I never saw such a lack of information about us. It just seems that he is unwilling to believe that a Negro preacher could have so much poetry in him. When you and I (who seem to be the only ones even among Negroes who recognize the barbaric poetry in their sermons) know that there are hundreds of

preachers who are equalling that sermon weekly. He does not know that merely being a good man is not enough to hold a Negro preacher in an important charge. He must also be an artist. He must be both a poet and an actor of a very high order, and then he must have the voice and figure. He does not realize or is unwilling to admit that the light that shone from GOD'S TROMBONES was handed to you, as was the sermon to me in *Jonah's Gourd Vine*.[6]

The review was typical of the book's reception by the white press. Everyone liked it, primarily for its rich language. Most reviewers also demonstrated their cultural bias, so much so that even their praise becomes suspect. Margaret Wallace, in the *New York Times Book Review*, assumed that all her readers were white, and wrote that John and Lucy were "part and parcel of the tradition of their race, which is as different from ours as night and day." The *Times Literary Supplement* read the English edition and found that the marriage "is described with a delicacy not often encountered in negro fiction." The *New Republic*'s review was entitled "Darktown Strutter." The *Boston Chronicle* said that the novel "presents openly the greatest problem of the Negro in all its universality: the utterly inescapable interrelation of sex, success, and society." What Hurston objected to in the *Times* review was criticism of John Pearson's characterization; the observation was that John's climactic sermon "is too good, too brilliantly splashed with poetic imagery to be the product of any one Negro preacher." Presumably no single uneducated black man could be so poetic, so powerful in his language-shaping art. Only *Opportunity* and the *Crisis* reviewed the book without a racist bias, and the *Crisis* objected to her imposition of folklore on the story.[7]

These reviews had to be disappointing, not because they were negative—in fact, all reporters praised the book—but for their ignorance of Hurston's purpose. Although she had no control over the racist misreadings, she had been very clear about what she was trying to portray in John, and somehow the message had gotten lost. She identified his ability to pronounce the Word as a culturally derived characteristic. Belligerently, she had originally titled the novel *Big Nigger*, hardly a casual decision. She was well aware of the controversy aroused by Van Vechten's *Nigger Heaven*, and her title could only have been meant to challenge readers into acknowledging the ethnic heritage John Pearson brought to Christianity.

Hurston was defiantly stating that a "nigger," supposedly a down-trodden, inarticulate, ignorant, semi-human being, was a Christian poet of extraordinary talent. That talent exposed the incredible irony that whites should ever call John such a name; his poetic gift also gave the label special significance when used by blacks among themselves. Her original dedication in *Jonah's Gourd Vine* stressed the courage of the John Pearsons of Afro-American history, creators of beauty in the face of such epithets: "To the first and only real Negro poets in America—the preachers, who bring barbaric splendor of word and song into the very camp of the mockers."[8]

John's poetic faculties are part of the esthetic matrix of black folk culture. Hurston surrounds her character with a world of metaphor and image that makes John's ability only a heightened example of a native esthetic. If it is the language-making faculty that best defines him, that is what also defines his world. John is a man who seeks beauty, lives intensely each moment, and loves language as an end in itself. Moreover, he lives in this way because his culture honors an improvisational oral art. He tells his wife, "Lucy, don't you worry 'bout yo' folks, hear? Ahm gointer be uh father and uh mother tuh you. You jes' look tuh me, girl chile. Jes' you put yo' pendence in me. Ah means tuh prop you up on ev'y leanin' side." His human inability to fulfill this promise does not detract from the poetry in its expression. Similarly, John's vulnerability to the "brute-beast" in him coexists with his ability to thank his God for living through another night:

> We thank thee that our sleeping couch
> Was not our cooling board,
> Our cover was not our winding sheet.

Such passages eventually add up to a theory of language and behavior: an ability to adorn with words the day-to-day ceremonies of living may indicate a life of profound wisdom despite observable human failings. Although a devout prayer coming from a lustful man might be thought hypocritical, John is never a hypocrite. He lives each moment sincerely, and his life deserves to be judged on its own terms. He is both spirit and flesh, a coexistence manifest in the image-making faculty that is John's special gift.

There is a contradiction at the center of *Jonah's Gourd Vine* that arises directly from Hurston's emphasis on the transcendent moment of language growing from this gift. John creates poetry, perceiving the world in striking images, but he can never really understand himself. He is a poet who graces his world with language but cannot find the words to secure his own personal grace. A captive of the community's need for a public giver of words, after he has served his neighbors he is washed out, voided, left only with instincts which he does not understand and for which he is condemned. No passage demonstrates the book's contradiction more sharply than the long sermon that John preaches on the same communion Sunday when he will renounce his pulpit. It is a linguistic tour de force; traditional metaphors and similes well known in the black community are skillfully improvised. In fact, the language is so powerful that the reader forgets that the sermon is intended as a climax to the novel. As we become captured by John's language, his personal crisis—whether to remain as a man of God—fades to the background. John's crisis is not important to the sermon; only his language compels, and it is this separation of confused self from inspired utterance that frustrates him.

The climactic sermon begins with the text of Zechariah 13:6, taken to be about the wounds of Jesus received in the house of his friends. This text then becomes part of a traditional sermon topic: the story of God's creation of the world and his gift of Jesus as an agent of salvation. Jesus loved man since the "foundations of the world," well before "the hammers of creation / Fell upon the anvils of Time and hammered out the / ribs of the earth." Christ's long-standing love makes his betrayal by his friends all the more tragic; and it causes John Pearson, at this moment the inspired agent of God, to call upon his allegorical faculties:

> I want to draw a parable.
> I see Jesus
> Leaving heben will all of His grandeur
> Dis-robin' Hisself of His matchless honor
> Yielding up de scepter of revolvin' worlds
> Clothing Hisself in de garment of humanity
> Coming into de world to rescue His friends.

It is "with the eye of faith" that John can see his saviour: "I can see Him step out upon the rim bones of nothing / Crying I am de way / De truth and de light." He can see him "grab de throttle of de well ordered train of mercy." John's sermon becomes a vision; the visionary cries out, "I can see-eee-ee," and his congregation shares in the sight. The vision is not an ethereal abstraction, but a living metaphor, created from blood, metal, and bones. John cannot only see, he can even hear:

> I heard de whistle of de damnation train
> Dat pulled out from Garden of Eden loaded wid cargo goin' to hell
> Ran at break-neck speed all de way thru de law
> All de way thru de prophetic age
> All de way thru de reign of kings and judges—
> Plowed her way thru de Jurdan
> And on her way to Calvary, when she blew for de switch
> Jesus stood out on her track like a rough-backed mountain
> And she threw her cow-catcher in His side and His blood ditched de
>   train
> He died for our sins.
> Wounded in the house of His friends.

These images and themes were familiar to most black congregations in the South, and many of them can still be heard in black churches. The train motif is well known; Bernard Bell has identified it, for example, as the source for the epic sermon from the Reverend Homer Barbee in Ralph Ellison's *Invisible Man*.[9] But the sermon itself is the important literary event at this point in the novel—not the fact that it is John's final sermon before his congregation. One could remove the sermon, place it in another context, and the language would command virtually the same response; the power of the passage is in the text, not the context. It is instructive to note that the sermon was taken almost verbatim from Hurston's field notes; this is the reason she told Johnson that it was "handed" to her. It does not grow from the novelist's trying to create an appropriate sermon for John's crisis. It was collected from the Reverend C. C. Lovelace of Eau Gallie, Florida, on May 3, 1929, and Hurston had published it before, in her *Negro* essay. Lovelace was apparently not giving his last sermon, and presumably he had a good relationship with his congregation. The sermon's power, then, is inherent. Its effect comes primarily from the self-contained text. Although it supports the theme of the black preacher as poet and represents John's inspired powers, it gives us few insights into John's interior struggle. His language does not serve to articulate his personal problems because it is directed away from the self toward the communal celebration. John, the man of words, becomes the victim of his bardic function. He is the epic poet of the community who sacrifices himself for the group vision.

This sermon scene reveals why the novel finally becomes as frustrating for the reader as for John. The book works at cross-purposes; it is a story of individual character in which language directs one away from the individual and toward the documentation of a communal esthetic. While John should be in harmony with his community—and is, at the moment of inspiration—usually he is at odds, although his poetic gift expresses the communal experience in its highest form. If the separation between John and his group were meant to be his tragedy, then John's individual story would affect us deeply. But John is not finally a tragic character, because this potentially tragic theme becomes subordinated to the cultural argument that is used to explain his struggle.

Hurston suggests that this lack of control over one's destiny is the obvious product of Afro-American history. Uprooted from his homeland, thrown into an alien culture, the African adapted as best he could to the barbaric institutions offered him by the white man. But the African heritage was never lost. It joined with white ideas, so that when white men's music wearied, Africa inspired, just as it did during John's sermons:

> "Hey you, dere, us ain't no white folks! Put down dat fiddle! Us don't want no fiddles, neither no guitars, neither no banjoes. Less clap!"
> So they danced. They called for the instrument that they had brought to America in their skins—the drum—and they played upon it. With their hands they played upon the little dance drums of Africa. The drums of kid-skin. With their feet they stomped it, and the voice of Kata-Kumba, the great drum, lifted itself within them and they heard it. The great drum that is made by priests and sits in majesty in the juju house. The drum with the man skin that is dressed with human blood, that is beaten with a human shinbone and speaks

to gods as a man and to men as a God. Then they beat upon the drum
and danced. It was said, "He will serve us better if we bring him from
Africa naked and thingless." So the bukra reasoned. They tore away
his clothes that Cuffy might bring nothing away, but Cuffy seized his
drum and hid it in his skin under the skull bones. The shin-bones he
bore openly, for he thought, "Who shall rob me of shin-bones when
they see no drum?" So he laughed with cunning and said, "I, who am
borne away to become an orphan, carry my parents with me. For
Rhythm is she not my mother and Drama is her man?" So he groaned
aloud in the ships and hid his drum and laughed.

The only problem with this passage is that it serves poorly its
novelistic context. There is no preparation for the intensity of
feeling; yet the rhythmic ceremony is intended to symbolize John's
dilemma. His concept of spirituality springs, as Larry Neal has
argued, "from a formerly enslaved communal society, non-
Christian in background, where there is really no clean cut
dichotomy between the world of spirit and the world of flesh."[10]
The significance of the passage for John's personal troubles is unclear, however, and its implications remain unfulfilled until the
penultimate paragraph of the book. There, when John's funeral
sermon is preached, the Kata-Kumba comes to have a special
meaning:

And the preacher preached a barbaric requiem poem. On the pale
white horse of Death. On the cold icy hands of Death. On the golden
streets of glory. Of Amen Avenue. Of Halleluyah Street. On the
delight of God when such as John appeared among the singers about
His throne. On the weeping sun and moon. On Death who gives a
cloak to the man who walked naked in the world. And the hearers
wailed with a feeling of terrible loss. They beat upon the O-go-doe,
the ancient drum. O-go-doe, O-go-doe, O-go-doe! Their hearts
turned to fire and their shin-bones leaped unknowing to the drum.
Not Kata-Kumba, the drum of triumph, that speaks of great ances-
tors and glorious wars. Not the little drum of kid-skin, for that is to
dance with joy and to call to mind birth and creation, but O-go-doe,
the voice of Death—that promises nothing, that speaks with tears
only, and of the past.
So at last the preacher wiped his mouth in the final way and said,
"He wuz uh man, and nobody knowed 'im but God," and it was
ended in rhythm. With the drumming of the feet, and the mournful
dance of the heads, in rhythm, it was ended.

Hurston demonstrates here John's conflicting impulses; she implies that his struggle is more than a personal conflict. Neal has argued that in adopting Christianity blacks still were "able to shape out of it unqiue forms of expression that reflected the most retrievable, thence the most important, aspects of the pre-Christian cultural memory."[11] By evoking this African past, the Kata-Kumba and the O-go-doe are meant to explain John's struggle. He is capable of great inspiration because he has access to a pre-Christian cultural memory. He is also capable of so-called Christian immorality, an immorality arising less from personal inadequacy, Hurston implies, than from the limitations of American culture, a civilization that denies the beat of the drum, as it denies John's manhood. Yet within the action of the novel it is primarily John's function as a giver of words that denies him the self-awareness that could lead to a resolution of his problem. Hurston was writing a traditional novel of character about internalized conflict, while denying her hero the possibility of discovering the cultural dilemma that created his frustration. It is not by chance that John is killed in a deus ex machina ending, driving into the side of a train, which is throughout the novel a symbol of the white man's mechanized world. He is doomed to cultural collision rather than to self-understanding.

It is John's lack of self-awareness that has troubled so many readers, as Nick Aaron Ford realized long ago. In his *Contemporary Negro Novel* (1936), Ford objected to *Jonah's Gourd Vine* because John's "rise to religious prominence and financial ease is but a millstone around his neck. He is held back by some unseen cord which seems to be tethered to his racial heritage. Life crushes him almost to death, but he comes out of the mills with no greater insight into the deep mysteries which surround him."[12]

Hurston had not yet worked out a way to fictionally resolve either the bicultural trade-offs inherent in being black in America or the relationship between the individual artist and the community that artist serves. Nor had she discovered a way to structure a novel around the image-making faculty, the suspended linguistic moment, and to sustain that structure through plot, character, setting—all the ingredients of successful fiction. *Jonah's Gourd Vine* is a fascinating first novel, written in three months, filled with the folklore Zora had been collecting, told out of the experience of her own family. Its beauty derives from its moments of traditional, poetic language. Although the sum may be less than the parts, the parts are remarkable indeed.

The $200 advance for *Jonah's Gourd Vine* did not go far, and throughout the fall of 1933 Hurston cast about for steady employment. She had been periodically presenting *From Sun to Sun* in the Florida area, and her skill in producing these concerts brought her to the attention of Mary McLeod Bethune, president of Bethune-Cookman College in Daytona Beach. In December, 1933, she was invited by Mrs. Bethune to establish a school of dramatic arts at Bethune-Cookman, "based on pure Negro expression."[13]

Hurston went to Daytona Beach in mid-January, 1934, with high hopes, but the whole experience proved disappointing. Mrs. Bethune, soon to become nationally known as an adviser to Franklin Roosevelt, was one of the most famous and powerful women in America, founder of the National Council of Negro Women. She had built Bethune-Cookman from a girls' training school to an accredited college, and she directed its affairs with single-minded purpose. Hurston, who did not submit well to authority and was never at ease as an academic, was very soon at odds with Mrs. Bethune. She claimed later: "I found it impossible to do anything worthwhile" because there was a "student body of only 226 and the same students were needed for all the choral groups, major athletics, social groups, *various* dramatic groups at the same time." Told to write a pageant for the school's thirtieth anniversary, she was given a "script that a member of the faculty had written who had no more idea of drama than I have about relativity." She wrote Locke that she had been "plugging away in the dark"—a statement she apparently meant to be taken literally; told to turn the old hospital building into a theater, she claimed to have difficulty even getting a light bulb for her office. She asked Mrs. Bethune for more autonomy and better physical surroundings. The president was pleased when Hurston got permission to give a dramatic performance at the previously segregated Daytona Beach auditorium; however, she wanted the school's anniversary pageant to be performed. The contest of formidable wills left Zora with the auditorium, but she had to depend upon her "personal popularity with the student body" to collect a troupe and organize a performance of *From Sun to Sun*. While it was again a success, by April, Hurston had "decided to abandon the farce of Bethune-Cookman's Drama Department and get on with my work."[14]

That work included taking some of her Florida performers to the National Folk Festival in Saint Louis for concerts between April 29 and May 2. In preparation for this trip, Zora wrote Walter White to inquire about the snakeskin costumes from *The Great Day* that he had been keeping in his apartment. She apparently had thought that White was going to send them earlier, but she had not asked about them for almost two years. Suddenly, on March 8, 1934, Hurston's resentment about her West Indian dancers, some of whom had performed in Hall Johnson's *Run Little Chillun*, spilled over onto White:

My dear Mr. White;

It is extremely difficult for me [to] understand your recent attitude towards me. The one question that stands out above the others in my mind is, why you feel that I am not due any answer about my costumes? I have thought about it intensely for months and still I am too dense to see why I should not have my things. I could understand the cupidity of Hall Johnson and those miserable wretches that he corrupted for his own ends, but I cannot see why any of it should touch *you*. I am determined to know.

Sincerely,
Zora Neale Hurston[15]

This episode is important only because it shows how much Hurston resented the Hall Johnson production of *Run Little Chillun*. Not only had the dancers joined the enemy; she also felt that some of the religious scenes were stolen directly from *The Great Day*. Hurston had developed an almost proprietary interest in folk drama, and she was extremely unhappy about people encroaching on her territory. Part of this objection was philosophical: she abhorred bastardized folk material that could not be white but that had lost its "gorgeously Negro" imagery. Part was possessive: Zora Hurston had produced *The Great Day*, Zora Hurston had collected the authentic folklore, Zora Hurston should have the fame that the

Hall Johnsons were reaping. Her prickliness on this matter may have been partially the wistfulness of the provincial who feels isolated from New York resources (while in Saint Louis she met the black actor Frederick O'Neal, and advised him to take his talent to New York rather than let it die in obscurity in the Midwest). Her resentment increased as others earned money and fame from folk entertainments, while her concerts struggled to find sponsors and performers. Hurston felt that she was laboring obscurely in the wilderness, while others, even when well meaning, corrupted black traditions.

Yet it was also true that up to now her hands had been tied; Godmother still maintained control over much of the material she had collected, and would do so until *Mules and Men* was published. One of the most important things about *Jonah's Gourd Vine* was that it produced a publisher for *Mules and Men*. Lippincott's could see the interrelationship between Zora's fiction and black folklore, and they were delighted to accept it as her second book. This gave Hurston a measure of financial security she had not had for some time. It is perhaps not surprising to find that her letters to Godmother went unanswered. She told Locke, "I assumed that she did not want to hear from me anymore." Zora was on her way; her success increased the longer she stayed independent of Mrs. Mason. She told Van Vechten that she wanted to give the concert at the folk festival even if there was no money in it: "It will increase my standing as a Negro folklorist outside of calling attention to me generally." The festival did bring a wider measure of national notice, and it provided good publicity for *Jonah's Gourd Vine*, published in May. She spent the summer in a cabin in a turpentine woods near Loughman, Florida, writing fiction and revising *Mules and Men* for a popular audience.[16]

Yet even at this juncture, about to be free of a relationship that had been ambiguous at best, Zora was reluctant to break off entirely. Mrs. Mason had grown increasingly frail, and by summer it was clear that she no longer intended to exercise control over her former charge; Hurston was finally at liberty to use the products of her labor as she saw fit. Still, she told Locke, "Instead of feeling less need of godmother and more independent as success approaches me, I need her more and feel her great goodness to me more deeply. If I am acclaimed by the world and make a million in money, I would feel still that she was responsible for it."[17]

In the fall of 1934 Hurston was contacted by a Chicago group interested in sponsoring another *Great Day*. On her way north she stopped in Nashville to give a small concert at Fisk University. She greatly impressed Fisk's president, Thomas Jones, who immediately began talking to her about the possibility of joining Fisk's faculty, perhaps after further study at Yale's School of Dramatic Arts. In October, at his urging, she formally applied for a job as a drama professor and sent him a long letter about herself. She explained that after returning to New York to organize her material for scientific publication, she "began to see the pity of all the flaming glory . . . being buried in scientific journals." This had led to *The Great Day*: "I had heard all of the Negro concert artists, both soloists and groups and was depressed by the fact that while they were often great artists in the white manner, they fell so far below the folk-art level of Negroes. I thought that it was because the material was lacking . . . later I found that to be true, but in addition it was thought that no Negro vocalist was an artist unless he or she could take good Negro music and turn it into mediocre white sounds." Describing her success at Rollins, she told how Wunsch and others had "believed with me, that if Negro drama is to exist, that it must come from the life of the people." When it arrives, such drama "will be the brightest flame in America." She added, "I would love to work out some of my visions at Fisk University."[18]

Hurston was being paid $500 for *The Great Day* in Chicago. She was provided living expenses and a secretary at the Chicago South Parkway YWCA. She titled the new show *Singing Steel* and drew her cast from local talent in YWCA classes. She also gave a number of lectures, leading to an interview by the *Chicago Daily News* on November 16 that simultaneously provided publicity for the show and asserted the Hurston philosophy of folk concerts. She told the reporter:

> When musicians arrange these songs they make anthems out of them. "I've got a rainbow wrapped and tied around my shoulder" becomes "Rain, rain, rain," and "bow, bow, bow" as the conductor manipulates his hands, in a way that would make the original Negro

singer listen as curiously as you do. But sing a song as they [the folk] sing it and everybody joins in. . . . It would be a tremendous loss to the Negro race and to America if we should lose the folklore and folk music, for the unlettered Negro has given the Negro's best contribution to America's culture.[19]

Singing Steel was given on November 23 and 24, 1934. Well received, the show was again almost identical to *The Great Day* and *From Sun to Sun*. Hurston was doing her part, she said, "toward debunking the current mammy-song–Jolson conception of the Southern Negro." The public response was not nearly so important, however, as the reaction of some officials of the Julius Rosenwald Foundation who saw the performance. Much impressed, they invited Hurston to apply for a fellowship to return to Columbia and study for a Ph.D. in anthropology and folklore. Since Fisk had begun to back away from her appointment to the faculty, apparently because of uneasiness over Zora's flamboyance and some of her past conflicts, the Rosenwald offer was fortuitous. The foundation was well known for its support of black students, and apart from the prestige, a fellowship meant that in the midst of the Depression she would have the opportunity to study without financial worry. When President Jones indicated that Fisk was backing out, she sent him a tart note telling of the fellowship and suggesting he give the job to John Work, the director of the Fisk Jubilee Singers, for "if he runs out of ideas he can always come to me under the guise of friendship and get some more."[20]

It was not that the dramatic presentation of folklore had begun to pale for Hurston; but it had become increasingly frustrating. *Jonah's Gourd Vine* had been well received, and *Mules and Men* was due to be published the next year; she was becoming known as an author. Yet some black people seemed reluctant to support her dramatic efforts—witness the rejections by Bethune-Cookman and Fisk—and what especially annoyed was the inability of audiences to recognize the thought behind her theatrical productions. Perhaps a Columbia Ph.D. could command more intellectual attention.

Hurston created folk drama and folk concerts for both money and fame. She had also thought through why the stage was an appropriate medium for this material. Her dramatic productions revealed the artistic content of the Afro-American heritage; they were intended to instill race pride. When bourgeois blacks found them "primitive," counterproductive in the fight against segregation, she became exceedingly unhappy. An article she wrote for the *Washington Tribune* on December 29, 1934, just before returning to Columbia, suggests the depth of this frustration. Under the headline "Race Cannot Become Great Until It Recognizes Its Talent," Hurston went to great lengths to show that Afro-American folk expression was not subordinate to Anglo-American high art. She pointed out that Shakespeare depended heavily on English tradition, that midsummer-night observances were just as much a part of English folklore and folkways as hoodoo practices and Brer Rabbit are a part of Afro-American folkways. She repudiated those psychologically captive blacks who thought that acquiring degrees and losing black dialect would be marks of intelligence. "Who knows what fabulous cities of artistic concepts lie within the mind and language of some humble Negro boy or girl who has never heard of Ibsen." She deplored the "intellectual lynching we perpetrate upon ourselves" in emulating whites, and ended: "Fawn as you will. Spend an eternity standing awe struck. Roll your eyes in ecstasy and ape his every move, but until we have placed something upon his street corner that is our own, we are right back where we were when they filed our iron collar off."

The "something that is our own" was Afro-American folklore. Hurston was not afraid to challenge the assimilationist politics of the era by emphasizing the cultural difference of black America. She later proposed that an African faculty be brought to America to teach music and dancing: "You see, no matter how much talent a Negro may have, if he is sent to a white conservatory he is ruined. He gains technique, yes. But he loses the flavor and quality that sets him apart from white artists. What should happen is that this native quality be increased rather than obliterated. That is the only way we can ever hope to add anything to Western arts."[21]

Hurston's attempt to study for a Ph.D. was completely unsuccessful, but the fault was not entirely hers. The Rosenwald Foundation offered her $3,000 over a two-year period to get the degree, then reneged on the offer a month later. The foundation officers decided that her degree plan was unacceptable, although Franz Boas had agreed to direct her studies and the plan had been drawn up with his assistance.

Hurston was ambivalent about going back to school. Only a month before the grant was awarded she had told Fisk that she did not want black folklore buried in scientific journals. Even with the fellowship assured, she still entertained the thought of chucking it all and traveling to China, the trip contingent upon whether she could sell a song to her friend Ethel Waters. She was also perfectly frank with the foundation. She was going back to school so that her dramatic and popular presentations of folk material would be taken more seriously:

> The major problem in my field as I see it is, the collection of Negro folk material in as thorough a manner as possible, as soon as possible. In order for the collection to [be] exhaustive, it must be done by individuals feeling the materials as well as seeing it objectively. In order to feel it and appreciate the nuances one must be of the group. In order to see it objectively one must have great preparation, that is if [one is] to be able to analyze, to evaluate what is before one.
>
> In my humble opinion, it is almost useless to collect material to lie upon the shelves of scientific societies. It should be used for the purpose to which it is best suited. The Negro material is eminently suited to drama and music. In fact it *is* drama and music and the world and America in particular needs what this folk material holds.[22]

Although this does not sound like the language of the dedicated scientist, Hurston still looked forward to the Columbia study. She wrote Boas that the "great news" was that she would be returning to work for her doctorate. Although her earlier efforts to get Mrs. Mason to pay for such study were unsuccessful, now she had plenty of support. The last paragraph of her letter shows the enthusiasm of the moment, and perhaps some of Zora's skill in soliciting Boas's sympathy:

> Now I realize that this is going to call for rigorous routine and discipline, which every body seems to feel that I need. So be it. I want to do it. I have always wanted to do it and nobody will have any trouble about my applying myself. I wonder if it ought not to be taken into consideration that I have been on my own since fourteen years old and went to high school, college . . . because I wanted to, and not because I was being pushed? All of these things have been done under most trying circumstances and I stuck. I have had two or three people to say to me, why don't you go and take a master's or a doctor's degree in Anthropology since you love it so much? They never seem

to realize that it takes money to do that. I had such a hard time getting the money to take my bachelor's that I could appreciate what it meant to attempt to attend a college on nothing. Another thing, it is hard to apply oneself to study when there is no money to pay for food and lodging. I almost never explain these things when folks are asking me why don't I do this and that. I have to make a living, and consequently I have to do the jobs that will support me. But oh, Dr. Boas, you dont know how I have longed for a chance to· stay at Columbia and study. Otherwise there would be no point to my using every thing possible to get this scholarship.[23]

After arriving in New York, Hurston and Boas began talking over what her course of study should be. She strongly resisted the normal graduate course work, both because of her experience and because most of the courses were in cultures unrelated to her interests. She remarked that "Pawnee is not likely to help me much in say, Alabama." It was finally agreed that she would take work in general ethnology for the spring, 1935, semester and the 1935–36 school year; she might also spend some time studying with Haitian expert Melville Herskovits at Northwestern. Then she would go into the field on a trip to Haiti, tracing hoodoo origins. She explained this plan in a series of letters to the foundation, some of which admittedly seemed slightly contradictory, because Boas kept changing his mind, perhaps at Zora's urging; in any case, the Rosenwald reaction was to withdraw its long-term support.

Hurston's relations with the Rosenwald Foundation and its president, Edwin Embree, had been curious from the beginning. A major reason for granting the fellowship was Embree's paternalistic feeling that the mercurial Zora needed the discipline of graduate study. He told Boas (who agreed with him) that he hoped "the brilliant Miss Hurston" could be "transformed" into a serious student. At the time of enrolling, Hurston quarreled with the foundation over its methods of dispensing money; she was totally dependent upon it for support, and its $100 payments would not enable her to pay the Columbia tuition at one time. The foundation's reply was to accuse her of being ungrateful.

When Embree was informed that Hurston would spend only three semesters in graduate school before entering the field, his response was to write her that "while these [arrangements] indicate that work can be arranged at Columbia of a fairly satisfactory character for the time being, they do not indicate a permanent plan on the basis of which we feel justified in awarding a longtime fellowship." In the same week when Hurston enrolled, he arbitrarily reduced the fellowship to $700, limiting it to the period from December 1, 1934, to June 30, 1935. At that point she could apply again if she wished, but there was no guarantee of support.

Hurston's reaction to this was private rage and deep depression. She thought of giving up the fellowship. She looked for a job, without success. At about the same time, a love affair went bad. She told Van Vechten in February, "I have lived thru a horrible period of grim stagnation. . . . My mental state was such that I could neither think nor plan. . . . I had got to the place I was talking to myself."[24] Her solution was a devious conciliation with the Rosenwald Foundation. She told Embree that the arrangements were satisfactory, made sure she was enrolled so that the $100 per month would be forthcoming, and then said good-bye to Columbia. She may also have resented Boas's attitude. He, like Embree, was trying to impose "the discipline of scientific study" on the effervescent student, and both of them were treating her like a first-year graduate student; yet she was the author of a published novel and a book of folklore.

By March, Boas was sending her notes asking where she was. On April 1 he complained, "I have been expecting to see you all this time." He might have had better luck checking the society columns, where Zora had become something of a celebrity. New York's *Amsterdam News* ran a feature on April 6 that summarized her activities while illustrating her gift for personal publicity. She stressed to the reporter that she was a member of the American Folklore Society, the American Ethnological Society, the American Anthropological Association, and the New York Academy of Sciences. She plugged *Jonah's Gourd Vine* and the forthcoming *Mules and Men*, adding, "I prefer writing while in bed at night. . . . Since I don't compose well at the typewriter, I prepare my manuscript in long hand, revise and revise, and then type it." She admitted to taking only one course in creative writing, and believed that it was "an absolute waste of time, for writing is a gift." She told of lectures scheduled in Minneapolis and Baltimore. When the interviewer asked for a list of her recent engagements, she willingly complied, prominently mentioning the tea held in her honor by her old

Barnard sponsor, Annie Nathan Meyer. Among those present had been Pearl Buck, Fannie Hurst, Robert Nathan, Bertram Lippincott, and Sir Gerald and Lady Campbell.[25]

Although this interview did not reveal it, most of her effort went into writing. The Rosenwald Foundation must have been startled to read in the New York *World Telegram* in February that she had "just about decided to pass [up] the proffered Julius Rosenwald Scholarship . . . and start in writing a book that would give her own people 'an awful going over,' particularly the ones who talk about the tragedy of being Negroes." Seldom attending classes, she worked hard. She told one correspondent in May that she was "working like a slave and liking it. But I have lost all my zest for a doctorate. I have definitely decided that I never want to teach, so what is the use of the degree. It seems that I am wasting two good years of my life when I should be working." "Working" meant writing, not studying, and she went about her labors. Her bitterness over the foundation's treatment of her surfaced later in response to one of its form letters requesting a report on her activities. She wrote Embree in June, 1935, what can only be termed a typical Zora letter:

> Gen. Del.
> West Palm Beach, Florida
> June 28, 1935
> Miami, Fla. July 1.
> Lemon City Station

My Dear Dr. Embree,

I am a little tardy with this letter but life has been rushing.

I want to express my appreciation for all that I was able to do under your grant.

You would understand that I would not be able to do anything important towards a doctorate with a single semester of work. So I did what could amount to something. I wrote two plays, both of which have a more than even chance of being produced in the fall. I wrote the first draft of my next novel which has already been accepted by my publishers. It was six months of most intensive labor, because I considered it *simply must* count constructively.

Now, since the first week in the month I have been south doing research with Alan Lomax, whom you know and we are doing some excellent recordings. Both of us feel that we belong together as workers. It is the chance I have wanted so long. Please accept my profound thanks for all that you have done thru the Foundation for me. It was short but important in my career.

Perhaps Dr. Jones [of Fisk] *did* feel badly over my letter, but so did I over his and all that it implied.

Most Sincerely,
Zora Neale Hurston
Belle Glade, Florida

lastest address:
(gen. Del. Lemon City Station, Miami, Florida.)

If the Rosenwald would like copies of the records we are making as beginning of a library of Negro folk expression, I'd be glad to arrange with Mr. John Lomax for copies to be made. I think it would be a wonderful collection if carried *far* enough, and could be [a] source for all the scientists who wish to work on such material *and* the Rosenwald is the organization to do it. Impertinent, eh? Perhaps, but stating fact.[26]

Hurston had signed on for the Lomax collecting trip after finishing the prepublication arrangements for *Mules and Men.* Lomax and a co-worker, Mary Elizabeth Barnicle, were collecting for the Music Division of the Library of Congress; Zora became indispensable to their efforts. As they followed with a recording machine, she led them to backwoods communities, and even convinced them to periodically wear blackface so that they could collect without interference from white authorities. The idea was not to fool black folks—who must have been amused by the strange sight—but to present a uniform color to white passersby. When a Maitland, Florida, sheriff, unimpressed by these cosmetics, arrested Lomax, Zora talked the man into releasing him. Lomax remembers her as a "macaw of brilliant plumage"; he felt especially close to her, sure that "she was almost entirely responsible for the success" of the first part of the expedition.[27]

Lomax was a relatively young folklorist, but he had already done important research, and he had learned much from his father, John, one of the earliest and most famous folklorists in America. It was father and son who brought a Texas ex-con named Huddie "Leadbelly" Ledbetter to New York and made him known to the world.

Alan Lomax was well aware of how crucial Zora was to his 1935 expedition. He wrote Oliver Strunk of the Library of Congress that she was "probably the best informed person today on Western Negro folk-lore." He explained in his report that, in June, "through Miss Hurston's influence we were soon living, in an isolated community on St. Simon's island, on such friendly terms with the Negroes as I had never experienced before." They went from there to Eatonville, where "Miss Hurston introduced us there to the finest Negro guitarist I have heard so far, better even than Lead Belly although of a slightly different breed." Writing to his father about this earlier part of the trip, Lomax told of how the three folklorists would move into a house in the community and invite folks to drop by: "They have thronged our house by day and night ever since we have been here. They have been perfectly natural and easy from the first on account of Zora who talks their language and can out-nigger any of them. She swaps jokes, slaps backs, honies up to the men a little when necessary and manages them so that they ask us for no money, but on the other hand cooperate in the friendliest sort of spirit."

These references are all to the early part of Lomax's expedition. Zora parted company with the group in Florida, after collecting in Belle Glade. She suggested that they go on to work in the Bahamas, which they did, but she refused to go along. She had grown to dislike Barnicle, a college professor from New York University, and their constant squabbling had come to a head over the woman's desire to photograph an Eatonville lad eating watermelon. Zora objected and elected to stay in Florida to do her own work.

The Rosenwald-Columbia fiasco was Hurston's final break with the formal study of folklore as an academic subject, and the Lomax–Library of Congress expedition was her last attempt to collect for scientific study. She might collect so that others could examine, but hereafter her primary interest in folk materials was as a source for journalism, drama, and fiction. She had always considered research only "formalized curiosity," a "poking and prying with a purpose." After 1935 she had relatively little interest in the formalities of the academic method.

It is relevant to ask why the scientific study of black folklore was so attractive in the first place, and how it came to coexist so easily with Hurston's long-standing commitment to the dramatization of Eatonville. Zora never became a professional academic folklorist because such a vocation was alien to her exuberant sense of self, to her admittedly artistic, sometimes erratic temperament, and to her awareness of the esthetic content of black folklore. If there is a single theme which emerges from her creative effort during the thirties—her five books, her fiction, her plays, her essays—it is that eventually immediate experience takes precedence over analysis, emotion over reason, the personal over the theoretical. She learned that scientific objectivity is not enough for a black writer in America, and she went on to expose the excessive rationality behind the materialism of American life, the inadequacy of sterile reason to deal with the phenomena of living. She forcefully affirmed the humanistic values of black life, contrasting them with the rationalized inhumanity of white society; she asserted early arguments for black cultural nationalism. Beginning with *Jonah's Gourd Vine*, her writing exhibits a studied antiscientific approach; in her nonfiction, even the most technical data is personalized. Her rejection of scholarly bias and scientific form was a process instead of a revelation; it occurred gradually, reflecting a deeply personal decision. Its cultural context is interesting, for Hurston's intellectual experience is in some ways a paradigm for the much-debated "crisis" of the black creative intellectual of the Harlem Renaissance.

Hurston was predisposed in favor of an anthropological conception of Eatonville simply because she was a creative writer. Although that sounds paradoxical, it is actually a logical product of the environment of ideas surrounding her. Black writers are especially vulnerable to the prescriptions which an idolatry of western European high culture imposes on American artists. They are urged to aspire toward a "raceless ideal" of literature, which, technically interpreted, has meant that they should not write about race, that they should not create Negroes but human beings—as if these were mutually exclusive categories. If they celebrate the ethnic heritage, it is said that they are not being universal, that they are engaging in propaganda. Such prescriptions were constantly offered during the

Harlem Renaissance, and some of its participants aided and abetted such dubious aims. Black writers have been historically badgered with such advice, the writer's success occurring in direct proportion to his ability to reject it. The attitude which invites the act of this prescribing, as well as the substance of the prescription, is a conception of the black condition as something which must be overcome, since it is somehow manifestly less than human—a habit of mind institutionalized as American racism. All black American writers confront in some way this attitude and its resultant phenomenon: the condition of black people. Thus, the dynamics of the culture make it as natural as breathing for the black artist to confront the issue of race.

In such a context, the attraction of a scientific conception for black experience becomes considerable for the writer-intellectual, especially for one who has taken part in the formal educational system. The educational process in America is essentially one of assigning and reinforcing class structures through the creation of an educated middle class. This acculturative process informed Hurston that black sharecroppers were peasants (a pejorative term, especially within the self-enterprise mythology of American agriculture), that superstition was a crutch of the ignorant, that her folk experience was quaintly interesting but hopelessly unsophisticated. But Zora *knew* that Joe Clarke and his Eatonville cronies were human beings of complexity and dignity, no matter what their grammar, no matter how unsophisticated their manner might be, no matter how much white interpretations distorted them. This knowledge typifies a dilemma facing the black intellectual: knowing this fact, how does one assert its truth and assign it meaning in the midst of a country whose institutions are structured to deny it? For Zora Neale Hurston, as for others, one way has been to assert black humanity by emphasizing its anthropological warrant, a particularly effective way of accounting for human truth in a technological society, and one which mostly sidesteps the purely esthetic issue of universality versus propaganda. Blacks can be measured, studied, and charted in the interests of proving the general equality of the races. One has only to cultivate a "genius for pure objectivity," as Franz Boas did, and let the evidence prove the absurdity of racial prejudice. Moreover, because anthropology also proves the exis-

tence of particular cultural differences while simultaneously posit-
ing a basic sameness in the human condition, one can maintain the
integrity of black culture without sacrificing it to the mythical
American melting pot. The scientific collection of black folklore
comes to prove black humanity as it asserts the beauty of the
culture; meanwhile, the artist who affirms the same thing is accused
of special pleading.

It seems plausible that one reason Zora Neale Hurston was
attracted to the scientific conceptualization of her racial experience
during the late twenties and early thirties was its prima facie
offering of a structure for black folklore. That is, it offered a pattern
of meaning for material that white racism consistently distorted into
stereotypes. A folksinger was a cultural object of considerable
scientific importance to the collecting anthropologist precisely because his folk experience affirmed his humanity, a fact that Hurston
could know subjectively as she proved it scientifically. The scientific attraction became so strong that she was led into seriously
planning a career as a professional anthropologist, and it continued
to affect her writing even after she had rejected such a possibility.
When she used Eatonville as fiction in *Jonah's Gourd Vine* and
folklore as personal narrative in *Mules and Men*, she was in the
process of rejecting the scientific conceptualization, but she had not
yet reached the esthetic resolution in fiction that characterized her
two masterpieces of the late thirties, *Their Eyes Were Watching
God* (1937) and *Moses, Man of the Mountain* (1939).

Hurston never denied the usefulness of her Barnard training, but
she made it clear that something more was needed for the creation
of art. As she once told a reporter: "I needed my Barnard education
to help me see my people as they really are. But I found that it did
not do to be too detached as I stepped aside to study them. I had to
go back, dress as they did, talk as they did, live their life, so that I
could get into my stories the world I knew as a child."[28]

NOTES

1. ZNH, *Dust Tracks on a Road* (Philadelphia: J. B. Lippincott, 1942), p. 217.
2. Ibid., pp. 217, 214, 218; ZNH, manuscript of *Jonah's Gourd Vine* (Schomburg Collection, New York Public Library).
3. ZNH, *Dust Tracks*, pp. 217–20.
4. ZNH to CVV, Feb. 28, 1934 (JWJYale).

5. ZNH to James Weldon Johnson, Apr. 16, 1934 (JWJYale).
6. Ibid., May 8, 1934 (JWJYale). The review was by John Chamberlain, *New York Times*, May 3, 1934, p. 7.
7. Margaret Wallace, "Real Negro People," *New York Times Book Review*, May 6, 1934, p. 6; review of *Jonah's Gourd Vine*, *Times Literary Supplement*, Oct. 18, 1934; Martha Gruening, "Darktown Strutter," *New Republic*, July 11, 1934, pp. 244–45; R.E.M.J., review of *Jonah's Gourd Vine*, *Boston Chronicle*, May 5, 1934; Andrew Burris, review of *Jonah's Gourd Vine*, *Crisis*, 41 (1934), 166; Estelle Felton, review of *Jonah's Gourd Vine*, *Opportunity*, 12 (Aug., 1934), 252–53. See also Josephine Pinckney, "A Pungent Poetic Novel about Negroes," *New York Herald Tribune Books*, May 6, 1934, p. 7. The reviews' emphasis on Hurston's language is similar to the way many scholars have treated ZNH herself: as a linguistic source; see, e.g., Clarence M. Babcock, *A Word List from Zora Neale Hurston*, Publications of the American Dialect Society, No. 40 (Tuscaloosa: University of Alabama Press, 1963).
8. ZNH, manuscript of *Jonah's Gourd Vine*.
9. Bernard Bell, *The Folk Roots of Contemporary Afro-American Poetry* (Detroit: Broadside Press, 1974), p. 57. Benjamin Brawley thought the sermon the primary merit of the novel (*The Negro Genius* [New York: Dodd, Mead, 1937], p. 258).
10. Larry Neal, introduction to *Jonah's Gourd Vine* (Philadelphia: J. B. Lippincott, 1971), pp. 6, 7. Neal's excellent introduction has considerably influenced my own thinking about this novel. For other interesting analyses of *Jonah's Gourd Vine*, see Addison Gayle, *The Way of the New World* (Garden City, N.Y., 1976), pp. 169–75; Arthur P. Davis, *From the Dark Tower* (Washington, D.C.: Howard University Press, 1974), pp. 113–20; and S. P. Fullinwider, *The Mind and Mood of Black America* (Homewood, Ill.: Dorsey Press, 1969), pp. 169–71.
11. Neal, introduction to *Jonah's Gourd Vine*, p. 7.
12. Nick Aaron Ford, *The Contemporary Negro Novel* (1936; rpt., College Park, Md.: McGrath Publishing, 1968), p. 99.
13. ZNH to CVV, Jan. 22, 1934 (JWJYale).
14. ZNH to Thomas E. Jones, Oct. 12, 1934 (Fisk); ZNH to AL, Mar. 24, 1934 (HUAL).
15. ZNH to CVV, Mar. 24, 1934 (JWJYale); ZNH to Walter White, Mar. 8, 1934 (LCMD).
16. ZNH to CVV, Jan. 22. 1934 (JWJYale); Frederick O'Neal to RH, Oct. 5, 1971; ZNH to AL, Mar. 24, 1934 (HUAL); ZNH to CVV, Mar. 24, 1934 (JWJYale).
17. ZNH to AL, Oct. 29, 1934 (HUAL).
18. ZNH to Thomas E. Jones, Oct. 12, 1934 (Fisk).
19. ZNH to Hamilton Holt, Oct. 8, 1934 (Rollins College Library); unidentified clipping, "Tea Honors Noted Author on Monday," ca. Sept.-Nov., 1934 (HCUFla); Frank L. Hayes, "Campaigns Here for Negro Art in Natural State," *Chicago Daily News*, Nov. 16, 1934; clipping, Dorothy Dockstader, "Book News," ibid., Oct. 25, 1934 (HCUFla) (this clipping appears to be mislabeled).
20. Hayes, "Campaigns Here"; unidentified clipping, publicity for *Singing Steel* (HCUFla); Edwin Osgood Grover, "The Story of Zora Neale Hurston, Author," typescript, July 21, 1971 (Rollins College Library); Thomas E. Jones to Charles S. Johnson, Dec. 18, 1934; Johnson to Jones, Dec. 21, 1934; ZNH to Jones, Dec. 29, 1934 (Fisk).
21. H.M.F., "Fighter against Complacency and Ignorance," *Barnard College Alumnae Magazine*, 36 (Autumn, 1946) 6–7.

22. See ZNH to CVV, Thanksgiving Day, 1934 (JWJYale); application for Rosenwald Foundation Fellowship, Dec. 14, 1934. The Rosenwald Fellowship narrative is written primarily from the following correspondence and documents in RosFisk: fellowship application, Dec. 14, 1934; budget, Dec. 19, 1934; account sheet, appropriation no. 3334–28; ZNH to EE, Dec. 29, 1934, Jan. 6, 8, 26, June 28, 1935; ZNH to Thomas E. Jones, Dec. 29, 1934; ZNH to Dorothy Elvidge, Jan. 18, 26, Feb. 7, 8, 11, 1935; ZNH to George R. Arthur, Feb. 5, 7, 1935; EE to ZNH, Dec. 19, 1934, Jan. 21, July 9, 1935; EE to Charles S. Johnson, Dec. 20, 1934; EE to FB, Jan. 2, Mar. 26, 1935; FB to EE, Dec. 27, 1934, Jan. 7, Mar. 20, Apr. 1, 1935; Elvidge to ZNH, Jan. 10, 21, 1935. Information pertaining to the Rosenwald Fellowship episode that does not come from these documents is noted normally.

23. ZNH to FB, Dec. 14, 1934 (APS).

24. ZNH to CVV, Feb. 6, 1935 (JWJYale).

25. FB to ZNH, Mar. 20, 1935 (APS); clipping, Thelma Berlack-Boozer, "Zora Neale Hurston Success as Author and Scientist," *New York Amsterdam News*, Apr. 6, 1935 (RosFisk).

26. Sally McDougall, "Author Plans to Upbraid Own Race," *New York World Telegram*, Feb. 6, 1935; ZNH to Edwin Osgood Grover, May 14, 1935 (HCUFla); ZNH to EE, June 28, 1935 (RosFisk).

27. RH interview with Alan Lomax, May, 1971, New York City. The narrative of the Lomax-Hurston-Barnicle expedition of 1935 is reconstructed from Lomax to Oliver Strunk, chief of the Music Division of the Library of Congress, Aug. 3, 1935 (LCAFS); the field recordings of the expedition (AFS 309–85) (LCAFS); and Alan Lomax to John Lomax, his father, June 18–Sept. 4, 1935 (eight letters) (Lomax Papers, Texas Collection, Archives, University of Texas library). Some of the field recordings are now available on LP: *Out in the Cold Again*, Library of Congress Series, Vol. 3, Flywright-Matchbox SDM 257, and *Boot That Thing*, Library of Congress Series, Vol. 4, Flywright-Matchbox SDM 258. See also Alan Lomax, "Zora Neale Hurston—A Life of Negro Folklore," *Sing Out!*, 10 (Oct.–Nov., 1960), 12–13.

28. McDougall, "Author Plans to Upbraid Own Race."

9 ⚞⚞⚞ Crayon Enlargements of Life

Seeing Eatonville with a child's eyes meant that the harsh edges of life in a Jim Crow South seldom came into view. There was a willfulness about Hurston's celebration of her native village, and it eventually brought her criticism. The publication of *Mules and Men* in the fall of 1935 marked the start of an extended controversy over the nature and value of her work. Critics argued that a pastoral conception in *Mules and Men* distorted the reality of black life in America, a complaint that would follow her the rest of her career.

Zora had returned to New York in August, anticipating the book's publication in early October. Having very little money, she searched for employment among the various federal programs of the Works Progress Administration. By the time *Mules and Men* reached the bookstores, she had signed on as a "dramatic coach" at $23.86 per week on the WPA's Federal Theatre Project in New York.[1]

The immediate reception of *Mules and Men* was mixed. The nature of both the praise and the dissatisfaction came to characterize Hurston's public reputation for the next twenty years. Reviewers liked the book and recommended its lively stories. The *Saturday Review* called it "black magic and dark laughter," stressing the "entertainment" value. But Zora had not intended the book as light reading, and some reviewers accepted her invitation to a more serious interpretation. Written by a black author, about black people, it was assumed to reveal "what the Negro was really like," a subject of immense fascination to whites and of obvious vested interest to black readers. The *New York Times* reviewer wrote that Hurston encouraged the reader to "listen in" while "her own people" were being "natural," something they could never be in the company of outsiders. A white southerner, he felt assured that "at the end you have a very fair idea of how the other color enjoys life." Even Henry Lee Moon of the NAACP, reviewing the book in the *New Republic*, urged a larger meaning. Zora had not presented the life of the race as he lived it in New York City, but he was willing to assert that *"Mules and Men* is more than a collection of folklore. It is a valuable picture of the life of the unsophisticated Negro in small towns and backwoods of Florida."[2]

Discussed on this basis for a few months, the book finally drew the public attention of Sterling Brown. Brown was one of the best poets in America, the author of *Southern Road*, a book of poems inspired by folk sources. A graduate of Williams College, holder of a Harvard M.A., and a teacher at Howard, Brown had collected folklore in the South. Although he had not spent as much time in the field as Hurston, he knew well the dusty roads she had traveled. His review did not appear until February of 1936, but its thoughtful criticism was symptomatic of the kinds of questions many people—especially black intellectuals—had begun to ask about Hurston's book.[3]

Brown stressed Zora's academic training and praised her rendering of the tales. He disliked some of the "sensationalism" in the hoodoo section, but on the whole found it worthy. He was less certain than Moon about the book's value as a portrait of black life. It was authentically done as far as it went, but the portrait of the South was incomplete; missing were the exploitation, the terrorism, the misery. Disputing Zora's claim that "the Negro story teller is lacking in bitterness," Brown reported that he had often found expressions of anger and animosity. He objected to her "socially unconscious" characters, whose lives are "made to appear easy-going and carefree." Where was the smouldering resentment so often characteristic of the black South? He concluded, *"Mules and Men* should be more bitter; it would be nearer the total truth."[4]

Many black intellectuals believed that books by black authors needed to tell the "total truth" to white America. Books about the race should aim to destroy the absurd beliefs and racist fantasies of the suppressing culture, and such books would necessarily at times be bitter. But even if Hurston had consciously tried to avoid bitterness, Brown's criticism was important. She had not been writing for pure entertainment—although publisher's demands may have veered *Mules and Men* in that direction—and she had offered a portrait of the race meant to be taken as a behavioral example. Her preface promised access to the interior of the black mind, a report on what blacks deliberately kept from whites. But if this was her purpose, why had she excised the sharper edges, the harsher tones, of her rural informants? Nowhere in *Mules and Men* was there a discussion of the stories told in Eatonville of the Ocoee riot of November, 1920. Only a few miles away, in a scene well remembered by the community, black people had been denied their voting rights; when some protested, a white mob had burned and killed. One victim, July Perry, became legendary by defending his family and property, killing two white men before he was lynched and left swinging from a telephone pole beside the road to Eatonville.[5]

Published in the same year as the Scottsboro trial, *Mules and Men* has a disembodied quality about it, as if it came from a backwoods so far to the rear that American social history of the twentieth century had not touched its occupants. At a time when the Communist party was recruiting large numbers of black people, primarily because it was the only political party in America advocating an end to segregation, and when Richard Wright and Langston Hughes were creating a proletarian literature, Zora Hurston had deliberately chosen not to deal with the resentment of the black community. Why?

The reasons were strategic and philosophic, although she later admitted that publisher's restrictions also played a part. Hurston had a conception of the black image in the popular mind, and she felt that it derived largely from a mistaken notion of the black folk. The total truth was relative, making the class struggle seem less important than the need for an altered perception of black folklore; the Ocoee riot was not folklore, but history. Afraid of being thought "one of the sobbing school of Negrohood," Hurston was determined to prove that black people did not devote their lives to a morose discussion of white injustice. She once complained about the "false picture" created by black writers dwelling on the race problem, producing writing "saturated with our sorrows." This picture was false because it distorted: "We talk about the race problem a great deal, but go on living and laughing and striving like everybody else."⁶ By leaving out "the problem," by emphasizing the art in the folkloric phenomenon, Hurston implicitly told whites: Contrary to your arrogant assumptions, you have not really affected us that much; we continue to practice our own culture, which as a matter of fact is more alive, more esthetically pleasing than your own; and it is not solely a product of defensive *re*actions to your actions. She felt that black culture manifested an independent esthetic system that could be discussed without constant reference to white oppression.

The price for this philosophy was an appearance of political naïveté and the absence of an immediate historical presence. *Mules and Men* really refers to an idealized Eatonville of Hurston's childhood memory. The town of the 1930s, hard hit by depression, seldom appears. Hurston privately acknowledged economic and racial realities, but the times called for a public indictment; her reticence offended those attacking racism by frontal assault. Zora's approach was oblique and open to misinterpretation. She chose to write of the positive effects of black experience because she did not believe that white injustice had created a pathology in black behavior, a position brought into sharp focus in the criticism of her career by a white radical, Harold Preece.

One of the charges Zora had faced was common to all folklorists, but special to her because she was black. What was the collector's responsibility to the folk who provided the lore? Preece, in an article in the *Crisis* entitled "The Negro Folk Cult," saw a kind of professional colonialism in the way Hurston "was devoting her literary abilities to recording the legendary amours of terrapins," when she should be enlisted in the revolution; she should "cast her lot with the folk," rather than simply mine their traditions.⁷

Preece's politics were more radical than Hurston's, but politics did not constitute the primary difference between them. At the root of their argument was a contrasting conception of black folklore. Preece saw black traditions as basically evasive; and no matter what their intrinsic beauty, this evasive factor predominated. While this quality might be admirable for "protective purposes," he felt that it impeded further racial progress. Trickster figures like John, outwitting the master through cunning, were less a symbol of strength

than the defensive creation of a psychologically captive and
economically deprived people. Preece sympathized with those
northern blacks who escaped the traditional culture, avoided the
folklorist, and resented Zora Neale Hurston: "For when a Negro
author describes her race with such a servile term as 'Mules and
Men' critical members of the race must necessarily evaluate the
author as a literary climber."[8]

Hurston's research convinced her that the intrinsic beauty of folk
expression was by far its most important element. The protest
impulse was not subordinated, but stylized so that it could survive.
A kind of art grew from a phrase like "mules and men" because a
collective esthetic impulse had transformed black people's identification with the mule—an overworked beast of burden—into a
special symbol. The phrase meant not only that black people were
treated as mules, but also that they were defiantly human—mules
and men. The identification itself demonstrated how a negative
relationship (slave : mule : beast of burden) could be transformed
into a positive identity (beast of burden : mule : slave : man), with
the content of the positive identification concealed from outside
understanding. "Mules and men" was a phrase that *signified*—it
had several meanings, many contexts.

From outside the race, a black person's identification with the
mule was appropriate; it implied that one knew his place. From
inside, the identification with the mule was only initially a recognition that one was being used as a beast of burden. Folklorist Alan
Dundes has explained how the folkloric process sometimes operated with a reverse anthropomorphism, which noted the similarity
between the mule's situation and that of the slave, then identified
mulish traits with black people. Mules were bought and sold by
massa just as slaves were. They were forced to work long hours just
as slaves were. But the mule also represented admirable characteristics for a slave society: individualism, stubbornness, strength,
and unpredictability. As Langston Hughes would later write, "I'm
like that old mule . . . Black / And don't give a damn! / So you got
to take me / Like I am." Many stories and sayings about mules
became allegories exhibiting the creative capacities of black
storytellers defying their treatment as animals. The phrase "mules
and men" never let one forget the perverse relationship with the

master— it could simultaneously repudiate the unnatural servitude and affirm one's natural human condition. Put another way, Preece's objection to Hurston's title went straight to the question of whether black folklore resulted from the protective pathology of servility or the creative genius of survival.[9]

Folk art and behavior were inseparable to Hurston because she saw the creative impulse as the highest form of the black survival mechanism. She identified drama as a "characteristic" of black behavior, explaining the dynamics this way: "Who has not observed a young Negro chap posing up a street corner, possessed of nothing but his clothing, his strength and his youth? Does he bear himself like a pauper? No, Louis XIV could be no more insolent in his assurance. . . . His posture exults, 'Ah, Female. . . . Salute me, I am strength.' . . . These little plays by strolling players are acted out daily in a dozen streets in a thousand cities, and no one ever mistakes the meaning."[10] The youth demonstrated the same sense of adornment that characterized black preachers and Eatonville storytellers: he was transforming his street-corner world into a stage. Hurston's emphasis was not on the economic system that seemed to make him a pauper, but on the drama that made him a king.

Hurston's critics of the thirties, concerned about the collapse of capitalism and its effects on black people, overlooked the implicit protest in her observations of this kind, and in much of her dramatic work as well. Zora joined the WPA Federal Theatre Project in the fall of 1935 not only because she sorely needed a job; she also still envisioned the stage as an appropriate vehicle for the affirmation of black lifestyles. Her celebratory manner confronted indirectly by asserting a positive view of black traditions. June Jordan has argued that this affirmative attitude is indeed an act of protest, given the American context.[11] Although not written specifically for the Federal Theatre Project, Zora's one-act play "The Fiery Chariot" illustrates her positive vision of the thirties. It attacks from an angle; yet its argument is forcefully direct, undercutting accepted interpretations about the origins of black Christianity while redefining the symbolism of good and evil.

In the notes to *Mules and Men* Zora observed that the devil in black folklore is not the terror he is in European folklore. Rather, he is a powerful trickster who often competes successfully with God. She added, "There is a strong suspicion that the devil is an extension of the story-makers while God is the supposedly impregnable white masters, who are nevertheless defeated by Negroes." This is a revolutionary principle, one which overturns the normative moral structure of the oppressing society. Bad becomes good, and vice versa, and this very perception protests the inadequacy of moral terminology in an oppressive culture. If God is a white man, the symbol of oppression, then white Christian claims to a God of love are dubious. Moreover, if the white man's power can easily be circumvented or defeated, often without punishment, the white man's God can hardly be a figure commanding instant, ungrudging obedience. The origin of the identification between black story-teller and devil trickster is almost impossible to discover and may even be an African survival. Its human logic is self-evident. Confronted with the hypocrisy and paradox of white Christianity's sanction of slavery, the slave might naturally identify with an opposing power. The linguistic effects of this identification, adapted through history, can be striking. When Sonia Sanchez titles a book of poems *We a BaddDDD People*, not only is she using black idiom, she is also reversing the vocabulary of moral dialogue by being true to the linguistic traditions of her race. Hurston's play "The Fiery Chariot" depends on this technique of ironic reversal. It illustrates how folklore can simultaneously affirm black life and protest white values.

Never published, "The Fiery Chariot" was first written in 1933 for inclusion in the Rollins performance of *From Sun to Sun*. Based on a widely known folktale Zora had collected in Florida, the action takes place on a plantation "before surrender." Ike is a tall black man, religiously inclined, who prays excessively each night for release from his life of toil and trouble: "Come Lawd, come in a good time and git yo humble servant and keer im to heben wid you. Come in yo' fiery chariot and take me way from dis sin-sick world. Massa work me so-ooo hard and Ah ain't got no rest nowhere." Tired of hearing this, Ole Massa decides to "see if he means what he prays," by dressing in a white sheet and knocking on Ike's door: "It's me, Ike, the Lord, I come in my fiery chariot to take you to heaven with me. Come right now, Ike." Going as slowly as possible to the door, Ike visibly starts when he sees the white being outside: "Oh, Lawd, you so white and clean, ah know you don't want me to go to heben wid you in dese ole dirty clothes. Gimme time to put on my Sunday shirt." After dressing, he asks the Lawd to step back from the door: "Oh, Lawd, the radiance of yo' countenance is so bright, ah can't come out by yuh." As he measures the distance between them, he gains more space: "Oh Lawd, heben is so high and ahm so humble in yo' sight, and yo' glory cloud is so bright and yo radiance is so compellment be so kind in yo' tender mercy as to stand back jes' a little bit mo'." Ike then exits in great haste, calling out, "If thou be a running death, ketch me." His child ends the play by asking if his father will be caught and taken to heaven; the mother assures him that the Lawd cannot outrun his father, "and him barefooted too."[12]

At one level, "The Fiery Chariot" is an example of Massa making fun of a superstitious black slave. But if Ike is being tricked, he is also a trickster, and the play ultimately makes fun of a religion which posits heaven as an otherworldly surcease from a life of slavery on earth. At another level of consciousness, listeners to the tale or viewers of the play could not help noticing that, despite his apparent religion, Ike readily adapts to the reality of the situation; his instinct for survival transcends his spiritual faith, leading him to improvise an escape. The direction of the play shifts at the moment Ike realizes he will have to extricate himself from the consequences of his prayers.

The accepted white cliché about the origins of the black Christian church has always been that the notion of heaven was particularly appealing to laborers in bondage. While this life may be hard, if one trusted in the Lord a better day was coming over Jordan. But in "The Fiery Chariot" the Lawd is exposed as a fraud and a sham, nothing but a plantation owner masquerading in a sheet; the image becomes as ludicrous as that of the white man with a rack of antlers on his head in *Mules and Men*. The slave is made fun of, but so is Massa. He is soooooo bright, soooo "white and clean," and the black man is soooo humble in his sight that the Christian support for white supremacy is exaggerated into mockery. Ike becomes foolish in direct proportion to his belief in the bogus white God, wise in direct proportion to his ability to alter that belief in the interests of survival. The good Christian hoping for release would presumably go passively; but even Ike's wife recognizes the unnatural hope in his religious exercises: "Every night heah, down on yo' rusty knees beggin God to come git yuh and take you to heben in his fiery chariot. You know you don't want tuh die a bit more'n Ah do." Coincidentally, as the story passed through history, Ole Massa's foolish wearing of a sheet assumed an additional satiric content, the apparel of the Ku Klux Klan made to appear ridiculous. Moreover, as folklorist Gladys-Marie Fry has documented, the tradition of a night-riding ghost, dressed in a sheet, was one that whites had manipulated during both slavery and Reconstruction to attempt to intimidate, an intimidation comically exposed in Hurston's folk play.[13] In sum, the white sheet represents fraud, with no capability to clothe with either power or divinity.

"The Fiery Chariot" and *Mules and Men* illustrate important black creative styles, appearing on the surface to avoid protest, but, in Hurston's eyes, protesting profoundly by saying that this is the more beautiful, the more viable, the more human tradition. Zora informed whites that their values faded in comparison with black values, for black people were much better at making their lives a thing of beauty. This was a philosophy that had dominated her earlier essays in Cunard's *Negro*. Black religious services are an example of native esthetics distinguishing black and white Christianity: "Prayers and sermons are tooled and polished until they are true works of art. . . . The prayer of the white man is humorous in its bleakness." Black dancers move with an angularity that becomes "dynamic suggestion" and involves the spectator in the movement. In comparison with whites, "the Negro must be considered the greater artist." Blacks might imitate whites, not out of a feeling of inferiority, but for the love of the art itself. The measure of the black man's creativity is his adaptation of the source: "While he lives and moves within the midst of white civilization, everything he touches is reinterpreted for his own use." On the other hand, white attempts to imitate indigenous black expression prove only the absence of a creative soul: "God only knows what the world has suffered from the white damsels who try to sing Blues."[14] Zora once told a lecture audience that "white people are inclined to more restraint" because "they lack imagination."[15]

Hurston brought this pride in black esthetics to the Federal Theatre Project, where she played a prominent part in organizing the New York City division's special Harlem unit. Many talented black theater people were employees of the project, and the atmosphere was bright with hope. Zora helped with the Harlem unit's first production, *Walk Together Chillun*, and Elmer Rice, the project's director, announced in the *New York Times* that her untitled play would be among the forthcoming offerings. The play was probably untitled because it had been written in a week's time to secure the federal employment. As the haste might imply, Zora's interest in the theater project was short-lived. By April, 1936, when the Harlem unit staged its most famous production—*Macbeth*, directed by Orson Welles with an all-black cast and a setting in Napoleonic Haiti—Zora was in the West Indies herself, the recipient of a Guggenheim Fellowship. She proposed "to make an exhaustive study of Obeah (magic) practices . . . to add to and compare with what I have already collected in the United States." Zora accepted the Guggenheim on March 18 and resigned her WPA job on March 20. In less than a month she was in Jamaica, ready to begin a year of intensive writing and collecting. As the Lafayette Theater reverberated with the voodoo drumming Welles had imposed on Shakespeare, Hurston sought out a living drama in the sound-filled nights of the Caribbean.[16]

Zora arrived in Kingston on April 14. En route she had stopped for a short time in Haiti, meeting a number of important government officials and making preparations for her return in September. Ten days later the Kingston *Daily Gleaner* ran a feature on the flamboyant visitor, photographing her in jodhpurs and riding garb, her hat at a rakish angle, ready for a sortie into the tropical bush. By the first week in May she had already begun "to gather material wholesale." Leaving Kingston almost immediately for the lush, green countryside, she had found that all she had to do was make her collecting intentions known: "Just squat down awhile and after that things begin to happen." She also made contacts with the upper class and was struck by the intraracial color-consciousness of the society and the sensitivity of the "coloureds," the light-skinned elite: "I have corrected several who called me a *coloured* person.

They wonder why we insist on being called Negroes." Annoyed at the tendency for mulattoes to speak only of their white male parent, she thought of writing an article about "this island where roosters lay eggs."[17]

This phrase became a chapter title in *Tell My Horse*, Zora's account of her trip; together with her correspondence, the book becomes a kind of diary for 1936–38. Her primary impression of Jamaica was of a hopelessly chauvinistic, assimilationist culture. She asked if the search for an ever-lighter race was the Jamaican answer to racial prejudice. If so, then "perhaps we should strike our camps and make use of the cover of night and execute a masterly retreat under white skins." Equally offensive was the male domination in the society. She was told repeatedly that "women who went in for careers were just so much wasted material"; that "we men do not need your puny brains to settle the affairs of the world"; that "wisdom-wise" western women should know that "being a woman [sexually] is the only thing that you can do with any real genius." The color-consciousness and the feminine oppression were inter-related, she noted, for it was the dark-skinned black woman who bore the brunt of both prejudices. If a woman was of no family, poor and black, "she had better pray to the Lord to turn her into a donkey and be done with the thing." She collected a bitter story of a young black girl, sexually used by her mulatto lover, then thrown away to preserve the "honor" of his marriage.

Zora had quickly learned about the treatment of women when she lost her letter of credit for the Guggenheim funds, along with $100 in cash, in a Kingston restaurant. The bank officials were condescending and uncooperative, and she worried that it meant the end to her fellowship. The experience was depressing not only because of the chauvinism of the police and the banking people, but also because it demonstrated her fiscal dependence: "I have no talents whatsoever in money and business matters. . . . I get too thoroughly immersed in my dreams. But somehow life is so organized that I find myself tied to money matters like a grazing horse to a stake."[18]

A new letter of credit was arranged, and the collecting continued. In late May she wrote Henry Allen Moe, director of the Guggen-

heim Foundation, that she had found a "gracious plenty," stressing that the Maroons of Jamaica "are worth a year's study in
themselves." Descendents of men who fought their way out of
slavery, the Maroons had resisted all subsequent attempts to reen-
slave them. One group, residing in the forbidding Saint Catharine
Mountains at Accompong, represented exactly the kind of isolated
community many folklorists hope to discover.[19]

Hurston spent much of her six months in Jamaica with these
Maroons, living among them quietly. They offered to stage various
dances for her benefit, but she declined: "I wanted to see their
culture and art expressions and knew that if I asked for anything
especially, I would get something out of context. I had heard a good
deal about their primitive medicines and wanted to know about
that. I was interested in vegetable poisons and their antidote. So I
just sat around and waited."[20] The waiting eventually paid off: she
was taken on a ritualistic hunt for a wild boar, and became friends
with the chief medicine man of the tribe. A politically astute,
ambitious man of extraordinary psychic power and herbal knowledge, he took her to a clearing on a hot summer afternoon and
demonstrated his abilities. Using only the power of his mind, he
willed to silence the thousands of croaking frogs of the nearby
jungle. Although Zora did not learn how he did it, there was no
questioning the effect. The sudden silence terrified.

This Maroon medicine man revealed to Hurston that there was
more to Jamaican folkways than the color-consciousness of the
upper class and the chauvinism of the male elite. She concluded
that "Jamaica is a seething Africa under its British exterior," and she
began to explore the African survivals manifest in the native religion. By the middle of June she had enough raw data to begin to
think about its organization:

> It has occurred to me to make a collection of all the subtle poisons
> that Negroes know how to locate among the bush and [in] the use of
> which they are so expert. No one outside the hoodoo or bush doctors
> know these things. But as I am learning day by day more and more I
> think that I will be doing medical science a great service to identify
> these weeds so that antidotes can be prepared. The greatest power of
> voodoo rests upon this knowledge. Some of these bushes are quite

marvelous. One of them I *know* will kill by being placed so that the wind will blow from it to the victim. Another can be rubbed on the clothing and enters thru the pores as soon as the victim sweats.[21]

Hurston stayed in Jamaica until September 22, 1936, visiting all the island's parishes, beginning the intensive indoctrination into obeah that was her primary purpose for the trip. She told Moe, "I have seen things!"[22] She watched old women conduct the sensual learning ritual that would prepare a young virgin for her wedding night. She also participated in two different "Nine Night" ceremonies intended to keep the spirit of the dead—the "duppy"— from returning to haunt the living. One of these ended in a naked, orgiastic dance climaxed by the sacrifice of a goat.

As exciting as these adventures were, after Hurston left Jamaica for Haiti, she discovered an entire system of belief that made Nine Night rituals look like child's play. She arrived in Port-au-Prince in late September. Her Haitian plan was to take a house up in the hills so that she could write during the periods when she was not finding things. She was fortunate in locating such a place, with a maid, Lucille, who was sympathetic and honest. But she was immediately confronted with such a wealth of material that she found it impossible to write up her research. In little less than three months she perfected her Creole, acquired a working knowledge of voodoo gods, attended a number of ceremonies presided over by a voodoo priest, or "houngan," and photographed an apparent zombie.

In December she took a trip to the beautiful Île de la Gonâve, near the harbor of Port-au-Prince. The local belief was that the island was formed when a whale bore a sleeping goddess on his back and that now the goddess held the formula of peace in her hand. Zora found the place enchanted, discovering "a peace I have never known anywhere else on earth." At night the luminous sea glittered like bushels of gems; the days were filled with languor, the air resting heavily on the rich green foliage.[23]

Haiti released a flood of language and emotion that Zora finally admitted to herself had been "dammed up" inside ever since her departure from New York. For seven straight weeks after her arrival she struggled to get it down on paper, sometimes writing late at night after a day of collecting. By the third week in December she had completed her second novel. She sent it to

Lippincott's, and when she returned to the United States mainland in March, 1937, plans were already underway for the novel's publication in the fall; the editors had found little need for revisions. The book was to be called *Their Eyes Were Watching God*.[24]

Their Eyes Were Watching God is a love story. The impetus for the tale came from Zora's affair with a man of West Indian parentage whom she had first met in New York in 1931 and then found again during her short-lived attempt at graduate school. The relationship was stormy, perhaps doomed from the first. He could not abide her career, but she could not break away. Her collecting trip with Lomax and her Guggenheim Fellowship were both intended to sever the relationship, to "smother" her feelings; both times her return brought them back together. As she admitted, "The plot was far from the circumstances, but I tried to embalm all the tenderness of my passion for him in *Their Eyes Were Watching God*."

This affair is instructive because it illustrates how Hurston used personal experience for her fiction. *Their Eyes Were Watching God* is autobiographical only in the sense that she managed to capture the emotional essence of a love affair between an older woman and a younger man. The prototype for the man, Tea Cake, was not a laborer, but a college student of twenty-three who had been a member of the cast for *The Great Day*. Handsome, lithe, muscular, he owned a smile that brightened rooms. But he was not a gambler and vagabond like Tea Cake; in fact, he was studying to be a minister, and the two of them held long conversations about religious issues. His quick intelligence and considerable learning no doubt attracted her as much as anything else. What Zora took from this relationship was the quality of its emotion: its tenderness, its intensity, and perhaps its sense of ultimate impossibility. Sooner or later it had to end, and when she left for the West Indies, she did so with a stoic toughness. The man she was leaving remembers that outwardly she was calm and that he was left hurt and confused, wondering if she was "crying on the inside." She gave him her answer in *Their Eyes Were Watching God*.[25]

Whatever its personal matrix, Hurston's novel is much more than an outpouring of private feeling. It is both her most accomplished work of art and the authentic, fictional representation of Eatonville she had been struggling for in *Jonah's Gourd Vine*. The novel culminates the fifteen-year effort to celebrate her birthright, a celebration which came through the exploration of a woman's consciousness, accompanied by an assertion of that woman's right to selfhood. By the time she wrote *Their Eyes Were Watching God*—or perhaps in the act of writing it, struggling to reconcile public career and private emotion—Zora Neale Hurston discovered one of the flaws in her early memories of the village: there had usually been only men telling lies on the front porch of Joe Clarke's store.

Their Eyes Were Watching God is about Janie Crawford, raised by her grandmother to "take a stand on high ground" and be spared the traditional fate reserved for black women as beasts of burden: "Ah been prayin' fuh it tuh be different wid you," Nanny tells her granddaughter. The search to fulfill through Janie her "dream of what a woman oughta be and to do" leads to Logan Killicks, owner of sixty acres, a house, and a mule. Older, looking "like a skullhead in the graveyeard," Killicks marries Janie shortly before the grandmother's death. When the marriage proves loveless, Janie searches for something or someone to represent "sun-up and pollen and blooming trees." She finds Joe Starks, an assertive, self-confident striver on his way to Eatonville, Florida, the town made "all outa colored folks," where a man can be his own boss. Joe intends to become a "big voice," and shortly after their arrival he buys 200 acres of land, sets up a store, secures a post office, and campaigns for mayor. Jody is the kind of man who has "uh throne in de seat of his pants," who "changes everything, but nothin' don't change him." He expects his wife to act like a mayor's wife, keep her place, subordinate herself to her master. The spirit of Janie's second marriage leaves the bedroom and takes "to living in the parlor," and she finally reacts to Joe's constant disparagement by publicly questioning his manhood. He dies a short time later, bitter over her revolt, shaken by the challenge to his authority.

Now a woman of means, Janie is beset by status-conscious suitors; but she rejects her class role and falls in love with Vergible "Tea Cake" Woods, a free-spirited laborer much younger than she. Tea Cake is a "glance from God"; he teaches her "de maiden language all over." To Tea Cake, Janie is the "keys to de kingdom."

Without the hypocrisy and the role-playing that characterized her other marriages, this love is strong enough to make both parties open and giving. Tea Cake accepts Janie as an equal. She travels with him from job to job, even though her money would enable them to settle comfortably in Eatonville. They eventually end up working happily together in the bean fields of the "muck," the rich black land reclaimed from Lake Okeechobee in the Everglades. Their bliss is short lived, for during their escape from a hurricane Tea Cake saves Janie but is bitten by a rabid dog. He develops rabies, and his illness drives him mad; eventually he attempts to shoot Janie. Reacting in self-defense, she shoots back, killing him, and then is tried and acquitted by a white jury. Janie is left at the end with the memories of a transcendent love and a wise awareness of its relativity. Yet she knows that Tea Cake will "never be dead until she herself had finished feeling and thinking."

This ending seems poorly plotted, and the narration shifts awkwardly from first to third person. But on the whole the novel is remarkable, with a consistent richness of imagery. Most critical commentary has either ignored this element or treated it superficially; yet the novel's effect depends largely upon the organic metaphors used to represent Janie's emotional life.[26] The imagery is introduced early, when the sixteen-year-old Janie is at the moment of sexual awakening. Using a symbol which will reappear often, Hurston identifies Janie with a blossoming pear tree. To the girl stretched on her back beneath the tree, the tree seems to represent the mystery of the springtime universe: "From barren brown stems to glistening leaf buds; from the leaf buds to snowy virginity of bloom it stirred her tremendously. How? Why?" As she lies there, "soaking in the alto chant of the visiting bees," the mystery is revealed: "The inaudible voice of it all came to her. She saw a dust bearing bee sink into the sanctum of a bloom; the thousand sister calyxes arch to meet the love embrace and the ecstatic shiver of the tree from root to tiniest branch creaming in every blossom and frothing with delight. So this was a marriage! She had been summoned to behold a revelation. Then Janie felt a pain remorseless sweet that left her limp and languid."

The orgasm described here comes to represent the organic union Janie searches for throughout her life: she wants "to be a pear tree—any tree in bloom." Yet events conspire to deny her a feeling of wholeness. Her hand-picked husband, Logan Killicks, is a "vision . . . desecrating the pear tree." Joe Starks does not "represent sun-up and pollen and blooming trees," but he does speak for a new life away from Killicks; Janie mistakenly thinks that perhaps he can become "a bee for her bloom." After Joe refuses to recognize Janie's autonomy, she discovers that she has "no more blossomy openings dusting pollen over her man, neither any glistening young fruit where the petals used to be." Tea Cake, however, embodies the organic union of completion: "He could be a bee to a blossom—a pear tree blossom in the spring. He seemed to be crushing scent out of the world with his footsteps." Tea Cake's only material legacy is a package of seeds he had meant to plant before his death. Janie vows to plant them for remembrance, commemorating the organic unity of their marriage with a living monument.

This organic imagery permeates the novel and suggests a resolution of time and space, man and nature, subject and object, life and death. In an episode borrowed from "Mule Bone," Hurston tells of a local mule, legendary for its meanness, that dies and is given a burial by the village. Dragging the mule to the swamp, the town makes a "great ceremony" of the interment with speeches and singing; one man even imitates John Pearson preaching a funeral sermon. They mock "everything human in death," then leave the mule to the buzzards. In a surrealistic scene, startling in a realistic novel, Hurston reports on the buzzards' conversation as the birds pick out the eyes "in the ceremonial way" and then go about their feast. Some commentators have criticized this scene for being an imposition of folklore on the narrative; but it is as natural for buzzards to speak as for bees to pollinate flowers, as for a human being to be a "natural man."[27] When not a part of the organic process of birth, growth, and death, one is out of rhythm with the universe. This is represented in the novel by Janie's dissociation of sensibility before she grows to consciousness. She discovers that "she had an inside and an outside now and suddenly she knew how not to mix them." She can sit and watch "the shadow of herself going about tending store and prostrating herself before Jody," but all the time "she herself is sitting under a shady tree with the wind blowing through her hair." Jody denies Janie participation in the mule's burial, and the restriction illustrates how she is out of touch with the cadence of nature. She tells Joe that "in some way we ain't natural wid one 'nother." Later, with Tea Cake, Janie feels in tune with natural process, just as she did under the pear tree as a child.

One might argue that Janie's finding the one true bee for her blossom is hardly a satisfactory response from a liberated woman. But the action is symbolic, demonstrating Janie's ability to grow into an adult awareness of self, and it is not until the imagery of the pear tree fuses with the motif of the horizon that this symbolic action is completed. Janie's romantic "dreams" of the pear tree are tempered by growth and time. What was thought to be the truth at puberty is gradually transformed by experience. Her childhood had ended when a neighbor boy failed to fulfill her romantic dreams. Killicks initiated her further, showing that "marriage did not make love. Janie's first dream was dead. So she became a woman." Joe Starks took Killicks's place, but Joe was a false dream too, "just something she had grabbed up to drape her dreams over." It is not until Tea Cake that her dream—now toughened by knowledge —can become truth. The reason is that Tea Cake suggests the horizon—he is the "son of Evening Sun"—and the horizon motif illustrates the distance one must travel in order to distinguish between illusion and reality, dream and truth, role and self.

Hurston claims at the beginning of the novel that men and women dream differently. For men, "ships at a distance have every man's wish on board. For some they come in with the tide. For others they sail forever on the horizon, never out of sight, never landing until the Watcher turns his eyes in resignation, his dreams mocked to death by time." Women, however, believe that the horizon is close at hand, willing it so: "Now women forget all those things they don't want to remember and remember everything they don't want to forget. The dream is the truth. Then they act and do things accordingly."

This complicated opening passage begins to make sense midway into the book, when Janie comes to an awareness that her grand-mother has pointed her in the wrong direction:

She had been getting ready for her great journey to the horizons in search of *people*; it was important to all the world that she should find them and they find her. But she had been whipped like a cur dog, and run off down a back road after *things*. It was all according to the way you see things. Some people could look at a mud-puddle and see an ocean with ships. But Nanny belonged to that other kind that loved to deal in scraps. Here Nanny had taken the biggest thing God ever made, the horizon—for no matter how far a person can go the horizon is still way beyond you—and pinched it in to such a little bit of a thing that she could tie it about her granddaughter's neck tight enough to choke her.

This second passage parallels the first in imagery and diction, demonstrating Janie's growing self-confidence in her own judgments and her realistic appraisal of her failed dreams. Only when thus prepared can she accept Tea Cake as an equal, without illusion, discovering love because she is finally accepted for herself. Tea Cake is certainly not an ideal husband, but he does grant Janie the dignity of self. On the final pages of *Their Eyes Were Watching God* Janie tells her friend, Pheoby, "Ah done been tuh de horizon and back and now ah kin set heah in mah house and live by comparisons." She has experienced the reality rather than dreamed it—"you got tuh *go* there tuh *know* there," she says—which means that the novel can end with an imagistic resolution of the distance between here and there, self and horizon. Escaping from a horizon that can be tied tight enough to choke, Janie peacefully gathers in the world: "She pulled in her horizon like a great fish-net. Pulled it from around the waist of the world and draped it over her shoulder. So much of life in its meshes! She called in her soul to come and see."

Janie's poetic self-realization is inseparable from Zora's concomitant awareness of her cultural situation. The novel also celebrates the black woman's liberation from a legacy of degradation. Janie's grandmother had given wrong directions because of her historical experience; she wants her granddaughter to marry Logan Killicks because of her own slave memories: "Ah didn't want to be used for a work-ox and a brood sow. . . . It sho wasn't mah will for things to happen lak they did." Janie's mother was also born into slavery, the offspring of the master, and Nanny had hoped that Emancipation would bring her daughter freedom. But she is raped by her schoolteacher, and Janie is conceived in the violence. Her mother leaves home a ruined woman, destroyed in spirit. Janie is left with Nanny, who sees the child as another chance: "Ah wanted to preach a great sermon about colored women sittin' on high, but they wasn't no pulpit for me. . . . Ah been waitin a long time, Janie, but nothin' Ah been through ain't too much if you just take a stance on high ground lak ah dreamed." Nanny "can't die easy thinkin' maybe de men folks white or black is makin a spit cup outa yuh." To her, Logan Killicks is "big protection" from this vision; when Janie complains about the absence of love, her grandmother responds, "Dis love! Dat's just whut's got us [black women] uh pullin and uh haulin' and sweatin' and doin from can't see in de mornin' till can't see at night."

Janie has, therefore, both a historical and a personal memory to react against in her search for autonomy. Much of the novel is concerned with her struggle to understand the inadequacy of her grandmother's vision. Tea Cake is not the means to self-understanding, only the partner of Janie's liberation from an empty way of living; she tells Pheoby: "Ah done lived Grandma's way, now ah means tuh live mine." Asked to explain, Janie says,

> She was borned in slavery time when folks, dat is black folks, didn't sit down anytime dey felt lak it. So sittin' on porches lak de white madam looked lak uh mighty fine thing tuh her. Dat's whut she wanted for me—don't keer whut it cost. Git upon uh high chair and sit dere. She didn't have time tuh think whut tuh do after you got up on de stool uh do nothin'. De object wuz tuh git dere. So Ah got up on de high stool lak she told me, but Pheoby, Ah done nearly languished tuh death up dere. Ah felt like de world wuz cryin' extry and Ah ain't read de common news yet.

The vertical metaphor in this speech represents Hurston's entire system of thought, her social and racial philosophy. People erred because they wanted to be *above* others, an impulse which eventually led to denying the humanity of those below. Whites had institutionalized such thinking, and black people were vulnerable to the philosophy because being on high like white folks seemed to represent security and power. Janie's grandmother had believed that "de white man is de ruler of everything as fur as ah been able tuh find out." She thinks that freedom is symbolized by achieving the position on high. Zora Hurston had always known, just as Janie discovers, that there was no air to breathe up there. She had always identified with what she called "the poor Negro, the real one in the furrows and cane breaks." She bitterly criticized black leaders who ignored this figure while seeking "a few paltry dollars and some white person's tea table." She once wrote that in her opinion some black leaders wanted most to be able to return from a meeting and say, "No other Negro was present besides me." This sense of racial pride had contributed much to *Their Eyes Were Watching God*: "I am on fire about my people. I need not concern myself with the few individuals who have quit the race via the tea table."[28]

Zora Neale Hurston had spent an entire career chronicling the cultural life of "the Negro farthest down," the beauty and wisdom of "the people"; she did not find racial liberation in the terms of white domination, or selfhood for the black woman in the arrogance of male supremacy. Black people became free not by emulating whites, but by building from the cultural institutions of the black community; women discovered an organic relationship with men only when there was consent between equals. This is the key to Janie's relationship with Tea Cake. In their very first meeting Janie apologizes for not being able to play checkers; no one has taught her how. She is surprised to discover that Tea Cake wants her to play, that he "thought it natural for her to play." When she resorts to role-playing in the competition, coyly asking him not to jump her exposed king, he jumps anyway, applying the rules of the game equally. In similar fashion they share the labor of the fields and the hardships of migrant life. While Jody would not let her take part in storytelling sessions, with Tea Cake it is perfectly natural for her to be a participant in oral tradition: "The men held big arguments here like they used to do on the store porch. Only here she could listen and laugh and even talk some herself if she wanted to. She got so she could tell big stories herself from listening to the rest."

It is important to note that Janie's participation comes after she has learned to recognize sexism, a necessary preliminary to her self-discovery. In the lying sessions on Joe's store porch, the philosophy of male dominance, often a part of black folklore, was everywhere present. Somebody had to think for "women and chillun and chickens and cows." Men saw one thing and understood ten, while women saw ten things and understood none. Janie eventually informs this male enclave that they will be surprised if they "ever find out yuh don't know half as much about us as you think you do." Her later life with Tea Cake, freely contracted for, without illusion (Tea Cake can be sexist, too), is a natural result of this developing consciousness.

Janie's verbal freedom might not seem such an important matter on the surface, but the reader should remember Hurston's conception of the store porch as a stage for the presentation of black folklore. The one time in the novel Janie takes over this male sanctuary, she is praised by the storytellers for being a "born orator. Us never knowed dat befo'. She put jus' de right words tuh our thoughts." However, Joe's sense of wifely propriety does not permit her repeat performances, and although "Janie loved the conversation and sometimes she thought up good stories," her husband forbids her to indulge. The storytellers are "trashy," because they lack his drive. As Janie later realized, "Jody classed me off."

When Hurston writes of Eatonville, the store porch is all-important. It is the center of the community, the totem representing black cultural tradition; it is where the values of the group are manifested in verbal behavior. The store porch, in Zora's language, is "the center of the world." To describe the porch's activities she often uses the phrase "crayon enlargements of life"—"When the people sat around on the porch and passed around the pictures of their thoughts for the others to look at and see, it was nice. The fact that the thought pictures were always crayon enlargements of life made it even nicer to listen to." It is on the store porch that the lying competition takes place, "a contest in hyperbole and carried out for no other reason." Borrowing from the verbal competition over Daisy in "Mule Bone," Hurston uses the store porch as the center of a courtship ritual which provides the town with amusement. Yet "they know it's not courtship. It's acting out courtship and everybody is in the play." The store porch is where "big picture talkers" use "a side of the world for a canvas" as they create a portrait of communal values.

The rhythms and natural imagery which structure the novel refer not only to liberation from sexual roles, but also to the self-fulfillment inherent in this sense of community. Janie's "blossoming" refers personally to her discovery of self and ultimately to her meaningful participation in black tradition. Janie discovers a way to make use of the traditions of slavery—her grandmother's memories—not by seeking to "class off" and attempt to "sit on high" as the white folks did, but by celebrating blackness. She asks the color-struck Mrs. Turner, "We'se uh mingled people and all of us got black kinfolks as well as yaller kinfolks. How come you so against black?" June Jordan calls *Their Eyes Were Watching God* the "most successful, convincing and exemplary novel of blacklove that we have. Period."[29] She is speaking of Janie's growth into an awareness of the possibilities of love between black men and black women —both individually and collectively, as selves and as members of a racial community.

Their Eyes Were Watching God responds in subtle ways to the criticism Zora had received. Certainly not a protest novel in the tradition of Richard Wright, parts of the book do capture the "smouldering resentment" of the black South. After the hurricane's destruction, a natural disaster the races suffer together, the white authorities are quick to reimpose supremacy by conscripting black men to bury the victims in segregated graves. Janie's trial has an arrogance about it; her freedom depends on the sanction of twelve white men who simply cannot understand her relationship with Tea Cake. The trial, however, is not grafted to the book to demonstrate the inequity of southern justice. It serves, rather, to illustrate the depth of Janie's discovery of self; for not only is she faced with a white power-structure irrelevant to her feelings, she is also blamed for the killing by Tea Cake's friends. She is not supposed to have the right of self-defense; they murmur that "uh white man and uh nigger woman is de freest thing on earth. Dey do as dey please." This is literally true for Janie, but only because she has become a complete woman, no longer divided between an inner and an outer self, a woman at home with the natural cycles of birth and death, love and loss, knowledge and selfhood. Janie's growth is Hurston's subject. Although that growth is affected by the racism surrounding her, white oppression is not the dominant factor in Janie's development. Zora is saying once again that it is arrogant for whites to think that black lives are only defensive reactions to white actions.

This very complicated argument was misinterpreted by almost all the novel's reviewers. The white establishment failed to recognize that her subject was purposefully chosen; they liked the story, but usually for the wrong reasons. Hershel Brickell in the *New York Post* compared Hurston favorably to D. H. Lawrence in her depiction of sensory experience. The *Saturday Review* called the novel "a simple and unpretentious story, but there is nothing else quite like it." Richard Wright, a Communist party member at the time, reviewed it for *New Masses*, complaining bitterly about the minstrel image that he claimed she was perpetuating. He admitted that "her dialogue manages to catch the psychological movements of the Negro folk-mind in their pure simplicity"; but as a Marxist intellectual working for social change, he felt that was counter-revolutionary. As with Sterling Brown, the lack of bitterness offended Wright: "Her characters eat and laugh and cry and work and kill; they swing like a pendulum eternally in that safe and narrow orbit in which America likes to see the Negro live: between laughter and tears."[30]

Wright's review had to hurt, and it no doubt fed Zora's lifelong suspicion of communism. But the review that infuriated came well after publication, in Alain Locke's January, 1938, *Opportunity* survey of the previous year's "literature by and about the Negro." Locke called the title magical and praised Zora's "cradle-gift" for storytelling. But he criticized the book because folklore was its "main point." Admittedly, it was "folklore fiction at its best"; but when was Hurston going to "come to grips with motive fiction and social document fiction"? Modern southern fiction had to get rid of condescension as well as oversimplification.

Zora's response was to write a malicious, angry portrait of Locke, which she insisted *Opportunity* publish and which they wisely refused. Openly libelous, the attack was unfair; the intensity of the invective was characteristic of the Hurston temper. She called the review "an example of rank dishonesty" and "a conscious fraud." She claimed that Locke "knows that he knows nothing about Negroes" and that he "pants to be a leader"; yet "up to now, Dr. Locke has not produced one single idea or suggestion of an idea that he can call his own." Her specific objection was to Locke's complaint that folklore intruded in the novel, detracting from the fiction, and she was enraged by his implication that the author condescended to her folk subjects. Zora claimed, in typical overstatement, that "there is not a folk tale in the entire book." She proposed, "I will send my toe-nails to debate him on what he knows about Negroes and Negro life, and I will come personally to debate him on what he knows about literature on the subject. This one who lives by quotations trying to criticize people who live by life." She felt that it was Locke, the Harvard Ph.D. and Oxford scholar, who condescended when he referred to the "pseudo-primitives" who were her folk characters.[31]

All of this was directed at a man who had helped Zora often. It shows the frustration of an author whose novelistic talents were deprecated because her fiction dealt with intraracial folkloric situations rather than with interracial confrontations—it was not "social document fiction." The difference in these perspectives is not between protest and accommodation, as Wright implied, but between different conceptions of the folk community. The difference is illustrated on the first page of *Their Eyes Were Watching God*. Janie has returned to Eatonville to tell her story; it is sundown and people are sitting on their porches: "It was the time to hear things and talk. These sitters had been tongueless, earless, eyeless, conveniences all day long. Mules and other brutes had occupied their skins. But now the sun and the bossman were gone, so the skins felt powerful and human." Just as Janie's struggle is to move beyond Nanny's observation that a black woman is "the mule of the world" into an awareness of her own humanity, so is Hurston's subject men rather than mules. Zora wrote of black life after the warrior stances preserving self-dignity in a hostile environment have been set aside for community fellowship. Folklore transmission is a natural product of this sense of security, for it is on these front porches that one's image can be turned from a negative to a positive identification ("I'm like that old mule / Black and don't give a damn / You got to take me / Like I Am"). Locke denied the validity of Zora's fictional environment when he claimed that she imposed folklore on reality rather than represented reality itself. It was natural for her response to be excessive, for she perceived a threat to her entire fictional world. Her fiction represented the processes of folkloric transmission, emphasizing the ways of thinking and speaking which grew from the folk environment. But it was fiction, not folklore. Zora replied to Locke by asserting, "To his discomfort I must say that those lines came out of my own head." Like Janie reacting to

Joe Starks, Zora Hurston was claiming her right to an autonomous imagination, both as a woman and as a member of the black American community. She was reacting in defense of a people who had been stereotyped as pseudoprimitive minstrels.[32]

NOTES

1. ZNH, transcript of employment (National Personnel Records Center, WPA Federal Theatre Project, New York City).

2. Jonathan Daniels, "Black Magic and Dark Laughter," *Saturday Review*, Oct. 19, 1935, p. 12; H. I. Brock, "The Full, True Flavor of Life in a Negro Community," *New York Times*, Nov. 10, 1935, p. 4; Henry Lee Moon, "Big Old Lies," *New Republic*, Dec. 11, 1935, p. 142.

3. Unidentified clipping, Sterling Brown, review of *Mules and Men*, Feb. 25, 1936 (JWJYale).

4. Ibid.

5. For Hurston's comments on the publisher's demands for *Mules and Men* see ZNH to CVV, Mar. 24, 1934 (JWJYale), and ZNH, "What White Publishers Won't Print," *Negro Digest*, 8 (Apr., 1950), 85–89. For the Ocoee riot story see "The Ocoee Riot," typescript, possibly by ZNH, Florida Federal Writers' Project (FHSP).

6. "Zora Neale Hurston," in *Twentieth Century Authors*, ed. Stanley Kunitz and Howard Haycraft (New York: H. W. Wilson, 1942), pp. 694–95.

7. Harold Preece, "The Negro Folk Cult," *Crisis*, 43 (1936), 364, 374.

8. Ibid.

9. See Alan Dundes's notes to Preece, "Negro Folk Cult," reprinted in *Mother Wit from the Laughing Barrel* (Englewood Cliffs, N.J.: Prentice-Hall, 1973), p. 37; LH, "Me and the Mule," *Negro Quarterly*, 1 (1942), 37.

10. ZNH, "Characteristics of Negro Expression," in *Negro: An Anthology*, ed. Nancy Cunard (London: Wishart, 1934), p. 39.

11. June Jordan, "On Richard Wright and Zora Neale Hurston," *Black World*, 23 (Aug., 1974), 5.

12. ZNH, "The Fiery Chariot," typescript play in one act (HCUFla). This is described in the program for *From Sun to Sun*, Feb. 11, 1933, as "an original Negro folk-play (a folk-tale dramatized by Zora Hurston)."

13. Gladys-Marie Fry, *Night Riders* (Knoxville: University of Tennessee Press, 1975).

14. ZNH, "Characteristics of Negro Expression," pp. 41, 42, 43, 46.

15. "Says Race Is Gifted," *St. Louis Argus*, Oct. 19, 1934 (report of a ZNH speech)(Schomburg Collection, New York Public Library).

16. "WPA Productions Scheduled by Rice," *New York Times*, Dec. 17, 1935, p. 30; ZNH to Edwin Osgood Grover, Dec. 29, 1935 (HCUFla); ZNH, application for John Simon Guggenheim Fellowship, Nov. 15, 1935 (GgFnd); employment transcript, "Zora Neale Hurston, WPA Federal Theatre Project, New York City" (National Personnel Records Center); ZNH to Henry Allen Moe of the Guggenheim Foundation, Mar. 18, 1936 (GgFnd).

17. ZNH to Henry Allen Moe, n.d. [received Apr. 20, 1936]; "U.S. Woman Anthropologist on Hoodoo Hunt in Jamaica," *Kingston Daily Gleaner*, Apr. 24, 1936; ZNH to Moe, n.d. [received May 5, 1936] (GgFnd). Quotations in this

reconstruction of Hurston's expedition to Haiti that are not noted come from her *Tell My Horse* (Philadelphia: J. B. Lippincott, 1938).

18. ZNH to Henry Allen Moe, May 22, 28, June 10, 1936 (GgFnd).

19. Ibid., May 22, 1936 (GgFnd).

20. ZNH, *Tell My Horse*, p. 36. Compare Hurston's account of the Maroons with Katharine Dunham's in *Journey to Accompong* (New York: Henry Holt, 1946).

21. ZNH to Henry Allen Moe, May 22, June 10, 1936 (GgFnd).

22. Ibid., Sept. 24, 1936 (GgFnd).

23. ZNH, *Tell My Horse*, p. 158.

24. ZNH to Henry Allen Moe, Mar. 20, July 6, 1937 (GgFnd); RH interview with Bertram Lippincott, Dec. 17, 1970, Penllyn, Pa.; RH interviews with Tay Hohoff, Dec., 1970, May, 1971, New York City. The manuscript of *Their Eyes Were Watching God* is dated Dec. 19, 1936 (JWJYale).

25. RH interview with "P" (name withheld by request), Jan. 15, 1976, New York City.

26. *Their Eyes Were Watching God* has received much critical treatment. Readers may wish to compare my own interpretation with the following: Jordan, "On Richard Wright and Zora Neale Hurston," pp. 4–10; Ellease Southerland, "Zora Neale Hurston," *Black World*, 23 (Aug., 1974), 20–30; Emma L. Blake, "Zora Neale Hurston: Author and Folklorist," *Negro History Bulletin*, 29 (Apr., 1966), 149–50, 165; Robert Bone, *The Negro Novel in America* (New Haven: Yale University Press, 1958), pp. 126–32; James W. Byrd, "Zora Neale Hurston: A Novel Folklorist," *Tennessee Folklore Society Bulletin*, 21 (1955), 37–41; Ralph Ellison, "Recent Negro Fiction," *New Masses*, Aug. 5, 1941, pp. 22–26; Hugh Gloster, *Negro Voices in American Fiction* (Chapel Hill: University of North Carolina Press, 1948), pp. 235–37; Evelyn Thomas Helmick, "Zora Neale Hurston," *Carrell*, 11 (June and Dec., 1970), 1–19; Ann Rayson, "The Novels of Zora Neale Hurston," *Studies in Black Literature*, 5 (Winter, 1974), 1–11; S. Jay Walker, "Zora Neale Hurston's *Their Eyes Were Watching God*: Black Novel of Sexism," *Modern Fiction Studies*, 20 (Winter, 1974-75), 519–27; Darwin T. Turner, *In a Minor Chord* (Carbondale: Southern Illinois University Press, 1971); Adam David Miller, "Some Observations on a Black Aesthetic," in *New Black Voices*, ed. Abraham Chapman (New York: Signet, 1972), p. 541; Roger Rosenblatt, *Black Fiction* (Cambridge: Harvard University Press, 1974); James O. Young, *Black Writers of the Thirties* (Baton Rouge: Louisiana State University Press, 1973), pp. 219–23; James R. Giles, "The Significance of Time in Zora Neale Hurston's *Their Eyes Were Watching God*," *Negro American Literature Forum*, 6 (Summer, 1972), 52–53, 60; Mary Helen Washington, "The Black Woman's Search for Identity," *Black World*, 21 (Aug., 1972) 68–75; Addison Gayle, *The Way of the New World* (Garden City, N.Y.: Doubleday, 1976), pp. 168–80. The last two critics cited are among the best commentators on the novel.

27. Turner, *In a Minor Chord*, p. 106.

28. ZNH to Mrs. Mason, Oct. 15, 1931 (HUAL).

29. Jordan, "On Richard Wright and Zora Neale Hurston," p. 6.

30. Herschel Brickell, review of *Their Eyes Were Watching God*, *New York Post*, Sept. 14, 1937; George Stevens, "Negroes by Themselves," *Saturday Review*, Sept. 18, 1937, p. 3; Richard Wright, "Between Laughter and Tears," *New Masses*, Oct. 5, 1937. Wright's conception of folkloric fiction was more

complicated than his review suggests; see his "Blueprint for Negro Writing," *New Challenge*, 2 (Fall, 1937), 53-65.

31. ZNH, "The Chick with One Hen," typescript (JWJYale). See also ZNH to James Weldon Johnson, n.d. [ca. Feb., 1938] (JWJYale).

32. LH, "Me and the Mule," *Negro Quarterly*, 1 (1942), 37; ZNH, "Chick with One Hen."

10 〰〰 Voodoo Gods and Biblical Men

Even while collecting in Haiti in the winter of 1936, Zora had concluded that much more needed to be done for a thorough voodoo book, and on January 6, 1937, she sent a formal application to the Guggenheim Foundation, requesting a fellowship renewal. She stressed that the "task is huge, so huge and complicated that it flings out into space more fragments than would form the whole of any other area except Africa. It is more than the sympathetic magic that is practised by the hoodoo doctors in the United States. It is as formal as the Catholic church anywhere. An ordinary volume of 100,000 words could only cover the subject by being very selective and brief. So you can see why a letter is difficult for me. It is like explaining the planetary theory on a postage stamp."[1]

A second fellowship was awarded in late March. Feeling that the proper voodoo book "has never been done, and it is crying to me to do it," Zora was grateful; she wrote that the "burning bush" flaming inside her could now be extinguished and her "ideal of achievement" attained. Trouble obtaining a passport delayed her departure, and she did not return to Haiti until May, arriving in Port-au-Prince via Panama steamer. She immediately made plans to return to the south of the island as soon as the seasonal rains subsided, and by July she was reporting, "The inflow has been so exciting and so full that there has been no opportunity for putting anything into final form."[2]

In the midst of this promising start something happened that would change her entire trip and seriously affect the book she hoped to write. As a foreign woman alone in a mysterious country, she had been warned often about studying the rituals of the Petro gods rather than the Rada gods. One of her best Haitian friends told her that she should not study randomly, that one needed a guide, for "some things were good to know and some things were not." The Rada gods were the good gods, or "loa," grouped around the supreme figure of Damballa, the "great source" of all life; they demanded only chickens and pigeons for sacrifice; there were no obligations incurred by what they did for a person. The Petro loa were terrible and wicked, powerful and quick; they could be made to do good things, but they worked only if one made great (some said human) sacrifices and promised to serve them. Petro gods were resorted to by many, but they were very much feared, for they were capable of extraordinary feats of possession. There was only a fine line between worshipping Petro gods and worshipping the devil, and one could not easily tell who was a true priest of voodoo, a "houngan," and who was a "bocor," or priest of evil. Hurston noted that "often the two offices occupy the same man at different times."[3]

With typical courage Zora had laughed off the warnings and continued, knowing some bad moments, but figuring them a small price to pay. A chicken being sacrificed in a ceremony for Papa Legba, god of the gate and crossroads, had leaped in its death agony and touched her: "My heart flinched and my flesh drew up like tripe." Once a man had become possessed by a Petro spirit, his face losing itself in a horrible mask as "a feeling of unspeakable evil" entered the room. Everyone felt it simultaneously: "The fear was so humid you could smell it and feel it on your tongue." Fortunately, the Rada houngan drove the spirit away and the man's "features untangled themselves and became a face again."[4]

Months after the initial warnings, in late June, 1937, she began to see what people had been hinting at. While deep in her studies in a remote part of the bush, she was taken violently ill; as she wrote privately, "It seems that some of my destinations and some of my accessions have been whispered into ears that heard. In consequence, just as mysteriously as the information travelled, I HAVE HAD A VIOLENT GASTRIC DISTURBANCE." She was in bed for two weeks, so shaken that she asked to be carried to the home of the American consul. She withdrew enough money from the bank to pay for the trip to the States. She told Moe, "For a whole day and a night, I'd thought I'd never make it."[5]

A case of the flu? A repetition of the intestinal disorder of a decade earlier? Or a poisoning? And if a poisoning, by natural or supernatural means? Zora Hurston was convinced that her illness and her voodoo studies were related. She had learned how horse hair chopped fine and put into one's food could kill, how gleanings from a curry comb were sometimes hidden in vegetables. A bocor knew which spiders and insects were poisonous, how a dried "gallowass" could create great harm. She backed off from continuing the intense research and began to make plans to finish *Tell My Horse* on American soil. She was forced to admit that she could "not pretend to give a full account of either voodoo or voodoo gods."[6] She had gone deeply enough into the Caribbean night.

Zora spent the next two months recovering and sight-seeing, and by September her usual optimism had returned. Her plan was to go to Florida "to polish off this volume. It is swelling up in me like a jeenie in a bottle, or like Southern Negroes would put it, like a barrel of molasses in the summertime." In Haiti the material had engulfed her, and she needed the perspective of home. She played with the idea of writing two books, one for the anthropologist and "one for the way I want to write it." Her plans for the compleat exposé of voodoo, however, had been permanently shelved. *Tell My Horse* was written by an author pulling her punches, trying to talk about matters that would entertain rather than startle.[7]

She arrived in New York in late September and stayed to help with publicity for *Their Eyes Were Watching God*, published on September 18. With support from the Guggenheim Foundation for the next six months, she was free from financial worries. She scheduled an appearance at the Boston Book Fair and thought of giving another *Great Day* concert in December, this time with much new Haitian material. However, Bertram Lippincott began to press her for the manuscript. She left for Florida in February, finished the book in mid-March while living in Maitland, and saw it scheduled for publication in October. Memories of the Haitian occupation by American marines were still fresh, and previous books about Haiti by Herskovits and Seabrook had proven popular; both she and Lippincott had high hopes for sales.[8]

Tell My Horse did not sell well. It is Hurston's poorest book, chiefly because of its form. She was a novelist and folklorist, not a

political analyst or traveloguist. Yet *Tell My Horse* is filled with
political analysis, often of a naïve sort, with superficial descriptions of West Indian curiosities. She reports a good deal of public
gossip as accepted fact, and she reveals a chauvinism that must
have infuriated her Haitian hosts. Zora consistently praises the
nineteen-year occupation of that country by American marines,
attributing solvency and political stability to the American influence. She complains about President Sténio Vincent's "Second
Independence Day" celebrating the marines' removal, observing
that the money could have been better spent to feed the peasants
red beans and rice. Although she should have known better, she
generalizes often: "There is a marked tendency [among Haitians]
to refuse responsibility for anything that is unfavorable." She reports that the "lying habit goes from the thatched hut to the
mansion," yet later praises the honesty of Lucille, her devoted
maid. She warns travelers not to pay anyone in advance in Haiti
unless one knows the person very well indeed. She gives a highly
poetic account of Haitian history by describing its legendary status
in oral tradition; she makes no attempt to compare these legends
with historical fact.

The voodoo sections, by contrast, are vivid and exciting, despite
the confusing accumulation of ceremonies and gods. Although the
book lacks a scholarly context that would distinguish Zora's adventures from the normal fare of the anthropological tourist, her two
weeks of violent gastric disturbance make for a serious, emotionally
charged presentation. Her voodoo reporting, as in the earlier accounts from *Mules and Men*, consistently treats voodoo as a legitimate, sophisticated religion. It is as old as creation: "It is the old,
old, mysticism of the world in African terms. Voodoo is a religion of
creation and life. It is the worship of the sun, the water and other
natural forces, but the symbolism is no better understood than that
of other religions." By stressing its religious nature, *Tell My Horse*
dignifies voodoo worship, removing it from the lurid and sensational associations held by the popular mind. Voodoo's sexual content becomes a dignified component of a complex belief on the same
order as the Virgin Birth. A houngan asks her, "What is the truth?"
and then answers with a ceremony in which the Mambo priestess
throws back her veil and reveals her vagina. Zora writes of the

reverence of the act: "The ceremony means that this is the infinite, the ultimate truth. There is no mystery beyond the mysterious source of life." The men in the ceremony express a decorous faith as they ritualistically kiss this organ of creation, "for Damballa, the god of gods has permitted them to come face to face with truth."

Perhaps the most revealing chapter in *Tell My Horse* deals with zombies. A government physician had warned that the secret of the zombies might cost her "a great deal to learn. . . . Perhaps it will cost you more than you are willing to pay." Accordingly, she is cautious in her observations: "What is the whole truth and nothing else but the truth about zombies? I do not know, but I know that I saw the broken remnant, relic, or refuse of Felicia Felix-Mentor in a hospital yard." Zombies were supposedly soulless bodies called back from the dead. A person of culture and refinement could become a mindless beast of burden, toiling naked in a banana field, without any hope of release. Loved ones would not be searching, because they had seen the person buried. While many believed that zombies represented only a superstitious fear held by the ignorant, Zora was not so sure. Whether the condition resulted from a bocor's sucking out the soul of a victim prior to death, administering a secret poison, or calling on some Petro god, she was willing to accept the existence of zombies as fact: "I know that there are zombies in Haiti."

Zora had been invited by one of her closest Haitian friends, Dr. Rulx Leon, director-general of the Service d'Hygiene, to travel to a government hospital to investigate the appearance of an apparent zombie. She did so, photographing this unfortunate being, and thinking long and hard about its meaning. Felicia Felix-Mentor had been buried in 1907; but in October of 1936 she was found wandering naked, muttering, "This is the farm of my father. I used to live here." The owner recognized the woman as his sister, buried twenty-nine years before. At the hospital she was a frightening sight to behold, cringing against a wall with a cloth hiding her face; she was "dreadfull. That blank face with the dead eyes. The eyelids were white all around the eyes as if they had been burned with acid." Communication was impossible, the sight of the human wreckage too much to endure for long. Zora went away, puzzled and uncertain about what she had seen. The Haitian doctors believed that some drug known only to a few bocors had produced a semblance of death, some secret "probably brought from Africa and handed down from generation to generation." But what could it be? "Nobody will tell who knows. The secret is with some bocor dead or alive."

Most of *Tell My Horse* falls short of the zombie account, and although reviewers were generally kind, the book's reception did not overwhelm. In *Opportunity* Locke referred to its "piquant thrills" and its "anthropological gossip." Anthropologists pointed out that Hurston's findings did not square with previous scholarship; Herskovits, for example, had claimed that the bocor was simply a magician. Newspapers and magazines praised the book but had questions about its curious mix of subject and style. The *New Yorker* found it "disorganized but interesting." Harold Courlander, writing in the *Saturday Review*, called it "a curious mixture of remembrance, travelogue, sensationalism and anthropology. The remembrances are vivid, the travelogue tedious, the sensationalism reminiscent of Seabrook and the anthropology a melange of misinterpretation and exceedingly good folklore."[9]

The period between completion of the *Tell My Horse* manuscript and the book's publication had been busy. A month after sending the manuscript to Lippincott's, Zora joined the Federal Writers' Project for the state of Florida. A unit of the WPA, the writers' project was the New Deal's answer to literary unemployment. Strongly supported by Mrs. Roosevelt, the project was begun in 1935 to provide jobs for hundreds of authors unable to practice their craft in a depression economy. Under federal leadership until 1939, then under state sponsorship until 1943, its roster of participants includes many of the most famous names in modern American literature: Conrad Aiken, Nelson Algren, Saul Bellow, Edward Dahlberg, Kenneth Fearing, John Cheever, Loren Eiseley, and Kenneth Rexroth. For the black writer the federal program was a particular boon, since hiring was often free of discrimination. Arna Bontemps, Sterling Brown, Margaret Walker, Willard Motley, Richard Wright, Frank Yerby, Katharine Dunham, Fenton Johnson, and Ralph Ellison found employment in its various divisions.

Zora became an editor for the Florida project on April 25, 1938, working on the preparation of the state's volume of the American Guide series. The guides were intended as American Baedekers, and many remain today invaluable introductions to unfamiliar states. She stayed on the Florida project for almost a year and a half, with one brief hiatus, and she cut a memorable swath. Operating out of the main office in Jacksonville, she would frequently leave for a week or more at a time, telling no one where she was going. It was assumed that she was collecting folklore for the Florida guide, but one was never sure. (It is clear now that she had also begun working hard on her next book, *Moses, Man of the Mountain*.) Admonished by the administrators for her truancy, she would reingratiate herself, pick up her weekly paycheck, and then sometimes disappear again. Her reputation on the project was that of an actress who loved to show off, a woman of remarkable talent and spirit, a loner, an uncooperative co-worker, an editor who hated to stay inside at her desk. [10]

Zora became heavily involved in collecting and editing material for a project book to be entitled *The Florida Negro*. Sterling Brown, the writers' project national editor of Negro affairs, had outlined for the states an ambitious program to research the true history and present status of the black American experience. One of the most notable results of his stewardship was *The Negro in Virginia*, a comprehensive account of black Virginians past and present; the Florida book was patterned after this Virginia volume. By June of 1938 Zora was acting as supervisor of the Negro unit of the Florida Federal Writers' Project, traveling to Washington to charm Henry Alsberg, the FWP director, into supporting the effort. She wrangled a salary increase for the supervisor and more travel money for the folklore collecting, and by July she was visiting black communities in the Everglades with a recording machine liberated from Washington despite a mountain of red tape. For the rest of her employment on the project, Zora worked on this book, eventually overseeing the compilation of a two-hundred-page volume. [11]

"The Florida Negro" has remained in manuscript, probably because it lacks a unifying structure. It contains many of the stories and songs Zora had collected before, as well as important slave narratives collected by the Florida FWP staff. The book was a composite effort of many editors, and Zora cannot be blamed for much of its sociological prose. The most interesting parts of the manuscript are clearly her work. She submitted a section on "Negro mythical places" such as "Diddy-Wah-Diddy"—where everything is in such a grand scale that "the dogs can stand flat-footed and lick crumbs off of heaven's tables"— and she spiced up a rather drab narrative with folksongs:

Oh, Angeline, Oh, Angeline
Oh, Angeline that great great gal of mine

You feel her legs, you feel her legs,
You feel her legs and you want to feel her thighs

You feel her thighs, you feel her thighs
You feel her thighs, then you fade away and die.

Less prurient but equally colorful were her tall tales about Florida weather: "They have strong winds on the West Coast too. One day the wind blowed so hard till it blowed a well up out of the ground. One day it blowed so hard till it blowed a crooked road straight. Another time it blowed and blowed and scattered the days of the week so bad till Sunday did not come till late Tuesday evening." Perhaps remembering Locke's attempt to affirm the spirituals as "classical" music by comparing them with Gregorian chants, she made sure that "The Florida Negro" included her notions on black music. In a section of the manuscript entitled "The Sanctified Church," Zora emphasized that the spirituals grew from a native black esthetic and could only be "twisted in concert . . . into Gregorian chants"; they were not "apocryphal appendages to Bach and Brahms."

In July of 1939, in a move long anticipated, federal sponsorship of the FWP was transferred to the states, and there was a large turnover in personnel. Zora had already begun to look for another job and had spent some time in Cincinnati doing a series of radio programs. She received an honorary doctor of letters' from her high school alma mater, Morgan State, in June. Armed with a new academic credential, she turned to the black colleges for employment and was hired by James Shepherd, president of North Carolina College for Negroes in Durham.

Dr. Shepherd, like Mary McLeod Bethune of Bethune-Cookman, had singlehandedly built North Carolina College from a small training school to an accredited college. He set the rules for his institution and did not always welcome differing views. A man of great energy and skill, he was one of the best-known black educators in the South. Shepherd and Zora began their association amiably enough, but they very soon crossed swords. Shepherd expected his faculty members to live on or near campus, to not make waves, and to conduct lives beyond reproach. Zora arrived in September, motoring up in a bright red convertible. She ignored campus housing, renting a cabin in the mountains outside of Durham; she explained that she needed the solitude to write. Hired to organize a drama program, she complained about the hour her classes were scheduled, and that none of the students knew that English 261 was to be a drama course. Fitful in her teaching—one day brilliant, the next preoccupied—she interested many students but never really progressed far with plans for presenting another *From Sun to Sun*. Shepherd urged her on, but after a concert was set for December 18, she begged off, saying there had been insufficient time to prepare a production. Frustrated by what she perceived as lack of support from the college administration, she urged Shepherd to provide a "proper frame . . . for me to work." That frame included courses in play writing, direction, and production. She told him that these were "the irreducible minimum if anything at all is to be accomplished, and I assume that you do want something accomplished or you would not have invited me to join the faculty in the first place." The upshot was that during the 1939–40 school year at North Carolina College for Negroes the director of dramatic productions never staged a single play. She and Shepherd were mutually glad to part company. She took her revenge in articles about black schools and their chronic need for money. In one, she unfairly characterized them as "begging joints," without laboratories or teachers; the usual begging joint had "little else beside its FOUNDER." In another, she waspishly referred to North Carolina College as "a one horse religious school" that had become the state college for blacks because of Shepherd's political influence. [12]

Zora's difficulties with Shepherd may have arisen in part from her activities outside the school. Less than a month after arriving, Zora made contacts with the Carolina Playmakers, a well-known dramatic group associated with the University of North Carolina at nearby Chapel Hill. In October she spoke at the fall meeting of the

Carolina Dramatic Association at the Carolina Inn, an event in itself in segregated North Carolina. She was introduced by Frederick Koch, director of the Playmakers, and although some members of the audience were prepared to scoff at a black woman's ideas, she charmed them all. Claiming that "our drama must be like us or it doesn't exist," Zora submitted a brief for a "native Negro drama." She had told her students, "We are going to try to make plays out of the Negro life in the Negro manner," and although she expected this to be disappointing, they responded enthusiastically because the plays given before had been incomprehensible. Her explanation was, "It's very hard to sell Park Avenue to a person who has never had any overstuffed furniture in his life." Flattering her white audience, she told them, "I want to build the drama of North Carolina out of ourselves. We want to follow in your footsteps. . . . We want you to help us. We are going to have to struggle against people who think if we don't do something highbrow we haven't accomplished anything." Her intent was to create a production company committed to dramatizing black folklore; just as the white group had performed a number of original plays about North Carolina mountain folk, so she hoped to "initiate among her race in this state a movement similar to that of the Playmakers."[13]

In the audience was Paul Green of the drama department at Chapel Hill, winner of a 1927 Pulitzer Prize for his drama of racial relations in the South, *In Abraham's Bosom*. (Green would later collaborate with Richard Wright on the dramatic version of *Native Son*.) A committed liberal at a segregated school who was known among black people for his racial sympathies, Green invited Zora to attend a play-writing seminar which met at his home each Sunday evening. Her presence offended one member of the class, a Daughter of the Confederacy from Alabama. Addressing the woman in his North Carolina drawl, Green was full of sympathy for her predicament, understanding how she felt, the painfulness of it. In all conscience he could not ask a southern lady to put up with such an indignity; it appeared she would have to leave. With the woman gone, Zora quickly became the "star," according to one of the class members. She and Green toyed with the idea of collaborating on a play called "John de Conqueror." Zora was so excited about the possibility that she soon began to shirk her teaching duties. She told

ZORA NEALE HURSTON
256

Green, "You do not need to concern yourself with the situation here at the school. I won't care what happens here or if nothing happens here so long as I can do the bigger thing with you. My mind is hitting on sixteen cylinders on the play now. . . . I see no reason why the firm of Green and Hurston should not take charge of the Negro playrighting [sic] business in America, and I can see many reasons why we should." As often with Zora, there was a bit of hustle in her solicitation, but the enthusiasm seems genuine. She continued to attend the class, despite the insults of Tarheel students as she drove her convertible through the tiny college town, a tam-o'-shanter tilted rakishly over one ear. "Hi, nigger," they shouted; "Hi, freshman," she replied.[14]

Shepherd and North Carolina College may have been disappointed in Zora's dramatic efforts, but they could hardly complain about the national publicity she brought to the school. During her first semester in Durham, in November, 1939, her novel *Moses, Man of the Mountain* was published by Lippincott's. Zora had been working on this book for a long time; five years earlier she had published a short story with the germ of its idea. Appearing in *Challenge*, a brave, short-lived black literary journal, in September, 1934, "The Fire and the Cloud" describes a dead and ascending Moses as half man, half god, a figure whose head is in the clouds on Mount Nebo, but whose practical concerns are those of his Israelites poised to cross the Jordan. We know that Zora worked on a novel during the semester the Rosenwald Foundation funded her study at Columbia, and submitted a draft to Lippincott's in the spring of 1935. In December of 1935 she told a friend she was working on a novel about Moses. Other tasks had intervened, and only after returning from Haiti and finding employment on the Florida Federal Writers' Project did she finally have time to complete the book. Working throughout late 1938 and early 1939, she produced a volume received with confusion at the time and with uncertainty ever since.[15]

Moses, Man of the Mountain is a large novel, by far Hurston's most ambitious book. It does not always achieve its own aspirations, but this is no excuse for its critical neglect. Even informed literary scholars have been misled by the novel; Robert Bone, for example, refers to it as a book of folklore. Only Darwin Turner, in an essay uniformly hostile to Zora, has assessed it properly: "If she had written nothing else Miss Hurston would deserve recognition for this book."[16]

Hurston attempts nothing less than to kidnap Moses from Judeo-Christian tradition, claiming that his true birthright is African and that his true constituency is Afro-American. Her audacity stemmed from a knowledge of the way legends grow and from the historical evidence indicating that Moses was probably Egyptian rather than Hebrew. In 1937, two years before *Moses* appeared, Freud had published two controversial essays in the famous German psychoanalytical journal *Imago*, which drew from sketchy historical evidence to assert not only that Moses was Egyptian, but also that the monotheistic religion he brought to the Hebrews originated with a heretical ruler of Egyptian antiquity.[17] The biblical account of the infant Moses' being placed on the water was known to be legendary—there are similar stories in a number of cultures, the most ancient being the legend of the founder of Babylon, who was borne secretly by his mother, placed in a basket, lowered into a river, and saved to found a nation. Hurston may have read Freud's articles, or she may have come to her vision independently; whatever her source, she clearly holds that Moses was an Egyptian whom Jewish myth undertook to transform into a Jew.

Although the novel depends heavily on the biblical narrative, Hurston dismisses the account of Moses' early survival; she presents it as a myth originating in a child's alibi. A male child is born to a Hebrew couple, Amram and Jochebed, already the parents of Miriam and Aaron, after the Egyptian masters have decreed the death of all male infants. They hide the unnamed baby for three months, then place it in a basket of bulrushes on the Nile. Miriam is instructed to watch, but falls asleep at her post; she awakens to discover that "the child and his basket were gone, that was all." Threatened with punishment for her negligence, she creates a child's fantasy about her baby brother's rescue by the Egyptian princess, a fantasy that quickly assumes the status of legend in an oppressed Hebrew community starved for symbols of power. This occurs despite the absence of corroborative evidence; when Moses' mother goes to the palace gates to ask to nurse the suckling child, Jochebed is informed that there is no new baby to be nursed.

Hurston's purpose is not so much to debunk a Judeo-Christian prophet as to remove him from scripture in order to relocate him in Afro-American tradition. Mosaic legends were not confined to Egypt or Palestine. Hurston's introduction cites Moses' stature throughout the Mediterranean area and Africa, especially among Africans who have suffered their own diaspora: "Wherever the children of Africa have been scattered by slavery, there is the acceptance of Moses as the fountain of mystic powers." In Haiti he is the father of Damballa, king of the Rada gods; elsewhere, Moses is the original conjurer, the greatest "power doctor" known to man. The symbol of his power—the staff that is a snake—is held by a "MIGHTY HAND" that commands nature to do his bidding.

Hurston's interest in Moses had been renewed in Haiti when she collected tales of Moses' supernatural powers that were neither in the Bible nor in any biography. In *Tell My Horse* she acknowledged the tradition of Moses as the great father of magic in Africa and Asia, and she speculated: "Perhaps some of his feats recorded in the Pentateuch are the folk beliefs of such a character grouped about a man for it is well established that if a memory is great enough, other memories will cluster about it, and those in turn will bring their suites of memories to gather upon this focal point, because perhaps, they are all scattered parts of the one thing like Plato's concept of the perfect thing."

To understand fully what Hurston attempted in this novel, one must remember the identification made by captive black slaves in America with the children of Israel in Egypt, and the resulting role that Moses played in Afro-American folklore. Black spirituals are full of references to Moses. Moses was "an infant cast away, by Pharaoh's daughter found." He goes down to Egypt land to tell ole Pharaoh to "let my people go"; "when Israel was in Egypt's land, they were oppressed so hard they could not stand." "Didn't old Pharaoh get los'," didn't "Pharaoh's army get drownded," when Moses led the chosen people to freedom? It is the slaves' identity as a chosen people that Hurston utilizes to tell Moses' story, an identity rich with complexity.

In one of the most important articles ever published about slave songs and slave consciousness, Lawrence Levine has demonstrated how the spirituals both before and after slavery "were the product of an improvisational communal consciousness. They were not, as some observers thought, totally new creations, but were forged out of many preexisting bits of old songs mixed together with snatches of new tunes and lyrics and fit into a fairly traditional but never wholly static metrical pattern. They were . . . *simultaneously* the result of individual and mass creativity. They were the products of that folk process which has been called 'communal re-creation' through which older songs are constantly recreated into essentially new entities."[18] This mutually supportive re-creation is the key to understanding Hurston's ambition in retelling the Moses story. Moses could be simultaneously the product of a mass creativity that had made him special to black people *and* the product of Zora Neale Hurston's improvised, poetic vision. Her fictional solo was being sung against a historical chorus created by those spiritual-makers whom James Weldon Johnson called "Black and unknown bards."

As Levine remarks, "The single most persistent image the slave songs contain . . . is that of the chosen people."[19] The spirituals identify the slaves as "de people dat is born of God": "we are the people of God," "we are de people of de Lord," "I really do believe I'm a child of God," "I'm a child ob God, wid my soul sot free." This identification should not be expected of a people told endlessly that they are members of the lowliest of races. But it was a pervasive identification, and it should call into question all theories about a slave mentality so internalized that slaves accepted the degraded image of self (the Sambo image) that whites attempted to force upon them. The chosen-people image demonstrates how the slaves created their own imaginative mental world, secure from a degraded status. That imaginative world was a place where unfettered creativity adapted a Christian pantheon to a slave's personal needs, a place where "de Lawd" was as intimate and as personal as African gods had been, a place where the heroes of the scriptures were life-size men. Biblical heroes so revered in white Christianity that they had lost the blood of humanity were reborn into the lusty creations of the Afro-American spiritual: Joshua fighting the battle of Jericho, Daniel being delivered from the lion's den, Gabriel blowing his trumpet, and Moses securing the release of a captive people.

This process of making the gods human and breathing life into ancient prophets provided Hurston with a way of looking at her material, with a fictional technique that could mediate between individual and mass creativity. The Moses story was a received narrative; the novelist made it her own by adapting the traditions of her people. Although admittedly Moses was man, not god, his role in Judeo-Christian tradition was remote, shrouded in biblical dignity. Once he was demystified, however, the analogy between biblical history and the black American past became real and immediate, an allegory relevant to the oppressive circumstances that black people encounter in any age. Hurston acts as a tradition-bearer for an Afro-American worldview in *Moses*, simulating the process of creation that had led to the spirituals, reaffirming the act of imagination that could make Moses African rather than Hebrew, a conjure man instead of a mere conduit for divine power. She identifies with the creativity that could make slaves a chosen people in the midst of a culture structured to deny them a sense of special status.

Having said this, however, and recognizing the dimension of her effort, one finally concludes that the attempt falls short of its goal. Hurston is unable to find a consistent tone that can treat Moses as both divine deliverer and common man, the Hebrew people as both a chosen sect and a collection of limited humanity. At times she seems content with small jokes when a situation calls for tragic irony. She is never quite sure if the outsider Moses is black or white, an uncertainty lending confusion to his racial statements. Told in a mixture of black dialect, colloquial English, and biblical rhetoric, Zora's story falls short of the greatness it might have achieved. She seems uncertain about how to resolve the tension between the Moses of mystical tradition, thought by some the original conjurer, and the Moses of biblical record, revered by the Jews as a law-giver and identified by the spirituals as God's emissary to oppressed peoples. Nevertheless, the book fascinates, making *Moses, Man of the Mountain* one of the more interesting minor works in American literary history.

Primarily a study of character, with Moses center stage, the novel turns the biblical Moses—whom Sir James Frazer described as "set apart," without human frailty, a "splendid but solitary figure"—into a very special hoodoo man subject to at least some of the defects of the human condition. Neither the Bible nor history tells anything of Moses' youth and rearing. In Hurston's book he grows up in the palace of his grandfather, the pharaoh; he is an outcast at court, suspiciously watched by his uncle, the heir to the throne. While others engage in palace intrigue, Moses studies the ways of man and nature with old Mentu, an illiterate but wise stableman. The older man has "answers in the form of stories for nearly every question that Moses asked"; he tells the lad "how it is that man can understand the language of the birds and the animals and the plants." Moses grows up an extraordinarily wise and imaginative youth, a child given to mysticism who presses the Egyptian priests to teach him their magic. He also frequently outwits his uncle, and after winning a war game by using cavalry to surround his uncle's chariots, Moses is appointed commander of the Egyptian armies. Drawing partially upon the account by the first-century historian Flavius Josephus that Moses was an Egyptian general, Hurston has him carry out his grandfather's expansionist policies with a lusty exuberance; Moses extends Egypt's dominion throughout the Middle East, submits to a marriage of convenience to an Ethiopian princess, and becomes a national hero.[20]

The life of a warrior eventually palls, and Moses becomes aware of the plight of the Hebrew slaves in the land of Goshen. He lobbies in the court for a more humane treatment and, as in the Bible, kills an Egyptian overseer who senselessly beat a Hebrew worker. The murder occurs at the same time his uncle, drawing upon the legends of a Hebrew in the palace, maliciously questions his birthright. Moses responds by forsaking the court and choosing self-exile. He travels to Midian, crossing the Red Sea at a secret point where the ebb of the tide leaves a dry walkway, and plans to live humbly the rest of his life in study of the natural world. Knowing that "the man who interprets Nature is always held in great honor," he vows "to live and talk with and know her secrets."

Moses' education really begins after he settles down to live with a Midianite priest, Jethro, the father of Zipporah, a beautiful woman of "tawny skin . . . luxuriant, crinkly hair," and "warm brown arms." Soon Zipporah is his wife, and Moses is studying even deeper magic from Jethro, for whom "other people's thoughts are like glass." After living among the tribe for twenty years, learning the native language, adopting the monotheism Jethro teaches, and exploring his magic, Moses embarks on a journey to Koptos to consult the secret Book of Thoth, which is guarded by a deathless serpent. The book, which "brings one to the Gods," is apparently preparation for the mission to the Hebrews that Jethro urges upon him. Shortly after Moses returns he encounters the burning bush in the wilderness and makes his promise to God to rescue the children of Israel from the rule of his uncle. The struggle with Pharaoh ensues, the plagues rain down, and the chosen people are finally emancipated after the Egyptian army drowns in the Red Sea. The tribes wander in the wilderness for forty years, quarrel with their leader, fall from faith, regain it, receive the laws and commandments, and eventually find themselves poised to enter the Promised Land. At this point, in a scene taken from the earlier short story, Moses ascends to Mount Nebo and utters his farewell, a figure of god-like powers who has lived very much of this earth.

Hurston works hard to demystify Moses. She describes his sentimental attachment to his mentor, his impulsive temper, his sometimes boastful righteousness (after settling a plague of lice on the Egyptians he tells Pharaoh, "I'd let them children of Israel go if I were you, but don't let *me* over-persuade you"), his shrewd political consciousness, and his continuing exasperation over the ingratitude of the people he has saved. She describes his emotions in universal terms: "Moses discovered he was two beings. In short, he was everybody boiled down to a drop. Everybody is two beings: one lives and flourishes in the daylight and stands guard. The other being walks and howls at night."

Hurston's most effective device for bringing Moses down to earth is the manipulation of his speech. In the first part of the novel Moses speaks in the proper diction of the Egyptian court; after living with Jethro for a number of years, he speaks more and more in the dialect of the rural black South. The effect is to reinforce Moses' human qualities at the very moment he is becoming less human, losing his husband-and-warrior image in the sanctity of his mission; this subtle shift both allies the outsider Moses with the people he will save and reminds us that a human being has been called to a god-like task. The elders of the tribes of Israel "done took notice" that

"Moses is getting so he talks our language just like we talk it ourselves." When they complain about their lot, he asks, "What makes you think you got to holler and cry about it. . . . We're assembled and gathered here to find out what you're all grumbling and mumbling about." Discovering that it is the lack of food, he rebukes them: "I had the idea all along that you came out here hunting freedom. I didn't know you were hunting a barbecue."

Moses' speech throughout the book is a marvel of folk wisdom and vivid expression. Confronted with Hebrew fickleness, he muses over how a leader deals with people. In language similar to that of Janie in *Their Eyes Were Watching God*, he notes: "You have to go to life to know life. God! It costs you something to do good . . . people talk about tenderness and mercy, but they love force." During the battle with the Amalekites, Moses raises his hands into the air to let his power flow to the people. But the battle is long, and Moses tires. He tells Aaron and Hur to hold up his hands: "Now you all, prop me up on every leaning side. Don't let my hands fall. . . . We're holding up the world with these hands." Not only does the speech echo the spiritual ("He's got the whole world in his hands"), but it also translates John Pearson's poetic expression of support for his wife into a ruler's need for the support of his people.

Moses has the capacity to hold the world in his hands because he is both the supreme magician of the universe and the appointed leader of the Hebrews. One of the most interesting and perplexing things about Hurston's Moses is his multiple role as the divinely designated leader of Israel, the possessor of nature's secrets, and the most powerful hoodoo doctor of antiquity. The journey to Koptos and the struggle with the deathless serpent occur without apparent divine intervention; Moses' personal powers enable him to read the Book of Thoth, to learn elemental truths: "He knows the ways and meaning of Light and he heard the voice of Darkness and knew its thoughts."

These roles of hoodoo man and divine leader are simply juxtaposed in the novel. Hurston gives no indication of whether Moses' power derives from the lessons of Jethro, from the Koptic snake he has commanded to meet him anywhere in the world, or from an all-powerful God who identifies himself as "I AM WHAT I AM." Jethro playfully shows Moses how to send a plague of frogs upon an unwanted guest. The Koptic experience is an archetypal trip to the underworld in which Moses receives what Joseph Campbell would call a "life-transmuting boon"; the adventure is supposed to give him "more power than any other man on earth." The God of the burning bush provides him with a staff of life that is both serpent and scepter, a rod that he will take in his right hand to turn Egyptian water into blood. What becomes obvious is that Moses is a man for all seasons, a priest, a conjurer, a messenger of God, an agent of the supernatural, an uncommon man with an understanding of nature. One source of power does not derive from any other; they all simply coexist.

These remarkable qualities cause Moses to transcend history, to enter the realm of legend. Indeed, one of Hurston's purposes in this novel apparently is to explain the legend-making, legend-transmission process. Belief tales regarded by their tellers as true, legends are created by people seeking to satisfy deeply felt personal needs, an irony of human history that Zora relishes for its comic moments. We all believe in legends because we need to, because they satisfy our innermost compulsions, because we want to find epic qualities in the most unlikely place—the affairs of the earth. Hurston seems to be saying that even when the extraordinary person like Moses comes along, he is subject not only to the whims of the legends that attach to him, but also to the frailties of those who would create him in their own image.

In *Moses, Man of the Mountain* the Moses legend begins with Miriam's alibi. The story, spread initially by the gossipy Jochebed, is believed because the Hebrews want to think that "we is kinfolks to Pharaohs now." It is only a short time before Miriam is convinced of the truth of her alibi, relating it far and wide. The Hebrews do not question too closely: "They wanted to believe and they did. It kept them from feeling utterly vanquished by Pharaoh." The idea of a Hebrew in the royal household even provides an explanation for cruelty, lending irony to the irrationality of racial hate: "Ho, ho! Pharaoh hates Hebrews does he? He passes a law to destroy all our sons and he gets a Hebrew child for a grandson. Ain't that rich." The Moses story leads to speculation about others who are passing ("The higher-ups who got Hebrew blood in 'em is always the ones to persecute us"), and rumors grow that Pharaoh's grandmother was

Hebrew; the people "had something to cherish and chew on, if they could say that they had a Hebrew in the palace." The story grows with being handled, until "men claimed to have seen signs at the birth of the child and Miriam came to believe every detail of it as she added them and retold them time and time again. Others conceived and added details at their pleasure and the legends grew like grass."

The legends pose a particular problem of belief for Moses himself. In the beginning he rejects the notion that he might be a Hebrew. When he hears that Miriam has come to the palace claiming to be his sister, he labels her story ridiculous. When his uncle and the court pick up the charge, he is furious. His anger leads directly to the impetuous killing of the Egyptian overseer and his decision to leave. But after his exile and his residence with Jethro, he is not so sure, and he begins to accept as possibility the legend of his Hebrew birth. He asks Jethro to renew the offerings at the tomb of his mother, the Egyptian princess, explaining, "She might not be my actual mother as they say. She might have adopted me from Assyria, or found me on the Nile or borne me. It doesn't matter to me for she was a real mother, loving and kind." By the time he has saved the Hebrews from Egypt and has wandered with them in the wilderness, Moses can see the blind chance in his being chosen to make the Hebrew fiction become a Jewish reality. After Miriam's death, he muses on this circumstance: "He wondered if she had not been born if he would have been standing here in the desert of Zin. In fact, he wondered if the Exodus would have taken place at all. How? If she had not come to the palace gates to ask for him and to claim him as a brother, would he have left Egypt as he did? He doubted it. He never would have known Jethro or married Zipporah, nor . . . led out a nation with a high hand, nor suffered as he had done and was doomed to keep on doing. A mighty thing had happened in the world through the stumblings of a woman who couldn't see where she was going."

At one level this is the cosmic joke in a semicomic novel—that Moses is less a true prophet than the captive of a yearned-for, self-fulfilling prophecy. But at this level Moses can serve neither biblical history nor Afro-American tradition. Moses did have a legitimate status, established biblically, as the great law-giver, the founder of modern Judaism. He also had a legitimate and honored status as the great emancipator, a role immortalized in the spirituals. Hurston legitimizes her hero by making his relationship with Jehovah, the monotheistic God given him by Jethro, an authentic religious experience. Moses is profoundly altered at the burning bush: "Life could never be again what it once was." He becomes a divine messenger, a law-giver, a man who successfully brings the "god of the mountain" to a people worshiping Egyptian deities because they are without a divinity of their own. Hurston seldom pokes fun at Moses' religious mission or his propagation of the faith. In fact, the parting of the Red Sea during the Exodus is called a miracle, even though earlier in the book it had been attributed to natural causes.

What Hurston does poke fun at, consistently and with great good humor, is the relationship between Moses the reluctant emancipator and a Hebrew nation suspicious of freedom. Because her use of black dialect and racial metaphor demands that we make the analogy between Hebrews in Egypt and Afro-Americans in the United States, the frequently ambivalent character of American racial relationships becomes the target for a gentle satire. Darwin Turner has claimed that "the chief art of the book is the abundant comedy"—perhaps an overstatement, but a useful corrective to those who have read the novel with a somber reverence for the biblical account.[21] Zora Hurston clearly held no such reverence.

The humor of *Moses, Man of the Mountain* functions in a number of ways. The spoken language of the novel becomes comic because it deflates the high seriousness of biblical rhetoric. One is not accustomed to hear Jethro charge Moses with the task of founding Jewish monotheism in quite such a colloquial and evangelical fashion: "How about them Israelites? They're down there in Egypt without no god of their own and no more protection than a bare headed mule. How come you can't go down there and lead them out? . . . Those people . . . need help, Moses. And besides, we could convert 'em, maybe. That really would be something—a big crowd like that coming through religion, all at one time." By placing racial relations in the perspective of antiquity, letting the early, Egyptian Moses represent a professional white liberal, Hurston lampoons the counsel of moderation. Moses tells truculent Hebrew

workmen complaining about their slavery: "This sort of thing is
what I am working for. Hebrew foreman first and keeping on up the
line until you have Hebrew state officials. But if you start leaving
work and creating disturbances you will find yourselves worse off
than you were, instead of better." Moses' overtures to the Hebrews
while he is still an Egyptian nobleman come straight from the
unconscious arrogance of white paternalism. He sounds like one of
the Negrotarians Zora had often seen in New York: "I am not your
bossman at all. I am your friend. I want you to act in such a way that
I can help you." When the men seem less than impressed with this
approach, Moses thinks he knows their emotions: "So! The will to
humble a man more powerful than themselves was stronger than
the emotion of gratitude. It was stronger than the wish for the
common brotherhood of man."

It is only after Moses has exiled himself, become radicalized, and
been appointed deliverer of the Hebrews that his rhetoric changes.
When it does, he encounters the supremacist mentality that had
attempted to justify slavery as a beneficent system. Pharaoh asks,
"What would slaves want to be free for anyway? They are being fed
and taken care of. What more could they want?" Quick to recognize
the danger in Moses' demands, he responds, "Why, that man is a
radical. He would have the common people talking about equality."

Hurston's satire is not all pointed from black toward white; some
is from black toward black. The same man who rejects Moses'
paternalism is also a big-talking street dude: "Did I tell that Prince
something," he brags. "I told his head a mess." Indeed, after Moses
has left Egypt, lived with Jethro, and returned to save the Hebrews, the satire shifts from being largely interracial to intraracial.
The psychological dependency that could grow from slavery is
referred to as one of the problems of the Exodus. Although Jethro
believes that "it stands to reason that anybody in slavery would be
glad to be free," his logic is refuted by many of the Hebrews'
actions. The price of freedom is simply too great for many, especially if it means fighting for it. Joshua tells Moses that his people
"was under the impression that you had found some god who was
going to save us. They didn't know you had to join the army." Even
Jehovah's granting of a favored-nation status and the promise of

divinely sanctioned laws is not enough to keep the tribes of Israel from falling back on transient, slave-time pleasures as soon as Moses goes up the mountain. They promise themselves "a real old down home Egyptian ceremony . . . with Aaron at the altar. Just like old times back home. And they tell me a breakdown and stomp is going to follow." Small bits of adversity are sometimes met with short memories: "Lawd, listen at that man! Here he done took and brought out us of Egypt where we was getting along just fine. We remember the nice fresh fish we used to get back there in Egypt every day. Nice sweet-tasting little pan-fish and a person could get all they could eat for five cents." Joshua, confronted with the reluctance of his people to fight for their rights, sounds like many a disillusioned black leader pondering the race. In a time-honored phrase of exasperated affection, Joshua mutters, "My People! My People. . . . My people just won't do."

Finally, however, one must be careful not to overemphasize the comic qualities of the novel; for, contrary to Turner's assertion, the final direction of the book is serious. Hurston makes fun of slave mentality because she agrees that the wandering in the wilderness was a necessary preliminary to real emancipation; only a new generation could enter the Promised Land. By the end of the book, as the crossing of the Jordan draws near, the theme of emancipation is hardly satiric. All the problems of a people struggling to liberate themselves from a heritage of bondage become crystallized in Moses' mind, illuminating both his effort and the people's task: "He had meant to make a perfect people, free and just, noble and strong, that should be a light for all the world and for time and eternity. And he wasn't sure he had succeeded. He had found out that no man may make another free. Freedom was something internal. The outside signs were just signs and symbols of the man inside. All you could do was to give the opportunity for freedom and the man himself must make his own emancipation."

This idea of emancipation is a major theme in *Moses, Man of the Mountain*. Although the historical identification is with Moses and the Hebrews, Hurston's contemporary message says that freedom can be delivered only by the self. Projected farther, the novel is about the deadly serious business of founding an Afro-American identity within a country structured to deny it. Perhaps this is why Hurston emphasizes the psychology of a slave generation, recreating the *mood* of the bondsman as he struggles toward survival and self-affirmation. Like slave women trying to hide and protect their children from sale, Hebrew women suffer their labor pangs in silence, lest their sons be ripped from them; they know that a cry in the night "might force upon them a thousand years of feeling." The slave's futility is the dominant tone of the early chapters; it leads to a depression of spirit that can cause one to seek solace in a white man's god, even when he knows that "anybody depending on somebody else's gods is depending on a fox not to eat the chickens." Slaves realize that there is "no way out but death," and that "you are up against a hard game when you got to die to beat it." Consequently, it was natural to hate; one man says, "That's what I hate 'em for too, making me scared to die." Such a person naturally looks upon a son's birth as something less than a blessing: "I hope I don't have another boy. . . . Even if the soldiers don't find him and kill him, I don't want him feeling like I feel. I want him to be a man."

Such passages suggest what a powerful novel *Moses* might have been if Hurston could have maintained a consistent attitude toward her material, building from her re-creation of the psychology of slavery to the discovery of the individual worth necessary for personal emancipation. It might have been a book that captured the psychological range of an oppressed people willing themselves a status as a chosen group and creating a divine messenger to lead them out of oppression. But it does not become this book: far too often Zora settled for the irony of one person's "leading" others to freedom, the human comedy in a people's thinking that they owned the one true god, the perverseness of human beings under an obligation to be grateful. Perhaps the best illustration of what the novel might have been is found in a passage describing the young Moses' crossing the Red Sea during his initial departure from Egypt:

> Moses had crossed over. He was not in Egypt. He had crossed over and now he was not an Egyptian. He had crossed over. The short sword at his thigh had a jewelled hilt but he had crossed over and so it was no longer the sign of high birth and power. He had crossed over, so he sat down on a rock near the seashore to rest himself. He had crossed over so he was not of the house of Pharaoh. He did not own a palace because he had crossed over. He did not have an Ethiopian Princess for a wife. He had crossed over. He did not have friends to

sustain him. He had crossed over. He did not have enemies to strain
against his strength and power. He had crossed over. He was subject
to no law except the laws of tooth and talon. He had crossed over. The
sun who was his friend and ancestor in Egypt was arrogant and bitter
in Asia. He had crossed over. He felt as empty as a post hole for he
was none of the things he once had been. He was a man sitting on a
rock. He had crossed over.

This is a passage about identity, in a book exploring group identity, and it illustrates how Zora Neale Hurston always had at creative command the black American esthetic tradition—a tradition
best represented by the forms growing from folk expression.
Humor here derives from the pun on *passing* (crossing over the
color line) and the reversal of the normal direction for crossing
(usually one passes for white). There is historical irony that Moses
can cross the Red Sea not as a miracle, but as a result of a natural
parting of the waters from the action of the tide. But the passage
refers most profoundly to the difficult process of constructing a new
identity from the ground up, with no blueprints to predict the final
shape of the edifice. Moses' life will be *transformed* into something
entirely new when he comes to identify with the oppressed; he
truly crosses over into a new and different land, one that will subject
him to the "laws of tooth and talon." His religion will change from
that of the Egyptian gods of the sun to that of the Hebrew god of the
mountain. It is, of course, a religious metaphor that Hurston is
using, referring to the crossing over from the sinner's bench to the
amen corner, from the heathen to the saved, from the state of the
unregenerate to that of the elect. It also has a secular context,
referring to the crossing over from slavery to freedom. Like a black
minister exhorting his congregation to cross over into a *new* life *in*
Christ, Hurston's prose not only uses the phrases, but also captures
the repetitive pattern and rhythm of the folk sermon—leaving one
to gasp for breath and interject the rhythmic *aaaah* of the black
preacher after each "he crossed over."

The passage is a tour de force, illustrating what Zora Hurston was
capable of when writing at the height of her personal powers,
simulating the communal creativity that was her special legacy.
Moses, Man of the Mountain is a noble failure; its author could not
maintain the fusion of black creative style, biblical tone, ethnic

humor, and legendary reference that periodically appears. *Moses* is the victim of its own aspirations, a condition that can be fairly said to characterize Zora Hurston's own life for the next decade.

NOTES

1. ZNH to Henry Allen Moe, Jan. 6, 1937 (GgFnd).
2. Ibid., Jan. 6, Mar. 20, 1937; Henry Allen Moe to Orange County Board of Health, Apr. 17, 1937; ZNH to Moe, May 23, July 6, 1937 (GgFnd); ZNH, Passport Records, U.S. State Department.
3. ZNH, *Tell My Horse* (Philadelphia: J. B. Lippincott, 1934), pp. 139, 179, 198. Hurston's discussions of Haitian gods sometimes differ from those of other scholars; see, e.g., Melville Herskovits, *Life in a Haitian Valley* (New York: Alfred A. Knopf, 1927), and Maya Deren, *Divine Horsemen: The Voodoo Gods of Haiti* (New York: Dell, 1972).
4. ZNH, *Tell My Horse*, pp. 173, 164–65.
5. ZNH to Henry Allen Moe, July 6, 1937 (GgFnd).
6. ZNH, *Tell My Horse*, pp. 254–57, 153.
7. ZNH to Henry Allen Moe, Aug. 26, 1937 (GgFnd).
8. ZNH to James Weldon Johnson, Nov. 5, 1937; Claude McKay to Johnson, Dec. 28, 1937, Feb. 21, 1938; Johnson to McKay, Feb. 18, 1938; ZNH to CVV, Oct. 23, Nov. 5, Dec. 1, 1937, Feb. 21, Mar. 26, 1938 (JWJYale); ZNH to Edwin Osgood Grover, Oct. 19, 23, 1937 (HCUFla). See also Herskovits, *Life in a Haitian Valley*, and W. B. Seabrook, *The Magic Island* (New York: Harcourt, Brace, 1929).
9. AL, "The Negro: 'New' or Newer," *Opportunity*, 17 (Feb., 1939), 38; *New Yorker*, Oct. 15, 1938, p. 71; Harold Courlander, review of *Tell My Horse*, *Saturday Review*, Oct. 15, 1938, p. 6.
10. ZNH transcript of employment, "WPA Project Service (Preparation of American Guide Series)," Federal Writers' Project (National Personnel Records Center); RH interview with Carita Doggett Corse, director of the Florida Federal Writers' Project, Feb. 25, 1971, Jacksonville, Fla.; Herbert Halpert to RH, Sept. 6, 1976.
11. Carita Doggett Corse to Henry G. Alsberg, director of the Federal Writers' Project, May 23, 1939 (LCAFS); Florida Federal Writers' Project Files (National Archives); Arthur Christopher of Christopher Publishing to ZNH, May 10, 1939; Lois Dwight Cole of Macmillan to ZNH, May 11, 1939; ZNH, "The Florida Negro," typescript (also called "The Negro in Florida" by FWP staff members) (FHSP). See also Jerre Mangione, *The Dream and the Deal* (Boston: Little, Brown, 1972).
12. RH interview with W. Edward Farrison, Apr., 1971, Durham, N.C.; RH interview with Dean Elder of North Carolina Central University, Apr., 1971, Durham, N.C.; Adele Ferguson Lafayette of Washington, D.C., to RH, Mar. 25, 1971; ZNH to James E. Shepherd, Dec. 14, 1939 (copy in possession of Paul Green); Darwin T. Turner, introduction to *Mules and Men* (New York: Harper and Row, 1970), p. 10; ZNH, "The Rise of the Begging Joints," *American Mercury*, 60 (Mar., 1945), 288–94; idem, "The 'Pet Negro' System," ibid., 56 (May, 1943), 599.
13. RH interview with Paul Green, Apr. 6, 1971, Chapel Hill, N.C.; "Drama

Group Concludes Meet, Zora Neale Hurston Featured," *Daily Tar Heel*, Oct. 8, 1939 (University of North Carolina Library).

14. Don Pope of Washington, D.C., to RH, n.d. [received Mar., 1971]; RH interview with Paul Green, Apr. 6, 1971, Chapel Hill, N.C.; ZNH to Green, Jan. 24, 1940 (in Green's possession).

15. ZNH to EE, July 1, 1935 (RosFisk); ZNH to Edwin Osgood Grover, Dec. 29, 1935 (HCUFla); ZNH, "The Fire and the Cloud," *Challenge*, 1 (Sept., 1934), 10–12.

16. Robert Bone, *The Negro Novel in America* (New Haven: Yale University Press, 1958), p. 126; Darwin T. Turner, *In a Minor Chord* (Carbondale: Southern Illinois University Press, 1971), p. 109. An excellent but generally overlooked analysis of *Moses* is Blyden Jackson's "Some Negroes in the Land of Goshen," *Tennessee Folklore Society Bulletin*, 19 (Dec., 1953), 103–7.

17. Sigmund Freud, "Moses an Egyptian" and "If Moses Was an Egyptian," chapters 1 and 2 of *Moses and Monotheism* (New York: Random House, 1939).

18. Lawrence Levine, "Slave Songs and Slave Consciousness: An Exploration in Neglected Sources," in *Anonymous Americans*, ed. Tamara K. Hareven (Englewood Cliffs, N.J.: Prentice-Hall, 1971), p. 107. Levine's article builds on the pioneering work of Sterling Brown, who has displayed extraordinary understanding of the creative process by which the folk produced spirituals. See Brown's introductory essay to chap. 11, "Spirituals," in *The Book of Negro Folklore*, ed. LH and Arna Bontemps (New York: Dodd, Mead, 1958), pp. 279–89.

19. Levine, "Slave Songs," p. 111. This paragraph owes much to Levine. See also John Lovell, *Black Song: The Forge and the Flame* (New York: Macmillan, 1972).

20. Sir James Frazer, *Folklore in the Old Testament* (New York: Hart Publishing, 1975), pp. 264–68; Flavius Josephus, *Antiquities of the Jews*, ed. William Whiston (Philadelphia: J. B. Lippincott, 1864), chap. 10. All quotations not noted are from ZNH, *Moses, Man of the Mountain* (Philadelphia: J. B. Lippincott, 1939).

21. Turner, *In a Minor Chord*, p. 111.

≈≈≈ **Ambiguities of Self,
Politics of Race**

Moses, Man of the Mountain received mixed reviews. Many newspapers and magazines liked it, finding it an unusual book; but Alain Locke called it "caricature instead of portraiture," and Ralph Ellison in *New Masses* said: "This work sets out to do for Moses what 'The Green Pastures,' did for Jehovah; for Negro fiction it did nothing." Zora had set high goals, and it was depressing to fall short. She told a friend, "I have the feeling of disappointment about it. I don't think that I achieved all that I set out to do. I thought that in this book I would achieve my ideal, but it seems that I have not yet reached it . . . it still doesn't say all that I want it to say."[1]

She was also troubled at the time by the failure of her second marriage. Like Janie Crawford in *Their Eyes Were Watching God*, she had wed a much younger man; on June 27, 1939, in Fernandina, Florida, she had stood before a county judge to be united with Albert Price III. Price was twenty-three and Zora was at least thirty-eight; they had met in Jacksonville where he was a WPA playground worker. While the age differential was a positive force for Janie and Tea Cake, it divided Albert and Zora. She filed for divorce in February, 1940, claiming bitterly that Price drank, refused to work, was often abusive, and refused to maintain a home. In his countersuit Price denied all these allegations, claiming that Zora had dragged him to the altar "in total disregard of the youth of the Defendant," and had promised that her "substantial income" would enable him to continue his college education. It is unclear whether the charges and countercharges had any validity, or whether they resulted from the formalized falsehood that divorce laws require. Certainly both sides posed for legal portraits; it takes a considerable act of imagination to see Zora as she represented herself in the complaint, a "meek and humble type easy to be imposed upon," the daughter of a Baptist minister who "never has used obscene language of any kind or under any circumstances." Although little is known of Price, it is equally hard to imagine him as a young innocent "enticed" into the marriage because Zora assured him "all that she wanted was his SWEET SELF." The court record sounds most plausible when it cites the resources that Zora might claim during a domestic quarrel: "The Defendant was also put in fear of his life due to the professed practice on the part of the Plaintiff in what is termed as 'Black Magic' or 'Voodooism,' claimed by the Plaintiff to have been acquired by her while living in Haiti and that she had the power both in spirits and in the uses of certain preparations to place individuals under certain spells and that if the Defendant would not perform her wishes she possessed the power to 'FIX HIM.'"[2]

The original divorce action was eventually withdrawn, and they were momentarily reconciled. Price traveled with Zora to Beaufort, South Carolina, on a folklore-collecting expedition during the summer of 1940, but they never really maintained a household. Although the divorce was not granted until November 9, 1943, the marriage was over after less than a year; the two of them never lived together more than two weeks at a time. Price stayed in Florida when Zora went to North Carolina to teach, and they apparently parted for good when she left South Carolina for New York in the late summer of 1940.[3]

The South Carolina expedition had begun as a study of religious trances in the sanctified church, a research project headed by the anthropologist Jane Belo. Zora's enthusiastic cooperation had helped Belo collect some "perfectly grand stuff in a very short time," and in the course of the field work Zora became fascinated by a new form of spirituals improvised by local church choirs from current events. When Belo left for New York, Zora urged her to send back recording equipment. In early May, Belo obtained a motion picture camera, with sound, and wrote that she was sending it; the rub was that the equipment was to be accompanied, as Zora put it, by "two very enthusiastic Jews who want to take the Spirituals for commercial purposes." She immediately warned Paul Green, "We can't let all that swell music get away from us like that."

Still thinking of a play they might do together, she urged him to send a recording machine before anyone else arrived. She was obligated to show the New Yorkers around, but "of course I am not going to lead them to the fattest and juiciest places nohow." If she could make her own recordings first, Hurston and Green would have "a great deal of raw music that we could work up from time to time as we needed it."[4]

The episode documents Zora's continuing hopes for a theatrical success, and her struggle to stay financially afloat. She could not alienate Belo because of the New Yorker's subsidy. Although the collaboration with Green had not produced anything (he wrote in his diary that he was afraid she lacked a dramatic sense), she had to keep him interested; an award-winning playwright, he had contacts among academicians, theatrical producers, and foundation people.[5]

In mid-career Zora Neale Hurston was still dependent on patronage, still committed to writing as a livelihood, still living mainly from hand to mouth. The author of five books, she had just spent a year teaching American drama to sophomores at a segregated southern college. She was separated from her husband and seeking a divorce. She had been harassed by racist fraternity boys when she arrived to lecture at the neighboring white campus. She felt put upon (rightly or wrongly) by the administrators who employed her. When the South Carolina collecting ended and the Hurston-Green collaboration fell through, she was ready to turn again to typewriter and publisher.

Zora spent the winter of 1940–41 in New York, lecturing, visiting old friends, and contemplating her next book. In a sense she was written out. Her folklore collecting had been reported on, Eatonville had inspired two novels, and her attempt to fictionalize biblical history had been unsuccessful. When she spoke with Bertram Lippincott about plans for a new book, he urged her to think about an autobiography; when she objected that her career was hardly over, he proposed that it be the first volume of a multivolume work.

In late spring, 1941, she moved to California at the urging of a rich friend, Katharine Mershon, who offered a place to live and write. She worked hard, completing a first draft of the book by mid-July. Uncharacteristically, the rewriting took almost a year, not only because Zora had found the autobiographical form difficult to sustain, but also because the Japanese attack on Pearl Harbor caused her to revise and delete much that she had written. While America sang "Praise the Lord and Pass the Ammunition," she would find no market for a book that spoke sarcastically of American marines who "consider machine gun bullets good laxatives for heathens who get constipated with toxic ideas about a country of their own." Nor could she refer to "that piece about trading in China with gunboats and cannons" that "we Westerners composed . . . long decades ago," which "Japan is now plagiarizing in the most flagrant manner. We also wrote that song about keeping a whole hemisphere under your wing. Now the Nipponese are singing our song all over Asia."[6]

Zora survived the year of revision with fitful employment. She served from October, 1941, to January, 1942, as a story consultant at Paramount Studios, trying to interest that firm in making movies of her novels. Then she lectured on the black college circuit. Finally she returned to Florida to live on her savings, settling in Saint Augustine to polish the autobiography, write plays, and "keep on eating." During the summer of 1942 she collected folklore throughout the state, returning to Saint Augustine in the fall. Her autobiography, *Dust Tracks on a Road*, was published in late November, 1942.[7]

Dust Tracks can be a discomfiting book, and it has probably harmed Hurston's reputation. Like much of her career, it often appears contradictory. Zora seems to be both an advocate for the universal, demonstrating that this black woman does not look at the world in racial terms, and the celebrant of a unique ethnic upbringing in an all-black village. *Dust Tracks* begins with Zora Hurston as she grows to adulthood, moving from rustic security toward college and career; approximately three-fifths of the book details this movement. She describes herself as a bright, combative, overly imaginative child who had a difficult time between her mother's death and her college success, but who persevered, and was served well by the values learned in Eatonville. Her rise from Florida sidemeat to caviar in Gotham is spiritedly told; the artistic, dramatic, eccentric Zora Neale Hurston, a master of figurative language, charms with transparently posed humility. The final two-fifths of the book self-consciously, and at times simplistically, ranges through love, religion, friendship; it explains why Zora Neale Hurston has "no race prejudice of any kind." When Zora selects a story from the repertoire of her life and narrates it for her audience, *Dust Tracks* succeeds. It fails when she tries to shape the narrative into a statement of universality, manipulating events and ideas in order to suggest that the personal voyage of Zora Neale Hurston is something more than the special experience of one black woman.

Those who do not like Hurston, or who wish to criticize her fiction, frequently claim that *Dust Tracks* shows how her folksiness eventually became both style and substance. Nathan Huggins believes the book demonstrates that she became the professional "folk Negro" whites needed. In a very hostile essay Darwin Turner has argued that *Dust Tracks* illustrates "her artful candor and coy reticence, her contradictions and silences, her irrationalities and extravagant boasts which plead for the world to recognize and respect her"; he concludes that it reveals "the matrix of her fiction, the seeds that sprouted and the cankers that destroyed."[8]

Turner is correct in one sense: the autobiography does reaffirm the vital source of her fiction. But it is hardly cankerous, and if the book displays Hurston's folksiness, it does so as an integral part of a complex personality. The matrix for Hurston's fiction was the front porch of Joe Clarke's Eatonville general store, where "big picture talkers" used the side of the world for a canvas as they painted "crayon enlargements of life." This matrix expanded to encompass sawmill camps, sanctified churches, jook joints, and voodoo ceremonies, as Hurston traced the soulful essence in the communicative behavior of those storefront talkers. That is the chief value of her autobiography—its documentation of the Eatonville scene and what it meant to a woman who would rise by force of will and talent to become nationally known. Turner has unfairly suggested that Hurston accomplished this feat by becoming a "wandering minstrel"; yet his dissatisfaction is understandable if one depends on her autobiography to provide the key to her life. Her total career, not her autobiography, is the proof of her achievement and the best index to her life and art. Only when considered in that total context can the book be properly assessed, for it is an autobiography at war with itself. Apparently written self-consciously with a white audience in mind, probably because of editorial suggestions, it illustrates the contradictions, ambivalence, and disappointment of Zora Hurston's personal and professional life in the early 1940s. As Zora admitted, "I did not want to write it at all, because it is too hard to reveal one's inner self," a remark that refers to both personal disclosure and the problems of autobiographical technique.[9]

Black American autobiography is a unique genre. Black autobiographers usually are people who have forged their identity despite attempts to deny them a sense of personal worth; the tension between individual and stereotype, between what one thinks of himself and what white society expects him to be, grants special energy to the autobiographical prose. The author, having escaped the self-deception and self-defeat that whites have hoped to impose, speaks from a position of privilege and responsibility; the autobiographical account is presumed to contain both lessons for black people—how to combat racism, how to affirm the self— and indictments for whites. One of the most acute students of black autobiography, Stephen Butterfield, argues that the self of black autobiography is generally not an individual with a private career, but a member of an oppressed social group with ties and allegiances to the other members. Butterfield offers a profile of the traditional black autobiography; he believes that it is both a bid for freedom and an attempt to communicate what whites have done. Normally it is characterized by political awareness, empathy for suffering, knowledge of oppression, and a sense of shared life, shared triumph, and communal responsibility.[10]

Almost none of these criteria applies entirely to *Dust Tracks*. Hurston's opinions on international politics were excised by editors, and the book's domestic politics sometimes appear naïve. She displays little empathy for suffering, suggesting that to dwell on discrimination is self-indulgent. She does not admit that oppression affects her, and she avoids describing it. She is very much aware of her private career. Only in the first portion of *Dust Tracks* does Hurston produce a traditional autobiography; she creates a sense of the shared life she knew in Eatonville as a black child.

Her technique for expressing this shared life is to speak in the village voice. When characterizing Eatonville's male hegemony, the Columbia anthropologist is nowhere present; her uncle Jim speaks for the store porch: "He maintained that if a woman had anything big enough to sit on, she had something big enough to hit on." The self-reliant career woman who had refused a traditional sexual role reports on Eatonville's homily for a "ruint" girl: "A pitcher can go to the well a long time, but its bound to get broke sooner or later." When death strikes her mother, the mature novelist describes the grim reaper in the pulpit poetry of the folk: "The Master-Maker in His making had made Old Death. Made him with big, soft feet and square toes. Made him with a face that reflects the face of all things, but neither changes itself, nor is mirrored anywhere. Made the body of Death out of infinite hunger. Made a weapon for his hand to satisfy his needs."

As brilliant as such a passage can be, the autobiographical self could not speak in this voice for an entire volume. Zora Neale Hurston did not remain in Eatonville, and as she admits, after her mother's death, "I was on my way from the village never to return to it as a real part of the town." She became an educated author, building a successful career for herself because she triumphed over obstacles placed in front of black women who happen to be Americans. From the publisher's point of view this success validated her autobiography; it served as a warrant to the reader that her life story had inherent interest. Yet Zora had spent a good part of her career proving that there were equally interesting lives, and in some cases equally powerful talents, on Joe Clarke's store porch and in Polk County sawmill camps. Did she become successful by rising above Eatonville, or by digging to its very soul? She found herself in the uncomfortable position of mediating between two spheres of experience, searching for an interpretive voice that would authenticate both Eatonville and Barnard, a West Indian houngan and a Guggenheim fellow. *Dust Tracks* eventually exposes Hurston's uneasiness over how to move beyond the Eatonville voice and, by implication, how to explain her fame and her townspeople's obscurity. She was trapped in *Dust Tracks* by the personal identification she cultivated as one of the folk, for it limited her freedom to account for her experience as a part of the larger world. What commentators like Darwin Turner and Nathan Huggins see as a personality defect, a professional folksiness, results mostly from the failure of the literary artist to fuse Eatonville and New York into an interpretive voice for her autobiography—a major reason the book should not be taken as the definitive statement of her character.

The problem of voice is illustrated in the following passage describing her parents' courtship:

> He was nearly twenty years old then, and she was fourteen. My Mother used to claim with a smile that she saw him looking and looking at her up there in the choir and wondered what he was looking at her for. She wasn't studying about *him*. However, when the service was over and he kept standing around, never far from her, she asked somebody, "Who is dat bee-stung yaller nigger?"
>
> "Oh, dat's one of dem niggers from over de creek, one of dem Hurstons—call him John I believe."
>
> That was supposed to settle that. Over-the-creek niggers lived from one white man's plantation to the other. Regular hand-to-mouth folks. Didn't own pots to pee in, nor beds to push 'em under. Didn't have no more pride than to let themselves be hired by poor-white trash. No more to 'em than the stuffings out of a zero. The inference was that Lucy Ann Potts had asked about nothing and had been told.

The anecdote begins straightforwardly; the famous author is narrating family history, an episode selected because it will help the reader understand her. Zora Neale soon takes over as a folk performer, sitting on Joe Clarke's porch, speaking the history in the colorful idiom of the oral tale-teller. Then, in the last line, performer and learned author confront each other in the same sentence: *inference* is a word of the educated elite; "had asked about nothing and had been told" emphasizes finality in the folk manner.

The passage may work as autobiographical statement, but it has serious implications. The egalitarian voice in such a passage announces, "See, despite my success, my ability to adopt the village voice shows that I am no different from any of my Eatonville brothers and sisters"—a sentiment that expresses the shared life of a racial community. But *Dust Tracks* also seems dedicated to describing the achievement of Zora Neale Hurston as an individual accomplishment, so much so, in fact, that the reader is reminded of a class differential: her townspeople did not become famous, while Zora Hurston did. As she becomes famous, her success is explained in terms that sever those racial and class identifications with rural black people that she admitted were the inspiration for her creativity, the source of her vivid language.

The same young girl who hung around Joe Clarke's store, learning folktales "that pleased me more than what I learned later on in Ethnology," also went fishing with a local white man who admonished her, "Don't be a nigger. . . . Niggers lie and lie." Yet his words did not offend, the interpretive voice claims: "I knew without being told he was not talking about race when he advised me not to be a nigger. He was talking about class rather than race. He frequently gave money to Negro schools." *Dust Tracks* has little or no reference to racial discrimination. Zora is superior to it; she refuses to let it affect her, since there is little she can do about it: "I too yearn for universal justice, but how to bring it about is another thing." (Anyone who would dwell on discrimination is guilty of Hurston's unpardonable sin, self-pity.) Zora refuses to write about the race problem: "My interest lies in what makes a man or a woman do such-and-so, regardless of his color."

The ultimate effect of ignoring the race problem is to imply that Zora Hurston's success resulted from either a mystical process or a personal transcendence of racial realities. She was different from her Eatonville friends, a very special person chosen by the gods for unusual things. She always had some "inside urge to go places," and her mother wondered "if a conjure woman hadn't sprinkled 'travel dust' around the doorstep the day I was born." She was compelled by unknown forces to "walk out to the horizon and see what the end of the world was like." The sign of her special fate was the mystical vision she claimed to have had at the age of seven:

> Like clearcut stereopticon slides, I saw twelve scenes flash before me, each one held until I had seen it well in every detail, and then be replaced by another. There was no continuity as in an average dream. Just disconnected scene after scene with blank spaces in between. I knew that they were all true, a preview of things to come, and my soul writhed in agony and shrunk away. But I knew that there was no shrinking. These last had to be. . . . So when I left the porch I left a great deal behind me. I was weighed down with a power I did

not want. I had knowledge before its time. I knew my fate. I knew that I would be an orphan and homeless. I knew that while I was still helpless, that the comforting circle of my family would be broken, and that I would have to wander cold and friendless until I had served my time. I would stand beside a dark pool of water and see a huge fish move slowly at a time when I would be somehow in the depth of despair. I would hurry to catch a train, with doubts and fears driving me and seek solace in a place and fail to find it when I arrived, then cross many tracks to board the train again. I knew that a house, a shotgun-built house that needed a new coat of white paint, held torture for me, but I must go. I saw deep love betrayed, but I must feel and know it. There was no turning back. And last of all, I would come to a big house. Two women waited there for me. I could not see their faces, but I knew one to be young and one to be old. One of them was arranging some queer-shaped flowers such as I had never seen. When I had come to these women, then I would be at the end of my pilgrimage, but not the end of my life. Then I would know peace and love and what goes with those things, and not before.

Zora added, "Time was to prove the truth of my visions, for one by one they came to pass." Interestingly, the visions take her only to the meeting with Mrs. Mason that enabled her to go south and begin folklore collecting. The "end of her pilgrimage" was the beginning of her career; and because her career was self-created rather than preordained, the reader is left to wonder about the ingredients of her success.

Although meant to explain Hurston's life, the visions do not successfully structure the autobiography. They fade into insignificance as the story unfolds. Although visions one and two serve as chapter endings, vision three is given only a single sentence; we encounter no further visions until Zora suddenly announces that six visions have now passed. The seventh vision is of her brother's house, which she fled to join the Gilbert and Sullivan troupe. There is no mention of the eighth. The ninth vision, the meeting with Mrs. Mason, is not identified as such in the published text, although the manuscript version reads, "She had been in the last of my prophetic visions from the first coming of them."[11] Visions ten through twelve are nowhere in sight, perhaps because—while claiming to see "twelve scenes flash before me"—her list ends with Godmother and number nine: "And last of all, I would come to a big house."

Did the visions occur? Probably. But if they were confirmed by subsequent events, why are they not more prominent? What the prophetic visions really do is direct us toward Zora Neale Hurston's contradictory understanding of her own success and her uneasy interpretation of it. Whether they occurred or not, they are inadequately integrated into the literary structure. While they may confirm the uniqueness of their recipient, they also are a key to Hurston's literary dilemma in her autobiography. She is searching for an appropriate voice for the post-Eatonville Zora Neale Hurston. The visions are a way to avoid confronting the reality of her own success, a fame wrested from a society that she admitted elsewhere confronted her with humiliating Jim Crow experiences. The paradoxes of *Dust Tracks*, the unanswered questions that ultimately make it a discomfiting book, grow from this deliberate refusal—after documenting the shared life of Eatonville—to interpret her later career in any context other than that of individual achievement. This does not mean, of course, that the book does not reveal the complicated Hurston personality.

How can Zora Hurston express herself as both one of the folk and someone special? How can she admit that discrimination may occur, but argue that it does not signify? How can her autobiography describe the drive to success of a black woman and not explain how she overcame the institutional racism and sexism of her society? How can Hurston claim identity with the masses, yet affirm the supremacy of the individual? Some of the answers are implicit in Larry Neal's observation that "she was no political radical. She was, instead, a belligerent individualist who was decidedly unpredictable and, perhaps, a little inconsistent."[12] Other answers stem from a paradox of personal pride. She may have been special, but she also believed that her hard-won success grew from the self-reliance, independence, and self-confidence inspired by familial and communal origins. These qualities helped her compete and brought her fame. To describe the discrimination she encountered might suggest that such self-reliance was a defensive reaction to white oppression; it might imply that racial discrimination worked, that it created compensatory black behavior. Absolutely obsessed with the fear that she might be found to engage in self-pity, Zora apparently believed that writing about the race problem might mean that Eatonville, an independent, self-governing black

community, could be misinterpreted as a self-defensive civic refuge from the white world.[13] To see her own drive for individual
achievement as having anything to do with "overcoming" meant
that her career became a prison; her success would be inseparable
from the race's oppressions, and her own highly developed pride
in her individual achievement would be explained in pseudopsy-
chological terms as an interesting form of "Negro pathology," or
"feminine aggression," or "overcompensation."

In the face of such questions, Hurston makes little attempt to
interpret the paradoxes of her life and art. She explains away all by
taking the position that she is what she is, an individual woman who
has come to stand apart from the racial fray. She sees no curse in
being black, no "extra flavor" in being white. She has learned, she
reports, that "skins were no measure of what was inside people,"
that "it took more than a community of skin color" to interpret life.
She laughs at both whites and blacks who claim special blessings on
the basis of race. This constitutes a fairly orthodox philosophy—
there are no differences between the races, so there is no reason
to segregate them—and the close reader discovers how Hurston
periodically manipulates her experience in Dust Tracks to present
an integrationist position. She overemphasizes the few whites who
were around Eatonville so that her all-black upbringing will not
appear segregated, purposely balances descriptions of white and
black friends (Fannie Hurst and Ethel Waters), takes pains to show
that black people can hate each other (just as she did her stepmother), and openly disavows any bitterness over past discrimination, asking only for equal opportunity from this day forward.

Yet Hurston's attitudes are never simple, and there is a revealing
parable in Dust Tracks, in the chapter entitled "My People, My
People." Zora describes her confusion as a child over the stock
phrases of black orators, such as "race consciousness," "race pride,"
"race solidarity." How did one reconcile race pride with folktales
about black people as monkeys, or with preferences for light-
skinned mates? She asked herself, "Were Negroes the great heroes
I heard about from the platform, or were they the ridiculous monkeys of everyday talk? Was it really honorable to be black?" The
question was answered when she saw her father and his friends

go to the woods behind Park Lake one night to rescue a missing neighbor reportedly held by the Ku Klux Klan. Armed and tense, they discovered that their brother was not being held, and when they returned, relieved, they released the tension with laughter. As Zora saw it, "The men who spoke of members of their race as monkeys had gone out to die for one. The men who were always saying, 'My skin-folks, but not kinfolks; my race but not my taste,' had rushed forth to die for one of these same contemptibles. They shoved each other around and laughed. So I could see that what looked like ridicule was really the Negro poking a little fun at himself. At the same time, just like other people, hoping and wishing he was what the orators said he was."

The passage introduces the expression Zora Hurston will end her autobiography with, ambivalently asserting a lack of racial perspective. She stated earlier that the phrase "racial consciousness" was meaningless, because "no Negro in America is apt to forget his race"; in her last paragraph she announces, "My kinfolks and my 'skin folks' are dearly loved. My own circumference of everyday life is there." In other words, Zora Neale Hurston is a proud black woman—she informs the reader, "You can consider me Old Tar Brush in person if you want to"—whose identity lies in her ethnic community. She also reassures whites that she has "no race prejudice of any kind," that her identity does not blind her, that she sees "the same virtues and vices" in blacks as in whites; this permits her to offer the "right hand of fellowship and love" to all, hoping for the same in return. The passage, however, does not end with the laying on of hands:

So I give you all my right hand of fellowship and love, and hope for the same from you. In my eyesight, you lose nothing by not looking just like me. I will remember you all in my good thoughts, and I ask you kindly to do the same for me. Not only just me. You, who play the zig-zag lightning of power over the world, with the grumbling thunder in your wake, think kindly of those who walk in the dust. And you who walk in humble places, think kindly too, of others. There has been no proof in the world so far that you would be less arrogant if you held the lever of power in your hands. Let us all be kissing-friends. Consider that with tolerance and patience, we godly demons may breed a noble world in a few hundred generations or so. Maybe all of us who do not have the good fortune to meet, or meet again, in this world, will meet at a barbecue.[14]

Ann Rayson claims that "said any other way, a comment like this would elicit considerable hostility from friends and foes alike. But . . . through style alone she can get away with saying things for which a straight [black] conservative . . . could never be forgiven."[15] Rayson may be right, but Hurston's comment is most revealing of the stylistic contradictions, arising out of the confusion of voice, that have been in the autobiography from the first. Like a member of the American Indian Movement telling whites at a bicentennial celebration that he is pleased the American immigrants could visit his country as guests for these past 200 years, Zora assures whites that they do not have to feel inferior just because they do not look like her. By ironically reversing the perspective, exposing the presumed standard of beauty, she documents the absurdity of the white norm. But having delivered that stroke, she immediately falls back upon the village voice to characterize the reality of white power—"You, who play the zig-zag lightning of power over the world, with the grumbling thunder in your wake"—and loses the cutting edge of her irony in an idealistic vision of breeding a noble world in a few hundred years, of all races meeting at an integrated barbecue in the great beyond. Her own language—the optative mood, the vagueness, the focus on a time and space beyond the here and now—reveals her uneasiness over the position in which she finds herself at the end of the book. Yet there is also a final twist, a concealed irony, that leaves one wondering just where both author and reader now find themselves. "A few hundred generations or so" is sufficiently futuristic to imply that the vision will never come true; the proximity of "godly demons" and "barbecue" causes one to think of Hades. Is Zora really telling her readers, "I'll see you in Hell"? Is it the fire next time?

Whatever its flaws, *Dust Tracks* is the book Zora Hurston wrote and permitted to be published. It should not be forgotten, however, that since she was a black author in a white publishing world, she felt especially subject to the constraints and controls of her editors. She once told an interviewer, "Rather than get across all of the things which you want to say you must compromise and work within the limitations [of those people] who have the final authority in deciding whether or not a book shall be printed."[16] The manuscript of *Dust Tracks* reveals that the book's inconsistency also results from Hurston's uncertainty over what her editors and white audience expected, a fact proven by those portions which never made it from manuscript to galleys, and which, if they had, would have given us quite a different autobiography.

The manuscript version of *Dust Tracks* displays a more self-assured, irreverent, and politically astute figure than the Zora Neale Hurston of the published book. It also exhibits some of the same disorganization and contradiction, but this is largely overcome by a tough-minded, let-the-chips-fall-where-they-may attitude. In the manuscript Zora consistently displays anger at colonialist oppression of nonwhite peoples. Writing while Western Europe was being terrorized by Nazi blitzkrieg, she admits, "All around me, bitter tears are being shed over the fate of Holland, Belgium, France and England. I must confess to being a little dry around the eyes. I hear people shaking with shudders at the thought of Germany collecting taxes in Holland. I have not heard a word against Holland collecting one-twelfth of poor people's wages in Asia." Moreover, she understood how colonialism was related to American racism. In another excised passage she points out that "President Roosevelt could extend his four freedoms to some people right here in America. . . . I am not bitter, but I see what I see. He can call names across an ocean, but he evidently has not the courage to speak even softly at home. . . . I will fight for my country but I will not lie for her."[17]

American democracy was a noble idea, but Zora had no illusions about how capitalism and colonialism had combined to emasculate the ideal: "As I see it, the doctrines of democracy deal with the aspirations of men's souls, but the application deals with things. One hand in somebody else's pocket and one on your gun and you are highly civilized. Your heart is where it belongs—in your pocket book. Put it in your bosom and you are backward. Desire enough for your own use and you are a heathen." Black people in power might be no more humane, she says, but it still "would be a good thing for the Anglo-Saxon to get the idea out of his head that everybody owes him something just for being blonde. I am forced to the conclusion that two-thirds of them do hold that view. The idea of human slavery is so deeply ground in that the pink-toes can't get it out of their system."[18]

The manuscript, in short, exhibits a different kind of woman from the Eatonville girl allowed to go public in *Dust Tracks*, and it helps explain why that book is often perplexing. One is forced to ask what sort of reputation Zora Hurston might have today, had she not felt compelled to respond to a Lippincott editor's note, written across the bottom of one of her pages: "Suggest eliminating international opinions as irrelevant to autobiography."[19]

Dust Tracks is a pivotal book in the Hurston canon because its public form became less than its private motive, a circumstance suggesting the drift of Zora's career throughout the forties. After *Dust Tracks* her mission to celebrate black folkways lost its public intensity. Although she still collected folklore occasionally, she seldom wrote about it. Her next book—an account of Florida crackers—would not be published for six years. She gave up fiction almost entirely to write essays for white magazines, and her journalism reflected the editorial lessons learned in the writing of her autobiography. Only when addressing a predominantly black audience did she feel the freedom to express the private self; in other cases she either tried to hit a straight lick with a crooked stick, masking her feelings in irony, or defused potentially troublesome racial issues with wit, humor, and stylistic ingenuity.

Dust Tracks was commercially successful. It did not offend whites, it sold well, most critics liked it, and it won the *Saturday Review's* $1,000 Anisfield-Wolf Award for its contribution to "the field of race relations."[20] More than at any other point in her life, Zora became a recognized black spokesperson, whose opinions were sought by the white reading public. Between 1942 and 1945 she published six articles in the *American Mercury* and one in the *Saturday Evening Post* (the *Post* bought a second article, "Miss Catharine of Turpentine," but did not print it); the *Reader's Digest* asked for an essay; and she told Carl Van Vechten, "I want to take a crack at the *New Yorker*. Do you think it can come off?" She wrote a friend in December, 1942, "I have assignments for several short subjects for magazines, and I am trying to get them all off of hand by

Christmas." Thinking about something for the *Reader's Digest*, she admitted that she was mainly interested in appearing there for the publicity, since publicity was part of the success of writing.[21]

Black writers often pay a price for this kind of popularity; for Zora it was the same price she had paid to make *Dust Tracks* more palatable. If her autobiography was less than it might have been, some critics were not hesitant to remind readers of that fact. Arna Bontemps noted that "Miss Hurston deals very simply with the more serious aspects of Negro life in America—she ignores them." Her old nemesis, Harold Preece, was even harsher, calling the book "the tragedy of a gifted, sensitive mind, eaten up by an egocentrism fed on the patronizing admiration of the dominant white world."[22]

Zora had also fielded brickbats for her public statements after the autobiography's publication. She had given an interview to the *New York World Telegram* that echoed her "raceless" posture in the book. She told the reporter: "I don't see life through the eyes of a Negro, but those of a person." She outraged many by claiming that "the lot of the Negro is much better in the South than in the North"—a reference, apparently, to patronizing northern liberals. But as frequently happened when Zora got warmed up, she went too far, asserting that "the Jim Crow system works." Roy Wilkins responded for the NAACP, calling such statements publicity-mongering to sell books: "Now is not the time for Negro writers like Zora Hurston to come out with publicity wisecracks about the South being better for the Negro than the North. . . . The race is fighting a battle that may determine its status for fifty years. Those who are not for us, are against us."[23]

Zora Hurston had acquired two audiences, represented by her *Dust Tracks* editor and by Roy Wilkins. After her autobiography's success, she tried to satisfy them both. This effort, largely doomed before it began, apparently affected her ability to write successful fiction, and her failures led to frustration and despair in the late forties. As a journalist Zora addressed herself to the racial complexities of America, but she never felt entirely free of publishing constraints; she always felt compelled to defend personal, sometimes conservative positions. She thought she knew very well "what white publishers won't print"—the title of one of her last essays—and she took care to anticipate any attacks on her uncompromising individualism.

Dust Tracks' last paragraph, whether the result of editorial pressure or authorial uneasiness, demonstrates Zora's usual public approach to black-white racial complexity; indirection, subtlety, humor. In 1939 she contributed an essay, "Now Take Noses" to *Cordially Yours*, a Lippincott volume prepared by that year's participants in the Boston Book Fair. A jeu d'esprit, filled with outrageous puns ("As a man nose so is he"), the essay has a serious racial purpose. It mocks all theories that would explain Roman conquests through the aquilinity of the Roman nose—could African civilization be explained by the "nose of Africa" sitting "in the shade of its cheek bones"?—or the attribution of cultural differences to any physical characteristic.

A similar playful rendering with a serious purpose was her short story "Cock Robin, Beale Street," which appeared in the *Southern Literary Messenger* for July, 1941. Told in the form of an animal tale, the story is narrated by Uncle July, who knows who killed Cock Robin. He is compelled to speak because white people have consistently misrepresented the circumstances: "Going round letting on dat Cock Robin was a bird . . . reading out of some kind of book how Cock Robin was a real true bird wid feathers on him and got kilt wid a arrow." Uncle July thinks that "dese white folks ought to talk whut they know and testify to what they see." He was right there when Cock Robin was killed, shot with a forty-four by Bull Sparrow outside Sister Buzzard's Shimmy Shack on Beale Street. The killing took place because ever since Cock Robin began hanging around, the "plain white eggs" the Sparrow family had lain for generations had lost their purity. Whenever Bull Sparrow left Mrs. Sparrow to go off on a worm hunt, he found another blue egg in his nest. Other birds remark on the same genetic mystery, and there is general agreement that Cock Robin got what he deserved: "Tain't no ifs and ands about it, Cock Robin was in de egg business."

Hurston's gentle mocking of the illusion of ethnic purity and the reality of American miscegenation was served well by the dialect and the folktale form of the story. Zora utilized the same technique to celebrate racial expression in her "Story in Harlem Slang," in the *American Mercury* for July, 1942—the only fiction she published between the completion of *Dust Tracks* and the appearance of her last novel in 1948. Speaking in what her editors term "Harlemese," Zora describes a day in the life of a Harlem hustler named Jelly, so called because "he put it in the street that where it came to filling that long-felt need, sugar curing the ladies' feelings, he was in a class by himself and nobody knew his name, so he had to tell 'em. 'It must be Jelly, cause jam don't shake.'" Jelly gets into "his zoot suit with the reet pleats" and skivers around to do himself some good, trying to score a meal. He gets involved in a bragging contest with a fellow hustler named Sweet Back, each "boogerbooing" the other until they are close to blows. Sweet Back warns, "I'm quick death and easy judgment"; Jelly replies, "I come on like the Gang Busters and go off like the March of Time." When they both try to pick up a "kitchen mechanic" on her day off (engaging in an urban courting ritual very similar to its rural counterpart in "Mule Bone"), they are unsuccessful; the woman, more than equal to their jive, "rocks on off with her ear rings snapping and her heels popping." The story ends with Jelly remembering the hot meals he left back in Alabama "to seek wealth and splendor in Harlem," forgetting in his hunger even "to look cocky and rich."

"Story in Harlem Slang" was less fiction than a linguistic study; a glossary of Harlem expressions was attached. The story touched upon a theme Hurston would often return to—that the North was no utopia, just as the South was not necessarily hell. Her biographical feature for the September 5, 1942, *Saturday Evening Post* profiled Lawrence Silas, a tough, shrewd, respected Florida cattleman. She introduces Silas by emphasizing the geography of his success: "Considering that Florida is in Dixie, it will sound like poker playing at a prayer meeting when you read that Lawrence Silas, Negro, is one of the most important men of the cow country. But that is the word with the bark on it. The cattlemen of the state have a name for him and it is good."

Hurston's journalism of the war years continually stresses such opportunities for black achievement, even when analyzing racist institutions designed to ignore it. In the May, 1943, *American Mercury* she chose the unfortunate title "The 'Pet Negro' System" to describe the way in which southern whites adopt certain blacks while vilifying the race in general: "The North has no interest in the particular Negro, but talks of justice for the whole. The South has no interest, and pretends none, in the mass of Negroes, but is very much concerned about the individual." Once that is understood, says Zora, "you can see why it is so difficult to change things in the South."

Her essay is about the complexity of race relations—"there are more angles to this race adjustment business than are ever pointed out to the public"—and about how neither posturing white southerners nor black civil rights workers can admit that the "pet Negro system" has contributed to a small, educated middle class who live on streets "of well-off Negro homes" and drive a "great number of high priced cars." Hurston condemns only faintly; she sees this system symbolizing a "web of feelings and mutual dependencies" between whites and blacks that "isn't half as pretty as the ideal adjustment of theorizers, but it's a lot more real and durable, and a lot of black folk, I'm afraid, find it mighty cozy." She thinks the system may indicate that "there are some people in every community who can always talk things over. It may be the proof that this race situation in America is not entirely hopeless and may even be worked out eventually." Knowing that her ideas are controversial, she concludes, "This is the inside picture of things, as I see it. Whether you like it or not, is no concern of mine. But it is an important thing to know if you have any plans for racial manipulations in Dixie."[24]

Although most black professionals in the South earned their status in spite of, rather than because of, white paternalism, "The 'Pet Negro' System" had a measure of uncomfortable truth to it, and it reinforced the twin Hurston themes of black individualism and black achievement. It is not surprising that she would complain about Bucklin Moon's *The Darker Brother* (1943), which painted a dismal picture of life in Harlem: "It gives a falsely morbid picture of Negro life. If his picture is true, how does he account for the thousands on thousands of wealthy, educated Negroes? . . . that awful picture does Negroes in general more harm than good. One might reason 'if the body of Negrodom is that weak and shiftless and criminal, no need to bother one's head about them.'"[25]

What Zora apparently hoped for, like many other black public figures during the war, was a mood of racial cooperation and a recognition of black people's patriotism. Her 1942 *Saturday Evening Post* feature saw cattleman Silas as a "symbol of the strength of the nation." His story "helps to explain our history, and makes a promise for the future. . . . He speaks for free enterprise and personal initiative. That is America." Yet even in her patriotism Hurston knew what was expected of black public figures. The *American Mercury* was very interested in her journalism and published a number of her essays, including a short piece about Cudjo Lewis (March, 1944) that was simply pulled from her files. One reason the magazine was so interested, however, was that Zora had proven herself an obliging author—apparently in the interests of placing a black perspective in the magazine. Her essay "High John de Conquer" in the October, 1943, *American Mercury* was offered as "some help to our brothers and sisters who have always been white." Blacks have put their labor and their blood into American causes for a long time, and "maybe now in this terrible struggle we can give something else. . . . We offer you our hope bringer, High John de Conquer." As a hero who helped slaves endure, High John played his tricks and made a way out of no way. The High John tales are often humorous because John gave the slave "something worthy of laughter and song." So "if the news from overseas reads bad . . . listen hard for John. . . . You will know then, that no matter how bad things look now, it will be worse for those who seek to oppress us. Even if your hair comes yellow, and your eyes are blue, John De Conquer will be working for you."

These are perfectly legitimate sentiments, but it is instructive to note that they are a part of the essay because the editor asked Zora to offer support for a nation at war. She told Locke, "What I did for the Mercury has no scholarship of necessity. Besides, the editor had to have it sugared up to flatter the war effort. That certainly was not my idea, but some times you have to give something to get something." Later, when she told this same editor that the North was just as prejudiced as the South, "he did not like it a bit. I am beginning to see that there is a great body of Northerners who sympathize with the South and want no corrections made. They have so long thought of themselves as holy angels as regards the Negro, that they object to being shown up as no better than the people whom they have denounced so long."[26]

Zora's journalism between 1942 and 1945 usually spoke favorably of an integrated society, or sought to alleviate ignorance by interpreting black subjects for a white audience. Not only did she offer

High John to an anxious populace; in "The Rise of the Begging Joints" (*American Mercury*, March, 1945), she also warned whites to beware of contributing to certain types of inadequate black schools. In all this reporting, Zora was acutely aware of the predominantly white mass-magazine audience and of what her editors expected. If she did not actually misrepresent her views, she seldom expressed her true feelings. The two essays she wrote for the *Negro Digest* in 1944 and 1945 provide evidence for this. (The *Digest*, which had been condensing most of the *American Mercury* pieces, eventually made her a contributing editor.) When addressing a predominantly black audience, Hurston's prose was much less oblique. In the June, 1944, *Digest* she contributed to a continuing series entitled "My Most Humiliating Jim Crow Experience," telling the story of her rejection by a specialist in internal medicine. The physician had examined her in a laundry closet, and "it was evident he meant to get me off the premises as quickly as possible." She went away feeling the pathos of Anglo-Saxon civilization: "And I still mean pathos, for I know that anything with such a false foundation cannot last. Whom the gods would destroy, they first make mad." The article reminds one of the experiences Zora might have used in *Dust Tracks*. She once told her agent, "Someday I am going to do a piece probing into why white men feel and believe that all females of darker hue are just dying to make them. It is astonishing. Maybe too much Kipling."[27]

Zora's harshest attack on American social institutions came after the war had ended and there was no longer a need to cloak feelings in the flag. In the December, 1945, *Negro Digest* she published an essay, "Crazy for This Democracy," that included at least some of the ideas edited out of *Dust Tracks*. Citing Franklin Delano Roosevelt's reference to the United States as "the arsenal of democracy," she wonders if maybe she heard incorrectly: although she has been told that democracy is wonderful, "I don't know for myself." Maybe FDR said "arse-and-all" of democracy. One proof of the mispronunciation lay in the American support for postwar Western colonialism in the Far East: "The Indo-Chinese are fighting the French now in Indo-China to keep the freedom that they have enjoyed for five or six years now." Hurston believes, "The ass-and-all of Democracy has shouldered the load of subjugating the dark world completely." She likes the idea of democracy and is "all for trying it out." She is "crazy for this democracy," and "the only thing that keeps me from pitching headlong into the thing is the presence of numerous Jim Crow laws on the statute books." Wanting to know how democracy really feels, "I am all for the repeal of every Jim Crow law in the nation here and now. Not in another generation or so. The Hurstons have already been waiting 80 years for that. I want it here and now." She ends the essay with a ringing challenge to a racist system: "I give my hand, my heart and my head to the total struggle. I am for complete repeal of all Jim Crow laws in the U.S. once and for all, and right now. For the benefit of this nation and as a precedent to the world. . . . Not in some future generation, but repeal *now* and forever."

Hurston's commitment to racial politics in the war years carried over to her private life. At the beginning of the war she had moved to Saint Augustine because it was "a quiet place to write," and things had gone well. She felt she was "working harder and more consistently now than ever in my life." She also taught part-time at the local black college, Florida Normal, where she did not get along with her new administrators any better than she had with Shepherd in North Carolina. When a dispute arose between the college president and the servicemen being trained at the school, she used her contacts to enter the quarrel. Walter White, then executive secretary of the NAACP, who had been accused of stealing Zora's dance costumes a decade earlier, must have been startled to receive an abrupt letter from her in November, 1942: "Well the Negroes have been bitched again! I mean this signal corps school which the government has set up here. It would be more than worth your while to look into the matter. Through pressure from you it was grudgingly granted. Fisk, Hampton, and Tuskegee asked for it. But it is stuck down here at the Florida Normal, a most insignificant school to begin with, and then there are inadequate living quarters for the men." Telling White of the men's complaints against the president, she added, "I feel the whole body of Negroes are being insulted and mocked. . . . There are Negro men here approaching genius in the field of radio, whom the mass of Negroes know nothing about but would be proud to hear of. . . . It concerns us all, and I really think something ought to be done."[28]

Zora did not stay in Saint Augustine long enough to see the argument settled. She did become close friends with the Saint

Augustine novelist, Marjorie Kinnan Rawlings, however, and invited Rawlings to speak to her class. The white woman was so dazzled by her companion that without thinking she invited her to tea at her husband's segregated resort hotel. Later, realizing what she had done, she gave special orders to the elevator man to take Zora immediately up to the Rawlings residence on the fourth floor. But Zora had lived in the South for a long time; she went in through the kitchen and walked up the stairs. Safe in the apartment she was her usual vibrant self, causing Rawlings to admit to her husband that she had never in her life had such a stimulating visit.[29]

Saint Augustine's gentle climate restored Zora's health; the sea breezes helped her recover from the malaria she had picked up near the Gulf of Mexico during the previous summer's collecting trip. Troubles at the college persisted, however, and early in 1943 she moved to Daytona Beach. The move was attended by her purchase of a houseboat, the *Wanago*, a twenty-year-old, thirty-two-foot houseboat cruiser with a forty-four horsepower engine. She invited Harold Jackman and Countee Cullen for a visit, warning that it had a small galley and a toilet that one could only squeeze into, "if your behind does not stick out too far." Zora would live on houseboats for the next four years, traveling up and down the Indian and Halifax rivers, renting a permanent berth at the Howard Boat Works in Daytona Beach. She admitted to Rawlings that although the boat was so small it was crammed with books and papers, "I have the solitude that I love." There were no elevators on the waterfront; the state of Florida had not gotten around to segregating boat yards, and Zora liked the way "all the other boat owners are very nice to me. Not a word about race."[30]

It was a romantic existence, and Zora loved it. Florida was home: "I love the sunshine the way it is done in Florida. Rain the same way—in great slews or not at all. . . . I dislike cold weather and all of its kinfolk: that takes in bare trees and a birdless morning." The boat also provided her with a base for fishing, one of her lifelong passions. She soon began work on an article about the history of the Indian River maritime traffic. She told a friend that she felt close to a big break and real money. In March, Howard University named her the recipient of their annual distinguished alumni award; she invited her friends to the ceremony and made a special trip to Washington to receive the honor.[31]

Zora spent the rest of 1943 and part of 1944 on her houseboat, secure in her solitude, but hardly isolated from the world outside. She joined the Florida Negro Defense Committee and was favorably impressed with the leaders of the state's black community. She sent a curious correspondence to the *American Mercury*, not to describe conditions that made the committee necessary, but to praise these men for throwing off "at least a hundred years of indoctrination" that says the black person "is an object of pity." At a meeting she attended nobody mentioned slavery or Reconstruction: "It was a new and strange kind of Negro meeting— without tears of self-pity. It was a sign and symbol of something in the offing."[32]

She also became involved in a program sponsored by Mary Holland, wife of Florida's governor, called Recreation in War; she spoke about her travels to GIs stationed (and segregated) in Florida, a striking figure in a leather vest, one of the few women the men had ever seen who wore pants for a public occasion.[33]

In a long letter to Alain Locke she denounced the Detroit "riot" of 1943 in which thirty-four had been killed. She proposed an article "showing that the basic trouble of that incident and others of its kind in the north arises out of the false premise that northerners love Negroes and that all the intolerance is in the south. I have been touching on it in everything I have done for some time because I have seen the tragedy coming out of millions of simple, (and not so simple) Negroes rushing north with the firm belief that all is permitted there, and finding it otherwise." She complained that northern whites, victims of nineteenth-century abolitionist rhetoric, wanted to believe in a racial fantasy: "They have the fixed idea we should all be sweet, long suffering Uncle Toms, or funny Topsys. When the real us shows up, there is disillusionment." The disillusionment leads to segregation because the white northerner is trapped: "He is caught between the folklore he has been raised on about Negroes and his actual feelings." For her part, she had no illusions: "The truth of the matter is that the Anglo-Saxon is the most intolerant of human beings in the matter of *any* other group darker than themselves."[34]

The houseboat and her writing were her real life; the independence they offered was probably the reason a marriage contemplated in early 1944 never came off. She needed no man when she had "achieved one of my life's pleasures by owning at last a house-boat. Nothing to delay the sun in its course. . . . The Halifax river is very beautiful and the various natural expressions of the day on the river keep me happier than I have ever been before in my life. . . . Here, I can actually forget for short periods the greed and ultimate brutality of man to man."[35]

In the spring of 1944 she left Florida for New York to work with Dorothy Waring, a white woman, on a script for a musical comedy to be entitled "Polk County." This was to be based roughly on the material from "High John de Conquer," *Mules and Men*, and "Mule Bone." The two women labored intensely for a number of weeks. Stephen Kelen d'Oxylion, Waring's husband (who was also the producer), hoped that the musical could be scheduled for Broadway in the fall. Zora lived at the Hotel Theresa in Harlem and came downtown to Waring's apartment to work. The first day she arrived, she was taken up in the service elevator; when the elevator man was reprimanded by her collaborator, he asked how he was to know whether she was a writer or a laundress. Zora, her face in a mask, assured both that the mistake was simply "amusing."[36]

Waring remembers particularly Zora's report of attending a literary tea where a pompous, professional hostess said to her, "Come right in, darling." Zora was not fooled: "You know that bitch didn't mean it, I wasn't her darling. She had known me five minutes but she was just leaning over backwards to impress me with liberal points of view—which I'm sure she didn't have. And I would have felt much more flattered if I had been Miss Hurston to her rather than darling." When Waring urged Zora to keep a "sort of Gershwinesque feeling" about their Polk County musical, Zora's reply was, "You don't know what the hell you're talking about."[37]

When the play script was finished, Zora returned to Florida, stocked up the *Wanago*, and began the fifteen-hundred-mile sea voyage to New York. Arriving in November, she took up residence in Manhattan, hoping to find further backing for the musical, which now looked as though it would never be produced. The *Amsterdam News* tracked her down, and, as usual, she provided good copy. Sensitive to criticism of her books, especially in the black community, she told the reporter the facts of life for a black author. A writer's "material is controlled by publishers who think of the Negro as picturesque," she said, and it was hard to break through that stereotype. The author of *Dust Tracks* knew the difference between a half-loaf and no loaf at all: "According to the philosophy of Miss Hurston, if one intends to be published it is not sensible to buck the will of the people who have final authority" over publishing a volume. The reporter inadvertently revealed how common criticism of Zora had become: "Perhaps in this statement might be found partial answer to those who hold that the things emphasized in her books do little credit to the Negro." Zora was quick to respond to her interviewer's nuances. She was not about to provide simplistic portrayals of black life: "There is an over-simplification of the Negro. He is either pictured by the conservatives as happy, picking his banjo, or by the so-called liberals as low, miserable and crying. The Negro's life is neither of these. Rather, it is in-between and above and below these pictures. That's what I intend to put in my new book."[38]

Zora's reaction to "so-called liberals" became an obsession in this period, perhaps because of their resistance to many of her ideas. She wrote Burton Rascoe of the Theatre Guild that she had infuriated at least two editors "who are 'friends' of the Negro" by telling them that "their condescension in fixing us in a type and place is a sort of intellectual Jim Crow." The politics of such liberals may have reminded her of the reception of her own books by the left-wing press. When liberals champion black people, Zora said, "they seek out and praise literary characters of the lowest type and most sordid circumstances and portray the thing as the common state of all Negroes, and end up with the conclusion that the whites, and particularly the capitalist whites are responsible for this condition. How sad is the state of Aunt Hagar's Children."[39]

There is considerable irony in Hurston's complaint about the portrayal of black low-life characters. When describing the sawmill camps of Polk County, she hyperbolically claimed that there was a killing in the jook each payday, leading to charges that this portrait of lower-class black folk represented all black people. But Zora had learned a good deal since *Mules and Men* about the complexity of American racial politics and the needs of a white audience; she had learned through bitter experience how that audience distorted the human portraiture of the black artist. What galled her was that now these white liberals claimed to be "better friends of Negroes than I." She explained, "I freely admit the handicaps of race in America.

But I contend that we are just like everybody else. Black skunks are just as natural as white ones." Her complaint was about the political effects of putting all black people in the skunk category; for "if our friends portray us as subhuman varmints, the indifferent majority can only conclude we are hopeless." All of this was highly offensive to a woman with an obsessive sense of individualism. She hated the righteousness of whites when patronizing the lowly Negro, and responded to it violently: "I say to hell with it! My back is broad. Let me, personally and privately, be responsible for my survival or failure to survive in this man's world. . . . I want no double standards of measurement . . . if I am a skunk, I meant to stink up the place. . . . If I am a walking rosebud, I did that too. I am a conscious being, all the plaints and pleas of the pressure groups inside and outside the race, to the contrary."[40]

Hurston's cry was the cry of any black person in America ever encouraged to feel invisible as an individual human being because of that defect of the inner eye that afflicts white viewers. As World War II neared its end, Zora must have taken time to evaluate how successful her efforts as a racial journalist had been, what kind of an impact she had made, what her own reputation had become. She had envisioned the ideal of a pluralistic American society; as with many black American intellectuals before her, the vision eventually blurred in the face of the necessity to defend one's individual identity. As the war dragged on, she became more and more depressed. About the time she was writing "Crazy for This Democracy" she divulged to folklorist Ben Botkin her present perception of the world:

> I do hope that all is well with you and yours. These do be times that take all you have to scrape up a decent laugh or so. I do not refer to the battlefields, but to this enormous pest of hate that is rotting mens souls. When will people learn that you cannot quarantine hate? Once it gets loose in the world, it rides over all barriers and seeps under the doors and in the cracks of every house. I see it all around me every day. I am not talking of race hatred. Just hate. Everybody is at it. Kill, rend and tear! Women who are supposed to be the softening influence in life screaming for the kill. Once it was just Germany and Japan and Italy. Now, it is our allies as well. The people in the next county or state. The other political party. The

world smells like an abbatoir. It makes me very unhappy. I am all wrong in this vengeful world. I will to love.[41]

Hurston's answer to her depression was expatriation in the tropical jungles of Honduras, a trip that became the biggest gamble of her life. She hoped to become the discoverer of an ancient Mayan city that few other persons had ever looked upon, and between 1945 and 1948 she invested much of her time, energy, and money in the project. Absolutely nothing resulted from it except her final, unsuccessful novel.

Zora had been contacted in the fall of 1944 by Reginald Brett, an English gold miner in British Honduras who had been impressed with *Tell My Horse*. He told Zora that he was the only person to have ever seen the ruins of the Mayan city, and assured her that if she could come and write about it, she would "be more acceptable to the Honduranians than any writer in America." Brett's information took Zora "just like a mule in a tin stable. I am pitching, rearing and kicking at the walls." She had to go even "if I have to toe-nail it all the way down there, and take my chances on eating and sleeping, someway and somehow after I get there."[42]

Her enthusiasm did not consume her common sense, however. She immediately applied for financial assistance from both the Guggenheim Foundation and the Library of Congress. While to both she stressed the folklore that could be collected among the primitive Indians, her real excitement was for the "mystery city." Her enthusiasm, as usual, was overwhelming, even if her description was vague: "No one knows how long this group of people have lived in this place, nor what their history is. But this town in the mountains has been there for centuries. No outsiders have ever been allowed to enter this place for any reason whatsoever. They even expel their own sick." Curiously, the "mystery city" was different from Brett's find, for she also told the Guggenheim Foundation she would explore "the Lost City up the Patuca River [that] my informant has discovered," stressing that it had not been "looted by the gold hunting Spaniards." Although she did not say so to the foundation people, Zora may have had hopes of striking it rich with buried treasure. Mayan burial grounds were also on her list of "explorations," and she hoped that their discovery would prove "as important intellectually as the finding of the tomb of Tut-Ankarkam." Zora wanted to stay in the field for two years. She told Ben Botkin at the Library of Congress, "Naturally, I must hoard every penny I can rake and scrape, beg and borrow. . . . I may even murder up a couple of old guys suspected of having research money in their pants and not donating." She advised Botkin to dash out of his office "combing files and records out of your teeth as you flee down the corridor, and come with me." She was afraid that "somebody might beat me to it if I have to wait."[43]

Unable to find funding immediately, Zora spent most of 1945 looking for money and writing a novel. Her physical surroundings were still pleasant in Daytona Beach; she took in the sun, sometimes eating a dozen oranges at a single sitting. She also bought a new boat, the *Sun Tan*. The warm Florida sky was clouded by sickness, however, when her "guts started raising Cain," and recovery was slow. She wrote Carl Van Vechten in July, 1945, "I have been sick with my colon and general guts for a long, long time, and really for a while I thought I would kick the bucket." However, she hoped that Van Vechten would go to Central America with her, since now "the sun is shining in my door."[44]

Zora's new plan depended upon her friendship with a Miami adventurer, Captain Fred Irvine, who had offered his twenty-seven-ton schooner for transportation and a base camp. Called the *Maridome*, the ship had both sails and engine; if they could use the wind most of the way, costs would be minimal. She assured Van Vechten that the relationship was platonic. Not only did Irvine seem to have plenty of admirers; she also knew that they would be together throughout the trip and that a romance would only cause trouble in the end. She added, "There will be lots of men down there too, and I am liable to run upon something that suits."[45]

The friendship between the white captain and the black author was unusual on the waterfront, and Zora protected it fiercely. One man, who remarked to her in conversation that he thought Irvine was an English Jew, was dealt with summarily: "I knew the bastard had race prejudice that must include Negroes as well as Jews, so I booted his hips right off my boat." Close to finishing the new novel, Zora postponed the Honduras trip, and Irvine became interested in other things.[46]

By September, 1945, Zora's new book was being rejected by

Lippincott's. She had wanted to do a serious book to be called *Mrs. Doctor*, on "the upper strata of Negro life, and had it 2/3rds done, when I think Lippincott (timid soul) decided that the American public was not ready for it yet." The novel she had finished used material from "Mule Bone" and "Polk County"; in it she returned to the "picturesque" Eatonville locale. The story dealt with "a village youth expelled from town by village politics going places, including Hell and Heaven and having adventures, and returning after seven years to achieve his childhood ambition of being a fireman on the Railroad, and the town hero." The publisher did not like the manuscript. Her editors were surprised at the sloppiness of the writing, at a different, strained quality in the prose. Her earlier novels had all been so effortless, with little revision, and now they wondered if she were written out, or lazy, or not caring as much. Both sides worked hard during the winter of 1945–46, but finally decided that the book should not appear. After one editorial conference in New York, Zora went to lunch with Bertram Lippincott; he was struck both by the poor service that seemed to come because of their integrated table and by the stares they were gathering from the other diners. Zora talked about the book and worked hard to give the appearance that she noticed none of the rudeness.[47]

With no book prospects in sight, Zora returned to the Honduras adventure. She secured her passport in June, indicating on her application that she would be leaving on the twenty-fourth of the month on a commercial liner. But lack of money again made the trip impossible, and she traveled to New York in search of work. She landed a job in the Harlem congressional campaign of Grant Reynolds, Republican candidate running against Adam Clayton Powell, and plunged into the work, operating out of a Harlem storefront. She also found time to do some community organizing, developing a "block mothers" plan which resembled current day-care programs. Zora told an interviewer: "It's the old idea, trite but true, of helping people to help themselves that will be the only salvation of the Negro in this country." Reynolds remembers her as an energetic campaigner, particularly effective in getting people from the arts involved in his candidacy; she seemed to know everybody, and she was valuable in securing financial backing for the campaign.[48]

After Reynolds's defeat in November, 1946, Zora stayed in New

After Reynolds's defeat in November, 1946, Zora stayed in New York, taking a room on 124th Street, but she accomplished little. The winter of 1946–47 was hard, her hopes of a trip to Honduras still unfulfilled, her last book rejected by her publisher. She did not even look up her old friend Van Vechten, admitting to him later: "The place was too much of a basement to Hell to suit me. Everybody busy hating and speaking in either brazen lies or using just enough truth to season a lie up to make their viewpoint sound valid. Not hating anyone, I felt entirely out of place. I am afraid that I got a little unbalanced. I got so it was torture for me to go to meet people, fearing the impact of all the national, class, and race hate that I would have to listen to."[49]

In the spring of 1947 things began looking up. Her friendship with Marjorie Kinnan Rawlings led to Rawlings's publisher, Scribner's, becoming interested in her work. In April she switched publishers, acquiring Maxwell Perkins as her editor. His purchase of the option on a new novel meant that she now had the money to go to Honduras, and she wasted no time making plans. She sailed on May 4, with high hopes that her adventure was about to begin.[50]

Zora settled on the north coast at Puerto Cortés, putting up at the Hotel Cosenza, a respectable but aging hostelry that would remain her base of operation for the next year. The inflation of the country frightened her, making her "feel half stranded already." Still, she was grateful to Honduras, "for it has given me back myself. I am my old brash self again." The brashness was soon evident in a blistering review of Robert Tallant's *Voodoo in New Orleans* she wrote for the October–December, 1947, issue of the *Journal of American Folklore*. Perkins died in June, and Zora lamented the death because she had looked forward to working with the great editor. But his passing did not stop her from laboring long hours on the Scribner's novel, and she postponed any full-scale anthropological adventures until after the work was finished. She did go "part of the way to the interior," making "a most sensational discovery which I am keeping under my hat until I get hold of a few hundred dollars."

It was much cheaper to sit and write at the Hotel Cosenza, noisy as it was with the shouts of children in the halls, than to outfit an expedition. By summer her money had run out, and she asked for more; an agreement to do some travel articles for *Holiday* had fallen through, and she was in need. She told Burroughs Mitchell, her new Scribner's editor, "Yes, PLEASE I do need some money for necessities. . . . A drab terror has settled upon me by reason of my situation, though possibly you can never know the feeling, never having been in a foreign country and finding yourself without. After the last few weeks, I do not think that a headless horror could add anything new to what I know about terror and fear."

Scribner's advanced a second $500 against royalties and restored her confidence. By September, 1947, a draft of the novel was finished and in the mail to New York. She could not decide on a title, suggesting *Angel in the Bed*, *Sang the Suwanee in the Spring*, and *The Seraph's Man*, among others. Referring to the idiom of the book's white characters, Zora foresaw that there might be problems: "I am conscious that the use of 'nigger' in the text will offend some Negro readers. However, I am objective in my observations, and I know, as they know honestly, that the heroine would have certainly used that word. However, as publisher, the discretion is yours."

With the major portion of the novel done, Zora's hopes of an expedition to the interior returned. She described it in detail to her editor, perhaps with the thought that the publishers might be interested in financing the venture:

My planned expedition is to find a lost city in the mountains of the Department of the Mosquitia, Honduras, which travellers have heard about for two hundred years, but has not as yet been seen. That is not because they searched and did not find. It is a forbidding area and for various reasons they did not try it. I have been told by the Indians, the only ones who really know anything about that vast area, that it is *there*. The average Honduranian knows nothing about it. They take no interest in such things. Even Copan was discovered by outsiders. The interior of the Mosquitia is avoided with a dread that almost amounts to awe and terror. I have been repeatedly warned not to venture there. They point out the dangers from tigres (jaguars), leones (pumas) and the deadly barbes amarillos (yellow-throats), fer-de-lances (snakes) and the cascabelles (rattlesnakes) and viboras palmas (palm tree vipers), mosquitoes and fevers, to say nothing of hostile Indians. None of these things impress me. Possibly all of these things do exist. I discount their quantity considerably. The area is even marked "unexplored" on the maps. A very sparsely populated region. But as an anthropologist, these reports tell me certain things. The civilization that had vanished from that area even before the coming of the Spaniards disappeared for some reason. I rule out conquest by more powerful Indian nations, because those people then would have settled there. I consider either crop failure over several seasons, or some epidemic, which naturally they had no way of controlling in those days. I am strengthened in this theory by hearing about the Icaques, a pueblo of Indians in the mountains near Cedros who fear infection so much that they permit no outsiders to enter, and avoid contact with others as much as possible. On the rare occasions when they buy cloth for garments, it is sterilized by being passed over flames before being taken into the pueblo. The seriously ill among them are expelled. They might easily be the remnants of some once great nation who fled the old location because of an epidemic. They might once have peopled the now avoided area. I am further strengthened by the universal legend here that some curse hangs over the area, and it is to be avoided. Very few of the Indians will go but so far. Certainly they do not fear the snakes and animals, for they deal with them all the time and effectually. I sense that it is some handed down legend of awe.

In the face of this, I am led to wonder. Catholicism was forced on the Indians by the Spaniards, and their old temples wrecked as far as the Spaniards knew about them. It is frankly admitted that they remained pagan in spite of that, and the conquerors frequently found them holding pagan rites even as late as the middle of the last century. They still do. You follow me, I know. There might be something back in there that is not meant for the Blanco's eyes. Being what they call here a Mestizo, (mixed blood) I am getting hold of some signs and symbols through the advantage of blood.

Zora's rewriting of her novel, now called *Good Morning Sun*, carried into December, and by that time the rainy season forestalled jungle explorations. At one point Puerto Cortés had eighteen inches of rain in three days, leaving Zora with nothing to do but "gnaw fingernails," stare at muddy streets, and listen to a group of American construction workers attempt to "bulldoze the natives."

Scribner's finally accepted the novel. The publishers wanted Zora in New York for final editorial decisions, wiring her the passage money in early February, 1948. She left Honduras on February 20, worked hard during the first two weeks of March, and saw the manuscript finished and accepted on March 17. The title had now become *Sign of the Sun*. A fall publication date was set. Zora spent the summer at Constance Seabrook's home in Rhinebeck, New York, then took a room on 112th Street to await the book's appearance. When finally published on October 11, 1948, the novel was titled *Seraph on the Suwanee*. It was a story of white southerners, with only random mention of black people.

Black authors have always had to suffer the arrogance of white critics, and often their success has depended upon the amount of resistance they offer to those self-appointed arbiters of the literary establishment. One of the most frequently voiced critical prescriptions is that the black author must transcend race in order to write universally. Even such a brilliant poet as Gwendolyn Brooks has been advised that if "being a Negro" is her only subject, then she is somehow prohibited from creating great literature. A white subject matter is offered as a remedy; the critics assume that the ultimate transcendence is to not write about black people at all, believing for some reason that white people carry no racial identity. Much fiction has been written in response to this prescription, and even a powerful writer like Richard Wright can fall victim to the suggestion, creating, for example, a very bad novel about a retired white insurance executive who commits murder after accidentally locking himself out of his apartment as he reaches, nude, into the hallway to pick up his Sunday *New York Times*. The peril in deliberately choosing a white subject is considerable. There is nothing which prohibits a black writer from creating successful white characters, and black literature is full of brilliant white portraits. But if the novelist consciously seeks to portray whites in order to validate his talent, to prove to the world there are no limits to his genius, the very assumptions of the decision become self-defeating. Black lives *are* universal, and black authors have not transcended but pushed deep into racial experience to prove it.[51]

In writing *Seraph on the Suwanee* Zora Neale Hurston largely turned her back on the source of her creativity. She escaped the stereotype of the "picturesque" black by giving up the celebration of black folklife, replacing the storytellers on Joe Clarke's porch with a family of upwardly mobile Florida crackers. She told her editor that she was proud of the book because it demonstrated her ability to write about both races, that it was "very much by design" that the book had primarily white characters. As early as 1942 she had told Carl Van Vechten that her "tiny wedge" in Hollywood gave her "hopes of breaking that old silly rule about Negroes not writing about white people. . . . I am working on a story now."[52]

Why did Hurston choose to write such a book? Because of the attraction of being labeled a "universal" novelist? Was it for the money? Transfixed by her "mystery city" in Honduras, she had written Scribner's, "This present book must be GOOD so that I can make money for the project that is burning my soul to attack." Was it a matter of racial politics? *Dust Tracks* had received much criticism, and she sometimes felt isolated and abused; one way to avoid criticism was to avoid writing about black people. Even if all these matters affected her decision, there remains another explanation for *Seraph on the Suwanee*. Biographical evidence suggests that Zora Hurston was groping toward a statement about marriage, and that the novel she created did not quite achieve what she wanted to say.

In *Dust Tracks* Zora pondered the sexual roles in marriage, explaining that her first marriage had been unsuccessful because of her desire for a career. The affair of the thirties that inspired *Their Eyes Were Watching God* became so intense because her lover was one of the few intellectual equals she had ever found; yet that relationship failed because she was unwilling to marry, assume a subordinate role, and give up her work. Hurston's independence had led her to rail in public life against "the natural apathy of women, whether Negro or white, who vote as their husbands do," and in private life at self-inspired Casanovas: "I may be thinking of turnip greens with dumplings, or more royalty checks, and here is a man who visualizes me on a divan sending the world up in smoke."[53] She discovered that in seeking temporary relationships she could not terminate them as a man would; she had to resort to deception: "If I get tired and let on about it, he is certain to become an enemy. . . . I have learned to frame it so that I can claim to be deserted and devastated by him. Then he goes off with a sort of twilight tenderness for me, wondering what it is that he's got that brings so many women down." She complained that while "under the spell of moonlight" she might "feel the divine urge for an hour, a day, or maybe a week." But male egos were too easily bruised to accept the transitory nature of her affection. Her second marriage apparently fell victim to such impermanence.

These relatively liberated attitudes inform and illuminate *Seraph on the Suwanee*. The novel is about Arvay Henson Meserve, a woman seemingly very different from Zora, whose life is defined by her marriage; Arvay is a woman searching for herself, trying to overcome a deep feeling of inferiority that leaves her believing she is not worthy of her strong, handsome, ambitious husband. Set in Florida between 1900 and 1930, the novel has little plot; basically, it is the story of Arvay's marriage to Jim Meserve and the problems that afflict it because of her uncertain sense of self and her husband's lusty, unthinking chauvinism. Jim Meserve rescues Arvay from a teenage withdrawal into repressed sexual hysteria by engaging to marry her, then raping her, then marrying her. Yet Arvay is infatuated with her husband, loves him fiercely, and worries that she will be unable to hold him. They migrate from the "teppentime forests" of northwest Florida to the citrus country, where Jim's energy carves out a good life for his wife and children. The road is not easy, for their first son, Earl, is retarded, and Jim rejects the child, while she protects him. This damages relations between Arvay and Jim and also affects Arvay's feelings toward their two normal children. She suffers guilt over Earl's handicap, seeing it as the price she must pay for once secretly desiring her sister's husband, and makes life difficult for Jim as a way to keep punishing herself. Jim, on the other hand, plays cruel tricks on Arvay, has no respect for her intelligence, and abuses the unusual power he holds over her.

As a teenager, Earl sexually attacks a neighbor girl, then hides in the "great swamp" near his home, a dark and murky wilderness that symbolizes the fearful tangle of Arvay's subconscious. When Jim tracks him down, Earl attempts to kill his father and is shot in order to save Jim; the sexual rivalry Arvay has created is symbolically acted out. After the death, Arvay retreats from the family, though she tries hard to understand her own withdrawal. Eventually she emerges to search for security in her responsibilities as a mother. Yet with her children grown, her mother's role is no longer necessary; her other son becomes a successful New York musician and her daughter marries a wealthy land developer. The novel ends inconclusively with Jim and Arvay in middle age. Jim has become a shrimp-boat captain, and Arvay has come to a kind of peace when she realizes that Jim, too, needs her mothering love.

Although narrated in the third person, the story is told largely through Arvay's consciousness, and the book offers a number of acute insights as Zora explores her psyche. It also contains vivid examples of the Hurston style; one character is described as having a face "as naked as a jay-bird in whistling time." The novel is not successful, however, because Arvay is not given a stature that will support the psychological burden she is asked to bear, and because the plot is frequently implausible (for instance, Jim becomes a shrimp-boat captain for the sole purpose of demonstrating Hurston's knowledge of shrimping). As Ann Rayson has admitted, in a sympathetic study of Hurston, "It is unfortunately easy to put *Seraph on the Suwanee* . . . in a ludicrous light."[54]

Hurston apparently created Arvay from two emotional sources: her knowledge of the inferiority she had been made to feel as a child, and her observations of the inadequacy felt by men when confronted by her own self-reliant, independent intelligence. Immersed in the writing of the novel in October, 1947, she wrote a long letter to Burroughs Mitchell explaining Arvay's characterization, indicating that part of Arvay's inadequacy grew from her inability to overcome childhood complexes about beauty. Zora used herself to illustrate the point: "Though brash enough otherwise, I got an overwhelming complex about my looks before I was grown, and it was very hard for a long time for me to believe that any man really cared for me. I set out to win my fight against this feeling, and I did. I don't care how homely I am now. I know that it doesn't really matter, and so my relations with others are easier."

Zora is talking, perhaps a bit defensively, about selfhood, about autonomous personality; the plot of *Seraph on the Suwanee*, interestingly, is about Arvay's doomed search for selfhood while married to a man who believes that "women folks don't have no mind to make up nohow. They wasn't made for that. Lady folks were just made to laugh and act loving and kind and have a good man to do for them all he's able, and have him as many boy-children as he figgers he'd like to have, and make him so happy that he's willing to work and fetch in every dad-blamed thing that his wife thinks she would like to have." Jim's opinions do not offend Arvay. In fact, they are attractive to her, and her only worry is that there may be a catch: "If she married Jim Meserve, her whole duty as a wife was to just love him good, be nice and kind around the house and have children for him. She could do that and be more than happy and satisfied, but it looked too simple."

It is too simple, of course, just as Zora knew it was simpleminded to submit to her lover's demand to give up her career. Neither Jim nor Arvay can be fully happy in such a subordination of roles, but neither quite realizes why. Arvay's ambivalence is dramatized during a scene in which she finds herself momentarily paralyzed, unable to act when her husband is in danger. Although the scene is awkwardly prepared for, its symbolism has a complicated reference, revealing the emotional tangle that can attend subordination. In action that reminds one of "Sweat," Hurston's 1926 story of marital hatred, Jim captures an eight-foot rattlesnake and holds it by its head, calling Arvay outside to witness his virility. He knows that Arvay has "a deep-seated fear and dislike of snakes," that "she shrank from worms even because they reminded her of snakes"; but he thinks he sees a chance "to do something big and brave and full of manhood" that will make Arvay love him. When the snake wraps itself around Jim's waist and threatens his life, Arvay cannot move: "She saw the imminent danger to her husband, her great love, the source of all the happiness that she had ever known, the excuse for her existence. And in this terrible danger, she went into a kind of coma standing there. . . . In her consciousness Arvay flew to Jim and slew that snake and held Jim in her arms like a baby. Actually she never moved. She could neither run to the rescue nor flee away from the sight of what she feared would happen."

This scene is almost topheavy with phallic and Christian symbolism. Arvay's inability to act is related to Jim's initial violent sexual assault, to her sublimated resentment over her role in their marriage, to the evil that Jim's sexuality represents to her fundamentalist Christian conscience, and to her own pleasure—and guilt—in their tempestuous intercourse. The immobility leads Jim to repudiate her. He leaves their bed and home, demanding of

Arvay what she both wants and fears: "I don't want that stand-still, hap-hazard kind of love. I'm just as hungry as a dog for a knowing and a doing love. You love like a coward. Don't take no steps at all. Just stand around and hope for things to happen right."

The fascinating thing about Arvay's characterization is that Hurston created it from the inadequacy she found in the men in her own life, transferring the feelings of inferiority she found in them to the wife of her novel. She told her Scribner's editor:

> I shall bring Arvay along her road to find herself a great deal faster. I get sick of her at times myself. Have you ever been tied in close contact with a person who had a strong sense of inferiority? I have, and it is hell. They carry it like a raw sore on the end of the index finger. You go along thinking well of them and doing what you can to make them happy and suddenly you are brought up short with an accusation of looking down on them, taking them for a fool, etc., but they mean to let you know and so on and so forth. It colors *everything*. For example, I took this man that I cared for down to Carl Van Vechten's one night so that he could meet some of my literary friends, since he had complained that I was always off with them, and ignoring him. I hoped to make him feel at home with the group and included so that he would go where I went. What happened? He sat off in a corner and gloomed and uglied away, and we were hardly out on the street before he was accusing me of having dragged him down there to show off what a big shot I was and how far I was above him. He had a good mind, many excellent qualities, and I am certain that he loved me. But his feeling of inferiority would crop up and hurt me at the most unexpected moments. Right in the middle of what I considered some sweet gesture on my part, I would get my spiritual pants kicked up around my neck like a horse-collar. I asked him to bring me all the clippings on my TELL MY HORSE, and he brought several and literally flung them at me. "You had read them," he accused, "and knew that they were flattering. You just asked me to get them to see how great you were." You know how many marriages in the literary and art world have broken up on such rocks, to say nothing of other paths of life. A business man is out scuffling for dear life to get things for the woman he loves, and she is off pouting and accusing him of neglecting her. She feels that way because she does not feel herself able to keep up with the pace that he is setting, and just be confident that she is wanted no matter how far he goes.

Millions of women do not want their husbands to succeed for fear of losing him. It is a very common ailment. That is why I decided to write about it. The sufferers do not seem to realize that all that is needed is a change of point of view from fear into self-confidence and then there is no problem.

This is revealing commentary, for *Seraph on the Suwanee* fails precisely because Zora seems incapable of moving Arvay "from fear into self-confidence." Arvay and Jim are reconciled after Arvay discovers how much Jim depends on her, after she finds that "inside he was nothing but a little boy to take care of, and he hungered for her hovering." She also learns how much there is to discover about herself: "And just like she had not known Jim, she had known her own self even less." This causes the book to end in apparent happiness; Arvay realizes that "all that had happened to her, good or bad, was a part of her own self and had come out of her." It is an unsatisfactory and unbelievable ending, however, because it is expressed in terms that vitiate Arvay's struggle toward selfhood. She can never define the self apart from her husband (Jim Me-serve is cleverly named); although she comes to greater self-confidence, discovering that she no longer needs to apologize for her cracker origins, or feel insecure about what she brings to her marriage, or spend her lifetime worrying if she is worthy, her possibilities for self-expression are extremely limited. She discovers in a climactic sunrise that "her job was mothering. . . . Yes, she was doing what the big light had told her to do. She was serving and meant to serve. She made the sun welcome to come on in, then snuggled down again beside her husband."

It is possible that Zora meant this last scene to be semitragic, Arvay descending into the trap of her marriage forever; but if so, it fails for lack of preparation. Although a chauvinist, Jim has also been given admirable qualities—courage, honesty, loyalty—one reason Arvay feels so inadequate. Jim and Arvay can never achieve the love between equals that Hurston idealized for herself, because Arvay is created without adequate potential. For some reason Zora could not grant Arvay the attainment of a truly independent selfhood, the kind that Zora Neale Hurston had established in her own life. In sum, *Seraph on the Suwanee* is an unsuccessful work of art, partially because Arvay's character promises a complexity of motive and a subtlety of action that is never realized. Just as Arvay begins to become interesting, she is lost again to domestic service.

If the role reversal described in her letter to Scribner's reveals Hurston's thoughts about male-female relationships, the novel has an interesting biographical matrix. Zora Hurston went through two marriages and a number of love affairs without finding a man secure enough to grant her both his love and her career. Although that male role has been reversed in the novel, *Seraph* does contain a statement about the sexual mythology of American culture: that this civilization produces very few adult human beings, even fewer adult marriages. *Seraph on the Suwanee* displays Zora Hurston's deep identification with both Arvay and Jim; yet she also felt compelled to expose their faults and renounce their characters. Zora understood Arvay's need for selfhood when confined to a traditional mother's role in a marriage limited by her husband's need to prove his manhood. She also understood Arvay's inferiority because she had been there herself, and had overcome a feeling of physical inadequacy; at the age of forty-six, and by all accounts a handsome woman, she still had to volunteer to listeners, "I don't care how homely I am now."

Zora also identified with Jim's exasperation over Arvay's inadequacy, for it was exactly the situation she had encountered with men. Jim's strength in the novel, his physical courage and his belief in self-reliance, are qualities that Zora consciously sought to demonstrate in her own personal relationships. She once told an interviewer, "I love courage in every form. I worship strength. I dislike insincerity, and most particularly when it vaunts itself to cover up cowardice."[55] However, Hurston also had to expose Jim's cruelty and the hollow center to his manly bearing, just as she had to divulge her revulsion for Arvay by not permitting her to escape the trap baited by her insecurity. Zora Neale Hurston demonstrates that both Arvay and Jim are captives of the sexual roles that afflict marriage, a social institution she eventually found unsuitable to her own life. Unfortunately, this understanding of the novel's complexity depends primarily upon extratextual evidence. The book itself is not nearly so interesting as the authorial emotions that coalesced in the creating of it.

What *Seraph on the Suwanee* finally illustrates is the new direction of Zora Neale Hurston's life during the late 1940s. She had turned away from the resources that had previously sustained and inspired her art. The main black characters in *Seraph*, Joe Kelsey and his wife and children, are only stick figures to be moved about for the purposes of the narrative, and at times they are mere stereotypes. Joe calls Jim Meserve "boss" and "quality," while Jim returns the compliment by affectionately calling Joe "you trashy rascal, you." The folklore that had graced Eatonville and provoked Hurston's celebration of black people now comes from the mouths of southern whites. She may have been only trying to show that there was cross-cultural borrowing of folklore in the South; but when Arvay's daughter says, "I don't care if he comes from Diddy-Wah-Diddy," or Jim Meserve assures Arvay, "You don't have to worry about a thing. You got a man who can bring it when he come," the context never seems quite right. It is worth remembering that at least one incident in *Seraph*—the curing of Arvay's "fits" with turpentine—originated in her anthology of Eatonville anecdotes published in the *Messenger* in 1926.

Hurston's anthropological studies had now become adventures, schemes to make her rich and famous, mother lodes to be mined for commercial purposes. Her political opinions had fallen victim to publishers' demands. Her journalism had become the captive of her own conception of public opinion. Only when speaking to a black audience did she feel safe to speak her mind in public, and she suffered from periodic depressions that were alleviated only by the solitude of a small houseboat or the strangeness of a foreign country. The woman who had traversed the rural South, living in turpentine camps and sawmills, playing jook songs on her guitar while packing a pearl-handled revolver in her purse, had traveled a long way down a dusty road, and her destination seemed much less promising by 1948 than it had a decade earlier. She told Marjorie Kinnan Rawlings that she had uneasy feelings about *Seraph*: "I am not so sure that I have done my best, but I tried. I need not tell you that my goal still eludes me. I am in despair because it keeps ever ahead of me."[56]

What happened after the publication of *Seraph on the Suwanee* made her goal seem ever more elusive, her travels even more doubtful.

NOTES

1. AL, "Dry Fields and Green Pastures," *Opportunity*, 18 (Jan., 1940), 7; Ralph Ellison, "Recent Negro Fiction," *New Masses*, Aug. 5, 1941, p. 211; ZNH to Edwin Osgood Grover, Oct. 12, 1939 (HCUFla). See also the reviews in *New York Herald Tribune Books*, Nov. 26, 1939; *Boston Transcript*, Nov. 18, 1939; *New York Times*, Nov. 19, 1939, p. 21; *New Yorker*, Nov. 11, 1939, p. 75; *Saturday Review*, Nov. 11, 1939, p. 11; *New York Post*, Nov. 9, 1939.

2. Marriage license, Albert Price III and ZNH, June 27, 1939, Marriage Book 10, p. 148 (Court Records, Nassau County, Fla.); F. Marjenhoff of Jacksonville, Fla., Department of Recreation and Public Affairs, to RH, Oct. 13, 1975; *ZNH v. Albert Price*, BOC Book 324, p. 441 (Public Records, Duval County, Fla.). Although Price had claimed to be older when married (and Zora had claimed to be born in 1910), in the 1939 divorce proceedings Price listed his age as twenty-three.

3. *ZNH v. Albert Price*.

4. Jane Belo to CVV, July 7, 1940 (JWJYale); ZNH to Paul Green, May 3, 1940 (in Green's possession). Hurston and Belo did make silent motion pictures, for there is such a film with the Belo Papers at the Museum of Natural History; Margaret Mead, administrator of the Belo estate, kindly made a copy of the film available to me.

5. Paul Green, Diary Notes, 1940-42, Feb. 11, 1940 (North Carolina Collection, University of North Carolina Archives).

6. Fannie Hurst to CVV, Sept. 17, 1940 (JWJYale); New York driver's license issued to ZNH, Feb. 10, 1941; ZNH to Edwin Osgood Grover, Dec. 30, 1941 (HCUFla); ZNH, *Dust Tracks on a Road* (Philadelphia: J. B. Lippincott, 1942), p. 221; manuscript of *Dust Tracks*, last page (dated July 5, 1941), p. 208 (JWJYale).

7. Peter Bergquist of Paramount Pictures Corporation to RH, Dec. 10, 1970; clipping, *Afro-American*, Apr. 18, 1942, relating that ZNH appeared as the guest speaker at the Fourth Annual Meeting of the Associated Women of Tuskegee (MSRC); ZNH to Edwin Osgood Grover, Apr. 15, 1942 (HCUFla); Harold Jackman to CVV, June 20, 1942 (JWJYale); ZNH to Henry Allen Moe, June 25, 1942 (GgFnd); ZNH to Roberta Bosley, Nov. 2, 1942 (JWJYale).

8. Darwin T. Turner, *In a Minor Chord* (Carbondale: Southern Illinois University Press, 1971), p. 91; Nathan Huggins, *The Harlem Renaissance* (New York: Oxford University Press, 1971), p. 133. See also Turner's introduction to *Dust Tracks on a Road* (New York: Arno Press, 1969).

9. Turner, *In a Minor Chord*, p. 89; ZNH to Hamilton Holt, Feb. 1, 1943 (HCUFla).

10. Stephen Butterfield, *Black Autobiography* (Amherst: University of Massachusetts Press, 1974), p. 3. This paragraph owes much to Butterfield.

11. ZNH, manuscript of *Dust Tracks*, chapter entitled "Friendship," p. 1.

12. Larry Neal, introduction to *Dust Tracks on a Road* (Philadelphia: J. B. Lippincott, 1971), p. xi.

13. See ZNH, "Negroes without Self-Pity," *American Mercury*, 57 (Nov., 1943), 601–3.

14. Ann Rayson, in "Dust Tracks on a Road: Zora Neale Hurston and the Form of Black Autobiography," *Negro American Literature Forum*, 7 (Summer, 1973), 39, calls this passage "both naïvely ridiculous and camp in a finely ironic self-parody."

15. Ibid.

16. Clipping, "Zora Neale Hurston Reveals Key to Her Literary Success," *New York Amsterdam News*, Nov. 18, 1944 (MSRC).

17. ZNH, manuscript of *Dust Tracks*, pp. 207–10.

18. Ibid., p. 210.

19. Ibid., p. 214.

20. *Saturday Review*, Feb. 20, 1943, p. 11. See the reviews in *New York Times*, Nov. 29, 1942; *New Yorker*, Nov. 14, 1942, p. 79; and *Saturday Review*, Nov. 28, 1942, p. 6.

21. ZNH to CVV, Nov. 2, 1942 (JWJYale); ZNH to Edwin Osgood Grover, n.d. [ca. Dec. 10, 1942] (HCUFla); ZNH to GgFnd, Sept. 12, 1944 (GgFnd).

22. Arna Bontemps, "From Eatonville, Florida to Harlem," *New York Herald Tribine*, Nov. 22, 1942; clipping, Harold Preece, "Dust Tracks on a Road," *Tomorrow*, Feb., 1943 (Schomburg Collection, New York Public Library).

23. Clipping, Douglas Gilbert, "When Negro Succeeds, South Is Proud, Zora Hurston Says," *New York World Telegram*, Feb. 1, 1943 (JWJYale); Roy Wilkins, "The Watchtower," *New York Amsterdam News*, Feb. 27, 1943. In fairness, it should be pointed out that Hurston later said that she had been misquoted; see Hugh Gloster, "Zora Neale Hurston, Novelist and Folklorist," *Phylon*, 4 (1943), 148, in which Gloster quotes a subsequent ZNH interview in the *Atlanta Daily World*, Mar. 3, 1943.

24. Marion Kilson, in "The Transformation of Eatonville's Ethnographer," *Phylon*, 33 (Summer, 1972), 112–19, argues that in essays such as this Zora was shifting from the perspective of an ethnographic artist to that of a critical ethnographer.

25. ZNH to Edwin Osgood Grover, Nov. 7, 1943 (HCUFla).

26. ZNH to AL, July 23, 1943 (HUAL).

27. ZNH to JPW, Mar. 7, 1951 (AWRH).

28. ZNH to Walter White, Nov. 24, 1942 (JWJYale); ZNH to Edwin Osgood Grover, n.d. [ca. Dec. 10, 1942] (HCUFla). I have not been able to confirm Hurston's employment by Florida Normal. Norton Baskin, husband of Marjorie Kinnan Rawlings, was sure that she had taught there, and Evelyn Thomas Helmick, in "Zora Neale Hurston," *Carrell*, 11 (June and Dec., 1970), 15, states that she taught creative writing there.

29. RH interview with Norton Baskin, Feb. 27, 1971, St. Augustine, Fla.

30. ZNH to Roberta Bosley, Nov. 2, 1942; ZNH to CVV, Feb. 15, 1943 (JWJYale); ZNH to Marjorie Kinnan Rawlings, May 16, Oct. 21, 1943 (SCUFla); ZNH to Harold Jackman, Mar. 29, 1944 (JWJYale).

31. "Zora Neale Hurston," in *Twentieth Century Authors*, ed. Stanley Kunitz and Howard Haycraft (New York: H. W. Wilson, 1942), p. 695; RH interview with Everette Hurston, Sr., Jan. 13, 1976, Bristol, Conn.; ZNH to Edwin Osgood Grover, n.d. [ca. Dec. 10, 1942]; ZNH to Hamilton Holt, Feb. 1, 1943 (HCUFla); *Howard University Bulletin*, Apr. 1, 1943, p. 6; ZNH to CVV, Feb. 15, 1943 (JWJYale).

32. ZNH, "Negroes without Self-Pity."

33. RH interview with Mary Holland, Feb., 1971, Bartow, Fla.

34. ZNH to AL, July 23, 1943 (HUAL).

35. The *New York Amsterdam News* reported on Feb. 5, 1944, that ZNH was engaged to marry James Howell Pitts of Cleveland, but apparently the marriage

never took place. I have been unable to find out much about this episode. ZNH to Henry Allen Moe, Sept. 8, 1944 (GgFnd).

36. RH interview with Dorothy Waring, May 21, 1971, New York City. The *New York Daily News* announced on July 31, 1944, that "Polk County, a Comedy of Negro Life," was being scheduled for fall production by Stephen Kelen d'Oxylion.

37. RH interview with Dorothy Waring, May 21, 1971, New York City.

38. Although the voyage from Daytona Beach to New York seems an arduous undertaking, especially for a small boat like the *Wanago*, Zora assured a *New York Amsterdam News* reporter on Nov. 18, 1944, that she had just arrived from Jacksonville a week earlier. The quotations in the paragraph come from this Nov. 18, 1944, article (clipping in MSRC).

39. ZNH to Burton Rascoe, Sept. 8, 1944 (Archives, University of Pennsylvania).

40. Ibid.

41. ZNH to Ben Botkin, Oct. 16, 1944 (LCAFS).

42. ZNH to Henry Allen Moe, Sept. 8, 1944 (GgFnd).

43. Ibid., Sept. 8, 18, 1944; ZNH to Ben Botkin, Oct. 16, 1944 (LCAFS).

44. Myrtis L. Hurston to RH, Aug. 30, 1976; ZNH to CVV, July 15, 1945 (JWJYale).

45. ZNH to CVV, July 24, 1945 (JWJYale).

46. Ibid.

47. Tay Hohoff to RH, Nov. 30, 1970; ZNH to CVV, Sept. 12, 1945 (JWJYale); RH interview with Bertram Lippincott, Dec. 17, 1970, Penllyn, Pa.; RH interviews with Tay Hohoff, Dec., 1970, May, 1971, New York City.

48. Passport application no. 96759, passport issued June 25, 1946 (Passport Records, U.S. State Department); RH interview with Grant Reynolds, May, 1971, New York City; H.M.F., "Fighter against Complacency and Ignorance," *Barnard College Alumnae Magazine*, 36 (Autumn, 1946), 6; clipping, James Fuller, "Harlem Portrait," *Pittsburgh Courier*, Sept. 28, 1946 (JWJYale).

49. ZNH to CVV, July 30, 1947 (JWJYale).

50. I have reconstructed the narrative of Hurston's trip to Honduras and her writing of *Seraph on the Suwanee* (New York: Charles Scribner's Sons, 1948) from the Hurston files at Scribner's. The files contain 102 items; I have depended primarily on the twenty-five letters from ZNH to Scribner's, most of which are to her editor, Burroughs Mitchell: ZNH to Max Perkins, May 20, 1947; ZNH to Burroughs Mitchell, July 31, Sept. 3, Oct. 2, "October Something Late," Dec. 5, 1947, Jan. 14, Feb. 3, 14, Aug. 5, 1948; ZNH to Whitney Darrow, July 30, 1948; Ann Watkins to Burroughs Mitchell, June 1, 1948. The manuscript of *Seraph on the Suwanee*, dated Mar. 17, 1948, and numbering 413 pages, is in HCUFla.

51. Quoted by Hoyt W. Fuller in "Towards a Black Aesthetic," in *The Black Esthetic*, ed. Addison Gayle (Garden City, N.Y.: Doubleday, 1971), p. 4.

52. ZNH to CVV, Nov. 2, 1942 (JWJYale); RH interview with Burroughs Mitchell, May, 1971, New York City.

53. H.M.F., "Fighter against Complacency and Ignorance," p. 7; ZNH, *Dust Tracks*, pp. 262, 263, 264.

54. Ann Rayson, "The Novels of Zora Neale Hurston," *Studies in Black Literature*, 5 (Winter, 1974), 1–11. See also James W. Byrd, "Zora Neale Hurston: A Novel Folklorist," *Tennessee Folklore Society Bulletin*, 21 (1955), 41.

55. "Zora Neale Hurston," *Twentieth Century Authors*, p. 695.

56. ZNH to Marjorie Kinnan Rawlings, n.d. [ca. Nov., 1948] (SCUFla).

12 ≋≋≋ The Pots in Sorrow's Kitchen

On September 13, 1948, New York police knocked at the door of Zora Hurston's room at 140 West 112th Street. They arrested her, drove her to precinct headquarters, and booked her, charging that she had committed an immoral act with a ten-year-old boy; the complaint had been filed by the Children's Society. The charge was false, but no one listened to her denials. The boy seemed sure of his story, the authorities convinced of her guilt; her emotional protests were what they expected. She offered to take a lie-detector test, but no one paid any attention.[1]

Burroughs Mitchell, her Scribner's editor, secured her release that evening. After spending the night at his home, she quietly moved to an apartment in the Bronx, leaving no forwarding address and hoping that no one would find her. With her publisher's help, she retained a lawyer, Louis Waldman, to represent her. Three weeks later she was indicted, solely on the boy's testimony.

Zora's emotions alternated between outrage and despair. Yet there was one ray of hope. Proceedings in children's cases were private, and the press had not yet discovered the story; the indictment, she hoped, would be dismissed before there was any publicity. She did not anticipate that an employee of the courts would take the news to New York's black newspapers. On October 15, after Zora pleaded not guilty before Judge Saul Streit of New York's General Sessions Court and was released on a $1,500 bond, a reporter for the *New York Age* caught up with her. Near tears, she emotionally denied "the impossible accusation" and was at a loss to explain the motives of the woman who had instigated her arrest. What shocked her was the way the judicial system took the word of a ten-year-old boy over that of an adult. Would they have done the same to a white person? she asked. "It smacks of an anti-Negro violation of one's civil rights. . . . If such an injustice can happen to one who has prestige and contacts, then there can be absolutely no justice for the little people of the community." Waving her passport in the air, she explained that she was in Honduras when the alleged acts were said to have taken place. She challenged the court to right its injustice, and promised, her voice shaking, "I intend to fight this horrible thing to the finish and clear my reputation."

Zora was accused of sodomy; the boy was the son of the woman who had rented her a room on 124th Street during the bleak winter of 1946–47, a period when Zora had avoided friends and lived quietly. Also accused were two other adults whom she had never met. At the pretrial hearing in Judge Streit's court, her attorney tried to pin the boy down to specific times and places. The youth first claimed that they had all gone to a coal bin each Saturday afternoon for over a year—a physical impossibility, since Zora had been in Honduras for most of this period. When pressed, the boy admitted that his memory might not be exact; but he claimed to definitely remember a meeting on August 15, 1948—a day Zora had been in Rhinebeck, New York, gathering material for an article. Still, the child seemed so forthright; the court believed that his testimony warranted a trial.

With the contradictory evidence established, Waldman went to Manhattan district attorney Frank Hogan and, in an unusual move for a defense lawyer, put all his cards on the table. He showed Zora's passport, told what refutation he could present, and asked Hogan not to prosecute in the interests of justice. Hogan conducted a thorough investigation. He discovered that the child was disturbed and that the mother resented Zora's advice, freely given two years before, that she take her son to Bellevue for psychiatric testing. The Children's Society had neglected to investigate carefully, and the district attorney became convinced of Hurston's innocence. After consulting with his staff, Hogan ordered the case dropped and the indictment dismissed.

By the time of the dismissal, in March, 1949, the damage had been done. A week after *Seraph on the Suwanee* was published—to rather good reviews—a national black newspaper had given the story lurid front-page coverage. The national edition of Baltimore's

Afro-American headlined Zora's troubles in its October 23, 1948, edition. At the top of the front page was the headline to another feature, "Police Seeking Bathtub Killer of Young Mother"; underneath, in large letters, was the headline "Boys, 10, Accuse Zora." Over the two-column story was the smaller "Novelist Arrested on Morals Charge. Reviewer of Author's Latest Book Notes Character Is 'Hungry for love.'" Beneath Zora's picture, set to the right of her story, was another headline, "Seven Milwaukee Men Held in Sex Case Probe. Teenage White Girls Illicitly Involved." The Hurston story itself was both inaccurate and sensational. The one boy had become three, while the charges were characterized as "particularly sordid." Most repulsive of all, the paper quoted Jim's plea to Arvay, "I'm just as hungry as a dog for a knowing and a doing love," and asked if Zora sought the same affection. A week later, after objections to such coverage, the *Afro-American* defended itself with haughty self-righteousness: "It is the *Afro's* belief that a hush-hush attitude about perversion has permitted this menace to increase."

Zora was ravaged by the story. Her world had collapsed, unfairly, unreasonably, in the ugliest possible way, just at the moment her new book was published. She was left with nothing to fall back on, and the depression was total. On October 30 she wrote bitterly to Carl Van Vechten: "The thing is too fantastic, too evil, too far from reality for me to conceive of it. . . . One inconceivable horror after another swept over me. I went out of myself, I am sure, though no one seemed to notice. It seemed that every hour some other terror assailed me, the last being the *Afro-American* sluice of filth." The "blow that knocked me loose from all that I have ever looked to and cherished" was the betrayal by a fellow black person, the court employee who peddled the story to the newspapers. The situation was so grim that Zora resolved to end it:

> But listen, Carl and Fania; I care nothing for anything anymore. My country has failed me utterly. My race has seen fit to destroy me without reason, and with the vilest tools conceived of by man so far. A society, eminently Christian, and supposedly devoted to super-democracy has gone so far from its announced purpose, not to *protect* children, but to exploit the gruesome fancies of a pathological case

and do this thing to human decency. Please do not forget that this thing was not done in the South, but in the so-called liberal North. Where shall I look in this country for justice?

This has happened to me, who has always believed in the essential and eventual rightness of my country. I have been on my own since I was fourteen, scuffling my way through high school and college, and as you know, I have never lived an easy life, but struggled on and on to achieve my ideals. I have believed in America; I have fought the good fight; I have kept the faith. . . .

All that I have ever tried to do has proved useless. All that I have believed in has failed me. I have resolved to die. It will take a few days for me to set my affairs in order, and then I will go . . . no acquittal will persuade some people that I am innocent. I feel hurled down a filthy privy hole.

It has been widely believed that the false morals charge was the beginning of the end for Zora Hurston, that her life unraveled in erratic acts, irrational wanderings, and personal incompetence, all leading downhill toward her death in 1960 as a penniless ward of the state. The impulse to romanticize has been overwhelming. One rumor held that she suffered from malnutrition. Although she died well fed in a county home, one reporter wrote that she spent her last, indigent days in a "third rate hotel." The facts are that Zora Neale Hurston did not commit suicide in 1948; after a brief depression, she recovered her usual enthusiasm for life. Between 1949 and 1951 she placed several articles in national magazines; between 1951 and 1956, living permanently in Eau Gallie, Florida, she found a kind of serenity, despite her poverty. The morals indictment scarred her, however, and pushed a woman with growing conservative instincts even farther to the right, making her suspicious and occasionally paranoid. It revealed the wisdom of maintaining good relationships with governmental establishments, the safety in having someone in authority on her side. She was never again so belligerently independent as she had been earlier. It is also true that for the last decade of her life she was frequently without money, sometimes pawning her typewriter to buy groceries, and that after 1957 she survived on unemployment benefits, substitute teaching, and welfare assistance. In her very last days Zora lived a difficult life—alone, proud, ill, obsessed with a final book she could not complete.[2]

But Zora Neale Hurston did not view her final years as uninterrupted tragedy, and we have a certain responsibility to acknowledge her toughness of spirit. Although she spent her last months in a county poorhouse, she was not necessarily any more tragic than her fellow inhabitants, who had also known good times and bad. Hurston had a full life that did not end all that differently from the way it was lived—with courage, and strength, and a compulsion for rejecting the commonplace and the everyday. Above all, it did not end in self-pity; in 1958 she refused to attend a Hurston family reunion because she was too proud to let any of her relatives know her need. When she died on January 28, 1960, Zora Hurston had lived "in Sorrow's Kitchen and licked all the pots," but there was no remorse; she once told her nephew, after he had blown fifteen hundred dollars, "Don't waste time and energy regretting that it is gone. Regret is the most useless emotion in the world." Near the end of her life she reminisced with her first husband: "It is interesting to see how far we both have come since we did our dreaming together in Washington, D.C. We struggled so hard to make our big dreams come true, didn't we? The world has gotten some benefits from us, though we had a swell time too. We Lived!"[3]

The morals charge went unreported in the major white newspapers and did little damage to the promising initial sale of *Seraph on the Suwanee.* Largely on the basis of *Seraph,* Scribner's paid $500 for an option on her next novel and began payments at $40 per week so that Zora could survive the winter. When the first 3,000 copies appeared not to be enough to supply demand, another 2,000 were ordered. The figures are especially impressive because many white bookshops in the South refused to carry Hurston's books. The publicity had effectively killed any promotional efforts on Zora's part, however; she would not subject herself to public scrutiny. Always a brilliant self-publicist, her presence usually had a considerable effect on sales. Now she appeared only on the Mary Margaret McBride radio show. Then she retired to the Bronx, brooded, and tried to lose herself in work.[4]

Zora wrote a great deal during the winter of 1948–49, but little of it was published, or publishable, and her mind was obviously on other things. After the indictment was officially dismissed, she began thinking again of Honduras, of the mysterious ruins that had eluded her before. A Central American jungle would be the perfect place to forget New York, a city she now thought of as "suicide for the creative artist." When her old friend Fred Irvine contacted her in July, it seemed the answer to her troubles. Always ready for adventure, Irvine had become the captain of a cargo boat, and he offered a way to leave the country. Zora joined him on the motor vessel *Challenger*, berthed along the MacArthur Causeway, near the Thirteenth Street bridge, dead across the bay from Miami's picture-book skyline. After a shakedown cruise to the Bahamas they leisurely began making plans for Honduras, and the Florida sun restored Zora's spirits. She told Mitchell, "I am feeling fine and in a working mood." She was meeting a number of waterfront characters who would provide colorful material.[5]

Zora floated on Biscayne Bay and sunned on the beach for the next five months, waiting for the Honduras expedition to begin. She arose early and strolled in a public park nearby, collecting coconuts or picking fruit from a sapodilla tree before the tourists arrived. And God kept his appointment with Miami every sundown: "Berthed on the East side of Biscayne Bay, I can look to the West side, which I never fail to come topside to do around sun set. Thus I get the benefit of His slashing paint brush all the way." New York faded away in the Florida dusk; wounds began to heal, although a residue of bitterness, a feeling of betrayal remained. Amused at having to explain that she was black, since people assumed she was a Latin American from the Argentinian boat docked nearby, Zora also told her editor, "I feel that I have come to myself at last. I can even endure the sight of a Negro, which I thought once I could never do again."[6]

The immediate problem was money. Irvine had a weakness for racetracks and he sometimes borrowed from Zora. Although she had sold a short story, "Conscience of the Court," to the *Saturday Evening Post* in June, her $900 payment had dissipated as they waited to sail. Irvine was unsuccessful in securing cargoes, and by January of 1950 it appeared that he might lose the boat as well. Zora left the waterfront with little cash and few prospects. Hard at work on the new novel for Scribner's, she was not dispirited, only broke.

She borrowed from friends and hustled a speaking date before county librarians, telling people that she would use the money to return to New York. But it was not enough. She decided to stay in Miami and finish the manuscript, renting what she called "a shabby, little studio." When this money ran out, she was forced to find a job, and her employment generated some unexpected and largely unwanted publicity.[7]

Zora hired out as a maid in a mansion on Rivo Island, one of Miami's most fashionable neighborhoods. She received thirty dollars a week plus room and board; her employer was kind, although not hesitant to advise her about what a maid should wear on her day off. It was not long before a *Miami Herald* reporter learned that Zora Neale Hurston was dusting bookshelves in the library while her mistress sat in the living room reading the *Saturday Evening Post*—and discovering a story written by her "girl."[8]

Such a feature had certified human interest, and it was picked up by the wire services. Intensely proud, Zora camouflaged the true reason for her employment by explaining that she had taken the job not for money, but as a break from writing: "You can only use your mind so long. Then you have to use your hands. A change of pace is good for everyone. I was born with a skillet in my hands. I like to cook and keep house. Why shouldn't I do it for somebody else a while? A writer has to stop writing every now and then and just live a little." She had another explanation, in case the first did not suffice. One might think her experience as a maid between the ages of fourteen and twenty had sufficiently acquainted her with domestic work; but she assured the reporter that she was here to learn "a great deal about a maid's life" so that she could begin a national magazine "for and by domestics." To her employer she had still another answer: she had large bank accounts overseas, where her books had been published in translation, but she refused to go abroad to spend them: "I'm not getting out from under the stars and stripes." Zora obviously knew what could be swallowed on Rivo Island; her employer said that she was impressed with Zora's "lack of pretensions, and a humility the like of which I have never encountered in an intelligent person." As for Zora, she counted the days until the job was over, telling Mitchell that the reporter had insisted on doing the story: "All I wanted was a little spending change when I took this job but it certainly has turned out to be one slam of a publicity do-dad."[9]

If the real reason for Hurston's domestic work was money, it was complicated by unhappiness over her writing. She may have revealed more than she intended when she told the *Herald* that she was temporarily "written out," and that with her eighth book and three short stories in the hands of her agent, she felt she should "shift gears" for the moment. The eighth book was "The Lives of Barney Turk," the story of a white youth who grew to manhood on a Florida truck farm, sought adventures in Central America, and ended up in Hollywood. The three short stories were about a Florida religious colony, a turpentine worker at a political meeting, and a mythological hunt for the reasons Swiss cheese has holes. Zora had started them all during the long winter of 1948–49 while preoccupied with the courts. The stories received a number of rejections and were finally forgotten. The novel was another matter. It was what she had worked on so hard during the winter while waiting to sail; she was still rewriting at Rivo Island, but the story would not come together.[10]

Not all of Zora's writing during this time was unsuccessful, but the struggle to remain solvent took its toll. There is a frantic quality about Hurston's work of the 1949–51 period, although she was almost as busy as she had been during World War II. In early 1949 she wrote a book review for the *New York Herald Tribune*, and in March of that year she completed "Conscience of the Court," the story which appeared a year later in the *Saturday Evening Post* and created such a stir on Rivo Island. Although not a very effective piece of fiction, the tale has its ironies. It tells the courtroom story of a lifelong family servant, a black woman named Laura Lee who is tried for assault after physically stopping a loan shark from illegally collecting a debt against her mistress. For a person who had been wrongfully charged in New York courts and forced, out of necessity, to work as a maid, it is a curious story indeed. It praises the white judge for releasing the black woman, and it presents Laura as almost a stereotypical loyal family retainer. The only moments of ambiguity come from Laura's pleasure in her violence ("All I did was grab him by his heels and frail the pillar of the porch with him a few times") and its curious ending. Laura returns home and performs "a ritual of atonement by serving," polishing the silver and expiating her guilt for doubting the white world. The ending makes one wonder about Zora's attitude toward her character; is she ironically revealing the psychological inadequacy of servitude, the dangers of unexamined loyalty? Any analysis is complicated by Zora's admission that the story was heavily edited by the *Post*'s staff, and by the knowledge that she badly needed to sell a story.[11]

One's suspicions of "Conscience of the Court" are reinforced by her April, 1950, article in the *Negro Digest*, for which Zora again enjoyed the freedom of addressing a black audience. "What White Publishers Won't Print" is one of her best essays, an amusing, salty account of relationships between black authors and white publishers. It may also inadvertently reveal how "Conscience of the Court," the story of a humble maid, was written to a formula Zora knew would sell. Although she is careful to avoid speaking personally, she must have remembered well Lippincott's rejection of her novel about "the upper strata of Negro life." She admits that she has been "amazed by the Anglo-Saxon's lack of curiosity about the internal lives and emotions of the Negroes, and for that matter, any non-Anglo-Saxon peoples . . . above the class of unskilled labor." Publishers find little market for stories "about the complicated emotions of minorities" because white audiences simply cannot conceive of non-Anglo-Saxons as anything other than stereotypes; they have created what Zora calls "the American Museum of Unnatural History," where the Jew is a Shylock, the Indian wears an eternal warbonnet, and blacks shuffle, pop, and roll their eyes. The stereotypes are self-perpetuating: "As long as the majority cannot conceive of a Negro or Jew feeling and reacting inside just as they do, the majority will keep right on believing that people who do not look like them cannot possibly feel as they do." Hurston asks why "the realistic story around a Negro insurance official, dentist, general practitioner, undertaker and the like" has not been published, and notes that "the average, struggling, non-morbid Negro is the best-kept secret in America."

"What White Publishers Won't Print," an effective brief for a bourgeois subject matter, illustrates again how Zora's career had changed. She had dropped the folk material that was the substance of her art, and she paid a heavy price. After 1948 she would never publish another book; Scribner's rejected both "The Lives of Barney Turk" and her next novel, "The Golden Bench of God," a story about hairdressing entrepreneur Madame C. J. Walker. Her last years were given to the futile effort to write a biography of the ruler of Judea in the first century B.C. Why did Zora Hurston turn away from those whom she called "the Negro farthest down," the people who had been her subject for more than twenty years? While she disliked the picturesque image that publishers had distorted from her work, probably the most immediate cause for the shift was her increasing interest in politics, and her understanding of the political implications in the reception of her folklore and fiction.[12]

Hurston wrote some unexpected political journalism in the early fifties. Fascinated by the political process since the Reynolds campaign against Adam Clayton Powell in 1946, Zora left Rivo Island in the middle of April, 1950, and became part of one of the most notorious campaigns in Florida history, the Democratic senatorial primary between Congressman George Smathers and Senator Claude Pepper. An old friend from Sanford, the same woman who once lent her money to mail *Jonah's Gourd Vine* to the publishers, put Zora in touch with the Smathers wing of the party, a group concerned about the Political Action Committee of the CIO and its organizing among black voters. Zora's experience working against Pepper and the CIO led to her angry article about vote-selling in Dade County, "I Saw Negro Votes Peddled." Writing at white heat just after the primary (which Smathers won), Zora was not the most objective reporter of the campaign; there is spite in the article, and perhaps sour grapes as well. Pepper had beaten Smathers badly in Miami's black neighborhoods. Her agent sent the piece to the *Saturday Evening Post*, the *American Mercury*, and the *Reporter*, and, when all else failed, thought of the *American Legion Magazine*. The Legion editors were delighted with its anti-Pepper tone and the implication that carpetbaggers had hoodwinked the black electorate; Pepper was a liberal whom the Legion opposed on principle, and they published the article in the election-month issue of November, 1950.[13]

"I Saw Negro Votes Peddled" is primarily addressed to black people, urging them to take the responsibilities of voting seriously.

Hurston did not trust the CIO effort, seeing big labor as a professional "friend of the Negro," and she resented those who would sell their vote for two dollars a head. Characteristically, she attributed such actions to an absence of self-respect: "There has to be an overload of self-pity and insufficient self-confidence and respect to cause a Negro with a ballot, the most potent weapon in a republic, to . . . sell his vote, then look for some 'friend of the Negro' to look out for his advancement."

What is hard to explain is why Zora Hurston would support Smathers over Pepper, or complain about vote-selling and fail to mention that systematic exclusion from the political process made it hard to take voting seriously. She had exaggerated the incidence of vote fraud; most black voters cast their ballot conscientiously. Lester Granger publicly complained that Zora's article pictured the black voter as "childishly gullible." There is also an accommodationist tone, for she emphasized Miami's black municipal court judge, its black policemen, and the many "modern and comfortable Negro homes" in the city. Yet the essay is consistent with Hurston's political views of the early fifties. The celebrant of black folkways became a political conservative in her later years, a right-wing Republican who supported Taft in the 1952 presidential primaries, questioned the landmark Supreme Court desegregation decision of 1954, and publicly endorsed Senator Spessard Holland, an old-line segregationist whom she considered a friend. But her politics were never simple. They must be understood both within the context of the times and within the development of an intricate, sometimes willful political philosophy.[14]

Hurston's conservatism grew primarily from three sources: an obsessive individualism that began with the self-confidence of Eatonville and expanded to generate great self-pride, almost a kind of egotism; a long suspicion of the Communist party and collectivist government, a suspicion that turned into mild paranoia during the McCarthy era, matching the mood of the country; and the social science philosophy that informed her folklore collecting.

The last source is by far the most complex. Zora had begun collecting folklore in the twenties with the conscious intent of celebrating the black folk who had made a way out of no way, like their folk heroes. She liberated rural black folk from the prison of racial stereotypes and granted them dignity as cultural creators. A black social scientist trying to destroy racial stereotypes held by the majority culture, she simultaneously urged black people to be proud of the folk heritage. This may sound commonplace today, but it was unusual then, since a common tactic for destroying white stereotypes was to document black literacy, cite the number of black college graduates, and describe the general black movement into the middle class. (The other side of the coin was to document all the discriminatory practices that denied equal opportunity and kept the black middle class from growing larger.)

Zora was concerned less with the tactics of racial uplift than with the unexamined prejudice of American social science.[15] She became a folklorist at a time when white sociologists were obsessed with what they thought was pathology in black behavior, when white psychologists spoke of the deviance in black mental health, and when the discipline of anthropology used a research model that identified black people as suffering from cultural deprivation. Hurston's folklore collections refuted these stereotypes by celebrating the distinctiveness of traditional black culture, and her scholarship is now recognized by revisionist scientists questioning the racial assumptions of modern cultural theory. John Szwed, for example, has shown how Boas's early assertion that race and culture were conceptually distinct eventually led anthropologists into a serious misapprehension. Once race and culture were separated, racial differences could be shown to be statistically insignificant. But while proving that there were no racial differences in mental capacity, anthropologists went on to claim that there were no significant *cultural* differences between the races. Out of a zeal to refute genetic racism, but with an ethnocentric bias, many argued that black Americans "shared essentially the same culture as white Americans, and where they differed, the differences could be accounted for exclusively as the result of environmental deprivation or cultural 'stripping,' but certainly not as the result of any normal cultural procedures." The implication grew that lower-class black Americans had no distinctive culture or subculture of their own.[16]

Hurston's collections addressed this theory and defiantly affirmed the cultural practices manifest in the folklore of "the Negro farthest down." She provided, as Szwed has suggested, an alternative view to the pathological theories, even before some of them were formulated. Because she was not a formal theorist, and because her books were meant for a popular audience, her theoretical assumptions about the distinctiveness of Afro-American culture were often masked, and did not receive the attention they deserved. Zora's method was presentational. She saw black Americans as cultural creators, and she documented the creation, not by amassing statistics for behavioral studies, but by presenting examples of oral tradition that expressed a behavioral system. Her attempt to distinguish black culture from white forecast the direction of much subsequent research; in the last thirty years the social sciences have begun to systematically collect the data that Zora Hurston indicated was there all along. We now have a body of "scientific" literature that provides evidence for the existence of a number of distinctive Afro-American cultural domains, including that domain of black esthetics which so interested her.

What has this to do with politics? Almost everything. As long as the culturally different behaviors of black people are treated as evidence of deviance, as failures on the part of individuals in the face of oppression, then the stereotype of black pathology becomes a grotesque monster looming behind American social legislation. White politicians want to believe in the notion of cultural deprivation, because it implies a social standard (white middle-class mores) and because it suggests that the racial tensions in the society are caused solely by poverty; they can attack material want among black people without having to confront the capitalism that created it, or the racism that helps perpetuate it. Hurston rejected the pathological stereotype because she knew that material poverty and ideological poverty were distinct entities, like apples and monkey wrenches. She saw ideological and esthetic poverty in the white middle class. This was why she claimed that black folksingers were ruined when they studied at white conservatories, and why she proposed that the Guggenheim Foundation fund a college of black music "to formalize and make respectable Negro musical methods": "Imagine Duke Ellington, Fats Waller, Louis Armstrong as guest professors! Ethel Waters, Bill Robinson, etc. Can't you see the whites who have ambitions in that direction running there?"[17]

Yet, despite Hurston's efforts, the pathological premise for most American social legislation remained the same during her lifetime and still holds today. Szwed calls it a "social science fiction monster" and cites a recent study that found that multipurpose room use in crowded slum housing prevents residents from developing "normal" middle-class kinship patterns. The political response might be to destroy the slum housing (urban renewal) and diminish the size of the family (funding for birth-control clinics and sex-education classes, and liberal abortion legislation). Yet the pathological premise for such action goes unexamined. In effect, the study argues that house type determines kinship patterns; its unstated premise is that a split-level house in a suburban tract produces "normal" family relationships. Zora Hurston spent the first twenty years of her career trying to show that normality is a function of culture, that an Afro-American culture exists, and that its creators lead lives rich with ideological and esthetic significance, a fact demonstrated by their folklore. She distinguished between the "Negro farthest down" and the "lowly Negro"; the first descriptive label implied a distinctive culture, while the second was a euphemism for the false notion of a "tragedy of color."[18]

Hurston's views were prophetic. If she was not a formal theorist, she possessed something the scholars lacked—a lifelong intimacy with the communicative behavior of Eatonville, a behavior that proved that her black neighbors were not deviant, pathological, or deprived, no matter how they might look to outsiders. As a result, she anticipated many ideas of modern black nationalists. Her portrayal of Eatonville in *Mules and Men* and *Their Eyes Were Watching God* says basically the same thing that Julius Lester would say thirty years later: "We are a distinct cultural group proud of our culture and our institutions and simply want to be left alone to lead our good, black lives." Hurston's 1937 plea that the Guggenheim Foundation establish a college of black music is virtually identical to Ishmael Reed's 1971 call for an end to the "Western Established Church of Art": "We propose the establishment of a black conservatory of music to be funded as generously by tax-supported foundations as white conservatories." She once reviewed a collection of African folklore and stressed how the language collected was for the ear, not the eye: "It is like the mass of Negro folk music, played by ear. It is from the pattern of the outdoors, the community . . . the shared life of the African village, a pattern that has not been entirely lost even in the Negro communities of the Americas." It is not surprising that Lester dedicated one of his books "in memory of Zora Neale Hurston, who made me glad I am me, and to H. Rap Brown."[19]

The critical question asked of Zora Hurston, however, was whether Eatonville was the whole story of black life in the South. This was what Sterling Brown meant when he spoke of the bitterness that would have made Zora's Eatonville closer to the "total truth." In a cultural sense her emphasis on Eatonville was appropriate, for the Afro-American culture ritualized and performed on Joe Clarke's store porch was replicated throughout the black South. But in a political sense it was not the whole story, for the gentle peace and communal security of Eatonville was not present everywhere. While Zora listened to folktales and heard her mother say, "Jump at the sun," Richard Wright threw rocks at white boys, then was beaten by his mother because she knew that if Richard fought whites as a boy he would be lynched as a man.[20]

Zora's problems came when she attempted in the late forties and early fifties to transfer her cultural perceptions to the political arena. If she could have found a political outlet for her cultural theories, she might have altered the premises of the American racial dialogue. But she made two mistakes. First, she interpreted all personal criticism in the context of her social science theories, refusing to admit that one could both celebrate Afro-American culture and deplore many of the conditions that helped to shape it; and second, she fixed her vision so narrowly on Eatonville that eventually she came to ignore the multiplicity of the southern black experience.

She was not a systematic political thinker. As Arna Bontemps once remarked, her politics conformed to the pattern of Eatonville—the Baptists versus the Methodists. She took things personally and defined herself in relation to those who opposed her. Roy Wilkins had called her publicity-hungry and implied that she did not support the race's struggles. Harold Preece, in the *Crisis*, accused her of engaging in a folk cult and forgetting about the economic conditions of the people she collected from. Alain Locke, connected with both the Urban League and the NAACP, called upon her to create a socially conscious fiction. Ralph Ellison and Richard Wright, both close to the Communist party, reviewed her books and accused her of caricature.[21]

This criticism was not always well meant, but the critics were intelligent, committed people who were worth taking seriously, and they represented a wide spectrum of political views. Zora's response was to group them all together, party members and NAACP conservatives, and interpret their criticism as resulting from a philosophical belief in the pathology of black life. She was an instinctive black nationalist—or at least a cultural nationalist—without quite realizing the implications of her position. Instead of transforming her observations about the distinct culture of black people into the idea of a distinct black political movement or a collective alternative to capitalism, Zora reacted to criticism by retreating from the brink to which her theories had led her. She found a personal litmus test for racial politics that tested for only two things—a pathological stereotype and an individual pride. In later life she came to interpret all attempts to emphasize black suffering, even the most angry protest, as the politics of deprivation, implying a tragedy of color in Afro-American life. If someone did not support her effort to celebrate the folkways of black people, he was assumed to have an insufficient pride in his own culture. The end result, as Larry Neal observed, was that "at one moment she could sound highly nationalistic. Then at other times she might mouth statements which in terms of the ongoing struggle for black liberation were ill-conceived and even reactionary."[22]

Hurston's opposition to the Communist party illustrates how her thinking developed. She had always been suspicious of the party, even in the twenties, when her friend Langston Hughes grew interested in it. The party line, she felt, said that American Negroes were so downtrodden that the Russians "deeply pitied" their case. Zora Hurston wanted none of this: "I was poor but I certainly did not feel pitiful." In 1938 she had reviewed Richard Wright's *Uncle Tom's Children* for the *Saturday Review* and complained about party propaganda. Wright had written his book after the liberating influence of Marxist thought granted insights into the economic and psychological oppression of his own southern experience, and his party sympathies offended his reviewer. Zora objected that "the reader sees the picture of the South that the Communists have been passing around of late. A dismal, hopeless section ruled by brutish hatred and nothing else. Mr. Wright's author's solution is the solution of the PARTY—state responsibility for everything and individual responsibility for nothing."[23]

By the early fifties, then, Zora Neale Hurston had long been at odds with communism, and it should not surprise that her anti-Communist sentiments surfaced during the "American nightmare," the era of Richard Nixon and Joseph McCarthy. Her support of Smathers probably had something to do with his allegations of Communist backing for Pepper. She had joined the American Writers' Association, a group organized to "protect the freedom" of non-Communist authors, and she once outlined an article, "My Race but Not My Taste," about Paul Robeson. She even thought that the false morals charge of 1948 might have been a Communist frame.[24]

In June of 1951 she published a second article in the *American Legion Magazine*, subtitled "Why the Negro Won't Buy Communism." Written at the magazine's request, its thesis is that black Americans resist communism because of the "raw flattery" and "insulting patronage" of party officials toward the "pitiable" black person. Standard anti-Communist fare, the article becomes most interesting when Zora digresses to object that black authors are promised publishing breaks for producing a formulaic, proletarian literature: "The formula was, you can't win, Negro, you can't win. Expanded, the poor, dear colored character starts off to be something in the world, but he or she gets trapped by our form of government and down he goes to the lowest depths like bottomless britches. Pity the poor, black brute . . . not his fault at all." Her second political essay of 1951, "A Negro Voter Sizes Up Taft," appeared in the December 8 issue of the *Saturday Evening Post*. Like the American Legion article, it was heavily edited by the magazine staff; it is the usual campaign rhetoric, full of praise and largely void of analysis. She likes Taft's logic and knowledge, cites his support among black politicians in Ohio, and speculates that if Taft had been in the Senate during the New Deal, we would have found out much sooner about the Communists in our midst.

Zora's support for Taft and her antipathy toward communism are easier to understand than her objections to the 1954 Supreme Court desegregation decision, but her opposition grew from the same premise. Zora could distinguish between the party and the NAACP—the civil rights organization had long been wary of communism—but she tested for social science philosophy and found the Association tainted. When she objected to the desegregation decision, argued by Thurgood Marshall of the NAACP before the Supreme Court, she did so on the grounds that the judgment implied a pathological stereotype. It implied, Zora said, that black students could learn only if they sat next to whites.[25]

On August 11, 1955, Zora expressed this belief in a letter to the *Orlando Sentinel*. It delighted rabid segregationists and was picked up by newspapers across the South, cited as proof that blacks did not really want integration. Hurston has been criticized for this document—and rightly so, since she ignored the inescapable evidence that black schools were inadequately and unequally funded. Yet her outburst was perfectly consistent, in her mind, with her pride in black institutions and her suspicion of attempts to integrate so that black students could be "uplifted" to white standards and a white way of life. The Supreme Court ruling, she said, implied that just like mules being led by a white mare, black students had to be led by white pupils and white teachers. She claimed to see the same thinking among Communists, and found it astonishing that the white-mare tactic should become law "just when the nation is exerting itself to shake off the evils of Communist penetration." If one believed that Florida's black schools did a poor job, Zora's argument ran, he believed that there was racial inadequacy. She claimed that the tactics of the NAACP contributed the pathos of race to this belief: "It is well known that I have no sympathy or respect for the 'tragedy of color' school of thought among us, whose fountainhead is the pressure group concerned in this court case."

Zora Neale Hurston, in her concentration on the individual, in her lifelong repudiation of pathological stereotypes, had developed a set of emotional code words that hardened into a political test. As the test became less and less flexible in her final years, it lost the ability to deal with changing situations or demonstrate a future vision. Zora's standard for comparison was always the Eatonville of her childhood, a proud, self-governing, all-black village that felt no need of integration and, in fact, resisted it so that an Afro-American culture could thrive without interference. She never quite acknowledged that there were few Eatonvilles, or that many black people had no opportunity to know the security of her birthplace. In her last years her personal political test failed to acknowledge either the diversity of the southern black experience or the need to react against the tyranny that could characterize that life. Larry Neal has stated, "When it came to the South, Zora could be an inveterate romantic. . . . We could accuse her of escapism, but the historical oppression that we associate with Southern Black life was not a central aspect of her experience." Zora's triumph was to generalize on the basis of Eatonville. This was valid and important, for it enabled her to document a distinctive black esthetic and refute the pathological stereotype. It also led, in her final years, toward political isolation. By the fifties Zora's repudiation of pathology had become rigid. If one spoke of "deplorable conditions," he tended, in Zora's view, to engage in self-pity. If one worked for integration, he tended to deny the value of existing black institutions. If one complained too loudly about racist social structures, he believed that it was a tragedy to be black. By the 1950s her nationalist prophecies were forgotten, her powers diminished, her individualism battered and scarred by events. What remained intact was the personal pride, a brave asset for a woman struggling for economic survival.[26]

If Hurston's politics are typically individual, they are also demonstrably human, and it is the human side of Zora's final years that explains more about her situation than any political analysis can ever do. Her work for Smathers produced a surprising offer; she was invited to ghost-write the autobiography of the congressman's father. Needing the money, she gave it a try, but found the task impossible. Not only was Judge Smathers irascible; she also felt that "he could not accept the reality that a descendent of slaves could do something in an intellectual way that he could not."[27]

She returned to "The Lives of Barney Turk." When it was rejected by Scribner's in the fall, she was stunned, finding herself "with a year's work gone for nothing." Friends in Belle Glade offered a place to stay for the winter of 1950–51; there she worked on a play and a novelette. The *American Legion Magazine* request for the article on communism came just in time, for she had bought a used car to explore the Everglades and found she had nothing to make payments with. She looked forward to establishing herself in housekeeping again: "Being under my own roof, and my personality not invaded by others makes a lot of difference in my outlook on life and everything. Oh, to be once more alone in a house."[28]

In March, 1951, Zora explained to her literary agent, Jean Parker Waterbury, that she was "cold in hand. That is a Negro way of saying penniless. And I do mean penniless. God! What I have been through. What I get for this article from the American Legion will just about pull me even. Just inching along like a stepped-on worm from day to day. Borrowing a little here and there." She asked Waterbury to prod the Legion people for early payment of her $540 because she was all too weary of going to the post office and turning away empty, "having to avoid folks who have made me loans so that I could eat and sleep. The humiliation is getting to be much too much for my self-respect, speaking from the inside of my soul. I have tried to keep it to myself and just wait. To look and look at the magnificent sweep of the Everglades, birds included, and keep a smile on my face."[29]

She was outlining the Taft article and expanding the novelette about the hairdressing empire into "The Golden Bench of God." Optimistic about the novel, she felt "more confident about this story than anything I have done since *Their Eyes Were Watching God*." Her plan was to make it a "truly indigenous Negro novel" of a kind never written before: "Punches have been pulled to 'keep things from the white folks' or angled politically, well to show our sufferings, rather than to tell a story as is. I have decided that the time has come to write truthfully from the inside. Imagine that no white audience is present to hear what is said."[30]

By May she was still working hard but feeling frustration; she was doing hack-like political essays while her career went nowhere: "The first thing too many Negroes do when they want to be writers . . . is to grab something from me, and then hate me for being alive to make their pretensions out a lie. And then take all kinds of steps to head me off. 'Block that Zora Neale Hurston!' is a regular slogan.

I go in the out of the way places and collect and gather, and then they sit on their rumps in New York and filch from me." She told her agent a few months later, "All I can say is that now and then I am attacked by a spell of withdrawal. Something keeps me from communicating with the outside world."[31]

When the Taft article was accepted in June, 1951, Zora made plans to leave Belle Glade. She was still without money, but the *Post* acceptance lifted her spirits, and this time she had no debts. The $1,000 that would soon arrive could be saved. She had found that the small, one-room cabin in Eau Gallie where she had written *Mules and Men* twenty years before was now available. Renting for only five dollars a week, it represented a link with a happier, more productive past. She moved in mid-June and began fixing up. The cabin had been neglected, the repairs were hard; but Zora was happy and preparing to work. She promised Waterbury "assorted scripts" very shortly. The *Post's* money had paid up her health and accident insurance for an entire year—an important item since she was beginning to suffer spells of stomach illness—and enabled her to bring in electricity, some secondhand furniture, and an icebox. She had plenty of groceries and a new pair of black slacks for wearing to town; she could avoid having to launder a dress to have something fresh to wear.[32]

Zora was so pleased with her new home that the Scribner's rejection of "The Golden Bench of God" two weeks after she moved to Eau Gallie hardly fazed her. She was most interested in telling Burroughs Mitchell about her place:

> Digging in my garden, painting my house, planting seeds, and things like that, makes me lazy about getting to the Post Office, and so I did not get your letter until Friday P.M. So belatedly I thank you for your editorial comments, and the time you spent reading the book. . . .
>
> I am very happily located. Here in this little house I wrote MULES AND MEN years ago, and have always intended to come back here to live. So now I am back in my little house, and though facing a paved street, two blocks of trees around me on three sides. No neighbor's radios and record-players to listen to. The place was quite shaggy when I arrived a month ago, but I have the joy of clearing it and arranging things like I please. About 15 cabbage palms and five shady

oaks as a background to start landscaping from. There is a flowing
artesian well about fifty feet of the house, and already I have arranged
a bit of ornamental water. I am planting butterfly ginger around it.
My eastern limit is a low pile of stone left from an old ice-plant.
Against the low line of stones I have planted pink verbena, and
around the palms and the park-like ground west of the stones, I have
scattered bright colored poppies. Going to let them run wild. The
Indian river, touted as the world's most beautiful river, is two blocks
to the east of me, and so there is ever a good breeze. As you know, it
is not really a river at all, but a long arm of the sea cut off by sand-bars,
at times less than a quarter mile wide from the Atlantic. The tropical
water is so loaded with phosphorus, that standing on the bridge at
night, every fish, crab, shrimp, etc., glows as it moves about in the
water. When the surface is disturbed, it scintillates like every brilliant jewel you can mention. . . .

Living the kind of life for which I was made, strenuous and close to
the soil, I am happier than I have been for at least ten years. I am up
at five o'clock and in bed around nine every night. I do hope and pray
that you and yours are experiencing something like my delirium
of joy.[33]

Zora lived in Eau Gallie for the next five years. In many ways it
was the most peaceful period in a turbulent life. She made plans to
put in a papaya crop, invited her nephew to come live with her,
began gaining weight, and became possessively attached to Spot, a
mottled brown and white terrier of dubious breed. She set up a
birdbath and feeder, listened to the cardinals and mockingbirds
each morning, was scolded by blue jays, and frequently carried oak
snakes away from the birds; she did not kill the snakes because they
were good ratters, and in the warm climate the wood rats would
invade the house if they got a chance. Her grounds became so
beautiful that tourists stopped to take pictures. She thought of
adopting a Japanese-American child fathered by a member of the
American occupation forces, then admitted that she did not want to
be tied down. She had hopes of buying the small cabin and the
surrounding acres, but was stymied because of her landlord's hesi-
tance (it was in a white area) and her lack of funds. She wrote
constantly and without much success. She started a sequel to *Dust
Tracks*, wrote a number of stories about Spot, did research in Vero
Beach for a piece on "Ginny" cows (a special breed of Florida beef

cattle), worked on an article about colonialism in Southeast Asia, tried to rewrite biblical tales, thought of an essay entitled "Do Negroes Like Negroes?" deploring the "lack of concerted action by the 15 million of us in the U.S.," and toyed with a tongue-in-cheek article about career women returning to their homes.[34]

What ate away at the "delirium of joy" was the absence of cash. Zora had a lifelong reputation for improvidence, and it is true that she did not have a banker's instincts. She was capable of giving a friend an expensive present, then asking for a five-dollar loan for lunch. She once paid back a small debt and then in the same letter asked for another loan. But Zora Hurston never earned much money. After Mrs. Mason's subsidy of 1927–32, she never held a job that lasted more than a year. Fellowships enable an author to write, but they do not make one rich. WPA employment is hardly the key to a personal fortune. Between 1949 and 1951, the period when the best records are available, she could not have earned over two thousand dollars per year, and her income sharply diminished thereafter. The simple fact is that Zora Hurston did not care that much, so long as she had enough to live on; during the Eau Gallie years her margin became increasingly thin. She told her agent, "I feel creative and in addition I have to make some money," an occupational coupling which undermined her judgment and eroded her style. Waterbury remembers that "she could write like an angel and yet be absolutely sloppy when she was desperate for money . . . she would lose all sense of perspective and judgment, and just as long as there were words on a page she felt that she could get some cash for it." When she tried to sell another story to the *Saturday Evening Post* the editors called it juvenile. She once pawned her typewriter to buy groceries, but assured Waterbury, "As soon as I get hold of money to get my machine out of hock, I will be in high spirits." Legal fees caused her to owe Scribner's $1,000, despite *Seraph's* sale of more than 4,600 copies. She survived on speaking dates, occasional reviews, a concert now and then, and what little came from subsidiary rights to her books. In 1952 Lippincott's paid her $37.87 in reprint fees; she seemed to sell well in Scandinavia, and translation rights brought in a bit more. Paying rent of twenty dollars a month, growing most of her own food, she managed to survive. A local white man, hearing of her work with

Judge Smathers, hired her to ghost an autobiography, but she backed out after the first payments when it became clear he intended the book as a diatribe against his ex-wife. For the most part she was simply amused at white visitors who implied that her comfortable cabin was a mere shack, her worn clothing a sign that she cared little about how she looked.[35]

Perhaps her most interesting experience during the Eau Gallie years was covering one of the era's most famous murder cases, the trial of Ruby McCollum, for the *Pittsburgh Courier*. Ruby McCollum was the black mistress of C. Leroy Adams, a white doctor and state senator in Suwannee County. Ruby's husband ran the county's equivalent of the numbers game, in Florida called *bolita*. In 1952 she shot Adams during a quarrel, then admitted that Adams had fathered one of her children and that she was pregnant by him again at the time of the shooting. In a notoriously unfair trial she was convicted of first-degree murder; after the Florida Supreme Court overturned the conviction, she was declared mentally incompetent and committed to a state hospital. Zora reported on the case, writing an extensive and extremely interesting biography of Ruby McCollum for the *Courier* after the trial ended. She and the *Courier* became active in Ruby's defense efforts, and she interested the white journalist William Bradford Huie into investigating the case. His book, *Ruby McCollum: Woman in the Suwannee Jail*, includes a section by Zora, a sensitive, angry, poignant account of the injustice.[36]

Zora might have been able to withstand her straitened circumstances if she could have kept her health. Eau Gallie compensated for much. But she had brought back from Honduras a "tropical fluke" from drinking impure water, and it periodically racked her system, making her so weak she could hardly lift her head. She experienced great swelling in the groin and under her arms, for which the doctors had no cure; there seemed to be little she could do except lie in bed and suffer. Eventually physicians decided that it must have something to do with the gall bladder infection that she had known periodically for the past ten years, and with the malady of the "colon and general guts" that she had known since the early thirties and that had stricken her in 1945.[37]

By 1956 Zora was middle-aged and considerably overweight, an author frequently without the money to support her ambition, or the physical energy to produce what talent compelled. This sickness and poverty make her efforts to finish her final book especially heroic. Called "Herod the Great," it was a project that had been germinating since 1945. In that year she wrote Van Vechten, "The story I am burning to write is one that will be highly controversial. I want to write the story of the 3,000 years struggle of the Jewish Peoples for democracy and the rights of man." She had been reading the Bible, Flavius Josephus, Spinoza, and contemporary Roman and Egyptian histories, all of which impressed her with the struggle of the Jewish people against the rule of their priests. Such a book was too large for an author planning to go to Honduras, but in Central America, Hurston did not forget the subject. In July, 1947, she told Van Vechten that she was writing a play about the fall of Jerusalem to Titus in A.D. 70: "It is a whale of a story. . . . The struggle of a handful of Jews against the mightiest army on earth, that they might be free to live their own lives in their own way." When she completed *Seraph* Zora submitted an outline to Scribner's for a book about "the history and philosophy of the Hebrews"; it was to be entitled "Just like Us" and would "bring about a revision of our Sunday School literature, and alter the slovenly and inimical attitude towards the modern Jew." One of the more interesting chapters was to be about Herod the Great, the ruler of Judea from 37 to 4 B.C. As described in the outline, Herod was a fascinating leader who "made friends and matched wits with Pompey, Crassus, Marc Anthony, Julius Caesar and Augustus Caesar and never came off second best." An ally of the Jewish people against their priests, Herod is pictured as one of those directly responsible for preparing Judea for democracy.[38]

When Hurston established herself in Eau Gallie and began to cast about for new projects, a dramatic version of the life of Herod the Great came immediately to mind. She asked Waterbury if Cecil B. De Mille, the producer of biblical epics, might be interested: "It needs Hollywood. It is a great story, really, and needs to be done. The man [Herod] had *everything*, good, bad and indifferent. Handsome, dashing, a great soldier, a great statesman, a great lover. He dared everything." By 1953 the Hollywood drama had become a major book, which Zora admitted had placed her "under the spell of a great obsession." She combed Flavius Josephus, the major source of information about Herod, and also Livy, Eusebius, Strabo, and Nicolas of Damascus. She wrote Bishop Fulton J. Sheen to ask for his advice and help, then became worried that he might steal her idea. She told Mitchell, "If I can only carve him out as I have conceived him, it cannot help from being a good book." Herod had once rejected Cleopatra's charms; he knew, Zora added, "perils which would have destroyed lesser men."

By mid-1954 the book was half-completed. She wrote Winston Churchill to ask if he would be interested in writing an introduction. By June, 1955, it was nearly finished, a revisionist biography revealing that Herod was not a butcher who murdered Bethlehem infants in an attempt to slay Jesus, but "a highly cultivated Hellenized non-Jew, the handsomest man of his time, the greatest soldier of Southwest Asia," who had "wider and more exciting experiences than any man who has yet appeared in history."

The subject was running away from its author; she no longer could control "the spell." When her Scribner's editors said that the manuscript had to be cut and focused, she resisted, unable to give up so much of her research. She had become possessed. The biography had now also turned into the comprehensive book about Jewish history first conceived a decade earlier. She told Mitchell, "When the reader gets some idea of this prolonged and intense struggle in Judea, he can realize, as he must, that the LIFE OF HEROD THE GREAT is not really the story of a man but of a movement which has ended up in Christianity on one hand and as the basis of Western Civilization on the other."

Zora was riding for a fall. In August, 1955, it came. Scribner's rejected the Herod manuscript, finding the book "disappointing" after her enthusiasm. What fascinates is how easily she took the rejection. She told Mitchell, "Please, please do not think that I feel badly. . . . I was astonished myself how easily I felt. Perhaps it is because I have such faith in the material and now my conviction that I can handle it. All is well." The first century B.C. had become a haven for an author who found herself without any way to publish her work. As events dealt harder and harder blows each year, she burrowed deeper into antiquity, as if the manuscript provided a way to avoid the unpleasant reality of her diminished circumstances. She not only maintained her enthusiasm, but also developed a recurring vision of growth in the writing. In mid-1957 she reported, "I have gone through a period that might appear outwardly unprofitable, but in reality extremely important. A taking-in period like the gestation of a prospective mother. Now, I am ready to give forth again. I feel that I have made phenomenal growth as a creative artist."

The pathos in such remarks is that the Herod the Great manuscript left at her death evinces no such growth, and it is easy to see why Scribner's rejected it. It was a good story—Zora's instincts were right. Herod's most recent biographer sees him as standing "at the confluence of the Jewish and Graeco-Roman civilizations," a man with "an astonishing record of public adventures and successes, and of private melodramas and disasters . . . a figure rising far above nearly all his contemporaries by the force and versatility of his talents." But her failing powers were not equal to the task. Zora's manuscript suffers from poor characterization, pedantic scholarship, and inconsistent style; the whole performance touches the heart by revealing a talent in ruins.

If her writing was less than she hoped, neither did her personal life justify the brave "all is well" she gave to Scribner's. Her landlord was trying to sell the house and land she had lived so comfortably with for the past five years. In March, 1956, he gave her notice. She left the second week in May, realizing that she needed to find a job. At the end of the month she received an award for "education and human relations" at the Bethune-Cookman commencement, standing tall and proud in her doctor of letters' robes. Two weeks later she was hired as a librarian in the space program at Patrick Air Force Base in nearby Cocoa. A clerk whose job was to keep track of technical literature, she was paid $1.88 per hour.[39]

Zora worked as a librarian for almost a year, hating every minute of it, quarreling with fellow employees, questioning the security of the base. She claimed that her Barnard B.A. made her stick out like a sore thumb. When a friend was fired, she insisted that "they went after me." She thought herself the "best educated and most culti-

vated person" among the library employees, resented the "Yan-
kees" who ran things, and sent periodic reports of office politics to
the President's Committee on Government Contracts. On May 10,
1957, she was terminated, her supervisor explaining that she was
"too well educated for the job."[40]

Zora moved to Merritt Island across the Indian River from
Cocoa, a body of land with a tropical climate and a surplus of
mosquitoes. She lived in a house trailer, drove along the beach in a
beat-up Willys station wagon, nursed a recently diagnosed stomach
ulcer, and worked again on Herod. She bravely announced that she
felt "a greater competence with the tools of my trade than formerly." Her eleven months at the air force base made her eligible
for unemployment, and she found that she could just make it on the
twenty-six dollars per week. She told Herbert Sheen that she
planned to go to New York, "but not to live permanently. . . . You
know about the literary parties, etc. that sap everything out of you."
Ernest Hemingway had once told her that she should live, as he
had, on the Isle of Pines off the Cuban coast; she thought of Merritt
Island and her house trailer as something equivalent. She found
herself in a retrospective mood: "I have no sentimental involve-
ments. I have no talent for business nor finance, but I do not mind
that. . . . I do take a certain satisfaction in knowing that my writings
are used in many of the great universities."[41]

By October her funds were low, and she applied unsuccessfully
for a job at the Air Force Missile Test Center in Cocoa. In December, C. E. Bolen, the owner of a local black weekly in Fort
Pierce, Florida, visited Merritt Island and invited her to write for
the paper. She moved to Fort Pierce, supplementing her unemployment checks with free-lance fees from Bolen's *Fort Pierce
Chronicle*. During the next two years she wrote a series of columns
entitled "Hoodoo and Black Magic," stealing episodes from her
earlier research. She also complained about farm laborers, praised
a local dairy, and called for an end to juvenile delinquency. In
February of 1958 she began substitute teaching at Lincoln Park
Academy, the segregated black public school of Fort Pierce; she
was not very successful and had several run-ins with students. She
lived in a house owned by her physician, Dr. C. C. Benton, at 1734
School Court Street, a squat, concrete-block structure fifty feet

square. She made the tiny, bare yard bloom with azaleas, morning glories, and gardenias, and put in a vegetable garden to raise collards and tomatoes. She labored on the Herod manuscript. Dr. Benton remembers how "she was always studying. Her mind . . . just worked all the time." A friend who free-lanced for the *Miami Herald* talked her into doing a feature article on the migrant workers who lived in Fort Pierce; but the essay was fragmented and unfocused, and the *Herald* editor wrote back that he presumed Zora Hurston had had ghost-writers for her books. In September she wrote to the David McKay Company to inquire whether the firm would be interested in publishing her manuscript on Herod; after reading her introduction, the editors decided they were not.[42]

Zora's health deteriorated badly after she moved to Fort Pierce. Dr. Benton, one of the few people who knew the full extent of her accomplishment, became a frequent visitor to School Court Street. He often stopped by after closing his office, and they would sit and talk for an hour or two. Sometimes Zora called him to ask for a ride to the grocery store, and he would buy her groceries. High blood pressure continued to bother her, a symptom of her weight; she now weighed over two hundred pounds. She loved to eat and was capable of sitting with a mound of ice cream, eating and talking until it all was gone. She still had the tropical fluke and the gall bladder attacks, her ulcer was not completely healed, and her obesity put a heavy strain on her heart.[43]

In early 1959 Zora suffered a stroke, which left her weak and without the ability to concentrate. In May she was forced to apply to the county welfare office for money to pay for her medicines. In June she began receiving food vouchers. She refused to inform her family of her illness or to let friends contact them. Writing occasionally for the *Chronicle* when she felt up to it, she slipped badly during the summer and fall. Her journalist friend, Marjorie Silver, became increasingly concerned about her condition. In earlier days they had talked for hours, knowing brilliant, wide-ranging conversations. Now Zora seemed spiritless, worn out, distracted.[44]

On October 29, 1959, Zora Neale Hurston entered the Saint Lucie County welfare home. She did not want to go, and had resisted for some time; but she had reached the point where she could do little for herself. Three months later, on the night of

January 28, 1960, she died of "hypertensive heart disease." Her name was misspelled Zora Neil Hurston on the death certificate, but no one noticed. She was an indigent woman who had prophesied her own ending when she said, "I am not materialistic. . . . If I happen to die without money somebody will bury me, though I do not wish it to be that way."

A week later someone did. Donations came from friends, publishers, and family until more than four hundred dollars was raised. A group of students who remembered their substitute teacher collected $2.50 in small change.

The services were held in the tiny chapel of the funeral home, and more than a hundred attended, sixteen of them white. The body was placed in an open casket. Zora was dressed in a bright pink dressing gown; fuzzy pink mules covered her feet.

At the funeral C. E. Bolen said, "Zora Neale went about and didn't care too much how she looked. Or what she said. Maybe people didn't think so much of that. But Zora Neale, every time she went about, had something to offer. She didn't come to you empty." The minister added, "They said she couldn't become a writer recognized by the world. But she did it. The Miami paper said she died poor. But she died rich. She did something."

Zora Neale Hurston was buried in the Garden of the Heavenly Rest, the city's segregated cemetery.[45]

The Master-Maker in His making had made Old Death. Made him with big, soft feet and square toes. Made him with a face that reflects the face of all things, but neither changes itself, nor is mirrored anywhere. Made the body of Death out of infinite hunger. Made a weapon for his hand to satisfy his needs. This was the morning of the day of the beginning of things.

But Death had no home and he knew it at once.

"And where shall I dwell in my dwelling" Old Death asked, for he was already old when he was made.

"You shall build you a place close to the living, yet far out of the sight of eyes. Wherever there is a building, there you have your platform that comprehends the four roads of the winds. For your hunger, I give you the first and last taste of all things."

We had been born, so Death had had his first taste of us. We had built things, so he had his platform in our yard.

And Now, Death stirred from his platform in his secret place in our yard, and came inside the house. . . .

Death finished his prowling through the house on his padded feet and entered the room. He bowed to Mama in his way, and she made her manners and left us to act out our ceremonies over unimportant things.

Zora Neale Hurston, *Dust Tracks on a Road*

NOTES

1. The story of the Hurston morals charge has been pieced together from a number of sources: my interviews in New York City with Burroughs Mitchell of Scribner's, with her lawyer, Louis Waldman, and with her agent, Jean Parker Waterbury, all in May, 1971; *Baltimore Afro-American* (national edition), Oct. 16, 23, Nov. 6, 1948; *New York Age*, Oct. 16, 23, 1948; ZNH to CVV, Oct. 30, 1948 (JWJYale); Charles Scribner to Waldman, Oct. 27, 1948; Waldman to Scribner's, Nov. 1, 1948; Mitchell to Waldman, Jan. 24, 1949; Waldman to Mitchell, Jan. 25, Mar. 21, 1949 (Scribner's).

2. See Alice Walker, "In Search of Zora Neale Hurston," *Ms.*, 3 (Mar., 1975), 79, and Alan Lomax, "Zora Neale Hurston—A Life of Negro Folklore," *Sing Out!*, 10 (Oct.-Nov., 1960), 12-13.

3. RH interview with Everette Hurston, Sr., Jan. 13, 1976, Bristol, Conn.; RH interview with Everett Hurston, Jr., June 23, 1976, Brooklyn, N.Y.; ZNH, *Dust Tracks on a Road* (Philadelphia: J. B. Lippincott, 1942), p. 288; ZNH to Everett Hurston, Jr., Oct. 12, 1951 (in Hurston's possession); ZNH to Herbert Sheen, Mar. 13, 1953 (Sheen Papers).

4. Interoffice memos, N. H. Snow to Burroughs Mitchell, Oct. 12, 1948, and E. Youngstrom to Mr. Merz, Oct. 5, 1948 (Scribner's); George Pfeiffer of J. B. Lippincott to Edwin Osgood Grover, Nov. 4, 1942 (HCUFla); Mitchell to ZNH, Sept. 9, 1948 (Scribner's).

5. ZNH to Herbert Sheen, June 28, 1957 (Sheen Papers); Burroughs Mitchell to ZNH, July 13, 1949; ZNH to Mitchell, n.d. [between Nov. 17, 1949, and Jan. 28, 1950] (Scribner's); ZNH to Helga H. Eason, Dec. 22, 1949 (Miami Public Library).

6. ZNH to Burroughs Mitchell, n.d. [between Nov. 17, 1949, and Jan. 28, 1950] (Scribner's).

7. RH interview with "B" (name withheld by request), Mar. 12, 1971, Miami, Fla. (the woman Zora worked for as a domestic after leaving Irvine's boat); ZNH, author's card (Watkins); ZNH to Burroughs Mitchell, Jan. 24, 1950 (Scribner's); Theodore Pratt, "Zora Neale Hurston," *Florida Historical Quarterly*, 40 (July, 1961), 38; ZNH to Helga Eason, Feb. 14, 1950 (Miami Public Library).

8. James Lyons, "Famous Negro Author Working as Maid Here Just 'to Live a Little,'" *Miami Herald*, Mar. 27, 1950.

9. Ibid.; RH interview with "B," Mar. 12, 1971, Miami, Fla.; ZNH to Burroughs Mitchell, n.d. [ca. Apr. 1, 1950] (Scribner's).

10. Lyons, "Famous Negro Author"; Burroughs Mitchell to ZNH, Oct. 10, Dec. 27, 1949, Jan. 10, Feb. 8, Mar. 14, 1950; ZNH to Mitchell, Feb. 3, ca. Apr. 1, 1950; JPW to Mitchell, Sept. 13, 1949; undated notes from Watkins concerning "The Lives of Barney Turk" (Scribner's); ZNH, author's card (Watkins).

11. ZNH, "At the Sound of the Conch Shell" [review of *New Day* by Victor Stafford Reid], *New York Herald Tribune Weekly Book Review*, Mar. 20, 1949; idem, author's card (Watkins); idem, "Conscience of the Court," *Saturday Evening Post*, Mar. 18, 1950, pp. 22-23, 112-22; ZNH to JPW, June 4, 1951 (HCUFla).

12. Burroughs Mitchell to ZNH, Oct. 3, 1950; JPW to Mitchell, June 4, 1951; Mitchell to ZNH, July 9, 1951 (Scribner's).

13. H. A. Leonardy to ZNH, Apr. 15, [1950] (HCUFla); RH interview with Leonardy, Feb., 1971, Miami, Fla.; ZNH, author's card (Watkins).

14. The charges of vote fraud caused considerable uproar in Miami. See "Negro Votes Sold Here, Author Says," *Miami Herald*, Oct. 25, 1950; "Negroes Heatedly Deny Votes Bought in Miami," ibid., Oct. 26, 1950; Bill Baggs, "Were Negro Votes Bought in Miami?," ibid.; clipping, Lester Granger column, *California Eagle*, Dec. 20, 1951 (JWJYale).

15. This paragraph and the following four are adapted from my "Folklore Field Notes from Zora Neale Hurston," *Black Scholar*, 7 (Apr., 1976), 39-47.

16. John Szwed, "An Anthropological Dilemma: The Politics of Afro-American Culture," in *Reinventing Anthropology*, ed. Dell Hymes (New York: Vintage, 1974), p. 158. My argument here leans heavily on Szwed's essay.

17. Ibid., p. 160; ZNH to Henry Allen Moe, Aug. 26, 1937 (GgFnd).

18. Szwed, "Anthropological Dilemma," pp. 163, 162.

19. Julius Lester, *Look Out Whitey! Black Power's Gon' Get Your Mama* (New York: Grove Press, 1969), p. 140; Ishmael Reed, "Ending the Western Established Church of Art," *Essence*, 1 (Jan., 1971), 15; ZNH, "Bible, Played by Ear in Africa [review of *How God Fix Jonah* by Lorenz Graham], *New York Herald Tribune Weekly Book Review*, Nov. 24, 1946; Julius Lester, dedication to *Black Folktales* (New York: Grove Press, 1970). Hurston certainly fulfills the definition of "cultural nationalism" given by Bracey, Meier, and Rudwick: "Cultural Nationalism contends that black people—in the United States or throughout the world—have a culture, style of life, cosmology, approach to the problems of existence, and aesthetic values distinct from that of white Americans in particular and white Europeans or Westerners in general" (John Bracey, Jr., August Meier, and Elliot Rudwick, *Black Nationalism in America* [New York: Bobbs-Merrill, 1970], pp. xxvi-xxvii).

20. See Richard Wright, *Black Boy* (New York: Harper and Row, 1945), chap. 3.

21. RH interview with Arna Bontemps, Nov. 18, 1970, New Haven, Conn.

22. Larry Neal, introduction to *Dust Tracks on a Road* (Philadelphia: J. B. Lippincott, 1971), p. xi.

23. ZNH to [Stuart Rose? of] *Saturday Evening Post*, Sept. 2, 1954 (HCUFla) (this letter is charred and the addressee is indecipherable; Rose was the *Post*'s editor); ZNH, "Mourner's Bench, Communist Line: Why the Negro Won't Buy Communism," *American Legion Magazine*, 50 (June, 1951), 15; idem, "Stories of Conflict" [review of *Uncle Tom's Children* by Richard Wright], *Saturday Review*, Apr. 2, 1938, p. 32.

24. The Smathers-Pepper campaign was hard hitting; playing on the rhetoric of the McCarthy era, Smathers had considerable success, it is claimed, by going to backwoods villages and calling Pepper a "somnambulist." There were many charges of Communist support for Pepper. See H. D. Price, *The Negro and Southern Politics* (New York: New York University Press, 1957); RH interview with Louis Waldman, May, 1971, New York City; ZNH, author's card (Watkins).

25. In a manuscript entitled "Which Way the NAACP" (copy lent to me by Marjorie Silver), Zora wrote, "The Charge so frequently flung that the NAACP is a Communist front outfit has not been proven. There is some kind of an affinity, however." This is a very hostile article towards the organization, and the "affinity," of course, is nonexistent. The right-wing praise for Hurston's attitude was considerable; not only did newspapers throughout the South reprint the letter, but she also received a card from a white supremacist group praising her stand and

describing the real meaning of the civil rights group's acronym: Negroes Are Advocating Communist Peace (HCUFla).

26. Larry Neal, "A Profile: Zora Neale Hurston," *Southern Exposure*, 1 (Winter, 1974), 161.

27. ZNH to Burroughs Mitchell, July 21, 1950 (Scribner's); RH interview with "B," Mar. 12, 1971, Miami, Fla. Frank Smathers's autobiography was eventually published: *It's Wonderful to Live Again* (Coral Gables, Fla.: Glade House, 1958).

28. Burroughs Mitchell to ZNH, Oct. 3, 1950 (Scribner's); ZNH to JPW, Mar. 12, 6, 1951 (AWRH).

29. ZNH to JPW, Mar. 12, 1951 (AWRH).

30. Ibid., Mar. 18, Apr. 9, May 1, 1951 (AWRH).

31. Ibid., May 10, Aug. 19, 1951 (HCUFla).

32. ZNH to JPW, June 4, 1951 (HCUFla); ZNH, author's card (Watkins); ZNH to JPW, July 9, 1951 (HCUFla).

33. ZNH to Burroughs Mitchell, July 15, 1951 (Scribner's).

34. ZNH to Everett Hurston, Jr., Oct. 12, 1951 (in Hurston's possession); ZNH to JPW, Feb. 13, 1951 (AWRH); ZNH to Burroughs Mitchell, July 15, 1951, May 1, 1952, Aug. 12, 1955 (Scribner's); ZNH to JPW, July 9, 1951 (HCUFla); ZNH to Mitchell, May 1, 1952 (Scribner's); ZNH to JPW, Aug. 19, 1951, Mar. 6, 1952 (HCUFla).

35. See Theodore Pratt, "Zora Neale Hurston," *Florida Historical Quarterly*, 40 (July, 1961), 37: "She was absolutely and completely improvident," a judgment often repeated by those who knew her. On the other hand, she urged friends and relatives with money to buy Florida property, which, if they had done so, would have made them rich. RH interview with JPW, May, 1971, New York City; Darwin T. Turner, introduction to *Mules and Men* (New York: Harper and Row, 1970), p. 10; ZNH, author's card (Watkins); ZNH to JPW, July 15, Sept. 13, Oct. 25, 1951, Mar. 6, 1952 (HCUFla); JPW to ZNH, May 23, 1953 (HCUFla); Burroughs Mitchell to William Bradford Huie, Mar. 10, 1960; memo, Apr. 28, 1954, showing "unearned balance" of ZNH account as $1120.68 (Scribner's); royalty statement, J. B. Lippincott to ZNH, Dec. 31, 1952 (HCUFla); ZNH to Helga Eason, Dec. 6, 1955 (Miami Public Library). In HCUFla there are two letters from white women who met Hurston at her home in Eau Gallie in 1955; they call her home a shack and state that Zora had reverted to her slave heritage by choosing to reside in a slave cabin.

36. William Bradford Huie, *Ruby McCollum: Woman in the Suwannee Jail* (New York: E. P. Dutton, 1956), pp. 89-101; William G. Nunn, Sr., of the *Pittsburgh Courier* to ZNH, Nov. 12, 1952 (HCUFla). Between Oct. 11, 1952, and May 2, 1953, ZNH published twenty stories about Ruby McCollum in the *Courier*. McCollum was released from the mental hospital in 1976 after a twenty-year fight to free her.

37. ZNH to JPW, Mar. 6, 1952 (HCUFla); ZNH to Helga Eason, Dec. 16, 1955 (Miami Public Library); ZNH to Margrit de Sabloniere, Dec. 3, 1955 (HCUFla).

38. In HCUFla there is a picture of Zora taken in the mid- or late fifties that is startling to anyone who has seen earlier pictures. She appears to weigh well over two hundred pounds.

The narrative of Hurston's effort to write "Herod the Great" has been compiled from a number of sources: ZNH to CVV, July 30, 1947, Sept. 12, 1955 (JWJYale); ZNH, "Just like Us," fourteen-page outline, typed; ZNH to Burroughs Mitchell,

Oct. 2, 1953, n.d. [ca. June-July], Aug. 12, 1955; ZNH to Miss Mousley, May 7, 1955 (Scribner's); ZNH to JPW, July 9, 1951; ZNH to Mary Holland, June 13, 1955 (HCUFla); ZNH to Herbert Sheen, June 28, 1957 (Sheen Papers); Michael Grant, *Herod the Great* (New York: American Heritage Press, 1971); ZNH, "Herod the Great," typescript, partially charred (HCUFla).

39. ZNH to Margrit de Sabloniere, Mar. 15, 1956; Richard Moore to ZNH, May 18, 1956; D. H. Goddard of Pan American World Airways to ZNH, telegram, June 13, 1956, and letter, n.d.; clipping, *Daytona Beach Morning Journal*, May 24, 1956 (HCUFla).

40. ZNH to Mary Holland, June 27, July 2, 1957 (HCUFla).

41. Ibid., June 27, 1957 (HCUFla); ZNH to Everett Hurston, Jr., Jan. 8, Mar. 31, 1957 (in Hurston's possession); ZNH to Herbert Sheen, June 28, 1957 (Sheen Papers).

42. Nelson Rutledge to ZNH, Oct. 29, 1957 (HCUFla); RH interview with C. E. Bolen, Feb., 1971, Ft. Pierce, Fla. The *Fort Pierce Chronicle* did not keep a back file in the late fifties, and I was unable to find copies of the paper for most of 1958. My search was conducted in a storage room piled from floor to ceiling with random, unordered copies of the paper for the previous fourteen years. For those *Chronicle* stories with Hurston's by-line that I did find, see the checklist of her writings in the Appendix. ZNH to M. Mitchell Ferguson, Feb. 27, 1958 (HCUFla); Walker, "In Search," pp. 87, 88; RH interview with Leroy Floyd, Feb., 1971, Ft. Pierce, Fla.; George Beebe to Doug Silver, July 9, 1958; ZNH to David McKay Publishers, Sept. 15, 1958 (HCUFla).

43. RH interview with C. C. Benton, Feb., 1971, Ft. Pierce, Fla.; Walker, "In Search," p. 88; Abbiejean Russell, welfare home coordinator, St. Lucie County Welfare Association, to RH, May 7, 1971; Leedell W. Neyland, *Twelve Black Floridians* (Tallahassee: Florida Agricultural and Mechanical University Foundation, 1970), p. 50.

44. Abbiejean Russell to RH, May 7, 1971; Walker, "In Search," p. 87; RH interview with Marjorie Silver, Feb., 1971, Ft. Pierce, Fla. See also Emma L. Blake, "Zora Neale Hurston: Author and Folklorist," *Negro History Bulletin*, 29 (Apr., 1966), 149-50, 165-66.

45. The facts of Hurston's death have come from a number of sources: Abbiejean Russell to RH, May 7, 1971; Walker, "In Search," pp. 87-88; certificate of death no. 60-004315, State of Florida; Marjorie Silver, "Friends Aid with Burial Expenses," *Miami Herald*, Feb. 6, 1960; RH interview with Sarah Peek Patterson, Feb., 1971, Ft. Pierce, Fla.; Theodore Pratt, "Zora Neale Hurston," *Florida Historical Quarterly*, 40 (July, 1961), 39-40. Pratt, who identifies himself as a good friend of Zora's, describes her as short, squat, and very dark skinned. In fact, Zora was between 5'5" and 5'7" and relatively light skinned—tan with freckles. Pratt deserves praise, however, for celebrating her career at a time when few others acknowledged her achievement.

Zora's disavowal of materialism is quoted from ZNH to Herbert Sheen, June 28, 1957 (Sheen Papers).

John Hurston and his second wife (Zora's stepmother), 1906. Courtesy of Everette Hurston, Sr.

Zora Neale Hurston, while a student at Howard University, 1919–23.
Courtesy of Herbert Sheen.

Zora Neale Hurston, while a student at Howard University, 1919–23.
Courtesy of Herbert Sheen.

Singers and dancers from *The Great Day*, 1932. Zora Neale Hurston is at the far right. Courtesy of Percival Punter.

Zora Neale Hurston, November 9, 1934. Photograph by Carl Van Vechten. Reproduced by permission of Carl Van Vechten Papers, Collection of American Literature, Beinecke Rare Book and Manuscript Library, Yale University.

Zora Neale Hurston, collecting from Rochelle French and Gabriel Brown, Eatonville, Florida, June, 1935. Courtesy of Library of Congress.

Zora Neale Hurston, at the Federal Writers' Project exhibit, 1938. Courtesy of Schomburg Center for Research in Black Culture, The New York Public Library, Astor, Lenox and Tilden Foundations.

Zora Neale Hurston, on a folklore-collecting trip, late 1930s. Courtesy of Jane Belo Estate.

Zora Neale Hurston, on a fishing trip, late 1930s or early 1940s. Courtesy of Everette Hurston, Sr.

Working As Maid He[...]

ZORA NEALE HURSTON

From the *Miami Herald*, March 27, 1950   Courtesy of John S.
Knight and the *Miami Herald*.

Zora Neale Hurston (*center*) and friends, probably in Fort Pierce, Florida, ca.
1958–59. The photograph was damaged by the fire that destroyed some of
Hurston's manuscripts after her death. Courtesy of Department of Rare Books
and Manuscripts, University of Florida Library.

Gravestone placed by Alice Walker in the Garden of the Heavenly Rest, August 15, 1973. Courtesy of Georgia Curry.

≋≋ Appendix: A Checklist of Writings by Zora Neale Hurston

BOOKS

This list includes American reprints, and the location of Hurston's manuscript, if known.

Jonah's Gourd Vine. Philadelphia: J. B. Lippincott, 1934. Reprinted, with an introduction by Larry Neal, Philadelphia: J. B. Lippincott, 1971. Manuscript in Schomburg Collection, New York Public Library.

Mules and Men. Philadelphia: J. B. Lippincott, 1935. Reprinted, New York: Negro Universities Press, 1969. Reprinted, with an introduction by Darwin Turner, New York: Harper and Row, 1970.

Their Eyes Were Watching God. Philadelphia: J. B. Lippincott, 1937. Reprinted, Greenwich, Conn.: Fawcett Publications, 1965. Reprinted, New York: Negro Universities Press, 1969. Reprinted, Urbana: University of Illinois Press, 1978. Manuscript in JWJYale.

Tell My Horse. Philadelphia: J. B. Lippincott, 1938. Manuscript in JWJYale.

Moses, Man of the Mountain. Philadelphia: J. B. Lippincott, 1939. Reprinted, Chatham, N.J.: Chatham Bookseller, 1974. Manuscript in JWJYale.

Dust Tracks on a Road. Philadelphia: J. B. Lippincott, 1942. Reprinted, with an introduction by Darwin Turner, New York: Arno Press, 1969. Reprinted, with an introduction by Larry Neal, New York: J. B. Lippincott, 1971. Manuscript in JWJYale.

Seraph on the Suwanee. New York: Charles Scribner's Sons, 1948. Reprinted, Ann Arbor, Mich.: University Microfilms, 1971. Reprinted, New York: AMS Press, 1974. Manuscript in HCUFla.

OTHER PUBLICATIONS

"John Redding Goes to Sea." *Stylus*, 1 (May, 1921), 11-22. Reprinted in *Opportunity*, 4 (Jan., 1926), 16-21.

"O Night." *Stylus*, 1 (May, 1921), 42.

"Poem." *Howard University Record*, 16 (Feb., 1922), 236.

"Drenched in Light." *Opportunity*, 2 (Dec., 1924), 371-74.

"Spunk." *Opportunity*, 3 (June, 1925), 171-73. Reprinted in *The New Negro*, edited by Alain Locke, pp. 105-11. New York: Albert and Charles Boni, 1925.

"Magnolia Flower." *Spokesman*, July, 1925, pp. 26-29.

"The Hue and Cry about Howard University." *Messenger*, 7 (Sept., 1925), 315-19, 338.

"Muttsy." *Opportunity*, 4 (Aug., 1926), 246-50.

"Possum or Pig." *Forum*, 76 (Sept., 1926), 465.

"The Eatonville Anthology." *Messenger*, 8 (Sept., Oct., Nov., 1926), 261-62, 297, 319, 332.

Color Struck: A Play. Fire!!, 1 (Nov., 1926), 7-15.

"Sweat." *Fire!!*, 1 (Nov., 1926), 40-45.

The First One: A Play. In *Ebony and Topaz*, edited by Charles S. Johnson, pp. 53-57. New York: National Urban League, 1927.

"Cudjo's Own Story of the Last African Slaver." *Journal of Negro History*, 12 (Oct., 1927), 648-63.

"Communication" [about the Fort Moosa settlement and Negro colony in Florida]. *Journal of Negro History*, 12 (Oct., 1927), 664-67.

"How It Feels to Be Colored Me." *World Tomorrow*, 11 (May, 1928), 215-16.

"Dance Songs and Tales from the Bahamas." *Journal of American Folklore*, 43 (July-Sept., 1930), 294-312.

"Hoodoo in America." *Journal of American Folklore*, 44 (Oct.-Dec., 1931), 317-418.

"The Gilded Six-Bits." *Story*, 3 (Aug., 1933), 60-70.

"Characteristics of Negro Expression." In *Negro: An Anthology*, edited by Nancy Cunard, pp. 39-46. London: Wishart, 1934.

"Conversions and Visions." In *Negro: An Anthology*, pp. 47-49.

"Shouting." In *Negro: An Anthology*, pp. 49-50.

"The Sermon." In *Negro: An Anthology*, pp. 50-54.

"Mother Catharine." In *Negro: An Anthology*, pp. 54-57.

"Uncle Monday.." In *Negro: An Anthology*, pp. 57-61.

"Spirituals and Neo-Spirituals." In *Negro: An Anthology*, pp. 359-61.

"The Fire and the Cloud." *Challenge*, 1 (Sept., 1934), 10-14.

"Race Cannot Become Great Until It Recognizes Its Talent." *Washington Tribune*, Dec. 29, 1934.

"Full of Mud, Sweat and Blood" [review of *God Shakes Creation* by David M. Cohn]. *New York Herald Tribune Books*, Nov. 3, 1935, p. 8.

"Fannie Hurst." *Saturday Review*, Oct. 9, 1937, pp. 15-16.

"Star-Wrassling Sons-of-the-Universe" [review of *The Hurricane's*

Children by Carl Carmer]. *New York Herald Tribune Books*, Dec. 26, 1937, p. 4.

"Rural Schools for Negroes" [review of *The Jeanes Teacher in the United States* by Lance G. E. Jones]. *New York Herald Tribune Books*, Feb. 20, 1938, p. 24.

"Stories of Conflict" [review of *Uncle Tom's Children* by Richard Wright]. *Saturday Review*, Apr. 2, 1938, p. 32.

"Now Take Noses." In *Cordially Yours*, pp. 25-27. Philadelphia: J. B. Lippincott, 1939.

"Cock Robin, Beale Street." *Southern Literary Messenger*, 3 (July, 1941), 321-23.

"Story in Harlem Slang." *American Mercury*, 55 (July, 1942), 84-96.

"Lawrence of the River." *Saturday Evening Post*, Sept. 5, 1942, pp. 18, 55-57. Condensed in *Negro Digest*, 1 (Mar., 1943), 47-49.

"The 'Pet Negro' System." *American Mercury*, 56 (May, 1943), 593-600. Condensed in *Negro Digest*, 1 (June, 1943), 37-40.

"High John de Conquer." *American Mercury*, 57 (Oct., 1943), 450-58.

"Negroes without Self-Pity." *American Mercury*, 57 (Nov., 1943), 601-3.

"The Last Slave Ship." *American Mercury*, 58 (Mar., 1944), 351-58. Condensed in *Negro Digest*, 2 (May, 1944), 11-16.

"My Most Humiliating Jim Crow Experience." *Negro Digest*, 2 (June, 1944), 25-26.

"The Rise of the Begging Joints." *American Mercury*, 60 (Mar., 1945), 288-94. Condensed in *Negro Digest*, 3 (May, 1945).

"Crazy for This Democracy." *Negro Digest*, 4 (Dec., 1945), 45-48.

"Bible, Played by Ear in Africa" [review of *How God Fix Jonah* by Lorenz Graham]. *New York Herald Tribune Weekly Book Review*, Nov. 24, 1946, p. 5.

"Jazz Regarded as Social Achievement" [review of *Shining Trumpets* by Rudi Blesh]. *New York Herald Tribune Weekly Book Review*, Dec. 22, 1946, p. 8.

"Thirty Days among Maroons" [review of *Journey to Accompong* by Katharine Dunham]. *New York Herald Tribune Weekly Book Review*, Jan. 12, 1947, p. 8.

"The Transplanted Negro" [review of *Trinidad Village* by Melville Herskovits and Frances Herskovits]. *New York Herald Tribune Weekly Book Review*, Mar. 9, 1947, p. 20.

Caribbean Melodies for Chorus of Mixed Voices and Soloists. With accompaniment for piano and percussion instruments. Arranged by William Grant Still. Philadelphia: Oliver Ditson, 1947.

Review of *Voodoo in New Orleans* by Robert Tallant. *Journal of American Folklore*, 60 (Oct.-Dec., 1947), 436-38.

"At the Sound of the Conch Shell" [review of *New Day* by Victor Stafford Reid]. *New York Herald Tribune Weekly Book Review*, Mar. 20, 1949, p. 4.

"Conscience of the Court." *Saturday Evening Post*, Mar. 18, 1950, pp. 22-23, 112-22.

"I Saw Negro Votes Peddled." *American Legion Magazine*, 49 (Nov., 1950), 12-13, 54-57, 59-60. Condensed in *Negro Digest*, 9 (Sept., 1951), 77-85.

"Some Fabulous Caribbean Riches Revealed" [review of *The Pencil of God* by Pierre Marcelin and Philippe Thoby Marcelin]. *New York Herald Tribune Weekly Book Review*, Feb. 4, 1951, p. 5.

"What White Publishers Won't Print." *Negro Digest*, 8 (Apr., 1950), 85-89.

"Mourner's Bench, Communist Line: Why the Negro Won't Buy Communism." *American Legion Magazine*, 50 (June, 1951), 14-15, 55-60.

"A Negro Voter Sizes Up Taft." *Saturday Evening Post*, Dec. 8, 1951, pp. 29, 150.

"Zora's Revealing Story of Ruby's First Day in Court." *Pittsburgh Courier*, Oct. 11, 1952.

"Victim of Fate." *Pittsburgh Courier*, Oct. 11, 1952.

"Ruby Sane." *Pittsburgh Courier*, Oct. 18, 1952.

"Ruby McCollum Fights for Life." *Pittsburgh Courier*, Nov. 22, 1952.

"Bare Plot against Ruby." *Pittsburgh Courier*, Nov. 29, 1952.

"Trial Highlights." *Pittsburgh Courier*, Nov. 29, 1952.

"McCollum-Adams Trial Highlights." *Pittsburgh Courier*, Dec. 27, 1952.

"Ruby Bares Her Love." *Pittsburgh Courier*, Jan. 3, 1953.

"Doctor's Threats, Tussle over Gun Led to Slaying." *Pittsburgh Courier*, Jan. 10, 1953.

"Ruby's Troubles Mount." *Pittsburgh Courier*, Jan. 17, 1953.

"The Life Story of Mrs. Ruby J. McCollum." *Pittsburgh Courier*, Feb. 28, Mar. 7, 14, 21, 28, Apr. 4, 11, 18, 25, May 2, 1953.

[The trial of Ruby McCollum]. In *Ruby McCollum: Woman in the Suwannee Jail*, by William Bradford Huie, pp. 89-101. New York: E. P. Dutton, 1956.

"This Juvenile Delinquency." *Fort Pierce Chronicle*, Dec. 12, 1958.

"The Tripson Story." *Fort Pierce Chronicle*, Feb. 6, 1959.

"The Farm Laborer at Home." *Fort Pierce Chronicle*, Feb. 27, 1959.

"Hoodoo and Black Magic" [column]. *Fort Pierce Chronicle*, July 11, 1958–Aug. 7, 1959.

UNPUBLISHED MATERIALS

"Barracoon." 1931. Biography of Cudjo Lewis, 117 pp. HUAL.

"Black Death." Short story submitted to 1925 *Opportunity* contest. CSJFisk.

"The Bone of Contention." Short story, 13 pp. HUAL.

"Book of Harlem." Short story, 7 pp. JWJYale.

"The Chick with One Hen." Character sketch, 2 pp. JWJYale.

"Eatonville When You Look at It." 2 pp. In "The Florida Negro."

"The Elusive Goal—Brotherhood of Mankind." Essay, 18 pp. HCUFla.

"The Emperor Effaces Himself." Character sketch, 7 pp. JWJYale.

"The Enemy." Personal experience, 10 pp. HCUFla.

"The Fiery Chariot." Play in one act, 7 pp. HCUFla.

"The Florida Negro." Manuscript prepared by ZNH and others for the Florida Federal Writers' Project. 183 pp. FHSP.

"Folklore." 11 pp. In "The Florida Negro." Copy in LCAFS.

"Goldsborough." 1 p. In "The Florida Negro."

"Herod the Great." Biography, 269 pp. HCUFla.

"Joe Wiley of Magazine Point." Folklore, 5 pp. HUAL.

"Maitland." 2 pp. In "The Florida Negro."

"The Migrant Worker in Florida." Journalism, 7 pp. HCUFla.

"Mule Bone: A Comedy of Negro Life." Play in three acts written with LH, 1930. Mimeographed copy in HUAL. Act 3 was published in *Drama Critique*, Spring, 1964, pp. 103-7.

"Negro Folk Tales." Folklore, 2 pp. LCAFS.

"Negro Legends." Folklore, 7 pp. LCAFS.

"Negro Mythical Places." 3 pp. In "The Florida Negro." Copy in LCAFS.

"Negro Religious Customs: The Sanctified Church." Folklore, 8 pp. FHSP. Copy in LCAFS.

"Negro Work Songs." Folklore, 5 pp. LCAFS.

"New Children's Games." 9 pp. In "The Florida Negro."

"Polk County: A Comedy of Negro Life on a Sawmill Camp, with Authentic Negro Music." Play in three acts written with Dorothy Waring, 1944. JWJYale.

"The Seventh Veil." Short Story, 34 pp. HCUFla.

"The South Was Had." Essay, 7 pp. HCUFla.

"Take for Instance Spessard Holland." Essay, 11 pp. HCUFla.

"Turpentine." 3 pp. In "The Florida Negro."

"Uncle Monday." 2 pp. In "The Florida Negro."

"Unique Personal Experience." 11 pp. HCUFla.

"Which Way the NAACP." Essay, 14 pp. In possession of Marjorie Silver, Ft. Pierce, Fla.

"The Woman in Gaul." Short story, 20 pp. HCUFla.

 Index